W9-CCK-297

THE ENCYCLOPEDIA OF

LEARNING DISABILITIES

THE ENCYCLOPEDIA OF

LEARNING DISABILITIES

Carol Turkington
Joseph R. Harris, Ph.D.
American Bookworks

Facts On File, Inc.

The Encyclopedia of Learning Disabilities

Copyright © 2002 by Carol Turkington

Facts On File, Inc.
132 West 31st Street
New York NY 10001

Library of Congress Cataloging-in-Publication Data
Turkington, Carol.
The encyclopedia of learning disabilities / Carol Turkington, Joseph R. Harris.
p. cm. — (The Facts On File library of health and living)
Includes bibliographical references and index.
ISBN 0-8160-4075-3 (hardcover: alk. paper)
1. Learning disabilities—Encyclopedias. 2. Learning disabled—Education—
United States—Encyclopedias. I. Harris, Joseph, 1951 Dec. 20– II. Title. III. Series.

LC4704.5 .T86 2001
371.9′03—dc21   2001040620

Facts On File books are available at special discounts when purchased in bulk quantities for businesses, associations, institutions, or sales promotions. Please call our Special Sales Department in New York at (212) 967-8800 or (800) 322-8755.

You can find Facts On File on the World Wide Web at http://www.factsonfile.com

Text and cover design by Cathy Rincon

Printed in the United States of America

VB FOF 10 9 8 7 6 5 4 3 2

This book is printed on acid-free paper.

CONTENTS

FOREWORD

Dr. Sam Kirk may have coined the term *learning disabilities* in 1963, but we know that problems in learning ability have been a part of the human condition for centuries. Indeed, there is evidence that as early as 3000 B.C., the Chinese recognized differences in learning ability among individuals and administered standardized tests to differentiate those candidates who were able to train for trades from those who were not.

Differences in the ability to learn became critically important to educators in the West at the beginning of the Industrial Revolution. Families left their farms and came to the cities in search of better lives and sent their children to school in hopes that they could eventually obtain the best jobs. Schools, no longer the exclusive privilege of the middle and upper classes, began to see their enrollments swell. Educators recognized that not all students could learn with the same degree of success. At the beginning of the 20th century, the first modern tests were developed to identify those students with learning problems who needed different educational services.

The presence of learning disabilities among prominent historical and contemporary figures has helped raise public awareness about learning disorders and has also helped remove some of the stigma associated with them. For example, the gifted French sculptor Auguste Rodin's teachers informed his parents that he was uneducable. In shame, his parents withdrew him from school and put him to work. President Woodrow Wilson was nine before he learned the alphabet and didn't learn to read until age 11. Thomas Edison's teachers referred to him as "addled," "abnormal," and "mentally deficient." Albert Einstein didn't learn to speak until the age of three, and was termed of "subnormal intelligence" by his teachers. Even as an adult, Einstein continued to struggle with what today would most likely be diagnosed as learning disabilities. Finally, the late vice president Nelson Rockefeller had such severe dyslexia that he was unable to read even his own speeches: he had to commit them to memory.

Before Kirk, there were as many theories of learning disorders as there were educators. Physicians emphasized learning disabilities as a result of neurological disorders and nervous system damage and advised medical treatment. Optometrists saw learning disabilities as deficits in visual perception of written symbols and recommended corrective lenses or ocular training. Speech and language pathologists defined learning disabilities as language-based and recommended language therapy. Psychologists assumed that learning disabilities were caused by emotional problems or faulty learning and emphasized psychotherapy or behavioral retraining. At last, educators saw learning disabilities as a result of faulty learning abilities or mismatches between instruction and students' learning styles and recommended diagnostic-prescriptive teaching that would match instruction with students' learning styles.

Kirk emphasized the role of information processing abilities in learning disabilities, and his views on learning disabilities continue to be among the more influential in the field nearly 40 years after he introduced them. His term *learning disabilities* replaced more antiquated terms, reflecting obsolete views of learning, such as

- word blindness
- reading (or math or spelling) retardation
- Strauss Syndrome
- brain dysfunction
- hard-of-learning
- six-hour retardation
- backwardness

In fact, until recently, there were still places in this country in which children were not identified as learning disabled: if they had adequate intelligence but still had learning problems, their schools labeled them "brain damaged" whether or not there was any evidence of neurological disorders.

But problems with identification were not the only obstacle affected individuals faced. Even if they were able to obtain diagnoses as learning disabled, there were few public schools in the country that provided any sort of special education, much less related services such as physical or occupational therapy. Individuals with learning disabilities had few of the rights or avenues to appeal schools' decisions regarding their education if they disagreed. Even in the early 1970s, in many places in the country, only the largest school districts had any classes for students with learning disabilities.

It was in the 1970s that American education changed radically for children with learning disabilities and all other types of handicaps. In 1975, President Gerald Ford signed Public Law 94-142 (since reauthorized as the Individuals with Disabilities Education Act). The law provided a legal definition of learning disabilities that emphasized a "severe discrepancy between potential and achievement" in specific academic areas. At the ceremony at which he signed the bill into law, President Ford made a prophetic comment that Congress would probably never authorize enough money to states to implement the new requirements. He was right. Since that time, many parents seeking the range of services they believe their children need have found themselves at odds with school districts that don't always have sufficient funding to implement the law.

Carol Turkington and I bring somewhat different but complementary perspectives to this book. Turkington is a professional journalist who specializes in writing on medical and psychological topics. I am a licensed and certified school psychologist, former school district special education director, and college instructor who teaches information pertinent to special education and school psychology on a graduate level. I was a second-year graduate student in school psychology when President Ford signed Public Law 94-142 into law, so I have been involved with the implementation of federal special education law from the beginning. I have helped school districts and families advocate for children with handicaps. As a special education director who has built special education programs in three school districts, I am quite familiar with the challenges that school districts face in implementing unfunded and underfunded mandates. As a school psychologist employed both by school districts and in private practice, I am very familiar with the challenges experienced by people with handicaps and by the people who love them. I have seen the difficulties they face in coping with handicaps and in struggling to obtain the services that they believe are appropriate and that the law demands. I have worked with attorneys to help many of them obtain Social Security Disability benefits and have worked with college counselors who have invariably been eager to help obtain appropriate educational accommodations. I have tried very hard to lend these perspectives to providing helpful information gained from nearly 30 years' experience in special education.

This book provides entries on a wide variety of terms and concepts related to learning disabilities that we hope parents, teachers, physicians, students, and others will find useful. We have tried to present terms ranging from the basic to the highly technical, from the matter-of-fact to the controversial, in a thorough but straightforward manner that allows readers to decide their positions on these issues for themselves. We have explained much of the "alphabet soup," such as LRE, IEP, PL 94-142, and IDEA that so confuses parents. We hope that we have provided information that readers will find helpful and informative in their attempts to navigate their way through this frequently confusing and controversial field.

—Joseph R. Harris, Ph.D.

INTRODUCTION

One in five children in the United States struggles with learning disabilities, a broad term that includes a wide range of problems with speech, language, reading, mathematics, concentration, and reasoning. The difficulties affect one out of every seven Americans, and every year another 120,000 students are diagnosed. Many thousands more are never properly diagnosed or treated, or don't get treatment because they are not considered eligible for services.

But not all learning *problems* are necessarily learning *disabilities*. Some children are simply slower than others in developing certain skills. This is why early identification and treatment are vital in treating symptoms of learning difficulties. Although most children have an occasional difficulty with learning or behavior, a consistent pattern of the problems that follow may suggest the need for further testing. A preschooler might be tested if the child has problems learning the alphabet; rhyming words; connecting sounds and letters; counting or learning numbers; being understood when speaking to a stranger; using scissors, crayons, or paint; reacting too much or too little to touch; using words or phrases; pronouncing; walking up and down stairs; talking or remembering names of colors; or dressing. In elementary school, children with learning disabilities may have trouble learning new vocabulary, speaking in full sentences, understanding conversation rules, retelling stories, remembering information, playing with peers, moving from one activity to another, expressing thoughts, holding a pencil, handwriting, handling math problems, following directions, remembering routines, learning, comprehending reading, drawing or copying shapes, deciding what information presented in class is important, modulating the voice, being neat or organized, meeting deadlines, or playing age-appropriate board games.

Adults with learning disabilities may have trouble with remembering new information, organization, reading comprehension, getting along with peers or coworkers, finding or keeping a job, having a sense of direction, understanding subtle jokes, making appropriate remarks, following directions, reading, writing, spelling, and math, self-esteem, using proper grammar, or meeting deadlines.

Although learning disabilities themselves have always been a part of the human condition, they have only recently been identified. Many of the symptoms experts consider to be learning disabilities were observed and described more than a century ago, but the term itself was coined by Samuel Kirk in 1963—less than 40 years ago. The discipline continues to evolve.

For much of this century, for example, conditions such as dyslexia have been called many different names, such as strephosymbolia and minimal brain dysfunction. But in the United States, it was really only with the advent of special education legislation and services in the 1970s that this label for a broad, complex, and often poorly understood range of learning problems came into common usage. Likewise, while less than a decade ago attention disorders were viewed primarily as a problem of hyperactive male children, today experts understand that attention deficit/hyperactivity disorder (ADHD) is far more complex, affecting many more girls, and extending into adulthood.

As recently as a generation ago, learning disabilities were poorly understood and often ignored. Even when parents were able to obtain special education services for their child, these services were often ineffective. With the advent of educational legislation, the quality of educational services has dramatically improved. The past two decades have also seen a dramatic increase in the scope and depth of research into the underlying issues involved in various learning disorders. Methods of investigation such as brain imaging and genetic research have begun to produce concrete support for scientific theories of the origin and nature of learning disorders. Within the past 10 years the role of medications in treating some disorders and the development of assistive technology has revolutionized the treatment of learning disabilities.

Even the terminology used in the area of special education has undergone dramatic change. The ways in which experts describe individuals and their learning have grown far more diagnostically accurate, and at the same time far more humane. Likewise, with the ongoing refinement of legislation to protect the rights of those with learning disabilities over the last 30 years, the terminology used in the field of special education has taken on legal as well as educational connotations.

This book has been designed as a guide and reference to a wide range of learning disabilities and to additional information and addresses of organizations that deal with learning disabilities. It is not a substitute for prompt assessment and treatment by experts trained in the diagnosis of learning disabilities.

Information in this book comes from the most up-to-date sources available and includes some of the most recent research in the field of learning disabilities, culled from leading textbooks and professional journals, in addition to the personal experience of the expert coauthors.

The book includes topics in three key areas:

learning disabilities and their treatment, such as

- in-depth discussion of academic skills disorders
- developmental speech and language disorders
- attention disorders
- ADHD
- stimulant medications

legal discussions of relevant topics, such as

- Americans with Disabilities Act
- Rehabilitation Act of 1973

school-related entries, such as

- independent education evaluations
- individualized education programs
- individualized transition plans
- assistive technology
- standardized assessments

Readers should keep in mind, however, that changes occur very rapidly in this field. A bibliography has been provided for readers who seek additional sources of information. All entries are cross-referenced, and appendixes provide additional information.

—Carol Turkington
Cumru, Pennsylvania

ENTRIES A to Z

ability grouping Placing children of similar ability in one group; also called "tracking" or "whole class ability grouping." Some experts believe ability grouping harms children with lower ability, who tend to perform more poorly in lower-track classes than in mixed-ability classes. At the same time, studies suggest that children of higher ability don't achieve more in tracked classes than in mixed-ability classes. Moreover, placing students with lower ability in tracked classrooms reduces self-esteem, with a particularly negative effect on students' sense of their own academic competence. Critics of tracking also maintain that the process reduces opportunities to develop relationships among students from different racial, ethnic, and socioeconomic groups, and has a negative effect on race relations.

Placement decisions about ability grouping are often made very early in a student's school career, and are often based on questionable data.

According to the NATIONAL ASSOCIATION OF SCHOOL PSYCHOLOGISTS, mixed-ability grouping can give all students equal access to an enriched curriculum and the highest quality instruction that schools have to offer, and avoids labeling and stigmatizing students with lower ability. It also promotes higher expectations for student achievement and reduces school segregation based on socioeconomic status, race, gender, ethnicity, or disability. Ideally, mixed-ability classes should not "teach to the middle" but should accommodate individual differences in learning styles, abilities, and interests. This type of grouping should include cooperative learning groups, peer tutors, flexible grouping practices, team teaching, multi-age groupings, and instruction in higher order thinking and problem-solving skills.

ability test Tests of ability, such as intelligence tests, measure an individual's ability to perform a task, manipulate information, or solve problems. Typically, tests of ability are used to assess specific performance abilities or potential for future learning, rather than stored information. Among the most commonly used ability tests are the WECHSLER INTELLIGENCE SCALE FOR CHILDREN, either revised or third edition (WISC-R or WISC-III), the Scholastic Aptitude Test (SAT), which is widely used in college admissions processes, and the Woodcock-Johnson-III (WJIII) cognitive battery, which is commonly used in public school settings to define a baseline of aptitude against which achievement can be measured in determining whether a learning disability is present.

Ability tests can be physical or mental. They can test verbal or nonverbal areas, and are also frequently used to assess potential employees for specific tasks. Depending on the nature of the test, a wide spectrum of individuals may be involved in administration. Specific clinical training in psychology is required in order to administer the Wechsler or other intelligence tests, while the Woodcock-Johnson may be administered by school guidance counselors with appropriate training. Standardized tests such as the SAT must be administered in specific contexts and according to specific testing procedures, but overseeing such tests requires no formal professional training.

Ability tests have particular importance in relation to the AMERICANS WITH DISABILITIES ACT, which protects individuals with disabilities from discrimination, especially in the workplace. Ability tests designed to assess mechanical abilities, clerical abilities, and other job-related abilities can prevent equal access. Individuals can request alternative assessment of their abilities if they can provide documentation of a disability and they are otherwise qualified for a position.

academic classes   The core classes in a student's program, such as reading, English, history, and mathematics. Children are generally moved into subject-area classes in elementary school, with different teachers for each subject. As students enter middle school, content areas take on more significance. Often, considerable reading, writing, and critical thinking are required in academic classes that may not be required of such electives as music, art, or physical education.

Typically, students with learning disabilities will perform significantly worse in academic classes involving reading and writing skills. This can be the result of problems with decoding, reading comprehension, or basic study skills. It's generally in academic classes where students with learning disabilities require accommodations or extra support. In fact, learning disabilities are usually first evaluated as a result of poor academic performance. For LD classification, federal law requires a severe discrepancy between *potential* (usually measured by IQ tests) and *achievement* (usually measured by *individual* achievement tests, never group standardized tests), as supported by anecdotal evidence of academic difficulties in the classroom.

academic skills disorders   Students with academic skills disorders often lag far behind their classmates in developing reading, writing, or arithmetic skills. These disorders can be divided into developmental reading disorder, DEVELOPMENTAL WRITING DISORDER, and developmental arithmetic disorder (DYSCALCULIA).

Developmental reading disorder (also known as DYSLEXIA) is quite widespread, affecting between 2 percent and 8 percent of elementary school children. The ability to read requires a rich, intact network of nerve cells that connect the brain's centers of vision, language, and memory. While a person can have problems in any of the tasks involved in reading, scientists have found that a significant number of people with dyslexia share an inability to distinguish or separate the sounds in spoken words. For example, a child might not be able to identify the word "cat" by sounding out the individual letters, c-a-t, or to play rhyming games.

Fortunately, remedial reading specialists have developed techniques that can help many children with dyslexia acquire these skills. However, there is more to reading than recognizing words. If the brain can't form images or relate new ideas to those stored in memory, the reader won't be able to understand or remember the new concepts. This is why other types of reading disabilities can appear in the upper grades when the focus of reading shifts from word identification to comprehension.

Writing, too, involves several brain areas and functions. The brain networks for vocabulary, grammar, hand movement, and memory must all work well if the child is to be able to write well. A developmental writing disorder may be caused by problems in any of these areas. A child with a writing disability, particularly an expressive language disorder, might be unable to compose complete, grammatical sentences.

Arithmetic involves recognizing numbers and symbols, memorizing facts such as the multiplication table, aligning numbers, and understanding abstract concepts like place value and fractions. Any of these may be difficult for children with *developmental arithmetic disorders*. Problems with numbers or basic concepts are likely to show up early, whereas problems that appear in the later grades are more often tied to problems in reasoning.

Many aspects of speaking, listening, reading, writing, and arithmetic overlap and build on the same brain capabilities, so it's not surprising that people can be diagnosed as having more than one type of learning disability. For example, the ability to understand language underlies the ability to learn to speak. Therefore, any disorder that interferes with the ability to understand language will also interfere with the development of speech, which in turn hinders learning to read and write. A single problem in the brain's operation can disrupt many types of learning activity.

Academy of Orton-Gillingham Practitioners and Educators
A nonprofit educational organization designed to maintain professional and ethical standards for practitioners and educators of the ORTON-GILLINGHAM APPROACH for the treatment of DYSLEXIA. The group also accredits training programs and practitioners and educators of the Orton-Gillingham approach. Incorporated in 1995 in New York by the Board of Regents of the University of the State of New York, the academy also sponsors continuing education programs and sponsors research relevant to Orton-Gillingham instruction.

Contact: PO Box 234, Amenia, NY 12501–0234; phone: (914) 373–8919; email: info@ortonacademy.org; website: http://www.ortonacademy.org

acalculia Also known as anarithmia, this is an acquired inability to do simple mathematics that does not involve normal difficulties with mathematics. Both oral and written calculations are commonly affected. The problem is caused by lesions usually caused by brain damage to the left parietal lobe.

Primary acalculia is an acquired problem in calculation that can't be explained by problems in writing numbers (AGRAPHIA), or by spatial disorganization for numbers. *Spatial acalculia* is the impaired ability to perform written calculations because of the failure to process spatial aspects of written problems properly. Spatial acalculia is

more often associated with right brain-hemisphere lesions.

accommodations Any modifications to an educational program to meet the needs of students with disabilities, or to provide access to individuals in the workplace. The AMERICANS WITH DISABILITIES ACT (ADA), IDEA, and Section 504 of the Rehabilitation Acts of 1973 (PL 93-112) and 1990, all require accommodations in one way or another so that qualified individuals with disabilities have access to educational and employment opportunities.

Although children with disabilities are protected under the INDIVIDUALS WITH DISABILITIES EDUCATION ACT and provided with special education services, college students aren't protected under IDEA. They must request accommodations under ADA or the Rehabilitation Act.

Under the ADA, the term "reasonable accommodation" may include

- making existing facilities readily accessible to people with disabilities
- job restructuring, part-time or modified work schedules, reassignment to a vacant position
- modifying equipment, examinations, training materials
- providing qualified readers or interpreters

For example, the ADA requires that someone with a physical disability who needs a wheelchair must be given a desk of the right width and height. However, someone with a disability must be "otherwise qualified" for the position. This means that a person who is blind can't be hired as an air traffic controller; antidiscriminatory legislation is designed to ensure that access is reasonable but not automatic.

However, employers and schools also have legal protection as to whether they are required to provide accommodations. For example, under the ADA an institution or employer may claim that modifications would impose a hardship under certain conditions. Those conditions include the following:

- the nature and cost of the accommodation
- the overall financial resources of the facility involved
- the number of employees
- the impact of the accommodation on the operation of the facility
- the overall size of the business
- the type of operation

Compliance with the ADA has been slow, especially because of the cost of removing physical barriers. Nonetheless, it is this legislation that provides the guidelines for accessibility as a UNIVERSAL ACCESS/DESIGN. For people with LEARNING DISABILITIES (especially for students enrolled in college), accommodations can be provided if a specific request is made to an institution's disability support office. Typical accommodations might include the following:

academic modifications: note-taking services, course requirement waiver or substitution, reduced course load

exam accommodations: extended time, alternative test formats, computer availability

auxiliary aids or services: taped tests, taped books, tutoring, writing or academic center support; remedial skills development courses or workshops; priority registration and course selection

In order to receive services or accommodations, students must have a recommendation from a psychologist based on a specific diagnosis. Program modifications may include waivers or course substitutions. The law states that accommodations should be made on a case-by-case basis, without compromising the academic standards of a program of study.

University faculty members vary in their willingness to provide accommodations to students with learning disabilities. Teachers should not question the need for accommodation nor are they legally allowed to ask for information about the specific disability, but they can decide if the accommodation is reasonable and how it will be implemented. Some studies have suggested that faculty are more willing to provide "teaching accommodations" such as allowing students to record lectures. They tend to be less eager to provide alternative exam formats because they are concerned with keeping academic standards high.

The U.S. Supreme Court has ruled on only one case pertaining to college access for students with disabilities. In *Southeastern Community College v. Davis* (1979), the Court upheld that a student with a hearing problem could be denied admission to a nursing program because the essential program requirements couldn't be modified. In this and subsequent case law, the courts have repeatedly deferred to faculty expertise regarding what constitutes the essential requirements of a program and whether these requirements can be waived.

See also AUXILIARY AIDS; Section 504 of the REHABILITATION ACT OF 1973.

accuracy　The correctness or precision in test performance. In general, the term "accuracy" is used with tests that measure different types of performance. For example, some reading tests measure both reading accuracy and reading rate; it's possible that a student might have markedly different scores for reading accuracy and reading rate.

Students with DYSLEXIA or a specific reading disability who have had some reading help could show a relatively high accuracy score compared to reading rate, showing that they are capable of decoding accurately but that they require more time to do so effectively. On the other hand, a student with an ATTENTION DEFICIT/HYPERACTIVITY DISORDER might score very high in terms of reading rate, but have a relatively lower level of accuracy, reflecting careless mistakes and inattention.

achievement   What an individual has learned; "achievement" generally refers to the kind of knowledge and skills that are taught in school. It may be measured by actual school performance or by STANDARDIZED TESTS of achievement. Achievement tests often focus on specific content areas such as grammatical structures or American history, or on general areas such as writing or reading comprehension.

Because the classification of "learning disability" depends on a discrepancy between achievement on standardized tests and intellectual potential, the concept of achievement is extremely important. Within most states, whether a person is recognized as having a learning disability and thus qualifies for special education services depends on a "severe discrepancy" between performance on standardized achievement and aptitude tests. Depending on which tests are used, the same student may score very differently, which can directly affect whether the student qualifies for services.

achievement test   Achievement tests are standardized measures of knowledge, information, or procedural learning (such as how to do something). This type of assessment is used to measure student learning in comparison to a norm.

Achievement tests may assess general academic skill areas, such as reading, writing, or mathematics, or they may test for content knowledge in a specific academic subject, such as biology or American history. Achievement tests are used by school systems to provide a standard measure of individual student performance, and to provide an aggregated measure of performance that enables school systems to evaluate their effectiveness. Achievement tests are also used as part of the diagnostic assessment of individuals to determine whether they have a learning disability and qualify for special education services.

ACID profile   A pattern of lower scores on specific subtests of the WECHSLER INTELLIGENCE SCALE FOR CHILDREN (WISC-III) or WECHSLER ADULT INTELLIGENCE SCALE (WAIS-III) that is associated with one subtype of LEARNING DISABILITY. This pattern of significantly low scores on the *A*rithmetic, *C*oding, *I*nformation, and *D*igit Span subtests has been associated with learning disabilities in reading, spelling, and arithmetic.

acoustic cortex   A part of the temporal region of the brain that receives all auditory stimuli.

active reading   Active reading refers to the process of reading in which students actively engage with the text by applying a variety of strategies. These might include the following:

- previewing the essay or chapter in order to get a sense of the whole
- underlining and/or highlighting main ideas, key terminology, and unfamiliar vocabulary
- margin-noting with main ideas or questions about the material
- outlining a chapter or essay after reading it, in order to show the relationship between ideas and sections
- paraphrasing the information
- summarizing main ideas

For individuals with learning disabilities, reading comprehension is often an area of weakness because of problems with vocabulary and background knowledge.

Using active reading skills can increase comprehension by exercising critical thinking skills and improving memorization. Research suggests that new information that is manipulated and rehearsed is more likely to be stored in long-term memory. The use of active reading skills helps individuals to understand the relationships between ideas, and to learn the information more efficiently and effectively. Teaching specific cognitive strategies, also known as STRATEGY INSTRUCTION, has been studied since 1960. Since then, other approaches have been developed for helping students with learning disabilities to more efficiently process information.

Studies also support the idea that children with learning disabilities don't have or can't apply the strategies for reading that more efficient learners do automatically. This emphasizes the need for explicit instruction in active reading, as well as many other skills.

ADA The acronym for the AMERICANS WITH DISABILITIES ACT.

adaptive behavior The ability of an individual to adapt to the expectations of society and a particular environment (such as the workplace or the classroom). Initially, the term was applied to those with DEVELOPMENTAL DISABILITIES.

A person's adaptive behavior is based on how well he or she has already mastered basic living skills. Rather than completing a series of tasks or test items, individuals are rated based on interviews with care providers, family, and teachers. The assessment of adaptive behavior is now considered important in the field of learning disabilities. Some research has indicated that children with learning disabilities often have problems with classroom adaptive behavior. These problems may involve difficulties with extroversion, creativity, curiosity, and completing tasks. Research suggests that these difficulties are not simply the result of academic failure, but relate to problems in adapting behavior to the classroom environment. Although this research is not conclusive, it does pose significant implications for mainstreaming students with learning disabilities.

adaptive behavior rating scale A standardized scale that measures a person's ADAPTIVE BEHAVIOR. The scale is determined after an interview that typically requires either teachers or parents to rate an individual on a wide variety of specific behavior, such as coping skills, use of language, development of peer relationships, the ability to stay focused, and so on. For example, questions in the "daily living" component might ask whether the person understands that hot things are dangerous, or whether the person can drink from a cup or glass without help.

Adaptive behavior scales are typically used in conjunction with intelligence tests, and are rarely used alone. These standardized behavior scales can provide important objective information about development and are considered to be more consistent than informal observations by a mental health professional. The most widely used adaptive behavior ratings scales are the Vineland Adaptive Behavior Scales and the American Association on Mental Retardation Adaptive Behavior Scales. Both tests have different forms for children and adults.

ADD See ATTENTION DEFICIT/HYPERACTIVITY DISORDER.

Adderall A stimulant medication prescribed for ATTENTION DEFICIT/HYPERACTIVITY DISORDER (ADHD) that is composed of dextroamphetamine and amphetamine. Adderall can be used in children over the age of three.

The drug can improve attention span and decrease distractibility, and also may decrease impulsivity, stubbornness, and aggression. The drug needs to be taken only once or twice a day, and while the effects may be noted immediately, it may take up to six weeks to achieve its full benefit.

Adderall is usually prescribed as part of a treatment plan that includes educational and psychosocial treatment. It is sometimes prescribed in cases in which Ritalin or other stimulant medications have been ineffective. Because it has a fairly slow onset of action, there may be less chance of Adderall causing or worsening tics.

Adderall had earlier been approved and marketed by another company under a different name, Obetrol, as a weight control medication.

The manufacturer was taken over by another company, which renamed the product Adderall in 1994. The drug was approved for the treatment of ADHD and reintroduced in 1996 as Adderall.

Side Effects

Most common side effects include appetite and weight loss, insomnia, and headache. Less frequently, a patient may experience dry mouth and nausea. Rare side effects include dizziness, irritability, stomach pain, increased heart rate, or hallucinations. As with most stimulants indicated for ADHD, there is a possibility of growth suppression and the potential for triggering motor tics and Tourette's syndrome; in rare cases, worsening of psychosis has been reported.

As with all other stimulants used in treating ADHD, one of the more troublesome side effects is a decrease in brain growth. Although there is something of a rebound effect once the child is removed from the drug, the rebound generally does not bring the child back to the same level on brain growth charts as prior to drug treatment.

Drug Interactions

Adderall should not be taken with the antidepressant MAO inhibitors, because serious (even fatal) interactions can occur. At least 14 days must pass between taking MAOIs and Adderall. Acidifying agents such as guanethidine, reserpine, and fruit juices can interfere with the absorption of Adderall, whereas substances such as Diamox (acetazolamide) increase absorption. Tricyclic antidepressants such as Tofranil become more potent when taken with Adderall. Thorazine (chlorpromazine), lithium, and Haldol (haloperidol) can interfere with the effect of Adderall.

See also STIMULANT MEDICATIONS.

ADHD See ATTENTION DEFICIT/HYPERACTIVITY DISORDER.

affect A visual representation of a person's feelings. Affect differs from mood, which is a pervasive, subjectively experienced emotion. An individual's affect conveys emotions through body language and facial expression, rather than through words. The affective component in learning disabilities is sometimes overlooked, but this may play a major role in helping to understand the nature of a person's learning needs.

For example, some individuals with learning disabilities or attention disorders may display what psychologists call a "flat affect," which means they don't reveal their underlying feelings. This may be interpreted by a teacher or parent as boredom or a lack of emotional engagement, when in fact it may be caused by delayed processing of verbal information or internal distractibility. Such a person may seem to be indifferent to discipline, when in fact the person really feels overwhelmed—and responds by shutting down. On the other hand, an individual may show a highly animated or inappropriate affect because of external stimuli, or because of internal problems with self control.

Affect is described in the following ways:

- blunted: significant reduction in the intensity of emotional expression
- flat: absence of any sign of emotional expression
- labile: repeated, rapid, abrupt shifts in expression
- restricted or constricted: mild reduction in the range and intensity of emotional expression

agnosia A defect in the ability to recognize and interpret complex objects or experiences; the stimuli are received, but their meaning is absent or distorted. Individuals with various forms of agnosia may be unable to recognize people or objects, despite the fact that their basic senses are normal. It is often caused by a lesion in a part of the brain called the angular gyrus.

For example, a person with visual agnosia may be able to describe what an object looks like, but still not recognize it; although the person's perceptual system may be intact, the individual has no meaningful associations with the object of perception.

Some types of agnosia are far more frequent. Visual agnosia (especially agnosia for faces, called prosopagnosia) is the most commonly encountered form of recognition disturbance. It is a disorder of recognition confined to the visual realm, despite normal visual perception and alertness, attention, intelligence, and language. Most patients can't recognize new visual stimuli that would normally have been learned after adequate exposure.

The condition of auditory agnosia is rarer, followed by the even less frequent tactile agnosia. A frequently encountered condition, which also conforms to the designation of agnosia, is a disturbance in the recognition of illness (anosognosia).

Agnosia bears some similarities to APHASIA, a condition characterized by problems in naming and describing objects. However, aphasia involves a disorder of language—individuals with aphasia don't improve their ability to name objects when information is presented in another way.

agraphia   An acquired impairment in writing or spelling that encompass a range of potential problems in the area of writing; also known as DYSGRAPHIA. These difficulties may be linked to problems in other areas of language functioning, or may be limited to the production of written language. Agraphia is an old-fashioned term; currently, these conditions are generally grouped under the category of disorders of written expression (see WRITTEN EXPRESSION, DISORDERS OF).

The term is usually used to describe instances of writing impairment due to a brain problem acquired after the person has learned to write. Writing impairments of developmental origin are usually considered as part of DYSLEXIA. Acquired impairments as a result of tremor or

other basic movement problems are usually not considered to be agraphia.

The disorder rarely occurs by itself, but appears together with more widespread language problems such as APRAXIA (problems carrying out physical movements involved in communication), dementia, or confusion.

Agraphia may involve one or several problems, such as the actual formation of letters, spelling, word selection, grammar, or arrangement of letters on the page. A patient with mild impairment may exhibit problems only with an increased number of spelling mistakes, but someone with a more advanced condition may be unable to write even single letters. Some people with agraphia may also have trouble writing numbers or other nonletter symbols, but others may be perfectly capable of number writing, for example, even if letter writing is impaired.

Types of Agraphia
People with *spatial agraphia* can't place writing on the page; this most often occurs as a progressive upward slant from the left to right side of the page and is associated with lesions of the dominant hemisphere. Someone with *micrographia* will write smaller and smaller letters over the course of a sentence; this problem is associated with Parkinsonism or Alzheimer's disease.

Most patients with APHASIA also have agraphia. In ALEXIA with agraphia, a patient distorts letters and has problems with spelling, in addition to reading impairment; this is associated with brain lesions in the left angular or supramarginal gyrus. In *Gerstmann syndrome,* loosely associated with brain damage in the parietal lobe, agraphia occurs with a number of other problems, including the inability to do simple arithmetic (ACALCULIA) and left-right disorientation. *Callosal agraphia* affecting the left hand only can follow brain lesions in the front half of the corpus callosum. *Phonological agraphia* involves a specific defect resulting in the inability to write pronounceable pseudowords.

Cause

Agraphia may be caused by almost any brain disease, but stroke, injury, tumor, and Alzheimer's disease are the most common. Agraphia is often one of the early behavioral signs of confusion due to metabolic problems or poisoning.

Diagnosis

The condition can be diagnosed with a simple writing test in which a patient copies a sentence, takes dictation, and spontaneously creates a sentence or two. A person with agraphia may still be able to write something learned extremely well (such as a patient's own name), and this should not be used to infer normal writing ability.

alexia   The loss of the ability to read caused by lesions on the brain or from other brain injury. Alexia is a separate condition from DYSLEXIA, and generally does not respond to treatment the way that dyslexia does.

While relatively pure cases of alexia occur, they usually are associated with APHASIA and problems in writing (AGRAPHIA). There are a number of different subtypes, but all types cause reading problems so that reading is slow or impossible, and comprehension of read material is impaired. In the United States, alexia almost always describes acquired defects in reading that occur as the result of a brain condition in a person who was previously literate.

Cause

The most common cause of acquired alexia is stroke. Other forms of brain disease, including tumors, inflammation, and head injury, can also cause alexia. In addition, there are some cases of degenerative disease (such as Alzheimer's) in which a reading problem occurs early.

American Association of University Affiliated Programs for Persons with Developmental Disabilities   National association with sites at major universities and teaching hospitals that support the independence, integration, and

inclusion of people with developmental disabilities and their families.

Contact: 8630 Fenton Street, Suite 410, Silver Spring, MD 20910; phone: (301) 588–8252; website: http://www.aauap.org.

American Association on Mental Retardation   National organization providing information, services, and support, plus advocacy.

Contact: 444 North Capitol Street, NW, Suite 846, Washington, DC 20001; phone: (800) 424–3688; (202) 387–1968; website: http://www.aamr.org.

American Speech-Language-Hearing Association (ASHA)   The professional, scientific, and credentialing association for more than 99,000 speech-language pathologists, audiologists, and speech, language, and hearing scientists in the United States. The organization provides information and referrals to the public on speech, language, communication, and hearing disorders.

Contact: 10801 Rockville Pike, Rockville, MD 20852; phone: (800) 498–2071 (voice) or (301) 897–5700 TTY; website: http://www.asha.org.

Americans With Disabilities Act (ADA), The   Legislation enacted in July 1990 that prohibits discrimination against individuals with disabilities. It guarantees equal opportunity for people with disabilities in jobs, public accommodations, transportation, and telecommunications, as well as other state services.

The ADA represents a significant addition to the scope of protections defined by the Civil Rights Act of 1964, which was not intended to protect the rights of individuals with disabilities. It also augments other laws that address issues of disability and access to education and employment opportunities, such as the INDIVIDUALS WITH DISABILITIES EDUCATION ACT (IDEA) and the REHABILITATION ACT OF 1973.

While the ADA covers many areas of possible discrimination (including schools), it is used primarily to protect individuals with disabilities on the job. The IDEA and CRA offer more specific protections and regulations in regard to schools and colleges.

On the job, employers are required to provide fair opportunities to individuals with disabilities if they are "otherwise qualified" for a position. For example, a person who is partly blind can't perform the essential functions of airline pilot. A person in a wheelchair, however, may be able to perform the essential functions of a bookkeeper, and therefore should not be discriminated against based on physical limitations.

Employers and schools may also be required to provide accessibility to buildings for those who have physical disabilities. Employers with more than 15 employees also may be required to provide accommodations for employees with specific needs based on their disability, such as equipment or more frequent breaks. "Disability" is an important term from a legal perspective, as it distinguishes those with temporary limitations or less severe limitations from those for whom a physical or mental impairment limits major life activities.

For people with LEARNING DISABILITIES, the ADA provides legislative support for accommodations within both educational and workplace settings. Unlike the federal legislation governing public education for children with learning disabilities, the ADA places a much greater burden of responsibility on the person seeking services or accommodations. The ADA also clearly protects educational institutions and employers from being required to provide accommodations that place unreasonable burdens or that represent significant lowering of educational standards. At the same time, the ADA also provides broad protection for individuals with learning disabilities in a wide variety of contexts.

analogy   A comparison between two different but related things. The ability to comprehend and create analogies is an important component of critical reasoning abilities. For example, an analogy might compare the biological process of a tree growing from small seed to tall oak, to the human process of development from infancy to adulthood. This analogy would be written:

SEED : OAK AS INFANT : ADULT

Another type of analogy is the visual analogy. For example, in a 2 X 2 cell grid, the two cells on the left might contain blue stars, and the top cell on the right might contain a green square. The person taking the test must then select which of several presented figures (including the correct green square) must go in the empty cell.

For some students with learning disabilities, understanding analogies may be very difficult. They may process information in fairly concrete ways, and miss more subtle connections between dissimilar things. Often, however, the ability to reason analogically is a relative strength for students with learning disabilities.

anarithmia   See ACALCULIA.

Angelman syndrome   A childhood disorder characterized by HYPERACTIVITY, seizures, laughter, and developmental delays. Initially presumed to be rare, it's now believed that thousands of children with Angelman syndrome cases have gone undiagnosed or misdiagnosed as CEREBRAL PALSY, AUTISM, or other childhood disorders.

In 1965, English physician Harry Angelman, M.D., first described three children with characteristics now known as Angelman syndrome, including stiff, jerky gait; lack of speech; excessive laughter; and seizures. Other cases were eventually published, but the condition was considered to be extremely rare and many physicians doubted its existence. The first reports from North America appeared in the early 1980s, and since then many new reports have appeared.

In the United States and Canada, there are about 1,000 diagnosed individuals, but it has been reported throughout the world among divergent racial groups. In North America, most cases seem to be of Caucasian origin.

Angelman syndrome is usually not recognized at birth or in infancy, since the developmental problems are hard to spot at that time. Parents may first suspect the diagnosis after reading about AS or meeting a child with the condition. The most common age of diagnosis is between age three and seven, when the characteristic behaviors and features become evident.

Symptoms

Hyperactivity and a short attention span are probably the most typical behaviors, which affect boys and girls about equally. Infants and toddlers may be continually active, constantly keeping their hands or toys in their mouth, moving from object to object. In extreme cases, the constant movement can cause accidental bruises. There may be grabbing, pinching, and biting in older children. A child's attention span can be so short that it interferes with social interaction, since the child can't pay attention to facial and other social cues.

Laughter is also quite common, which seems to be a reaction to physical or mental stimuli. Although AS children experience a variety of emotions, apparent happiness is most common. Parents may first notice this laughter at the age of one to three months. Giggling, chortling, and constant smiling soon develop and appear to represent normal reflexive laughter, but cooing and babbling are delayed.

Other symptoms include

- developmental delay
- severe speech impairment with almost no use of words
- movement or balance disorder
- easily excitable personality, often with hand-flapping movements
- abnormally small head
- seizures

Treatment

Persistent and consistent behavior modification helps decrease or eliminate unwanted behavior. In milder cases, the child's attention may be good enough to learn sign language and other communication techniques. For these children, educational and developmental training programs are much easier to structure and are generally more effective.

Most children don't receive drug therapy for hyperactivity, although some may benefit from use of medications such as methylphenidate (RITALIN).

Angelman Syndrome Foundation Foundation provides information on diagnosis, treatment, and management, and offers support and advocacy through education, information exchange, and research. The group also offers local contacts and a newsletter.

Contact: 414 Plaza Drive, Suite 209, Westmont, IL 60559; phone: (800) IF.ANGEL or (630) 734–9267; website: http://www.angelman.org.

angular gyrus A part of the brain that plays an important part in language processing. It is involved in recoding visual information so that this information can be interpreted as auditory code. Some research suggests that during reading tasks the brains of individuals with DYSLEXIA may be less active than nondyslexics in the angular gyrus, as well as in a part of the brain called WERNICKE'S AREA.

anomia The inability to find the correct word. Anomia is Latin-derived and means "without a name" or "unnamed." It is a type of aphasia that involves the loss of ability to recall words, such as the names of objects, persons, activities, and so on.

anoxia The total deprivation of oxygen. In general, it refers to the ways in which oxygen deprivation damages the brain. Brain damage caused by anoxia can range from subtle learning disabilities to profound mental retardation, depending on severity.

Anoxia during birth may cause brain damage that affects the ability to learn. Brain damage resulting from anoxia may also occur from any situation in which a person is deprived of oxygen for a significant period of time.

antecedent event   One of the three key elements (the other two elements are behavior [response] and consequence [reinforcement]) of the BEHAVIORAL UNIT, a model at the core of behavioral psychology. The antecedent event is the stimulus that results in a response. For example, a teacher's cue to sit quietly at a desk and take out paper and pencil might be viewed as an antecedent event designed to stimulate the students to take out paper and pencil (response).

antisocial personality disorder   A type of personality disorder characterized by disregard for the feelings and rights of others. Patterns of irresponsibility, aggression toward others, and impulsive "acting out" in social situations recur and interfere with a person's ability to function in society. Antisocial personality disorder exists in 2 percent to 3 percent of the general population, and is three to four times more common in men than in women. The popular term "sociopath" has replaced the older term "psychopath" for a person with this disorder.

People with this disorder may be in trouble with the law and have trouble maintaining interpersonal relationships. Antisocial personality disorder is an adult diagnosis that is often given to individuals (typically male) who were diagnosed with CONDUCT DISORDER as children. Research suggests that antisocial personality disorder can coexist with ATTENTION DEFICIT/HYPERACTIVITY DISORDER (ADHD).

Cause

Research suggests that the condition may be caused by an interaction between a genetic predisposition and environment, since other risk factors include regular exposure to substance abuse and criminal behavior, as well as a childhood characterized by chaotic, neglectful, harsh, or abusive parenting. Attention deficit/hyperac-

tivity disorder and conduct disorders in childhood can herald the subsequent development of antisocial personality disorders in adulthood.

Symptoms

Although the diagnosis is limited to people over age 18, there is always a history of antisocial behavior since age 15, including repetitive lying, truancy, delinquency, and substance abuse. As an adult, there is a pattern of unlawful behavior, failure of job and family responsibility, reckless personal behavior, promiscuity, failure to sustain long-term relationships, and aggressive behavior. Superficial charm and wit can be highly developed and skillfully used. Symptoms of antisocial personality disorder include

- impulsiveness and a lack of concern for consequences
- pattern of criminal behavior
- lying and deceit for personal profit or pleasure
- lack of empathy
- irritability, aggressiveness, and violent behavior
- disregard for safety or responsibility
- lack of remorse

Treatment

Drug treatment has not proven to be helpful. The fact that antisocial personality disorder develops early and is the natural way these patients define themselves makes treatment more difficult. Effective treatment must address a person's basic behavioral patterns, attitudes, relationship styles, and function. In most cases, antisocial personality disorder can respond to therapy, but changing habits of thought, feeling, and behavior requires extensive and repetitive examination, evaluation, and relearning. Definitive inpatient treatment must be provided in a specialized hospital unit so that a patient's problems with the inability to trust, to fantasize, to feel, and to learn can be addressed.

Some experts believe that the single most effective factor in helping individuals with antisocial personality turn their behavior around is a close, personal relationship with a significant older mentor, to whom the antisocial person looks as a role model.

Typically, most antisocial persons don't actively seek therapy; instead, they usually come to treatment as a result of court orders. However, outlook for successful treatment is poor.

anxiety   A feeling of apprehension, fear, or worry not connected to a specific threat. Many experts believe that anxiety is a learned response to stress. For example, a child who has been stung by a bee will run away crying on the next appearance of a flying buzzing insect. Should the avoidance continue to be reinforced, the anxiety continues.

Cognitive psychologists believe that anxiety is the result of inappropriate thinking about circumstances. For someone who has an irrational fear of snakes, a picture of a snake can cause anxiety even though it's not possible to be hurt by a two-dimensional picture.

People with learning disabilities may often have accompanying problems with anxiety, especially in connection to schoolwork. Reading aloud, taking timed tests, or trying to start a writing assignment all may trigger anxiety and cause even further problems with the required task. Someone experiencing a high level of anxiety may "freeze up" and find it impossible to perform at all, or may show signs of restlessness and agitation, leading to erratic and inconsistent performance.

There is also a significant link between attention deficits and anxiety. To some degree, it can be hard to tell the difference between the two. An inability to focus and sustain attention may often lead to anxiety, and anxiety itself can make it very difficult for a person to pay attention to a task. In some cases, attention deficit disorders coexist with anxiety disorders.

It's also possible for someone with an anxiety disorder to be misdiagnosed as having ADHD. In evaluating ADHD, a differential diagnosis for anxiety may be important. It is equally important that those who work with individuals with ADHD take into account the possibility that anxiety may underlie some expressions of learning, communication, and social difficulties.

aphasia   A language disorder characterized by profound difficulties with both expressing and understanding language. Individuals with aphasia experience problems understanding language; there are problems with word-finding ability, and speech may be incoherent. There is often a combination of naming, fluency, comprehension, and repetition deficits that are accompanied by reading and writing impairments (AGRAPHIA). However, aphasia does not include speech disorders. Most patients have disturbed language function rather than complete loss of language.

Caused by damage to the temporal or frontal lobe in the brain, aphasia may be the result of a stroke, brain injury, or infection. Its severity can vary; some people can't communicate at all, while others may have problems with just one aspect of language (such as word retrieval).

Types of Aphasia

There are a number of types of aphasia that are characterized by different symptoms:

- amnesic: word-finding difficulties that imply words have been "forgotten"
- anomic: problems with naming ability sometimes called nominal aphasia or amnesic aphasia
- conduction: fluent aphasia with severely impaired repetition but relatively preserved language comprehension, with word-finding difficulties. Patients with conduction aphasia have difficulty reading aloud but they may have relatively good comprehension.
- global: involves loss of nearly all fluency, comprehension, repetition, reading, and writing. Large brain lesions in both Broca's and Wernicke's area (and nearby tissue) are usually involved.

- jargon: characterized by fluent speech that may be incomprehensible. Speech contains numerous incorrect word selections with significant repetition. Jargon aphasia is an acute expression of Wernicke's aphasia.

- mixed transcortical: a rare subtype in which patients are unable to name, read, and write.

- nonfluent: effortful speech production and lack of normal emotional tone or quality in speech. Nonfluent aphasia includes Broca's aphasia, global aphasia, transcortical motor aphasia, and mixed transcortical aphasia.

- posterior: fluent aphasia, also known as Wernicke's aphasia. The term is no longer widely used.

- pure motor: nonfluent speech with largely preserved language functioning demonstrated by the ability to write. It is also called apraxia of speech.

- transcortical motor: nonfluent aphasia characterized by preserved repetition and relatively preserved language comprehension

- transcortical sensory: fluent aphasia in which language comprehension is severely impaired. It may occur in the later stages of Alzheimer's disease.

aphasia, developmental   A term used to describe an individual whose difficulties in learning to speak are severe and pervasive. Developmental APHASIA is generally linked to a problem in the central nervous system present since birth, as opposed to acquired aphasia, which describes the loss of the ability to speak due to brain damage.

aphasoid   A mild or moderate retardation in the development of language competence, associated with mild problems in expressing language (APHASIA).

aphemia   Loss of the ability to speak. In this condition, written communication is possible, but spoken communication is impossible. Both speech and written words are understood, however. Some experts use the term interchangeably with motor aphasia.

apraxia   A general term describing impairment of the ability to carry out physical movements involved in communication. Children with this problem have trouble transmitting the speech message from their brain to their mouths, and have problems translating their thoughts into a correct sequence of movements using their mouth, tongue, and lips. A child with apraxia of speech can have speech that is very limited and unclear, making it difficult for others to understand the child. This is not something a child will outgrow, but with early speech therapy by a trained speech-language pathologist, many children with apraxia are capable of learning to speak clearly and communicate effectively. However, without the necessary and appropriate therapy, children with apraxia may never speak clearly and experience a lifetime of frustration.

Some forms of apraxia involve impairments in the ability to use gestures or movement in nonverbal communication, such as waving or pointing.

aptitude   An individual's ability to learn, without reference to specific instruction or prior knowledge. Aptitude is most often measured by STANDARDIZED TESTS such as intelligence tests (for example, the WECHSLER INTELLIGENCE SCALE FOR CHILDREN) or cognitive batteries of tests that also include achievement components (such as the Woodcock-Johnson). Other important aptitude tests include the Scholastic Aptitude Test (SAT) and the American College Test (ACT), each of which plays a prominent role in college admissions.

Determining whether someone has a learning disability is generally based on a discrepancy between achievement and aptitude, as measured by standardized tests. Consequently, tests of aptitude such as the WISC and the Woodcock-

Johnson play a central role in determining who is eligible to receive special education services.

aptitude test   A measurement of a person's ability to learn, typically using tests for specific abilities in order to predict achievement in these areas. For example, the Scholastic Aptitude Test (SAT) is commonly used to assess potential ability to succeed in college.

See also APTITUDE.

arcuate fasciculus   A pathway of fibers in the parietal lobe of the brain that connects WERNICKE'S AREA with BROCA'S AREA. When this connection first develops at about age two, children become able to form words into sentences. If it is damaged, the child will be able to understand words that are heard or read but won't be able to repeat them. This condition is called conduction APHASIA.

arithmetic disability   A subtype of a specific learning disability that relates to computational arithmetic skills, rote learning or memorizing, writing, or difficulties with fine motor coordination. Federal law differentiates two subareas of arithmetic disability: mathematics calculation and mathematics reasoning.

There can be a variety of reasons for problems with arithmetic. The more severe subtypes (such as DYSCALCULIA) are based in the brain and relate to visual spatial ability. For others, mathematics ability is impaired by cognitive difficulties or poor information processing.

Those affected with arithmetic disability have a particular cognitive and neuropsychological profile that is different from those with primarily reading deficits, although the two disabilities may coexist in a single individual.

arousal regulation   The regulation of arousal and alertness is associated with the frontal lobe and the BASAL GANGLIA in the brain. Difficulties in regulating arousal have been connected to

ADHD, and in some theories are seen as the central deficiency in attention disorders. There is some evidence that the way in which Ritalin and other stimulants help a person with ADHD is by stimulating the basal ganglia.

A person who has problems with arousal regulation may have difficulty staying alert and focused, and may also have problems with over-arousal and difficulty falling asleep at an appropriate time. For some individuals, difficulty with arousal regulation may be so severe that they may be classified as having a sleep disorder.

articulation   The production of speech sounds. In the human body, speech is produced through the combined work of several organs, including the larynx (voice box), tongue, lips, and pharynx. The respiratory system is also involved in producing basic speech sounds.

Articulation also involves other aspects of speech production, including intonation and enunciation of specific sounds. Difficulties with articulation are sometimes associated with language-based learning disorders, or with speech-language disabilities.

A person who has difficulty pronouncing certain sounds may have a speech disorder, rather than a specific language disorder. In order to produce speech, a person must coordinate muscle movement, including the respiratory system and larynx. Articulation skills and remediation of speech disorders are addressed by a SPEECH/ LANGUAGE SPECIALIST.

articulatory phonetics   The study and classification of speech sounds based on the way they are produced by the vocal cords.

Asperger's disorder (Asperger syndrome)   A condition characterized by sustained problems with social interactions and social relatedness, and the development of restricted, repetitive patterns of interests, activities, and behaviors. The disorder is named after Hans Asperger, a

Viennese pediatrician who first documented this cluster of characteristics in the 1940s.

It is believed to be a milder variant of AUTISM, but without the delays in cognitive or language development. In 1994 Asperger's was first classified as a pervasive developmental disorder (a designation that includes autistic disorder).

Many children with pervasive developmental disorders such as Asperger's disorder also meet the diagnostic criteria for ATTENTION DEFICIT/ HYPERACTIVITY DISORDER (ADHD). However, ADHD should not be diagnosed when there is Asperger's, since all the ADHD symptoms can be attributed to the other condition. Clinicians who overlook other symptoms of Asperger's tend to diagnose these children as ADHD.

Like many learning disorders, Asperger's is believed to be more common in males, although more research needs to be done to understand its genetic origins. According to the National Institutes of Health, Asperger disorder occurs in one out of every 500 Americans—more often than multiple sclerosis, Down syndrome, or cystic fibrosis. It is estimated that more than 400,000 families are affected by this condition.

Symptoms

Often there are no obvious delays in language or cognitive development, or in age-appropriate self-help skills. While these individuals possess attention deficits, problems with organization, and an uneven profile of skills, they usually have average and sometimes gifted intelligence.

Individuals with Asperger's syndrome may have problems with social situations and in developing peer relationships. They may have noticeable difficulty with nonverbal communication and an impaired use of social gestures, facial expressions, and eye contact. There may be certain repetitive behaviors or rituals. Though grammatical, speech is peculiar due to abnormal inflection and repetition. Clumsiness is prominent both in speech and physical movements. Individuals with this disorder usually have a limited area of interest that usually excludes more age-appropriate, common interests. Some examples of these single-minded obsessions may include cars, trains, Russian literature, door knobs, hinges, astronomy, or history.

Asperger's vs. Autism

When compared to autism, Asperger's disorder usually appears later in life, with less severe social and communication problems. Clumsiness and single-minded interests are more common, and verbal IQ is usually higher than performance IQ (in autism, the reverse is usually true). The outcome is usually more positive than for autism.

Cause

While biological factors are of crucial importance in the etiology of autism, so far brain imaging studies with Asperger's cases have found no consistent pattern or evidence of any type of lesion, and no single location of any lesion.

Associated medical conditions such as fragile-X syndrome, tuberous sclerosis, neurofibromatosis, and hypothyroidism (sluggish thyroid) are less common in Asperger's disorder than in classical autism. Therefore, scientists suspect there may be fewer major physical brain problems associated with Asperger's than with autism.

Treatment

While there is no cure, early intervention has been proven to be effective. The need for academic and social supports increases through the school years, and by adolescence many children develop symptoms of depression and anxiety. It is important to continue supports into adulthood to ensure affected adults can lead productive lives.

Symptoms can be managed using individual psychotherapy to help the individual to process the feelings aroused by being socially handicapped. Other treatments may include parent education and training, behavioral modification, social skills training, educational interventions, and medication. Drug therapy may include the following:

- hyperactivity, inattention, and impulsivity: stimulants such as methylphenidate, dex-

troamphetamine, methamphetamine, pemoline, clonidine, and tricyclic antidepressants
(desipramine, nortriptyline)

- irritability and aggression: mood stabilizers
(valproate, carbamazepine, lithium), beta
blockers (nadolol, propranolol), neuroleptics
(risperidone, haloperidol)

- preoccupations, rituals, and compulsions:
antidepressants (fluvoxamine, fluoxetine,
clomipramine)

- anxiety: antidepressants (sertraline, fluoxetine, imipramine, clomipramine, nortriptyline)

Contact online: http://www.aspergers.com

**Asperger Syndrome Coalition of the United
States** A national nonprofit support and advocacy organization for ASPERGER'S DISORDER and
related disorders that is committed to providing
the most up-to-date and comprehensive information on the condition.

Contact: PO Box 49267, Jacksonville Beach,
FL 32240.

assessment A general term that covers a wide
range of activities, instruments, and approaches
involved in evaluating prior performance,
describing present abilities and behaviors, and
predicting future performance and behaviors.
"Assessment" differs from "testing," which
reflects performance on particular tasks at a specific time. Instead, "assessment" interprets overall patterns and relationships among testing
results and other observations.

In the area of learning disabilities and special
education, assessment generally has two purposes. The first is to classify the nature of the
problems an individual is experiencing and to
provide a diagnosis. The second involves planning treatment, including instruction, social and
behavioral interventions, and medications (in
the case of ADHD).

Traditional assessment procedures tend to
focus on STANDARDIZED TESTS, including tests of

ability and tests of achievement. A typical school
assessment might include an intelligence test
(such as the WISC-III or Stanford-Binet) and
ACHIEVEMENT TESTS (such as the Woodcock-
Johnson battery).

The typical assessment in special education
includes individual tests measuring intelligence,
achievement, behavior and adaptive behavior.
Other assessments may be added depending on
the nature of the child's disability.

A neuropsychological assessment might
include a more comprehensive group of tests
designed to identify functioning in specific areas
such as memory or visual processing. In most
cases, such standardized testing is used together
with case histories, interviews, and details on
actual performance at school, among friends,
and at home. In some cases, assessment may also
incorporate testing in specific areas of brain
function. Assessment may also include testing
designed to identify emotional, psychological,
and personality factors that may be involved in
learning difficulties.

The field of assessment is in a state of continuous development in order to discover more
accurate methods of evaluating performance
and behavior. Portfolios may be used as an alternative to assessing a student's academic achievement. Evaluators may assess an individual's
ability to learn—rather than test for what the
person already knows. Finally, contemporary
assessment may also focus on an individual's
abilities in the areas of strategy development and
problem solving.

Types of Assessment

"Authentic assessment" is usually done at
school, and places demands on the individual
linked to the actual academic program, such as
reading from a passage assigned in class and
answering questions about it, giving a short
speech about an experience or a topic assigned
in class, or solving mathematics problems that
have a real-life component.

"Performance assessment" is similar to authentic assessment; it is intended to evaluate

how well a student performs in relationship to the actual school curriculum. This sort of assessment is typically part of a teacher's effort in evaluating students' performances on assigned tasks. Portfolio assessment is an increasingly common form of performance assessment, used to measure student progress in reading, writing, and mathematics over time. Portfolio assessment involves collected multiple samples of a student's work over time, keyed to the specific objectives of the curriculum and derived from a wide range of different activities.

"Dynamic assessment" evaluates what students already know plus their ability to learn new skills, strategies, and information. For this, a student might be given, as a baseline, a set of problems to assess initial performance, followed by a similar set of problems after instruction. Assessment of this sort may help to more accurately predict a student's potential to learn and to be successful.

Assessment of problem-solving and strategy development is related to dynamic assessment in that it attempts to evaluate a student's ability to learn, rather than to create a static picture of what a student already knows. Assessment of this sort attempts to identify student's ability to reflect on their own knowledge and strategies, and to develop new strategies and problem-solving procedures based on this. Students who performs well on an assessment of this sort, but performs poorly on more standard or traditional assessment measures, may be demonstrating a gap between the quality of their school experience and their actual potential to learn and succeed. Likewise, a student who has significant problems in assessment of this sort may require much more extensive and focused school interventions.

In general, assessment is an area in which the field of learning disabilities is continuing to change and develop. New developments in this area are likely to include continued questioning of the usefulness of intelligence testing and the discrepancy formula for defining learning disabilities. There will be greater focus on both tra-ditional testing and on more performance-based approaches to measuring a student's actual academic capabilities.

assistive technology Any technology that enables an individual with a LEARNING DISABILITY to compensate for specific deficits. This includes a broad scope of learning tools ranging from the use of tape recorders to voice-activated software programs. Since the onset of the age of computers, assistive technology often refers to computer technology.

Computers are extremely useful to everyone, but they are especially important to people with learning disabilities because they offer powerful and flexible tools for reading and writing. For example, computers allow individuals to find ways to become independent learners. At any point in the writing process, computer software programs can provide the help that once was provided by a teacher, tutor, or parent.

However, not all uses of technology are helpful for everyone. With a wide range of ever-changing products in the market, one of the hardest tasks is to link the most effective technology with an individual's learning profile.

Many people see assistive technology as a way of circumventing deficits; for example, a student with writing problems that make taking notes in class virtually impossible may be allowed to tape the lecture as a way of bypassing this area of weakness. After all, the goal is to learn the information from the lecture—not to improve note-taking skills. This is what is referred to as a *compensatory approach.*

In a *remedial approach,* technology is used to directly address skill deficits. For example, in this approach the same person who relied on taped lectures could use a keyboarding program to improve note-taking skills.

Furthermore, the two approaches are not necessarily mutually exclusive. In many cases, the use of assistive technology to bypass a problem also improves the area of weakness at the same time. For example, students who tape a

FORMS OF ASSISTIVE TECHNOLOGY AND USES FOR INDIVIDUALS WITH LEARNING DISABILITIES

Technology	Strengths	Limitations	LD Characteristic
Word Processing	• Circumvents handwriting and spelling difficulties • Easily allows: - deleting - inserting - moving - copying text • Allows information to be arranged graphically into charts and tables • Can customize text by size, color, style	• Does not directly improve spelling • Spell check and grammar check can be confusing or distracting • Spell/grammar check can give a false sense of accuracy	• Writing aversion • Handwriting difficulties • Visual weakness • Short-term memory weakness
Spell Checker	• Identify misspelled words • Suggest correct spellings	• Proper nouns are flagged as spelling errors • Does not catch errors that are real words/homonyms • Suggestions for severe misspellings are unhelpful	• Poor spellers • Some phonological awareness • Strong visual discrimination
Word Prediction	• Limits the amount of keyboarding • Used in conjunction with synthesized speech can be very useful in spelling • Assist spelling/word choice during writing rather than during revisions	• Can interrupt the flow of writing • Visually similar words are displayed	• Severe spelling problems • Eye-hand/keyboarding difficulties
Voice Recognition	• Transcribes spoken language into text	• Does not work with 100% accuracy	• Oral language skills exceed written language
Outlining/Semantic Webbing	• Provides visual-graphic structures to show relationships among ideas • Allows ideas to be "dumped" into the program and then organized later	• Weak in terms of spelling/word processing functions	• Visual learner • "Big Picture" learners • Difficulties generating ideas • Difficulties moving from generating ideas to starting papers
Screen Reader/ Synthesized Speech	• Enables user to hear text on computer screen spoken aloud • Uses a computer (synthesized) voice • Scan or import text • Improves decoding and fluency • Some versions provide study skills and active reading support • Allows users to hear what they have written • Helps identify errors in syntax and spelling	• Unnatural speech voices can be distracting • Uses significant computer memory when used with other programs	• Poor spellers • Oral language skills exceed written language

lecture may be sketching written notes (by pencil or keyboard) at the same time. Later, students may revisit the tape to supplement written notes, while improving writing skills in class.

The following chart outlines some of the most commonly used assistive technologies.

Because computers allow users to control, customize, and manipulate the learning environment, more so than static text environments, assistive technology offers flexibility and options to individuals with learning disabilities. While it isn't the only answer, the explosion in modern technology has made an enormous impact on the lives of individuals with learning disabilities who have access to such tools.

Assistive Technology Act of 1998 This law, also known as PL 105–394, replaced the Technology-Related Assistance for Individuals with Disabilities Act of 1988. This new act, authorized through fiscal year 2004, addresses the assistive-technology needs of individuals with disabilities.

See also ASSISTIVE TECHNOLOGY.

Association on Higher Education and Disability An international, multicultural organization of professionals committed to full participation in higher education for persons with disabilities. The association promotes education, communication, and training through numerous training programs, workshops, publications, and conferences. AHEAD was founded in 1977 to address the need and concern for upgrading the quality of services and support available to those with disabilities in higher education.

Contact: University of Massachusetts–Boston, 100 Morrissey Boulevard, Boston, MA 02125–3393; phone: (617) 287–3880; website: http://www.ahead.org.

astereognosis Deficient ability to recognize objects by touch alone. It involves the inability to discriminate shape, texture, weight, and size of objects. Astereognosis often occurs with lesions in the parietal lobe of the brain.

ataxia The complete or partial inability to control or coordinate body movements; this may include an unsteady gait and poor coordination of speech. Ataxia is caused by a group of rare, hereditary diseases known as the hereditary ataxias, which vary in age of onset and severity of symptoms. They are generally characterized by breakdown of the cerebellum, brain stem, and spinal cord.

Another type of ataxia (nongenetic ataxia) can be acquired as a result of multiple sclerosis, alcoholism, or other diseases.

There is no direct relationship between ataxia and learning disabilities, although developmental disabilities are common with the problem. Ongoing evaluation, diagnosis, and educational assessment are necessary. In acquired ataxia, there may be specific treatments for the underlying diseases.

attention The focus of consciousness on something in the environment, or on a sensation or an idea. Attention includes a number of elements that are essential to all activities, including the following:

- arousal: being ready to receive stimuli
- vigilance: being able to select stimuli from those presented over a period of time
- persistence or continuity: being able to sustain a mental effort and select stimuli that are presented often
- monitoring: checking for and correcting errors

The length of time in which a child can pay attention to something (the attention span) increases with age, interest, and intelligence level.

Breakdowns in these different elements can cause a variety of problems. A breakdown in vigilance, for example, might cause someone to select or focus on the wrong details. A breakdown in monitoring might lead to repeated careless errors. Persistence or continuity is necessary for a complex task to be completed.

attention deficit/hyperactivity disorder (ADHD)

A condition that may occur in both children and adults who consistently display inattention, hyperactivity, and impulsivity. People who are inattentive may have trouble keeping their mind focused, and may get bored with a task after just a few minutes. Those who are hyperactive seem to feel restless and are constantly in motion, finding it hard to sit still. People who are impulsive have a problem with curbing their immediate reactions and tend to act before they think. Other symptoms may include problems in school, with friends, and with behavior.

ADHD and LEARNING DISABILITIES frequently occur together, but they are not the same. Learning disabilities include difficulty with receiving, organizing, understanding, remembering, and offering information. ADHD involves difficulty with paying attention to information. Between 10 percent and 20 percent of all school-age children have learning disabilities. Of those with learning disabilities, between 4 percent and 12 percent of all school-age children will also have ADHD, making it the most common childhood neurobehavioral disorder.

Although ADHD is a common childhood behavioral disorder, it can be difficult to diagnose and even harder to understand. Once viewed as a disorder of childhood primarily involving hyperactivity and the inability to pay attention, ADHD is now seen as a lifelong condition that may not include physical restlessness or hyperactive behavior at all. It may also be a source of unusual talents or giftedness in specific areas.

In recent years, there has been growing interest in ADHD as well as concern about possible overdiagnosis. In surveys among pediatricians and family physicians across the country, wide variations were found in diagnostic criteria and treatment methods for ADHD. Indeed, the definition and treatments of ADHD continue to evolve; over the past decade, there has been an extraordinary surge in the level of focus on ADHD and in the incidence of diagnosis among children and adults. It is likely that the present level of understanding of the disorder, as well as current methods of diagnosis and treatment, will continue to develop rapidly in the coming years.

Once thought to be a disorder primarily affecting young hyperactive boys, ADHD is both more complicated and more pervasive. In particular, experts now know that children don't typically "outgrow" the condition, nor does it affect only males. The present gender ratio ranges from 3 to 1 to 7 to 1 males to females, but this is hampered by inconsistent standards for diagnosis and insufficient research samples.

Cause

ADHD is presumed to be a brain condition that affects between 3 percent and 7 percent of the population. Since the early 1990s, scientists have worked to pinpoint the differences found in brain scans between the normal brain and the ADHD brain. Recently, scientists have been able to localize the brain areas involved in ADHD, finding that areas in the FRONTAL LOBE and BASAL GANGLIA are reduced by about 10 percent in size and activity in children with ADHD.

Studies in the past few years have shown that boys with ADHD tend to have brains that are more symmetrical. Three structures in the brains of boys with ADHD were smaller than in non-ADHD boys of the same age: prefrontal cortex, caudate nucleus, and the globus pallidus. The prefrontal cortex is thought to be the brain's "command center"; the other two parts translate the commands into action.

There is evidence that not only are some of the structures slightly varied, but also the brain may use these areas differently. Watching brain scans, researchers discovered that boys with

ADHD have an abnormal increase of activity in the frontal lobe and certain areas below it. These areas work in part to control voluntary action. This meant that the ADHD boys were working harder to control their impulses than non-ADHD boys. Once given Ritalin, this abnormal activity quieted down. This effect was not seen in the non-ADHD boys. This means that Ritalin may act differently on ADHD brains compared to "normal" brains.

Although brain scans (called functional magnetic resonance imaging or fMRI) are expensive and may not be covered by insurance, they may provide a more accurate way to diagnose ADHD. As scientists explore more of the brain, ADHD may be thought of more as a disorder than a behavioral problem.

DOPAMINE pathways in the brain, which link the basal ganglia and frontal cortex, also appear to play a major role in ADHD. The National Institute of Mental Health released the results of a major clinical trial focusing on ADHD, which found that medication, which boosts the level of dopamine in the brain, is the most successful type of treatment.

Experts believe that at least some cases of ADHD may be inherited, and that it may involve both brain structures in the frontal lobe related to attention, impulse control, and EXECUTIVE FUNCTIONS, as well as neurotransmitters and subtle imbalances in brain chemistry. Other children may experience abnormal fetal development that affects the areas of the brain controlling attention and movement.

Diagnosis

ADHD is primarily diagnosed through a combination of individual and family history, individual behavioral assessments, and information about behavior from parents, teachers, and others. Some tests also contain factors for inattention, distractibility, and memory that can be affected by ADHD, and may contribute to a diagnosis.

In addition, certain medical conditions such as hypothyroidism, juvenile diabetes, and seizure disorders must be ruled out as causes for the child's inability to pay attention. Increasingly, psychologists and physicians are reluctant to make the diagnosis alone, favoring a joint diagnosis after they have gathered all necessary medical, psychological, and behavioral information.

Formerly called attention deficit disorder, with or without hyperactivity, this disorder was recently renamed attention deficit hyperactivity disorder (ADHD) and includes three subtypes:

- **inattentive subtype** (formerly known as attention deficit disorder, or ADD) with signs that include being easily distracted, an inability to pay attention to details, not following directions, losing or forgetting things like toys, notebooks, or homework
- **hyperactive-impulsive subtype** (formerly known as attention deficit hyperactivity disorder, or ADHD) includes fidgeting, squirming, blurting out answers before hearing the full question, difficulty waiting, running or jumping out of a seat when quiet behavior is expected
- **combined subtype** (the most common of the subtypes) includes those signs from both of the subtypes above, and can be seen with or without hyperactivity

To be considered for a diagnosis of ADHD, a child must display these behaviors before age seven and the behaviors must last for at least six months, and they must be considered "maladaptive." For a diagnosis, the behavior must also negatively affect at least two areas of a child's life (such as school, home, or friendships).

ADHD is diagnosed using the criteria in the *Diagnostic and Statistical Manual of Mental Disorders,* fourth edition (DSM-IV). Diagnostic criteria include:

Inattention

- often fails to give close attention to details or makes careless mistakes in schoolwork, work, or other activities

- often has difficulty sustaining attention in tasks or play activities
- often does not seem to listen when spoken to directly
- often does not follow through on instructions and fails to finish schoolwork, chores, or duties in the workplace (not due to opposi- tional behavior or failure to understand instructions)
- often has difficulty organizing tasks and activ- ities
- often avoids, dislikes, or is reluctant to engage in tasks that require sustained mental effort (such as schoolwork or homework)
- often loses things necessary for tasks or activ- ities (such as toys, school assignments, pen- cils, books, or tools)
- is often easily distracted by extraneous stimuli
- is often forgetful in daily activities

Hyperactivity-Impulsivity
- often fidgets with hands or feet or squirms in seat
- often leaves seat in classroom or in other sit- uations in which remaining seated is expected
- often runs about or climbs excessively in situ- ations in which it is inappropriate (in adoles- cents or adults, may be limited to subjective feelings of restlessness)
- often has trouble playing or engaging in leisure activities quietly
- is often on the go
- talks excessively
- often blurts out answers before questions have been completed
- often has difficulty awaiting turn
- often interrupts or intrudes on others

The American Academy of Pediatrics recently developed new guidelines for the diagnosis of ADHD with input from a panel of medical, men- tal health, and educational experts. The new guidelines, designed for primary care physicians diagnosing ADHD in children aged six to 12 years, include the following recommendations:

- ADHD evaluations should be performed by the primary care clinician for children who show signs of school difficulties, academic underachievement, troublesome relationships with teachers, family members, and peers, and other behavioral problems.
- Questions to parents, either directly or through a previsit questionnaire, regarding school and behavioral issues may help alert physicians to possible ADHD.
- In diagnosing ADHD, physicians should use DSM-IV criteria, which require symptoms to be present in two or more of a child's settings, and that the symptoms interfere with the child's academic or social functioning for at least six months.
- The assessment of ADHD should include in- formation obtained directly from parents or caregivers, as well as from a classroom teacher or other school professional, regarding the core symptoms of ADHD in various settings, the age of onset, duration of symptoms, and degree of functional impairment.
- Evaluation of a child with ADHD should also include assessment for coexisting conditions: learning and language problems, aggression, disruptive behavior, depression, or anxiety.
- Because as many as one-third of children diag- nosed with ADHD also have a coexisting con- dition, other diagnostic tests (sometimes considered positive indicators for ADHD) have been reviewed and considered not effective. These tests include lead screening, tests for generalized resistance to thyroid hormone, and brain image studies.

Of course, all children sometimes have trou- ble paying attention, following directions, or being quiet, but for children with ADHD, these behaviors occur more frequently and are more disturbing.

Symptoms

Although the primary symptoms associated with ADHD are inattention, distractibility, and hyperactivity, some current researchers now recognize ADHD as a condition that primarily affects impulse controls that delay response to external or internal stimuli. The inability of impulse controls to delay response has a significant effect on memory and executive functions that involve holding verbal or visual information in mind in order to process it, reflecting on previous experience and learning to change behavior based on it, and reconstituting prior emotional states as a means to self-understanding and development.

Symptoms of ADHD may include failing to sustain attention while playing or performing tasks, difficulty completing tasks, difficulty with organization and planning, difficulty with impulsive behavior, such as blurting out answers, acting inappropriately, and/or fidgeting and restlessness. There may also be an inability to self-monitor or self-regulate behavior, and an impaired sense of the passage of time. Individuals with ADHD frequently have difficulty getting started, lose focus, and do not finish projects. Short- and long-term planning abilities may be greatly diminished, and disorganization can result from an inability to mindfully plan, act, and complete even the most basic tasks, such as cleaning a room. Individuals with ADHD often display risk-taking or conflict-seeking behaviors, and may exhibit poor judgment in social or interpersonal contexts.

At the same time, individuals with ADHD may also display paradoxical behaviors, such as the ability to focus intensively on a task over a period of time; very strong intellectual, verbal, and problem-solving skills; and extraordinary creativity. Characteristically, both types of behavior may occur within a single place, such as a class or work environment. Because the performance of individuals with ADHD can be strong, especially when they are very interested, subsequent failure to perform at the same level is often perceived as a lack of self-discipline or effort.

The symptoms for ADHD must be pervasive and long-lasting, usually appearing before age seven. Adults who are diagnosed late in life often report severe and lifelong problems in school, job, or with personal relationships. They may feel misunderstood and are frequently misdiagnosed, given the range of varying symptoms that can develop as a result of an attention disorder.

ADHD and Other Disorders

ADHD can coexist with a number of psychological conditions, including conduct disorders, mood disorders (such as depression), anxiety disorders, and impulse control disorders (such as eating disorders and alcohol abuse). Some children may be depressed as a result of having ADHD, whereas others may have a mood disorder that exists independently of ADHD. Nearly half of all children with ADHD also have oppositional defiant disorder, characterized by stubbornness, outbursts of temper, and defiance.

Many children with ADHD also have a specific learning disability, which means that they might have trouble mastering language or other skills, such as math, reading, or handwriting. Although ADHD is not categorized as a learning disability, its interference with concentration and attention can make it even more difficult for a child to perform well in school. The issue of coexisting conditions makes diagnosis, treatment, and understanding of ADHD particularly complex.

Treatment

There is no cure for ADHD, but a combined program of medication and behavioral therapy can help and is often prescribed to treat ADHD. With the advice and cooperation of a child's pediatrician, teachers, counselors, and family members, the child can have a normal life in spite of this disorder.

Medication

For most children and adults with ADHD, medication is an important part of treatment that isn't used to "control" behavior but to ease the symptoms of ADHD. Stimulants appear to work by altering the levels of transmitters in the brain by which the different nerve cells communicate.

Between 70 and 80 percent of children with ADHD respond positively to these medications, with improvements in attention span, impulsivity, and behavior, especially in structured environments. Some children also demonstrate improvements in frustration tolerance, compliance, and even handwriting. Relationships with parents, peers, and teachers may also improve.

This medication may also be effective in adults who have ADHD. The reaction to these medications can be similar to that experienced by children with ADHD—a decrease in impulsivity and an increase in attention. Many ADHD adults treated with medication report that they are able to bring more control and organization to their lives. Other medications, such as antidepressants, can be helpful when depression and phobic, panic, anxiety and/or obsessive-compulsive disorders are present.

The drugs usually include regular, fairly small doses of stimulants such as RITALIN (methylphenidate), DEXEDRINE, Dextrostat (dextroamphetamine), ADDERALL (single entity amphetamine), or CYLERT (pemoline). While these drugs can be addictive in teenagers and adults, they don't seem to be addictive in children. Nine out of 10 children improve on one of these stimulants; so if one does not work, others are tried. It may seem strange to give stimulants to children with hyperactivity and attention deficit problems, but instead of making the child act out more, these drugs reduce the hyperactivity and increase the attention span. The drugs also help children with ADHD control their behavior. A child using these drugs actually becomes quieter and more attentive.

Sometimes, however, none of these medications work. In this case, some children may respond well to antihistamines usually prescribed for allergies, or to antidepressants like Elavil, Prozac, Tofranil, or Norpramin. Clonidine, a drug normally used to treat high blood pressure, may ease some symptoms of ADHD. With any of these medications, adjusting the dosage for each child is vital for treating the symptoms of ADHD.

Side Effects

Stimulant drugs do cause side effects. Most doctors feel the potential side effects should be carefully weighed against the benefits before prescribing drugs to children with ADHD. While taking these medications, some children may lose weight, have stomachaches or have less appetite, and temporarily grow more slowly. Others may have trouble falling asleep and become irritable. Some doctors worry that stimulants may worsen the symptoms of TOURETTE'S SYNDROME, although recent research suggests this isn't true. Many doctors believe if they carefully monitor a child's height, weight, and overall development, the benefits of medication far outweigh the potential side effects. Side effects that do occur can often be handled by reducing the dosage.

Unfortunately, the long-term effects of taking these drugs are not known. Cylert may cause more serious side effects and is therefore not considered to be a first-line medication for ADHD. Otherwise, side effects are usually dose related.

Drug Controversy

Still, the use of stimulants for children with ADHD—especially Ritalin—is not without controversy. Critics worry that Ritalin and other stimulant drugs are prescribed unnecessarily for too many children, since many things—including anxiety, depression, allergies, seizures, problems at home or school—can make children seem overactive, impulsive, or inattentive. They argue that many children who don't have ADHD are drugged anyway as a way to control disruptive behaviors.

Critics also worry that so many of the nation's children are given these drugs without any real understanding of the future side effects. Although Ritalin is one of the most commonly prescribed drugs for children, there are concerns about its long-term effects.

There are no studies on children who have taken Ritalin for more than 14 months. Ritalin affects the brain in a way very similar to cocaine, one of the most addictive substances known. Critics worry that the child who takes Ritalin may be more likely to use illegal drugs in the future, or that he or she might be more likely to smoke as an adult. These concerns are fueled by research showing that rats who were exposed to stimulants were more likely to choose cocaine, suggesting that early exposure to some drugs may make a person more likely to abuse drugs in the future. However, the data on whether there is a link between Ritalin and later substance abuse are controversial, and some researchers insist that ADHD children are not more likely to use drugs of any type later in life.

Behavioral Treatment

Many experts believe that the best way to manage the symptoms of ADHD is to combine drug treatment with behavioral methods. Medication can help to control some of the behavior problems that may have led to family turmoil, but more often there are other aspects of a child's problem that medication won't affect.

Even though ADHD primarily affects a person's behavior, the simple fact of having ADHD can trigger serious emotional problems as well. Some of these children have very few experiences that build their sense of worth and competence. If they're hyperactive, they're often punished for being disruptive. If they are too disorganized and unfocused to complete tasks, they may be branded "lazy." If they are impulsive, shove classmates, and interrupt, they may lose friends. If they are unlucky enough to have a related conduct disorder, they may get in trouble at school or with the police.

The daily frustrations that are a part of having ADHD can make people feel abnormal or stupid. In many cases, the cycle of frustration and anger has persisted for so long that it may take years to alleviate.

For this reason, parents and children may need special help to develop techniques to manage behavior patterns that have become ingrained. In such cases, mental health professionals can help the child and family develop new attitudes and ways of relating to each other.

Behavior treatments include coaching, a process of individual support that focuses on understanding maladaptive patterns of behavior, identifying goals and strategies for change, and providing consistent reinforcement and feedback. For younger children, such an approach may involve behavioral rating scales, consistent feedback, and reinforcement for positive behavioral change. For adults, the approach may focus on identifying and describing goals and strategies. In either case, focusing on the role of individual responsibility and choice is a vital component, as is developing a consistent pattern of feedback and reinforcement.

In individual counseling, the therapist helps children or adults with ADHD learn to feel better about themselves. The therapist can also help people with ADHD identify and build on their strengths, cope with daily problems, and control their attention and aggression.

In group counseling, people learn that they are not alone in their frustration and that others want to help. Sometimes only the child with ADHD needs counseling, but often the entire family can benefit from support. If the child is young, parents can learn techniques for coping with and improving their child's behavior.

Several intervention approaches are available and different therapists tend to prefer one approach or another. Knowing something about the various types of interventions makes it easier for families to choose the best therapist for their own situation.

In psychotherapy, patients talk with the therapist about their thoughts and feelings, explore problem behaviors, and learn different ways to handle their emotions. If someone who has ADHD wants to gain control of symptoms more directly, more direct kinds of intervention are available.

Cognitive-behavioral therapy helps people directly change their behavior instead of concentrating only on understanding their feelings and actions. The therapist may help an individual learn to think through tasks and to organize work, or may encourage new behavior by giving praise each time the person acts in the desired way. A cognitive-behavioral therapist can use these techniques to help an ADHD child learn to control his fighting, or an impulsive teenager to think before speaking.

Social skills training can help children learn new behaviors by watching the therapist model appropriate behavior, like waiting for a turn, sharing toys, or responding to a bully.

Support groups can also be helpful, linking people who have common concerns. Many adults with ADHD and parents of children with ADHD find it useful to join a local or national support group. Many groups deal with issues of children's disorders. Members of support groups share frustrations and success, and provide referrals.

Because ADHD affects all aspects of a child's home and school life, experts recommend parent education and support groups to help family members learn how to help the child cope with frustrations, organize environments, and develop problem-solving skills. Special parenting skills are often needed because children with ADHD may not respond as well to typical parenting practices, especially punishment. Instead, children with ADHD should learn how to reinforce their positive behaviors themselves, and learn how to solve problems. Children who take medications and practice these behavior techniques do better than those who rely on medication alone.

Parenting skills training, offered by therapists or in special classes, gives parents tools and techniques for managing their child's behavior. One such technique is the use of "time out" when the child becomes too unruly or out of control. During time outs, the child is removed from the agitating situation and sits alone quietly for a short time to calm down. Parents may

also be taught to give the child quality time each day, in which they share a relaxed activity. During this time together, the parent looks for opportunities to point out what the child is doing right and to praise strengths and abilities. An effective way to modify a child's behavior is through a system of rewards and penalties. The parents (or teacher) identify a few desirable behaviors that they want to encourage in the child, such as asking for a toy politely. The child is told exactly what is expected in order to earn a small reward, which is given when he performs the desired behavior. The goal is to help children learn to control their own behavior and to choose the more desired behavior. The technique works well with all children, although children with ADHD may need more frequent rewards.

Parents also may learn to structure situations in ways that will allow their child to succeed. If a child is easily overstimulated, parents may try allowing only one or two playmates at a time. If the child has trouble completing tasks, parents may help the child divide a large task into small steps, then praise the child as each step is completed.

Stress management methods such as meditation, relaxation techniques, and exercise can increase the parents' tolerance for frustration, enabling them to respond more calmly to their child's behavior.

Other behavioral treatments that may be helpful in treating children with ADHD include play therapy and special physical exercise.

Although play therapy may help a child who has fears and anxieties, these are not the key problems among most ADHD children. Special physical exercises usually try to boost coordination and increase a child's ability to handle activities that can be overstimulating. Most ADHD children do have problems in these areas, but this is not the cause of ADHD. While these exercises may help, they seem to work mostly because they get parents to pay more attention to the child, which boosts self-esteem.

Controversial Treatments

In addition to more traditional treatments, there are a range of controversial therapies that may sound reasonable. Some come with glowing reports, and a few are outright quackery. Some are developed by reputable doctors or specialists but, when tested scientifically, results can't be proven.

One of the most widely used controversial treatments is a special diet based on the unproven idea that certain foods cause ADHD. These diets look at specific groups of foods, such as additives, sugar, and foods to which children are commonly allergic, such as corn, nuts, chocolate, shellfish, or wheat. While there is scientific evidence that these diets don't work, many parents strongly believe they help. Some of these diets are healthy and won't hurt, but most experts agree that no special diet alone can solve the problems of ADHD and should not be used as the only treatment for a child's behavior.

Other types of treatment that have not been shown scientifically to be effective in treating the majority of children or adults with ADHD include

- biofeedback
- allergy treatments
- drug treatments for inner-ear problems
- megadoses of vitamins
- chiropractic treatments
- yeast infection treatment
- eye training or special colored glasses

Education

ADHD occurs in children with all levels of intelligence, yet even bright or gifted children with ADHD may experience school failure. Despite their natural ability, problems with inattentiveness, impulsivity, and hyperactivity often lead to poor grades, retention, suspension, and expulsion. Without proper diagnosis, accommodations, and intervention, children with ADHD are more likely to experience negative consequences.

Children suspected of having ADHD must be evaluated at the school's expense and, if found to be eligible, provided services under either of two federal laws, the INDIVIDUALS WITH DISABILITIES EDUCATION ACT, Part B (IDEA), and Section 504 of the REHABILITATION ACT OF 1973. These two laws guarantee children with ADHD a free and appropriate public education. Both laws also require that children with disabilities be educated, to the maximum extent appropriate, with children who do not have disabilities. Because there are different criteria for eligibility, different services available, different procedures for implementing the laws, and different procedural safeguards, it is important for parents, educators, clinicians, and advocates to be well aware of the variations among these laws and to be fully informed about their respective advantages and disadvantages.

The most substantial difference between these two laws is that eligibility for IDEA mandates that a child have a disability requiring special education services, while eligibility for Section 504 may occur when the child needs special education or related services. Because of this distinction, children covered under Section 504 include those who typically either have less severe disabilities than those covered under IDEA, or have disabilities that do not neatly fit within the categories of eligibility under IDEA. Most students classified as ADHD are served under the Rehabilitation Act.

Some of the services that could be provided to eligible children include modified instructions, assignments, and testing; help from a classroom aide or a special education teacher; ASSISTIVE TECHNOLOGY; behavior management; and the development of a behavioral intervention plan.

Adjustments may be necessary for a child with ADHD in the classroom, such as having the child sit in front of the room so as to help him pay better attention. The teacher can try to limit open spaces in the classroom, which may encourage hyperactive behaviors. Teachers should provide clear instructions and have the child write down homework assignments in a notebook. Both parent and teacher should keep oral instructions brief and provide written instructions for tasks that involve many steps.

Formal feedback (such as a star chart) can be used to reinforce positive behaviors and progress even if it falls a little short of the goal. The child should work hard on organization, establishing daily checklists.

Parents and teachers also can help the child with ADHD

- control impulses: urge him to slow down when answering questions and to check his homework before turning it in.
- foster self-esteem: the child should be encouraged, and not be asked to perform a task in public that is too difficult.
- design a specific behavior program: focus it on a few unacceptable behaviors with clear and consistent consequences. These consequences should not be publicly humiliating (hand signals can warn a child that his behavior is inappropriate).
- encourage active learning: have the child underline important passages in her school books as she reads and to take notes in class.

Even when suspended or expelled, children covered by IDEA are still entitled to education services that meet the standards of a free appropriate education. Parents can request an impartial due-process hearing when they disagree with a school's decision.

Under a separate provision, a child can remain in the then-current educational placement until all administrative proceedings are concluded (unless the child has brought a weapon or drugs to school, or is proven to be substantially likely to harm himself or others).

If a child's behavior interferes with learning, IDEA requires that a functional behavior analysis be conducted and a positive behavior plan be developed. IDEA prohibits schools from suspending such a child for more than 10 days or expelling students whose behavior results from their disability, unless drugs or weapons are involved or the child is a danger to himself or others.

attention deficit/hyperactivity disorder in adults
ADHD has been recognized and treated in children for almost a century, but only in the last few decades have experts realized that ADHD often persists into adulthood. In fact, up to 70 percent of children diagnosed with ADHD will continue to have symptoms that significantly interfere with school, work, or social functioning throughout their adult lives.

ADHD in adults is sometimes viewed as a "hidden disorder" because the symptoms are often concealed by problems with relationships, organization, mood, substance abuse, or employment.

Symptoms
To be diagnosed with ADHD as an adult, an individual may

- fail to pay close attention to details
- make careless mistakes at work
- fidget or squirm
- have trouble paying attention in tasks or fun activities
- leave a seat in situations where seating is expected
- not listen when spoken to directly
- feel restless
- not follow through on instructions and fail to finish work
- have problems engaging in leisure activities quietly
- have trouble organizing activities
- feel "on the go" or "driven by a motor"
- avoid, dislike, or be reluctant to perform work that requires sustained mental effort
- talk excessively
- lose things
- blurt out answers before questions have been completed

- be easily distracted
- be impatient
- be forgetful in daily duties
- interrupt others

Diagnosis

Since these symptoms are common to many other psychiatric and medical conditions, adults should never try to diagnose themselves but should seek a comprehensive evaluation from a qualified professional or a team with experience in ADHD. This team may include a behavioral neurologist or psychiatrist, a clinical psychologist or an educational psychologist. Evaluation for ADHD should include a comprehensive clinical interview surveying ADHD symptoms, and a comprehensive history of health, school, work, and mental problems, including any medications, social adjustment, and general day-to-day function. This should not simply be a brief, surface-level exam, but an in-depth survey that should require at least one or two hours. Ideally, the interview should rely on several people, including a parent or significant other, if possible. It is also imperative that the clinician rule out other psychiatric diagnoses that may better explain symptoms.

A proper diagnosis can help adults better understand their problems and the reasons for lifelong symptoms. Proper diagnosis and effective treatment can improve self-esteem, job performance, and social relationships. Many adults with ADHD are offered protection under the AMERICANS WITH DISABILITIES ACT of 1990, which prohibits job discrimination for anyone with a physical or mental impairment that substantially limits one or more major life activities, such as school and job.

Treatment

Although there is no cure for ADHD, treatment can help an individual manage symptoms. The best treatment plan combines medication, education, behavioral, and psychosocial treatments. Several studies suggest that counseling can be effective in treating adults with ADHD, helping the patient identify how the disability might be linked to a history of below-average performance and trouble in personal relationships. Therapy also can help control mood swings, stabilize relationships, and alleviate guilt and discouragement. This long-term combined treatment approach can help affected adults lead more satisfactory and productive lives.

Attention Deficit Information Network, Inc.

A nonprofit organization offering information to families of children and adults with Attention Deficit Disorder (ADD), and to professionals, through a network of AD-IN chapters. AD-IN was founded in 1988 by several parent support group leaders. Today it acts as a community resource for information on training programs and speakers available to those who work with individuals with ADD.

The organization also presents conferences and workshops for parents and professionals on current issues, research, and treatments for ADD and makes an annual, post-secondary scholarship award.

Contact: 475 Hillside Avenue, Needham, MA 02194; phone: (781) 455–9895; website: http://www.addinfonetwork.com

attention span A phrase commonly used to refer to a person's ability to sustain attention, maintaining focus and alertness over a period of time. It is also referred to as sustained attention. Individuals with ADHD are often seen as having a "short attention span," though in reality such individuals may be capable of sustained attention when presented with information that engages them. The breakdown in attention lies in the ability to distinguish between essential and nonessential information.

For example, Mary (who does not have ADHD) pays attention to the teacher's lesson while Jim, who has ADHD, is noticing that the car driving by the school is making a strange sound and there is a grasshopper sitting on a rock outside the classroom window.

attribution The ways in which an individual understands the sources of success, difficulty, or failure. Often, people with learning disabilities attribute their successes and failures to factors they don't control, such as luck, the nature of the task, or their own inadequacies. By contrast, successful learners tend to attribute failure or success to their own level of effort and perseverance, and see themselves as having control over the outcomes of their work.

Attribution theory provides an approach to understanding the difficulties with motivation experienced by some people with learning problems, and also suggests that direct guidance in changing attribution styles may be helpful to those with learning disorders.

atypical learner A general term for a child who is different from the typical student in physical, intellectual, social, or emotional development, and who differs in mental characteristics, sensory abilities, communication abilities, or social behavior to the extent that special education services are required for the child to develop.

See also SPECIAL EDUCATION.

audiologist A licensed or certified specialist trained to identify and measure hearing loss and rehabilitate those with hearing and speech problems. Audiologists also can fit hearing aids. A child who is experiencing learning problems, especially in early grades, may see an audiologist in order to identify or rule out physiological factors.

Audiologists are trained to determine where hearing loss occurs, and to assess the effect of the loss on the ability to communicate. They also offer hearing aid evaluation and orientation, auditory training, training in speechreading techniques, and speech counseling. Audiologists aren't physicians, and thus can't treat infections or other ear diseases.

Audiologists work in a wide variety of settings, including universities, hospitals, schools, medical offices, and private practice. Since most school districts require some type of hearing screening tests for their students, audiologists serve as directors of these programs and work with teachers to help with special educational needs of students with hearing problems. In schools with special classes for students with hearing problems, audiologists equip and maintain classroom amplification systems.

audiology The study of hearing and hearing disorders. It involves identification and assessment of hearing, including the nature and degree of hearing loss and the rehabilitation of individuals with hearing disorders, with an emphasis on the communication skills.

auditory discrimination The ability to distinguish one speech sound from another, and to identify whether words are the same or different. People with problems in auditory discrimination have difficulty distinguishing between words that sound alike or differ in a single phoneme, such as between the words "bake" and "make" or "lick" and "like." In order to read efficiently, a child must be able to distinguish one sound from another, especially those sounds that match letters in the alphabet.

Children with problems in this area may find it difficult to learn to read or understand spoken language, follow directions, and remember details. Problems with auditory discrimination may be part of a group of problems in the area of auditory perception that can have a significant effect on learning, especially in the area of reading development, and on academic and social performance.

In addition, a serious weakness in auditory discrimination in the classroom setting can be confused with inattention, as the child appears not to have listened closely.

See also PHONEMIC AWARENESS; INFORMATION PROCESSING DISORDERS.

auditory figure-ground discrimination The ability to pick out important sounds from background noise. Some disorders of attention are associated with auditory figure-ground discrimination difficulties. Children with problems in this area may find it harder to separate meaningful sounds from background noise. For example, a child may not be able to easily isolate the words spoken by a teacher standing at the front of the classroom in the presence of sounds made by children playing in the next room or the traffic outside.

Problems in this area may be physiological or may have to do with selective attention and filtering problems.

In order to be successful, a child with this condition will need to stay focused on auditory information in order to complete tasks.

See also FIGURE-GROUND DISCRIMINATION; FIGURE-GROUND DEFICITS.

auditory memory The ability to store and retrieve information presented as sounds, most important in the acquisition of language. An individual who has problems with auditory memory might not be able to follow a sequence of oral directions, or to remember and discuss information presented in a class. In general, difficulties in the area of auditory memory are common among those with diagnosed learning disabilities, especially in the area of reading.

There are two kinds of auditory memory, long- and short-term. Long-term auditory memory is the ability to recall something heard long ago. Short-term auditory memory is the ability to remember something heard very recently. Children with problems in this area may find it difficult to remember people's names, memorize and recall telephone numbers, follow multistep spoken directions, or recall stories or remember words from songs.

auditory perception The ability to process and make sense of information that is received as sound. Involving recognition and interpretation, rather than hearing itself, auditory perception is related to the ways in which the brain recognizes and discriminates sounds in order to make sense of them.

Problems with auditory perception are frequently associated with language disorders and may have a significant effect on an individual's language development in areas such as reading, expressive language, and receptive vocabulary. These problems are a major factor in language learning disabilities.

auditory processing The full range of mental activity involved in reacting to sounds (especially speech sounds) and in considering their meanings in relation to past experience and to their future use.

auditory sequencing Also called auditory sequential memory, this is the ability to remember verbal items presented orally in the sequence in which they were presented.

Children with auditory sequencing problems may have trouble learning the alphabet or the months of the year. Difficulties with such basic auditory sequencing tasks may persist into later childhood or adulthood if not recognized and treated. In addition, subtle difficulties with auditory sequencing may persist throughout life.

Auditory sequencing is measured by tests such as digit span and memory for sentences and nonsense syllables. People with auditory sequential memory problems may also have difficulty following a series of instructions. However, such a problem may be confused with or coexist with attention problems. Such an attention problem may also be marked by an inability to respond correctly to a series of verbal directions.

autism This complex developmental disability (known correctly as autistic disorder) typically appears during the first three years of life. The result of a neurological disorder that affects the functioning of the brain, autism and its associated behaviors have been estimated to occur in as many as one in 500 people. This means that more than a half-million Americans have autism or some other form of pervasive developmental disorder. Its prevalence rate makes autism one of the most common developmental disabilities. The condition is four times more common in boys than in girls and is not related to race, ethnic origin, family income, lifestyle, or education.

Autism significantly impairs a child's ability to communicate and socialize with others. While severity and symptoms vary according to age, the disorder is significant and sustained. Children with autistic disorder demonstrate little interest in friends or social interactions, often failing to develop verbal and nonverbal communication skills. Typically, these children function at a low intellectual level; most experience mild to severe mental retardation. However, this is by no means true for all individuals with autistic disorder; the condition may be accompanied by average or strong abilities in an isolated area such as reading or computation.

During the course of childhood and adolescence, children with this condition nevertheless usually make some developmental gains. Those who show improvement in language and intellectual ability have the best overall outlook. Although some individuals with autism are able to live with some measure of partial independence in adulthood, very few are able to live entirely on their own.

Cause

Autism impacts the normal development of the brain in the areas of social interaction and communication skills. Although a single specific cause of autism is not known, current research links autism to biological or neurological differences in the brain. In many families there appears to be a pattern of autism or related disabilities—suggesting a genetic basis to the disorder—although at this time no gene has been directly linked to autism. Scientists think that the genetic basis is complex and probably involves several combinations of genes.

Autism is not a mental illness or a behavior problem, and it's not caused by bad parenting. No known psychological factors in the development of children have been shown to cause autism.

Symptoms

Autism is a spectrum disorder, which means that the symptoms and characteristics of autism can appear in a wide variety of combinations, from mild to severe. Although autism is defined by a certain set of behavior, children and adults can exhibit any combination of behavior in any degree of severity. Two children with the same diagnosis can act very differently from one another and have varying skills.

Children and adults with autism typically have problems in verbal and nonverbal communication, social interactions, and leisure or play activities.

- Communication: language develops slowly or not at all; uses words without attaching the usual meaning; communicates with gestures instead of words; short attention span
- Social Interaction: spends time alone rather than with others; shows little interest in making friends; less responsive to social cues such as eye contact or smiles
- Sensory Impairment: may have overly sensitive sight, hearing, touch, smell, and taste
- Play: lack of spontaneous or imaginative play; does not imitate others or initiate pretend games
- Behavior: may be overactive or very passive; throw tantrums for no apparent reason; show an obsessive interest in a single item, idea, activity, or person; lack common sense, show aggression, often has difficulty with changes in routine

The disorder makes it hard for children to communicate with others and relate to the outside world. There may be repeated body movements (hand flapping, rocking), unusual responses to people, or attachments to objects and resistance to changes in routines. In some cases, there may be aggressive or self-injurious behavior. Autism may affect a child's range of responses and make it more difficult to control how body and mind react. Sometimes visual, motor, or processing problems make it hard for these children to maintain eye contact, and some use peripheral vision rather than looking directly at others. Sometimes touching or being close to others may be painful to a person with autism. Because they can't make sense of the world in a normal way, people with autism may experience anxiety, fear, and confusion.

In addition, people with autism may have other disorders that affect brain function, such as epilepsy, mental retardation, Down syndrome, or genetic disorders such as fragile X syndrome or Tourette's. Many people diagnosed with autism will also be mentally retarded, and between 25 and 30 percent may develop a seizure pattern.

Although there is no standard type of person with autism, these children can learn and function productively and show gains from appropriate education and treatment.

Diagnosis

Diagnostic categories have changed over the years as research progresses and as new editions of the DSM (*DIAGNOSTIC AND STATISTICAL MANUAL*) have been issued.

Because there are no medical tests for autism, an accurate diagnosis must be based on observing the person's communication, behavior, and developmental levels. However, because many of the behaviors associated with autism are similar to other disorders, various medical tests may also be ordered to rule out or identify other possible causes of symptoms.

Because the characteristics of the disorder vary, a child should be evaluated by a team including a neurologist, psychologist, developmental pediatrician, speech/language therapist, learning consultant, or other professionals experienced in autism. Problems in recognizing

autism often lead to a lack of services to meet the complex needs of these individuals.

It's important to include a history from parents and caregivers in coming to an accurate diagnosis. Some people with autism may seem to have developmental disabilities, a behavior disorder, problems with hearing, or eccentric behavior. It's important to distinguish autism from other conditions, since early identification is required for an effective treatment program. While there is no "cure" for the brain abnormalities that cause autism, patients can learn coping mechanisms and strategies to ease various symptoms. Some of these symptoms may lessen as the child ages and others may disappear altogether. With appropriate treatment, many problem behaviors can be changed so that the person may appear to no longer have autism. However, most patients continue to show some faint symptoms to some degree throughout their entire lives.

Treatment

Early intervention is crucial and can provide dramatic improvements for young children with autism. While various preschool models may differ, all emphasize early, appropriate, and intensive educational interventions for young children. Other common factors may be

- some degree of inclusion, mostly behaviorally based interventions
- programs that build on the interests of the child
- extensive use of visuals to accompany instruction
- structured activities
- parent and staff training
- transition planning
- follow-up

Because of the nature of autism, no single approach can ease symptoms in all cases. Therapies include applied behavior analysis, auditory integration training, special diets, discrete trial teaching, medications, music therapy, occupational therapy, physical therapy, sensory integration, speech/language therapy, and vision therapy.

Studies show that individuals with autism respond well to a highly structured, specialized education program tailored to individual needs. A well designed treatment approach may include work on communication and social skills, sensory integration therapy, and applied behavior analysis by autism experts.

More severely ill children may require a structured, intensive education and behavior program with a one-on-one teacher to student ratio. However, many other children with autism may do well in a normal education environment with appropriate support.

In addition to an academic program, children with autism should be trained in functional living skills at the earliest possible age. Learning to cross a street, to buy something in a store or ask for help are critical skills, and may be hard even for those with average intelligence. Training is aimed at boosting a person's independence and providing opportunity for personal choice and freedom.

Prognosis

Contrary to popular belief, many children and adults with autism can make eye contact, and can show affection and demonstrate a variety of other emotions in varying degrees. Like other children, they respond to their environment in both positive and negative ways.

With appropriate treatment, some behaviors associated with autism may lessen over time. Although communication and social problems will continue in some form throughout life, difficulties in other areas may improve with age, education, or stress level. Many individuals with autism enjoy their lives and contribute to their community in a meaningful way, as they learn to compensate for and cope with their disability.

Some adults with autism live and work independently in the community, and can drive a car, earn a college degree, and even get married. Some may need some support only for daily

pressure, while others require a great deal of support from family and professionals.

Adults with autism may live in a variety of residential settings ranging from an independent home or apartment, to group homes or supervised apartment settings with other family members, or more structured residential care. More and more support groups for adults with autism are appearing, and many patients are forming their own networks to share information, support each other, and speak for themselves. Individuals with autism are providing valuable insight into the challenges of this disability by publishing articles and books and appearing on TV to discuss their lives and disabilities.

Autism Society of America A nonprofit organization that seeks to promote lifelong access and opportunities for persons within the AUTISM spectrum and their families, to be fully included, participating members of their communities through advocacy, public awareness, education, and research related to autism.

Founded in 1965 by a small group of parents, the society is the leading source of information and referral on autism and the largest collective voice representing the autism community for more than 33 years. Today, more than 24,000 members are connected through a volunteer network of over 240 chapters in 50 states.

Contact: 7910 Woodmont Avenue, Suite 300, Bethesda, MD 20814–3015; phone: (800) 3AUTISM, x150; (301) 657–0881; website: http://www.autism-society.org.

Autism Society of America Foundation (ASAF) A fundraising organization founded in 1996 by the AUTISM SOCIETY OF AMERICA, the largest and oldest organization representing people with AUTISM. ASAF was established to raise and allocate funds for research to address the many unanswered questions about autism.

The ASAF has implemented action on several autism research priorities, developing up-to-date statistics; developing a national registry of individuals and families with autism who are willing to participate in research studies; and implementing a system to identify potential donors of autism brain tissue for research purposes and to facilitate the donation process. In addition, the foundation contributes money for applied and biomedical research in the causes of and treatment approaches to autism.

Contact: 7910 Woodmont Avenue, Suite 300, Bethesda, MD 20814–3015; phone: (800) 3AUTISM, x127 or (301) 657–0881, x127; website: http://www.autism-society.org/foundation/foundation.html

automatization   A form of learning in which a skill or procedure becomes automatic and virtually unconscious. Most people experience some degree of automatic skills, such as driving a car, forming letters, spelling common words accurately, and performing simple arithmetic equations.

Individuals with learning disabilities may have difficulty with automatic skills, taking longer to develop automaticity with such basic skills as spelling, decoding, and handwriting, and requiring more repetition, practice, and reinforcement.

This means that people who experience inadequate automatization may take longer to complete academic tasks, and expend an enormous amount of mental energy on relatively low-order elements of an assignment, leaving little

capacity to work on more complex components such as problem-solving or coming up with new ideas.

auxiliary aids   Accommodations made to help students with disabilities, such as taped books, voice recognition software, and note-takers. Under Section 12102 [Section 3] of the AMERICANS WITH DISABILITIES ACT, the term "auxiliary aids and services" includes the following:

> qualified interpreters or other effective methods of making aurally delivered material available to people with hearing problems;
> qualified readers, taped texts, or other effective methods of making visually delivered materials available to people with visual impairments;
> acquisition or modification of equipment or devices
> other similar services

Determining what auxiliary aids may be necessary to provide access is primarily the role of the individual seeking such accommodations, working with human resources personnel, compliance officers, or college disability support services. Providing specific auxiliary aids must be based on documented disabilities.

See also ACCOMMODATIONS.

background knowledge Information an individual has acquired through previous learning and experiences that creates a familiar context in which to learn new ideas. Activating background knowledge before introducing a new concept is a learning strategy that improves comprehension by connecting new information to existing information.

Many individuals with learning disabilities don't have good background knowledge due to poor reading, memory, or comprehension skills. Children who haven't developed age-appropriate decoding skills won't have the reading rate and fluency they need to understand what they read. For these children, the energy and focus needed to decode words makes reading inefficient and interferes with reading comprehension. In addition, children who spend significant time in resource rooms learning basic skills miss out on practicing the use of background information in areas such as history, geography, and literature.

Through remediation of basic skills, many individuals with learning disabilities are able to develop the skills required to perform high school and college-level academic work. However, many find that they aren't successful in higher level courses because they don't have solid background knowledge in certain areas.

back to basics movement An educational movement emphasizing explicit instruction in basic academic skills. Increasingly, this movement represents the preferences of parents in public school districts, although it is often at odds with contemporary teacher-instruction practices in colleges and universities.

"Back to basics" includes such elements as a phonics approach to teaching reading and attention to rote memorization of math facts.

basal ganglia A part of the brain located under the center of the cerebral cortex and above the thalamus. Although it isn't directly connected to the spinal cord, it plays an important role in movement and sensory information. The basal ganglia includes the caudate nucleus, globus pallidus, putamen, subthalamus, substantia nigra, and red nucleus.

basal reader A look-say model of reading instruction designed to teach reading in a structured sequence. Through practice, students memorize key words that are repeated throughout the text. Basal readers often begin in first grade, using simple words for simple stories, becoming more difficult until about the sixth or seventh grade. Teachers often use additional materials such as workbooks and teacher editions to deliver reading instruction and skill development.

basic skill A fundamental ability necessary to function on a daily basis. The mastery of basic skills is necessary to progress to higher levels of achievement. Academically, basic skills include speaking, spelling, reading, writing, and arithmetic.

The basic skills of children with a LEARNING DISABILITY are often not uniformly developed.

This makes the achievement of more advanced academic skills like problem solving more difficult to achieve.

For children with learning disabilities, basic skills training may emphasize social skills, study habits, attention training, and other specific tasks that assist in the development of independence and self-esteem.

behavioral rating scales for ADHD   A major assessment instrument that can help an examiner identify ADHD behaviors; used to evaluate an individual for attention deficit/hyperactivity disorder (ADHD). These rating scales are typically filled out by parents or teachers, and sometimes by the individuals being evaluated. Behavioral rating scales generally contain items intended to assess attention and distractibility, such as "daydreams," "easily distracted," and "doesn't pay attention."

These scales are generally reliable and easy to use, but they can't make a precise analysis of the various components of attention. Some commonly used scales are the Connors' Parent and Teacher Rating Scales, the Child Attention Profile, and the ADHD Rating Scale.

behavioral unit   The center of behavioral psychology's theory of behavior management. The behavioral unit consists of three elements: antecedent (stimulus), behavior (response), and consequence (reinforcement).

In behavior management, a person's response is the target behavior of the individual, situated between two sets of environmental influences. Changing a behavior involves carefully and systematically analyzing each of these three components.

This approach is the core of direct instruction techniques: teachers provide specific lessons, assess target behavior (response), and then either reward or repeat the stimulus until the child masters the lesson.

Individuals with learning disabilities often require the structure and objectivity inherent in a behaviorist approach to instruction. Even young children are capable of understanding the fundamental principles underlying this approach, and how to achieve the desired consequence.

Critics of behaviorist approaches typically agree that it is effective, but suggest that other approaches are needed to help develop more complicated thinking and problem-solving skills, since some research suggests that children with learning disabilities aren't efficient or organized in their approach to learning. While individuals with learning disabilities require explicit instruction in order to learn basic skills, they also require a range of instructional techniques.

behavior modification   The application of rewards or punishments as a way of reducing or eliminating problem behavior, or to teach people new responses. Behavior modification is based on the idea that since all behavior is learned, with appropriate treatment it also can be *unlearned* by using positive or negative consequences.

Behavior modification is used by psychologists, social workers, teachers, and other professionals to change an individual's reaction to a situation. There are two major approaches to behavior modification, one based on the work of the late psychologist B. F. Skinner, the other based on the work of psychologist Albert Bandura.

Skinner believed that all behavior is learned by interacting with the environment, and that bad behavior is learned the same way normal behavior is learned. Skinner believed that rewarded behavior is likely to be repeated, and punished behavior is likely to be avoided. Therefore, a behavior modification program will set up a program that rewards specific desired behaviors.

Bandura's approach emphasizes learning through imitation, believing that a person can learn to avoid an unpleasant situation without experiencing it. Individuals can also learn new skills by watching and imitating others. Bandura emphasizes the effectiveness of role models who speak and act consistently, and this applies especially to working with young children.

Modeling specific social skills or strategies, communication patterns, and other behaviors is especially important for children with learning disabilities, who require specific direct instruction as well as consistent modeling. Because children with learning disabilities often present behavior issues in the classroom, often a consequence of their frustration with learning, it is important that teachers and parents have consistent approaches to helping these children learn more appropriate and effective behaviors.

Bender Visual-Motor Gestalt Test A test of visual-perceptual and motor development for children aged five to nine and a half years old. This test measures visual-motor ability using nine geometric figures for the child to copy one at a time. The drawings are then scored depending on any distortions of shape, rotations, integration difficulties, and too many dots or extra lines.

The test is useful only for younger children since those over age eight can usually reproduce all the designs perfectly. After age eight, the test is helpful only in distinguishing whether a child's perceptual motor maturity is below that of an eight-year-old.

bias When used to describe a psychometric test, bias denotes "unfairness." Bias can involve any sort of group membership, such as race, social class, gender, age, and so on. Bias in standardized testing can be detected and, when it cannot be eliminated, its effects can be measured so that scores can be fairly interpreted.

Most test makers review items for obvious biases, such as offensive words, but many forms of bias are not superficial. While some test makers also use statistical bias-reduction techniques, these techniques can't detect underlying bias in the test's form or content. As a result, critics say,

biased cultural assumptions built into the test as a whole may not be exposed or removed by test makers.

bilateral motor coordination The ability to use arms and legs in a symmetrical, coordinated manner. An individual needs to have adequate motor coordination to ride a bike, catch a ball, or swim.

bilingual approach Teaching in two languages—a person's native language and a second language. The philosophy behind using a bilingual approach in teaching children who don't speak English is to allow students to learn academic courses in their native language while introducing a second language. Gradually, more and more information is taught in the second language. For students with learning disabilities, learning in an environment with two languages may be difficult.

bipolar disorder Popularly known as "manic depression," this condition is characterized by manic episodes alternating with depression. Mood swings are often dramatic and unpredictable. Because the manic periods (with impulsive behavior and bursts of energy) can be similar to symptoms of ATTENTION DEFICIT/HYPERACTIVITY DISORDER, a good diagnosis is important for anyone experiencing repeated episodes of mania or depression. The feelings of depression, inadequacy, fatigue, and sadness are also similar to emotions experienced by individuals with other disorders.

While everyone experiences normal mood changes during everyday life, bipolar disorder is a medical condition in which people have mood swings totally unrelated to things going on in their lives. These swings affect thoughts, feelings, physical health, behavior, and functioning.

Bipolar disorder affects about 1 percent of the adult population of the United States. It's in the same family of illnesses (called "affective disorders") as clinical depression. Unlike depression, which affects more women than men, bipolar disorder seems to affect men and women equally. For a clinical definition of bipolar disorder, symptoms must include one or more manic episodes accompanied by one or more major depressive episodes, which usually occur in cycles.

Bipolar disorder usually begins in adolescence or early adulthood, although it can sometimes start in early childhood or as late as the 40s or 50s. However, when someone over 50 has a manic episode for the first time, the cause is more likely to be a problem that just mimics bipolar disorder (such as a brain condition or the effects of drugs, alcohol, or some prescription medications).

Cause

There is no single, proven cause of bipolar disorder, but research strongly suggests that it is often an inherited problem related to a lack of stability in the transmission of nerve impulses in the brain. This biochemical problem makes people with bipolar disorder more vulnerable to emotional and physical stresses. This means that if a person experiences stress, substance abuse, lack of sleep, or too much stimulation, the normal brain mechanisms for restoring calm functioning don't always work properly.

Bipolar disorder tends to run in families, and a number of genes have been linked to the condition, suggesting the presence of several different biochemical problems. If one parent has bipolar disorder and the other doesn't, there is a one in seven chance that the couple's child will develop it. The chance may be greater if one spouse has several relatives with bipolar disorder or depression.

Symptoms

A person with bipolar disorder may experience any or all of four different kinds of episodes: mania, low-level mania (hypomania), depression, or a combination ("mixed state"). Bipolar disorder can seriously affect a patient's marriage, family, and job. Divorce rates are much higher in patients with bipolar disorder (about two to three times higher than in normal subjects).

Mania (manic episode) This episode often begins with a pleasant sense of high energy, creativity, and social confidence, which become more severe until it develops into a full-blown manic episode. People with mania typically lack insight and deny that anything is wrong, angrily blaming anyone who suggests otherwise. A manic episode is characterized by feeling unusually euphoric or irritable for at least a week, plus at least four (and often almost all) of the following symptoms:

- needing little sleep yet having great amounts of energy
- talking fast
- having racing thoughts
- being easily distracted
- having an inflated feeling of power, greatness, or importance
- doing reckless things without concern about possible negative consequences, such as spending too much money, inappropriate sexual activity, or making foolish business investments
- psychotic symptoms in very severe cases, such as hallucinations or delusions

Mild mania (hypomania) This milder form of mania causes similar but less severe symptoms, which often begin with someone feeling better and more productive than usual and then usually build into a full-blown mania or crash into depression.

Depression (major depressive episode) To be considered a full-blown "major" depressive episode, a person will feel sad and lack interest for at least two weeks, in addition to at least four other symptoms:

- trouble sleeping or sleeping too much
- loss of appetite or eating too much
- problems concentrating or making decisions
- feeling slow or agitated

- feeling worthless or guilty
- loss of energy; fatigue
- thoughts of suicide or death
- hallucinations or delusions (in severe cases)

Mixed episode The most disabling episodes are those that include symptoms of both mania and depression at the same time, or that alternate often during the day. A person in this condition will feel excited or agitated but also feel irritable and depressed.

Types of Episodes

Untreated patients with bipolar disorder may have more than 10 total episodes of mania and depression during their lifetime. Often, five years or more may pass between the first and second episode, but the time periods between subsequent episodes get shorter and shorter. But people don't all experience bipolar disorder in the same way. Some people have equal numbers of manic and depressive episodes; others have mostly one type or the other.

The average person with bipolar disorder has four episodes during the first 10 years of the illness. Men are more likely to begin with a manic episode, while women tend to experience depression first. While a number of years can elapse between the first two or three episodes of mania or depression, without treatment most people eventually have episodes more often. Sometimes these follow a seasonal pattern, but a few people cycle frequently or even continuously through the year.

Episodes can last days, months, or sometimes even years. On average, without treatment, manic or mild manic episodes last a few months, while depressions often last well over six months. Some individuals recover completely between episodes and may go many years without any symptoms, while others continue to have low-grade but troubling depression or mild swings up and down.

There are two main types of bipolar disorder:

- Bipolar I: the "classic" form of the condition that most often involves widely spaced, long-lasting bouts of mania followed by long-lasting bouts of depression.
- Bipolar II: at least one episode of mild mania (hypomania) and one major depressive episode.

Although the shifts from one state to another are usually gradual, they can be quite sudden. In this so-called rapid-cycling form of the disorder, a person can experience four or more complete mood cycles within a year's time. Some rapid cyclers can complete a mood cycle in a matter of days (or more rarely, hours). Rapid cycling occurs in between 5 percent and 15 percent of patients.

It's also possible for someone who has bipolar disorder to experience a "mixed state," which means their mood includes some characteristics of depression and some of mania or mild mania.

While there are rare documented cases of mania without depression, the DSM-IV does not currently include a category for just "mania." Using DSM-IV to diagnose the condition, a person with symptoms of mania will almost always be diagnosed as bipolar.

Diagnosis

Typically, people with bipolar disorder see three or four doctors over at least eight years before being correctly diagnosed. The earlier the diagnosis and proper treatment, the quicker people can be helped and the more likely they will be able to avoid suicide attempts, alcohol and substance abuse, and other personal problems. In addition, some research suggests that the earlier the treatment the better the outcome; evidence indicates that the more mood episodes a person has, the harder it is to treat each subsequent episode and the more frequent episodes may become. (This is sometimes referred to as "kindling.")

Treatment

While there is no cure for bipolar disorder, a combination of drug treatment and therapy can lessen the frequency, severity, and consequences of symptoms and improve functioning between episodes. The two most important types of medication used to control the symptoms of bipolar disorder are mood stabilizers and antidepressants; other medications can help ease insomnia, anxiety, restlessness, or psychotic symptoms.

Mood stabilizers are used to improve manic symptoms, but they also may sometimes ease depression as well. They are the mainstay of long-term preventive treatment for both mania and depression. Three mood stabilizers are widely used in the United States: lithium, valproate, and carbamazepine. Each of the three affects the body differently, so that if one doesn't work another may prove to be better. For all three, blood tests determine the correct dose.

Traditionally, lithium has been the primary drug treatment for patients with bipolar disorder. Discovered to be effective in 1949, it has been widely used since the mid-1960s for prevention and treatment. Valproate and carbamazepine are newer drugs used for bipolar disorder since the late 1970s.

Although mood stabilizers (especially lithium) can ease depression, many patients also need a specific antidepressant to treat the depressive episode. However, antidepressants alone can sometimes trigger a manic attack or rapid cycling. For this reason, antidepressants are given together with a mood stabilizer.

Although electroconvulsive therapy (ECT) has received negative publicity, it can be the safest and most effective treatment for psychotic depression. ECT may also be needed if a patient is severely ill and can't wait for medicine to work, if there have been several unsuccessful attempts with different antidepressants, or if the patient is pregnant or has a health condition that makes drug therapy less safe. Like all treatments, ECT has potential side effects, including a short-term memory loss.

Hospitalization may be needed but usually lasts only a week or two, and can prevent self-destructive, impulsive, or aggressive behavior. During a depressed phase, hospitalization may be needed if a person becomes suicidal. Hospitalization is also used for people who have medical complications that make it hard to monitor medication or for those who can't stop using drugs or alcohol. Early recognition and treatment of manic and depressive episodes can lower the chances of hospitalization.

Side Effects

At least half of those who take medication have side effects, especially if high doses and a combination of medicines are needed. Lower doses and fewer medicines help offset symptoms, but some people may have severe enough side effects to require different medicine. Although side effects tend to be worse early in the treatment, some people who have taken lithium for 20 years or more can suddenly develop side effects as they age. Valproate or carbamazepine make excellent alternatives as long as the switch is made gradually. Valproate appears to cause the fewest side effects during long-term treatment.

Prevention

Successful management of bipolar disorder can be challenging, especially if a patient wants to stop medication because he feels better, doesn't like the side effects, or misses the "highs." A patient who stops medication probably won't have an acute episode right away, but eventually a relapse will probably occur. And each episode runs the risk of making it harder to manage subsequent flare-ups.

Sometimes a diagnosis of bipolar disorder is not clear after just one episode, and medication can be tapered off after about a year. However, if a patient has had only one episode of mania but has a very strong family history, or if the episode was severe, experts believe the patient should probably take medication for several years—or for life. After two or more manic or depressive episodes, experts strongly recommend taking preventive medication indefinitely.

About one in three people with bipolar disorder will be completely free of symptoms by taking lithium, valproate, or carbamazepine for life, and most people become ill much less often, much less severely, with each episode.

birth weight, low Low-birth-weight infants are at risk for a wide range of behavior and learning problems, and assessment and intervention are feasible well before the child might be diagnosed as needing special education services.

Recent research has suggested that extremely low-birth-weight children from age seven through adolescence have poorer reading and math skills; children whose birth weight was less than two pounds lagged behind their peers academically, and displayed other subtle behavioral characteristics that undermined their efforts at school. Poor motor skills and neurological immaturity were defined in many of the children.

This is becoming more of a concern since modern medicine can now save many infants with very low birth weight who would have died 15 years ago. In fact, infants whose birth weight was as low as one pound eight ounces, born after 24 weeks of gestation, have survived in neonatal intensive care units.

Many neonatal intensive care units have follow-up programs to assess the development of children and initiate early intervention strategies, as needed. Unfortunately, physicians traditionally have not received much training in the area of child development and disabilities, although pediatric and family practice training programs today include rotations in child development and rehabilitative services for children. Such assessments are vital since some studies have found that middle-class, low-birth-weight children may not require special education services if they received strong parental support. Early childhood educational partnerships between home and school are essential to help keep low-birth-weight infants on target in their development.

blending Stringing sounds (phonemes) together to create sounds and words.

See also PHONICS.

borderline intellectual functioning An IQ between 70 and 85, in the absence of functional or adaptive problems; sometimes considered in the "slow learner" educational category. Earlier classifications referred to this IQ range as borderline mental retardation. Neither term is linked to borderline personality disorder.

borderline personality disorder A pervasive pattern of instability in interpersonal relationships and self-image, with marked impulsivity, beginning by early adulthood.

Because the impulsivity and inappropriate behavior of this condition may mimic symptoms of ATTENTION DEFICIT/HYPERACTIVITY DISORDER, a diagnosis by an experienced clinician is important.

Borderline personality disorder affects one in 50 people in the United States. The name "borderline personality disorder" was given because experts once thought the condition fell somewhere between neurosis and psychosis on the mental illness continuum. Professionals who are educated about BPD all agree that the name should be changed as it does in no way describe the disorder.

Symptoms

This type of personality disorder leads to intense feelings of abandonment, poor self-image, and unrealistic expectations of others. Moodiness and angry outbursts may be common, and the individual may seem depressed or suicidal. The hallmark of the disorder is chronic instability, affecting relationships with family members or colleagues, and a lack of close, long-term interpersonal relationships that can add to a sense of isolation and abandonment.

Cause

Although some experts believe the condition is a true personality disorder acquired from childhood trauma, research does not support this theory. While the exact cause is still unknown, more and more research has discovered that BPD is highly genetic. Mothers who have the condition are five times more likely to give birth to an affected child compared to a mother without BPD.

Treatment

Recent research has shown that medications can significantly relieve the suffering of borderline patients when used in combination with psychotherapy. Treatment may be some combination of antipsychotic or antianxiety drugs, antidepressants, and psychotherapy. Due to their suicide attempts, or brief psychotic episodes, borderline patients frequently are hospitalized.

brain imaging   Imaging technology that offers a way of identifying structural and metabolic differences between the brain functions of individuals with learning and attention disorders and normal subjects. In turn, imaging research offers an increasing potential for clarifying the factors underlying learning problems in terms of brain chemistry and physiology.

These techniques will play an increasingly prominent role in research into learning and attention disorders, and may also become more important in the assessment of individual cases.

For example, recent research into brain imaging is producing important new information about how children learn to read and do arithmetic. Scientists now have a fairly good idea of what areas of the brain are activated in certain skills. These scanning techniques may one day also help teachers objectively decide which are the best methods to help children learn.

In the future, brain scanning may provide ways to understand the effectiveness of various training techniques, although there will probably not be one technique that will be better than another in all children under all circumstances and for all languages.

Brain imaging studies also can reveal specific LEARNING DISABILITY problems. In research at the National Institute of Mental Health (NIMH), brain imaging has revealed dramatic evidence of a deficit in the brain's visual system in people with DYSLEXIA, a disorder that affects the reading ability of millions of American schoolchildren and adults. While it has been commonly believed that only the language related areas of the brain are affected in dyslexia, this study adds to the growing body of research pointing to dysfunction of another portion of the brain as well.

The research confirms that people with dyslexia, hobbled by problems with reading, writing, and spelling, have trouble processing specific visual information. It also confirms that dyslexia is a discrete brain disorder, not a by-product of a poor education. If confirmed by additional research, functional brain imaging could be used as a tool for early and accurate diagnosis of this common and disabling disorder.

According to the research team, the anatomical changes underlying these functional differences may occur during the early stages of development, when regional functional specialization occurs. Future research will provide further insights into the details of visual and language deficits and their effects on reading.

Types of Scans

MRI   a technique capable of projecting images of multiple sections of the brain onto a video screen, indicating the shape and location of various structures of the brain. Functional magnetic resonance imaging (fMRI) represents a technological advance over MRI that allows for noninvasive study of the human brain at work. The technique of functional magnetic resonance imaging is based on the principle that blood flow increases in active areas of the brain at work.

Brain electrical activity mapping (BEAM) an advance over electroencephalogram (EEG) procedures, allowing researchers to convert the electrical brain waves that individuals produce in response to various stimuli into visual form, and map these.

Positron emission tomography (PET)   an approach that permits researchers to measure metabolic activities and changes within the brain.

brain injury, traumatic   Damage to the brain may be caused by a wide range of factors, including damage before birth as a result of maternal illness, substance abuse, or medications; loss of oxygen at birth or because of an accident such as near drowning; stroke or other medical conditions such as tumors; and physical injury. Brain injury may be associated with learning disabilities.

Traumatic brain injury is a federally recognized disabling condition that can change how a student learns and acts in school. The degree of dysfunction varies with the type and location of injury and with the age of the child. School personnel traditionally have had little exposure to this condition, and there is great potential for problems to occur due to lack of knowledge and miscommunication.

Even a mild brain injury such as a concussion or whiplash can cause serious learning and behavioral impairments. Headaches, sleep, concentration, memory, vision, mood, and irritability are but a few of the many continuing problems caused by head injury. The combination of the many thinking and emotional disorders caused by brain injury seriously undermine the ability to learn and fit in.

Children tend to make what appears to be a "good" physical recovery from brain injuries, but parents, teachers, and doctors may be surprised by the behavioral, learning, and emotional problems that soon follow. Due to the nature of the persistent problems that typically follow traumatic brain injury, such as restlessness, disinhibition, and impulsivity, many children with this condition are misdiagnosed as ATTENTION DEFICIT/HYPERACTIVITY DISORDER (ADHD).

Assessment

Assessment procedures, including tests of intelligence, academic achievement, and social/emotional functioning, should be conducted by a multidisciplinary team to determine the special services that may be needed. Appropriate placement should depend upon the specific characteristics of the child. INDIVIDUALIZED EDUCATION PROGRAM objectives should be developed first for achievement over short periods of time.

Modifications in teaching style and methods, testing, behavior management techniques, length of lessons and homework assignments, and student expectations may all be necessary.

Symptoms

Depending on the region of the brain affected, the conditions associated with brain damage or brain injury may vary widely. Physical and mental problems may be severe or highly selective and localized in cases where trauma occurred in a particular brain region. Relatively mild brain injury may express itself more subtly in conditions that have to do with language, behavioral controls, and judgment, or other higher cognitive functions.

Because each injury is unique, some patients may not experience all the symptoms. The impact of the injury really depends on where in the brain the trauma occurred.

Cognitive Symptoms

- problems processing information (decreased speed, accuracy, and consistency)
- shortened attention span
- problems understanding abstract concepts
- impaired decision-making ability
- inability to shift mental tasks or to follow multistep directions
- memory loss
- problems in expressing thoughts and understanding others, inappropriate word selection

Perceptual Symptoms

- change in vision, hearing, sense of touch, smell, or taste
- loss of sense of time and space
- spatial disorientation
- altered sense of balance
- increased pain sensitivity

Physical Symptoms

- persistent headache
- extreme mental or physical fatigue

- disorders of movement, including spasticity or tremors
- seizures
- sensitivity to light
- sleep disorders
- paralysis
- speech that is not clear due to poor control of the muscles in the lips, tongue, and jaw, or poor breathing patterns

Behavioral/Emotional Symptoms
- irritability and impatience
- reduced tolerance for stress
- lack of initiative, apathy
- dependence
- denial of disability
- aggression, cursing, inappropriate sexual behavior
- inflexibility
- stronger or weaker emotional responses

See also BRAIN INJURY ASSOCIATION.

Brain Injury Association Organization offering advocacy, support services, and research.

Contact: 105 North Alfred Street, Alexandria, VA 22314; phone: (703) 236–6000. website: http://www.biausa.org.

Broca, Paul Pierre (1824–1880) This brilliant French surgeon and anthropologist was born in Sainte-Foy-la-Grande, France, in 1824. A child prodigy, he held baccalaureate degrees simultaneously in literature, mathematics, and physics, and entered medical school when he was only 17 years old, graduating three years later. Soon he became a professor of surgical pathology at the University of Paris and a noted medical researcher in many areas, and by age 24 he already was showered with awards, medals, and important positions. In his early

work he studied cartilage and bone, in addition to cancer, the treatment of aneurysms, and infant mortality.

He was a superb brain anatomist, making important contributions to the understanding of the limbic system, but he was best known for his discovery of the speech center (now known as BROCA'S AREA) in the third circumvolution of the frontal lobe. He studied the brains of aphasic patients (people who can't talk).

A kind and gentle man with a huge propensity for work, he wrote hundreds of books and papers (53 of them alone on the brain), and he was also concerned with health care for the poor. Near the end of his life, he was elected a lifetime member of the French Senate, and also was a member of the French Academy, holding honorary degrees from many universities around the world. He died in Paris in 1880, probably of a brain aneurysm.

Broca's aphasia A problem encountered in speaking, although spoken words are understood. Also called expressive aphasia, the condition occurs with lesions in the motor strip of the frontal lobe.

See also BROCA'S AREA.

Broca's area A section of the left frontal lobe that is involved in the production of language and directs speech via the motor cortex. Damage to this area results in Broca's aphasia, a speech disorder characterized by the ability to understand language but difficulty in speaking fluently.

Broca's area processes syntax and structural complexity of language. Individuals with neurological damage to this area are unable to understand and make grammatically complex sentences.

Brown v. Board of Education of Topeka The major court ruling on desegregation of public schools in the United States, ending the doctrine of "separate but equal" and requiring integration of schools with "all deliberate speed." It was delivered on May 17, 1954, by the U.S. Supreme Court, which ruled unanimously that racial segregation in public schools violated the Fourteenth Amendment to the Constitution. This amendment states that no state may deny equal protection of the laws to any person within its jurisdiction.

The 1954 decision declared that separate educational facilities were inherently unequal. Based on a series of Supreme Court cases argued between 1938 and 1950, *Brown v. Board of Education of Topeka* completed the reversal of an earlier Supreme Court ruling (*Plessy v. Ferguson,* 1896) that permitted "separate but equal" public facilities. The 1954 decision was limited to the public schools, but it was believed to imply that segregation was not permissible in other public facilities. However, the decision did not actually abolish segregation in other public areas, such as restaurants and restrooms, nor did it require desegregation of public schools by a specific time. It did, however, declare the permissive or mandatory segregation that existed in 21 states to be unconstitutional. While it was a giant step toward complete desegregation of public schools, even partial desegregation of these schools was still very far away.

In the early 1950s, racial segregation in public schools was widespread across America. Although all the schools in a given district were supposed to be equal, most black schools were far inferior to their white counterparts. In Topeka, Kansas, a black third grader named Linda Brown had to walk one mile through a railroad switchyard to get to her elementary school, even though a school for whites was only seven blocks away. When Linda's father, Oliver Brown, tried to enroll her in the white elementary school, the principal of the school refused.

Topeka's branch of the National Association for the Advancement of Colored People (NAACP) was eager to assist the Browns, as it had long wanted to challenge segregation in public schools. Brown was the right plaintiff at the right time, and other black parents joined Brown; in 1951 the NAACP requested an injunction that would forbid the segregation of Topeka's public schools.

The U.S. District Court for the District of Kansas heard Brown's case from June 25 to 26, 1951. At the trial, the NAACP argued that segregated schools sent the message to black children that they were inferior to whites; therefore, the schools were inherently unequal. The board of education's defense was that because segregation in Topeka and elsewhere pervaded many other aspects of life, segregated schools simply prepared black children for the segregation they would face during adulthood. The board also argued that segregated schools were not necessarily harmful to black children; great African Americans such as Frederick Douglass, Booker T. Washington, and George Washington Carver had overcome more than just segregated schools to achieve what they achieved.

Because of the precedent of *Plessy v. Ferguson,* which allowed separate but equal school systems for blacks and whites, the court felt "compelled" to rule in favor of the board of education.

Brown and the NAACP appealed to the Supreme Court on October 1, 1951, and their case was combined with other cases that challenged school segregation in South Carolina, Virginia, and Delaware. The Supreme Court first heard the case on December 9, 1952, but failed to reach a decision. In the reargument, heard from December 7 to 8, 1953, the Court requested that both sides discuss "the circumstances surrounding the adoption of the Fourteenth Amendment in 1868." The reargument shed very little additional light on the issue. The Court had to base its decision not on whether the authors of the Fourteenth Amendment had desegregated schools in mind when they wrote the amendment in 1868, but on whether desegregated schools deprived black children of equal protection of the law when the case was decided, in 1954. On May 17, 1954, Chief Justice Earl Warren read the decision of the unanimous Court:

We come then to the question presented: Does segregation of children in public schools solely on the basis of race, even though the physical facilities and other "tangible" factors may be equal, deprive the children of the minority group of equal educational opportunities? We believe that it does . . . We conclude that in the field of public education the doctrine of 'separate but equal' has no place. Separate educational facilities are inherently unequal. Therefore, we hold that the plaintiffs and others similarly situated for whom the actions have been brought are, by reason of the segregation complained of, deprived of the equal protection of the laws guaranteed by the Fourteenth Amendment.

The Supreme Court struck down the "separate but equal" doctrine of *Plessy* for public education, ruled in favor of the plaintiffs, and required the desegregation of schools across America.

Bruininks-Oseretsky Test of Motor Proficiency   An assessment for children aged four and a half through 14 $^1/_2$ that measures large- and fine-motor development on subtests that check running speed, balance, coordination, muscle strength, visual tracking, speed of motor response, coordination of eye and hand movements, hand speed, arm speed, and hand and finger dexterity.

C

cadmium and learning disabilities   See ENVIRONMENTAL TOXINS.

case history   An essential element of any assessment that represents a record of the person's family, health, developmental, educational, psychological, and social experiences. Typically, the creation of a case history involves the analysis of records as well as interviews with parents, teachers, and the individual. Case histories are an important component of assessment in all cases of learning or psychological difficulty.

central auditory processing disorders   Hearing difficulties due to fundamental problems in thought processing as well as to deficits in auditory perception.

cerebellum   A prominent hindbrain structure important for coordinating and integrating motor activity.

cerebral cortex   The most complex area of the brain, the cerebral cortex is the convoluted covering of the two hemispheres; also known as gray matter. The body's control and information processing center, it's organized into four lobes: frontal, parietal, occipital, and temporal, each concerned with different functions.

It is divided into two equal halves (or spheres) called hemispheres. The left hemisphere processes information logically; for example, it helps a person read, speak, and write language or compute an equation. The right hemisphere is responsible for more processing of spatial information, such as recognizing a friend's face or appreciating a piece of artwork. In other words, the right hemisphere sees the forest (the big picture) while the left hemisphere sees the trees (details).

Because the brain carries out many different functions, its cells are also specialized. Different types of neurons are distributed across different layers of the cortex in arrangements that characterize the several areas of the hemispheres, each one with its own functions.

The cerebral cortex represents a highly developed structure concerned with the most familiar functions associated with the human brain, including intelligence and personality, interpretation of sensory impulses, movement, and the ability to plan and organize.

Its distinctive shape arose during evolution as the volume of the cortex increased more rapidly than the cranial volume, so that the entire brain structure folded in onto itself.

cerebral palsy   A condition caused by injury to the parts of the brain that control the ability to use muscles. Most often, the injury happens before or during birth, or soon afterward. A child can have mild, moderate, or severe cerebral palsy. In mild cases, a child simply may be clumsy. With moderate CP, a child might walk with a limp and require a special leg brace or a cane. More severe CP can affect all parts of a child's physical abilities, and the child may need to use a wheelchair and other special equipment.

49

Sometimes children with CP can also have learning problems, problems with hearing or vision, or mental retardation. Usually, the greater the injury to the brain, the more severe the CP, but the condition doesn't worsen over time, and most children with CP have a normal life span.

About 500,000 Americans have some form of CP; each year 8,000 infants and nearly 1,500 preschool-age children are diagnosed with the condition.

Symptoms

There are three main types of cerebral palsy: spastic, athetoid, and a combination of these two types known as "mixed."

Spastic CP is the most common form and is characterized by extremely tight muscles, with stiff movements of the legs, arms, or back. Children with this form of CP move their legs awkwardly, turning in or scissoring their legs as they try to walk.

Athetoid CP (also called dyskinetic CP) can affect movements of the entire body. Typically, this involves slow, uncontrolled body movements and low muscle tone that make it hard for the person to sit straight and walk.

Mixed CP is a combination of the symptoms listed above. A child with this form has some muscles that are too tight and others that are too loose, creating a mix of stiffness and involuntary movements.

In some cases of cerebral palsy, only the legs are affected (diplegia) or only half the body (hemiplegia).

Treatment

With early and ongoing treatment the effects can be reduced. Children younger than age three benefit from early intervention; older children can get special education services through public schools. Typically, children with CP may need different kinds of therapy, including:

- physical therapy: to help develop stronger muscles, with emphasis on walking, sitting, and keeping his or her balance

- occupational therapy: to help develop fine motor skills such as dressing, feeding, writing, and other daily living tasks
- speech-language pathology: to help develop communication skills

A variety of special equipment may help. This may include braces to hold the foot in place when the child stands or walks or custom splints to help a child use the hands. A variety of therapy equipment and adapted toys can help children play, and activities such as swimming or horseback riding can help strengthen weaker muscles and relax the tighter ones.

Surgery, Botox injections, or other medications can help lessen the effects of CP, but there is no cure for the condition.

Education

A child with CP can face many challenges in school and is likely to need individualized help. For children up to age three, services are provided through an early intervention system. Schools work with the child's family to develop an individualized family services plan (IFSP). The plan describes the child's unique needs as well as the services the child needs. The plan will also emphasize the unique needs of the family, so that parents and other family members will know how to help their young child with CP. Early intervention services may be provided on a sliding-fee basis, meaning that the costs to the family will depend upon their income.

For school-age children (including preschoolers), special education and services will be provided through the school. School staff will work with the child's parents to develop an INDIVIDUALIZED EDUCATION PROGRAM (IEP), which is similar to the family services plan in that it describes the child's unique needs and necessary services. Special education and related services, which can include physical and occupational therapy and speech-language pathology, are provided free.

In addition to therapy services and special equipment, children with CP may need ASSISTIVE

TECHNOLOGY, like communication devices such as voice synthesizers, or communication boards with pictures, symbols, letters, or words attached. The child communicates by pointing to or gazing at the pictures.

Other types of technology may include electronic toys with special switches or sophisticated computer programs operated by simple switch pads or keyboard adaptations.

The INDIVIDUALS WITH DISABILITIES EDUCATION ACT (IDEA) guides how early intervention services and special education and related services are provided to children with disabilities. Under IDEA, cerebral palsy is considered an "orthopedic impairment"—a severe impairment that affects a child's educational performance.

channel   One way to refer to the sensory mode through which information is taken in and processed, as in the "auditory channel" or "visual channel." Individuals often show a preference for a specific sensory channel.

See also LEARNING MODALITIES; MULTIPLE INTELLIGENCES.

Child Behavior Checklist   This type of behavioral questionnaire contains a list of behavioral problems that are rated by the parent as "not true," "somewhat true," or "very true." Children are compared with others of the same age on anxiety, depression, hyperactivity, and so on. Because it is helpful on any behavior checklist to obtain input from several teachers and parents, self-report and teacher forms are also available. Because each teacher and parent is likely to see the student from a different perspective, the best overall view of the child's behavior is obtained by comparing many different viewpoints.

child psychiatrist   A physician who specializes in the treatment of children and adolescents. Unlike psychologists, psychiatrists can prescribe medication. Typically, either a child psychiatrist or a pediatrician will be involved in the prescription of medication for attention deficit disorders.

Children and Adults with Attention Deficit/ Hyperactivity Disorder (CHADD)   A nonprofit organization founded in 1987 in response to the frustration and sense of isolation experienced by parents and their children with ADHD. At that time, there were very few places for support or information, and people misunderstood ADHD. Many clinicians and educators knew little about the disability, and individuals with ADHD were often mistakenly labeled a behavior problem, unmotivated, or not intelligent enough.

From one parent support group in Florida, the organization grew dramatically to become the leading nonprofit national organization for children and adults with ADHD. Today the organization continues to be run by volunteers, with the support of a small national staff, and offers education, advocacy, and support.

Contact: 8181 Professional Place, Suite 201, Landover, MD 20785; phone: (301) 306–7070; website:: http://www.chadd.org

child study committee   A group of school members who review and decide plans of action for students. Typically, a student is referred to the child study committee because of concerns about school performance, either academic or behavioral. The committee usually consists of at least three people, including the school principal or a delegate, the teacher or teachers, and a special educator or school counselor.

chunking   A strategy for enhancing memory by grouping similar information, because smaller "chunks" are easier to remember than larger sequences of information. For example, a telephone number is typically remembered in chunks of three: the area code, the exchange, and the individual four-digit number, which is far easier to remember than a 10-digit number.

classroom management The array of strategies and techniques a teacher uses to manage the range of learning needs and behaviors that may exist within a given class. Effective classroom management keeps discipline problems to a minimum and addresses them effectively, and provides a safe, secure space for learning that appropriately responds to a variety of learning styles.

clinical observation The study and analysis of an individual's behavior and performance in a clinical setting. This observation may involve analysis of behaviors during testing, mood and behavior during a clinical interview, or the observations of behavior in more open-ended assessment contexts, such as play in the case of young children. Clinical observation is an important component of assessment.

closure The idea that information processing and perception typically strives for making things whole. For example, in a CLOZE PROCEDURE test (a form of assessment used to measure various reading comprehension skills), individuals read sentences in context; if they understand, they have little difficulty finding correct responses.

cloze procedure A form of assessment used to measure various reading comprehension skills. In a passage of sentences, words are replaced with spaces for the reader to fill in, using contextual cues and the reader's understanding of a variety of language patterns.

Code of Federal Regulations (CFR) All of the federal regulations that explain, expand on, and are used to implement federal laws. Federal regulations contained in the CFR often define terms that are used in laws but aren't clearly defined; the CFR also may specify how a program mandated by law is to be administered. Federal regulations are cited by volume and section number in the CFR.

coding This term refers to the ways in which information is represented so it can be placed in and retrieved from long-term memory. When something is seen or heard, it must be associated with existing knowledge or organized if the information to be useful. Research suggests that some people with a LEARNING DISABILITY don't encode information well.

cognition The process of knowing, thinking, problem solving, remembering, reasoning, planning, and making judgments. It includes the acquisition and manipulation of knowledge, usually by means of symbols.

Cognitive scientists are concerned with this human ability. They are less concerned about the fact that cognition can't be directly observed; instead, they consider the neurological events that allow the process to occur.

cognitive ability A general term that refers to the broad cluster of mental skills involved in learning, thinking, and processing information. Examples of cognitive abilities include memory, attention, language development, comprehension, problem solving, critical analysis, and concept formation.

Although it's possible to generalize about the overall cognitive ability of an individual, it is far more important and valuable to understand the ways in which specific cognitive functions interact and depend on one another, and to assess strengths and difficulties in a more specific and fine-grained fashion.

cognitive style The preferred way an individual processes information, usually described as a personality dimension that influences attitudes, values, and social interaction. Unlike individual differences in abilities that describe peak performance, styles describe a person's typical mode of thinking, remembering, or problem solving. Having more of an ability is usually considered beneficial, while having a particular cognitive style simply denotes a tendency to behave in a certain manner.

Field Independence/Dependence

A number of cognitive styles have been identified and studied over the years; field independence/field dependence is probably the most well known. Individuals view the world in different ways. Those who are called "field-dependent" perceive the world in terms of larger patterns and relationships, whereas those who are "field-independent" perceive the world in terms of discrete individual elements—they look at the pieces that make up the whole.

Most schools in Western culture favor a field-independent approach, rewarding students who tend to work and organize information on their own. These learners are objective in that they make what is being studied into an object to be analyzed and understood.

Studies have identified a number of connections between this cognitive style and learning. For example, field-independent individuals are likely to learn more effectively by studying by themselves, and are influenced less by social reinforcement.

college admission and learning disabilities

More and more students with learning disabilities are enrolling in two- and four-year colleges and universities, doubling from 15 percent to 32 percent since 1985. Currently, nearly one-third of all freshmen with disabilities report having learning disabilities.

However, universities have different purposes, entrance criteria, programs, and requirements for certifications, associate degrees, and baccalaureate degrees. As a result, students with learning disabilities who want to go to college need to prepare in high school long before their senior year.

First, students with learning disabilities who want to go to college need to learn strategies to help them plan, complete, and evaluate projects, to apply strategies flexibly, and modify or create strategies to fit new learning situations. There

are many ways to do this, such as allowing more time to complete tests or projects, listening to audio tapes of textbooks while reading, and so on.

Legal Rights

High school students with learning disabilities must understand their rights under Section 504 of the REHABILITATION ACT and the AMERICANS WITH DISABILITIES ACT (ADA), which guarantee the civil rights of people with disabilities, and how these differ from the rights and services they receive under the INDIVIDUALS WITH DISABILITIES EDUCATION ACT (IDEA).

IDEA is the legislation that guarantees a free, appropriate public education and governs how special education services will be provided to students with disabilities in elementary and secondary schools. Under IDEA, the school is responsible for identifying and testing students with disabilities, and for monitoring services. These special education services, which are described in detail in a student's INDIVIDUALIZED EDUCATION PROGRAM (IEP) and individualized transition plan (ITP), could significantly change the requirements of the "standard" high school academic program. Requirements for high school diplomas may be changed under IDEA as well. For example, depending on the particular disability, some students may not need to take certain language, mathematics, or science courses that are usually required courses for a diploma. However, IDEA does not apply to higher education; colleges and universities don't offer "special" education.

Under Section 504 and the ADA, universities can't discriminate against a person because of disability, and must provide reasonable modifications, accommodations, or aids to enable qualified students to participate in college programs. A university, for example, may provide readers, notetakers, extra time to complete exams, or alternate test formats. Decisions about the exact accommodations a college would provide are made on a case-by-case basis. Exactly what they offer is up to the college, as long as it is effective.

Colleges and universities are not required by law to provide aides, services, or devices for personal use or study.

In addition, colleges aren't required to design special academic programs for students with disabilities, but they must provide services so that qualified students with disabilities will have equal access to the regular academic program. After equal access is provided, it is a student's own responsibility to succeed. Section 504 and the ADA don't require colleges to change their requirements for either admission or graduation.

After high school, the level of responsibility about special services changes. Once a student has been admitted to college, it is the student's responsibility to provide documentation of a disability. The college won't provide any accommodation until a student:

1. requests services from the office (or person) on campus responsible for providing services to students with disabilities
2. provides documentation of disability. For the student with a learning disability, such documentation is often a copy of the testing report and/or a copy of the IEP or ITP.

Confidentiality

To protect the privacy of student records, the Family Educational Rights and Privacy Act (FERPA) was passed in 1974 and later amended several times. FERPA (also known as the Buckley Amendment) gives students the right to access their educational records, consent to release a record to a third party, challenge information in those records, and be notified of their privacy rights. FERPA affects all colleges that receive federal funds. FERPA protects a student's record from being shared (without the student's permission) with "curious" faculty, administrators, other students, the press, or anyone without a legitimate reason for seeing the record. For example, faculty members don't have a right to access information about a student's disability; they need to know only what accommodations are necessary to meet the student's disability-related needs, and then only with permission of the student.

Preparing for College

Under the IDEA, the IEP for each student receiving special education services must include a statement of the transition services needed. Students with learning disabilities who plan to go to college should participate in the transition planning process.

College Options

Hundreds of colleges and universities have comprehensive programs on campus specially designed for students with learning disabilities. Staffed by experts, these programs may offer tutoring or counseling services. Since the services provided in such programs are more than they are required to offer under Section 504 and ADA, many colleges and universities charge for these services. Services required by Section 504 and ADA are provided at no cost.

It is also possible that such programs have their own separate admission requirements. Students who wish to learn more about such programs should either call and ask if such a program exists on campus, or check guidebooks that contain listings of such programs.

IDEA requires reevaluations to be conducted at least every three years; therefore, high school students with learning disabilities ought to have a comprehensive reevaluation close to graduation to ensure that the documentation they take with them is up to date. Students and parents should discuss the documentation in order to understand what it conveys about the student's strengths, weaknesses, and recommended services.

Many high schools routinely destroy copies of student records after a number of years. Since students with learning disabilities will need copies of some items in their records to show to the college or university as documentation of their disability, they should be sure to have complete copies of all records.

Students with learning disabilities should consider various college options as well as their academic strengths and weaknesses in planning their high school program. Students seeking admission to selective institutions MUST meet the criteria set by the college.

Successful college students with learning disabilities report that high school courses teaching keyboard skills and word processing are especially important. A high school transcript displaying successful completion of a wide array of courses (science, math, history, literature, foreign language, art, music) is attractive to selective college admissions staff. Involvement in school or community sponsored clubs, teams, or performances also enhances a college admission candidate's application.

Students with learning disabilities may benefit from mini-courses in study skills, assertiveness training, and time management. It is very important to list the accommodative services in the ITP, since the types of accommodations students may receive when taking standardized college admission tests or licensing examinations may depend on the evidence of having received them in high school.

Colleges and universities are not required to change admission requirements, nor are they required to alter program requirements for students with learning disabilities once they have been admitted. While colleges and universities need to give consideration to requests of students with learning disabilities for course waivers and substitutions, such waivers and substitutions are not often granted. If the campus academic committee determines that a course is not an essential component of the student's major, a waiver may be granted. Substitution with courses that convey the essential elements of the requirement (such as substituting a course in the culture of another country for a course in foreign language) are more readily granted than waivers. However, if a course is an essential element to the degree sought, it is unlikely that a waiver or substitution would be granted. Therefore, passing such a course would continue to be a requirement for graduation.

Admission Testing

With proper documentation, high school students with learning disabilities may take standardized college admission tests such as the PSAT, SAT, and ACT with certain accommodations, including:

- individual administration of the test
- audiocassette tape or large-print test editions
- special answer sheets
- extended testing time

However, the procedures for accommodations in each of the standardized tests vary, and students should contact the agency that administers each standardized test for specific information. It is the responsibility of the student to request information and accommodations. Any accommodation given by a testing agency to a student with a learning disability is designed only to give that student equal footing in the testing environment. It is then every student's responsibility to do well. Tests taken by students with disabilities are scored in the same fashion as those taken by students without disabilities. Scores of tests taken with accommodations are so noted when they are reported to the schools.

Disclosure

A student will need to decide whether or not to disclose the disability. Colleges may invite applicants for admission to indicate the existence of disabilities on the application form, but may not require this information. Should a student reveal a disability, this information alone can't be used as a basis for denying admission. On the other hand, colleges don't have to change their admission requirements or standards. This means that having a learning disability does not entitle a student to a place in college.

However, by disclosing the disability, the student may explain possible discrepancies within admission documents, such as a transcript with top grades but low SAT scores. Such discrepancies are typical of a student with a learning disability, but if an admissions committee isn't aware of the disability, admission may be denied.

Of course, disclosing a learning disability doesn't guarantee admission, but it can offer the chance to include additional insights.

communication delay   Speech and language patterns that develop normally but at a slower pace than would be typically expected.

communication disorder   A problem in being understood or in understanding. Students with a communication disorder can quickly fall behind in class, and have problems in vocabulary, memory, and problem solving. Many also encounter difficulty in social situations. While experts aren't sure how many children have communication disorders, estimates suggest it may affect about 5 percent of the school-age population. Early identification of a communication disorder is essential. Communication disorders can be grouped into two main categories—hearing disorders, or speech and language disorders.

A hearing disorder affects the ability to hear sounds clearly. Such disorders may range from hearing speech sounds faintly, or in a distorted way, to profound deafness. Speech and language disorders affect the way people talk and understand, and may range from simple sound substitutions to the inability to use speech and language at all.

Hearing Disorders

Hearing disorders may be caused by a wide variety of problems either at birth or any time thereafter. Profound hearing loss from birth or at an early age makes the acquisition of spoken language very difficult. However, deaf infants and children all go through the same developmental speech stages in acquiring gestural language, such as the recognized language of American Sign Language.

Hearing loss acquired through disease, injury, or noise may be more subtle, but if not treated it may interfere with a child's ability to acquire spoken language.

Speech/Language Disorder

Evidence of a speech and language disorder may be seen when a person's speech or language significantly differs from that of others of the same age or background, or when there is a marked impairment in a person's ability to express himself.

Speech and language disorders may be caused by a broad range of factors, such as hearing loss, cerebral palsy, severe head injury, stroke, or heredity. Often, the cause is unknown.

See also APHASIA; EXPRESSIVE LANGUAGE DISORDERS; MIXED RECEPTIVE-EXPRESSIVE LANGUAGE DISORDER.

comorbidity   A medical term that refers to a relationship or association between one condition (such as ADHD) and other psychological or learning disorders. For example, DYSLEXIA is comorbid with ADHD in as many as 40 percent of children with ADHD. ADHD may also be comorbid with substance abuse disorders, depression, OBSESSIVE-COMPULSIVE DISORDER, and BORDERLINE PERSONALITY DISORDER.

The term suggests that one disorder may be linked with others in a relationship that is not fully understood. For effective treatment, a diagnosis must assess all possible learning and psychological problems. If more than one condition is present, treatment must take into account all of the existing conditions.

compensation   A change in action, behavior, or attitude that is based on the influence of a disability or disorder. In learning, compensation is the development of skills or strategies to help strengthen a weak area or disability. Compensatory strategies can develop over time in order to learn successfully or more efficiently.

comprehension   The ability to recognize and understand information. There are different types of comprehension (such as listening comprehension, reading comprehension, and picture comprehension), and an individual may perform differently in varying comprehension areas.

For example, an individual's listening comprehension may be stronger or weaker than his reading comprehension, and an individual with poor comprehension of verbal material may be much stronger in the area of social comprehension.

In academic settings, comprehension is often associated with intellectual potential and intelligence. However, comprehension involves a number of subcomponents, and it is important to be cautious in assessing the factors that may underlie comprehension problems. For example, listening comprehension difficulties may arise from problems in the area of auditory processing, rather than difficulties with reasoning. Likewise, problems with reading comprehension may be caused by underlying decoding problems and unfamiliarity with the material, or limited general knowledge.

Some learning disorders such as nonverbal learning disabilities may involve significant deficits in the area of social comprehension, resulting in large part from difficulties in processing visual-spatial information.

comprehension monitoring A term that refers to the fact that, as a student reads, he notes whether he is beginning to form a concept of the meaning of the passage and adjusting the reading processes accordingly.

comprehension strategy In reading, a systematic sequence of steps for understanding text. However, there is little consensus in the research literature on what constitutes a comprehension strategy, which also may include teaching techniques such as mapping or diagramming, used to help students become strategic readers.

compulsion An irresistible urge to perform an action over and over.

computer assisted instruction (CAI) A form of individual learning that offers instruction, practice, and feedback delivered by software programs. CAI is a somewhat dated term that was used when computers were a relatively new phenomenon in classrooms. Now that most learning environments have integrated computer tools into instruction, the term is becoming obsolete.

CAI applies to any computer hardware or software that enhances learning, as opposed to ASSISTIVE TECHNOLOGY, which refers specifically to computer-based learning aids for people with various kinds of disabilities.

Computer assisted instruction can offer a useful means for practice of newly developed skills, and is most effective when facilitated by a skilled instructor. CAI can be a useful and motivating means of improving skills because of the graphic and interactive nature of most programs.

concentration Focused attention. Someone who is concentrating on a task must both sustain attention over time and also hold information in active working memory. Concentration requires a higher level of arousal than attention or vigilance, because of the requirement for processing in working memory on a continuing basis.

Although "concentration" is not a clinical term, it may be used in descriptions of task performance in order to describe the level of active processing of relevant information and a high level of filtering out distractions.

concept A mental representation used to group things or ideas by their shared attributes. The term "concept" reflects a central element in COGNITION. Humans conceptualize information by first absorbing it and then organizing or classifying it.

A concept can be a concrete or abstract mental representation. The concept of "dog" is concrete —understanding that specific animals, although different in size, appearance, and behavior, can be grouped together as a "dog" category. Concepts are often understood to be abstract, as well, such as the concept of "justice." In understanding the term "justice," an individual must be able to apply a current use of the word to background knowledge and prior experience. While there may be no specific, agreed-upon mental representation or image for "justice," individuals store a range of information that allows them to retrieve an assortment of applications and meanings in order to help them understand.

Being able to form a concept is a cognitive process of abstraction. As individuals experience the world, they make inferences about the things in it. When a person perceives that qualities are similar and can be placed in the same class, concepts are formed. This process involves understanding a set of relevant features or qualifiers that can be used to represent a concept.

Concepts can be formed verbally or nonverbally—it may be easier to visualize a poodle than it is to describe a poodle. Verbal concepts are associated with ideas that are easier to describe with words than visually. Nonverbal concepts are easier to envision than to describe with words.

Individuals with learning disabilities can have difficulty with concept formation. They are likely to have difficulty if concepts are presented in a way not suited to their strongest learning style. If they are visual learners, they may have difficulty with concepts that are explained only verbally. Individuals with language-based learning difficulties may benefit from presentations that are more visual.

concept imagery The ability to imagine the whole. Concept imagery is directly related to oral and written language comprehension and critical thinking.

See also CONCEPT IMAGERY DISORDER.

concept imagery disorder A problem with visualizing related to language comprehension. The ability to imagine is directly related to oral and written language comprehension and critical thinking. Individuals with good comprehension report that they form mental images easily, but students with poor comprehension report that they see nothing when they read, or see only a few fleeting images. This means it's difficult to connect to the entire concept of what is read or heard.

Students with this problem grasp a few facts, but get lost after a few sentences when they read or listen. They can recall some specifics, but cannot generalize and create a "whole" from the information.

Symptoms of the disorder include:

- poor reading comprehension
- poor oral language comprehension
- inability to follow oral directions
- weak expressive language
- weak higher order thinking skills
- poor problem solving

conceptual disorder Problems in thinking, memorizing, and organizing thoughts in relation to problem solving, following or producing logical sequences, or the ability to formulate and express concepts.

This problem may make it very hard for a student to understand written material or spoken information and seriously interfere with school performance. In general, conceptual disorders may be part of a specific learning disability, rather than an isolated learning problem.

Concerta An extended-release form of methylphenidate (RITALIN) for ATTENTION DEFICIT/HYPERACTIVITY DISORDER. Approved to be given only once a day, this version of the drug eliminates the ups and downs that often come with traditional medications. Concerta is designed to give a very smooth sustained release and then to shut off after 10 to 12 hours, so that the child's appetite and sleep are normal at end of the day.

Concerta is the first of the slow-release medications to be created for ADHD. Several others are expected to be introduced in 2002.

Concerta is approved for the treatment of ADHD in children over age six. It is to be taken in the morning, before a child leaves for school. The drug overcoat dissolves within an hour, providing an initial dose of methylphenidate, which is then released gradually in a smooth pattern, improving attention and behavior throughout the day. The advanced system was designed to help a child maintain focus without in-school and after-school dosing. Due to its controlled release, Concerta minimizes the fluctuating levels of medicine in the blood associated with other medications when they are taken more than once per day.

Concerta should not be taken by patients who have significant anxiety, tension, or agitation, since the drug may make these conditions worse. It should not be used by anyone who

- is allergic to Ritalin or any of the other ingredients
- has glaucoma
- has tics
- has TOURETTE'S SYNDROME or a family history of Tourette's syndrome
- takes a prescription monoamine oxidase inhibitor (MAOI)

Ordinarily, Concerta should not be given to patients with preexisting severe gastrointestinal narrowing, and it should be used with caution by anyone with a history of drug dependence or alcoholism. Chronic abuse can lead to psychological dependence.

concrete operational stage The third of the four stages in Piaget's theory of cognitive development. This stage occurs from ages six or seven to about 11, during which the child learns to think logically about concrete events. During this period, the child will learn to consider several features of a task or situation rather than to focus on only the most obvious. At this stage children can mentally go through a series of steps to solve

a problem and then reverse the series, returning to the beginning of the problem.

They are able to classify objects into subcategories and to place objects into a sequence based on a variety of qualities such as height, weight, or age. They also come to understand that objects remain the same in terms of mass and number when their shape or arrangement changes.

Research has confirmed that Piaget's sequence of the acquisition of various characteristics at this stage is generally accurate.

concrete thinking A type of thinking in which the individual is unable to understand the similarities between situations, seeing each situation as different.

conduct disorder Extremely disobedient behavior in young adults, including vandalism, theft, lying, and drug use. Typically diagnosed in young boys, conduct disorders are characterized by antisocial behavior and patterns of "acting out" at home or at school. The child may have difficulty learning how to solve problems or to establish peer relationships.

Individuals with conduct disorder are more likely to attract attention from teachers and parents, to be referred for services, and to receive some treatment at an early age for their misbehavior.

There is a high correlation between conduct disorder and ATTENTION DEFICIT/HYPERACTIVITY DISORDER (ADHD). Individuals with both disorders are particularly at risk for continuing social and emotional difficulties into adulthood.

Cause

Research suggests that the most severe cases of conduct disorder begin in early childhood, especially in the presence of inconsistent rules and harsh discipline, lack of enough supervision or guidance, frequent change in caregivers, poverty, neglect or abuse, and a delinquent peer group.

Treatment

Because antisocial behavior in children and adolescents is very hard to change after it has become ingrained, the earlier the problem is identified and treated the better. Some recent studies have focused on promising ways to prevent conduct disorder among children and adolescents who are at risk for developing the disorder, since most of these children are probably reacting to events and situations in their lives.

confidential file   In relation to special education, a confidential file is a limited-access file maintained by the school that contains evaluations and any other information related to special education placement. Parents have the right to know the information contained in a confidential file and to have copies of any materials.

configuration   The visual shape of a word, including elements such as the height, depth, or width of various letters, and the overall length of the word. Word configuration may be used in sight-word reading as a cue in word-attack skills.

Connors Parent/Teacher Rating Scales–Revised   These two types of behavioral questionnaires are checklists—one for parents, one for teachers—on which they can rate a variety of behavior problems on a four-point scale. Several versions of this scale are available; the 48–item parent scale and the 39–item teacher scale are both standardized. Because many of the items on the hyperactivity scale involve acting out and other annoying behaviors, this scale may not identify the child who is well socialized but has attention deficit and hyperactivity. Behavioral characteristics include

- antisocial
- anxiety
- conduct disorder

- disorganized
- hyperactive
- learning problems
- obsessional
- psychosomatic
- restless

constructional apraxia   The inability to assemble, build, draw, or copy accurately.

context clues   Using information in a sentence or paragraph surrounding a new term to help the reader understand that term. There are several items to look for when searching for context clues, including

- a punctuation mark (such as a comma or dash) that may signal that information is being presented about the new term.
- key words: words such as "or" and "that is" may signal that a definition is to follow.
- definition: sometimes the meaning of a new term may be made clear by reading the entire paragraph in which it appears.

Learning to use context clues to gain meaning is an important reading skill. A student who is able to use the context to identify an unknown word, grasp the meaning of a word, or comprehend a passage read, will become a good reader.

contextual reading   Reading that is performed using narrative text (paragraphs, stories, articles) rather than words in isolation. Assessing the way in which an individual reads contextually is essential to developing an accurate picture of the person's reading ability.

Determining a person's fluency is important in developing an overall reading program. Increasing the volume of reading (especially reading for pleasure) is considered essential to improving contextual reading abilities.

continuum of services A range of services from least amount of change in a student's educational program to institutionalization. In the past, it was a common practice in many school districts either not to provide any special education at all or to provide only a very few placement options.

With the passage of the INDIVIDUALS WITH DISABILITIES ACT (IDEA) schools were required to provide any necessary placement options such as resource classes, self-contained classes, or INSTITUTIONALIZATION.

contralateral Relating to opposite sides. The human brain is contralateral in nature, since areas on one side of the brain are concerned with sensory and motor processes on the opposite side of the body. For example, left brain activity regulates physical movement on the right side of the body.

convergence A way of thinking that combines existing information and knowledge to solve a problem in an analytical and rational manner. It is most useful for problems that can be solved algorithmically or that have a single correct answer.

convergent retrieval memory The location of highly specific information in memory on demand, such as in word-finding, spelling tests, or solving arithmetic equations. Trying to locate the precise word to describe a phenomenon, or attempting to recall the answer to a simple multiplication problem, are both examples of convergent retrieval memory at work. Individuals with learning disabilities often have trouble with these types of tasks.

Convergent retrieval memory is the opposite of divergent retrieval, in which there may be many possible appropriate responses.

coordination The effective control of muscles in the body to perform smooth, voluntary, and complex movements. This is accomplished through regulating muscle groups by the motor control areas of the brain and the accompanying motor and sensory nerves.

Difficulties with the development of gross motor coordination in early childhood may be an early sign of a learning disability; problems with fine-motor coordination may have a significant impact on some academic activities, such as the development of handwriting skills.

A coordination disability affects fingering, feeling, grasping, pinching, and handling. Tasks that may be impaired include typing, writing, eating, bathing, grooming, dressing oneself, telephoning, handling money—in general, any task that includes use of the hands for manipulation.

corporal punishment Any intervention that is designed to, or likely to cause physical pain in order to stop or change behavior. In the United States, the most typical form of school corporal punishment is the striking of a student's buttocks with a wooden paddle by a school authority because the student disobeyed a rule.

More than half of all states ban the use of corporal punishment in schools because of its harmful physical, educational, psychological, and social effects on students. In states where it is allowed, many school boards voluntarily prohibit it. Yet, almost a half million children are being hit each year in public schools—a disproportionate number being minority children and children with disabilities.

Most experts agree that corporal punishment contributes to the cycle of child abuse and pro-violence attitudes of youth by teaching that it is an acceptable way of controlling the behavior of others. While discipline is important, effective alternatives are available to help students develop self-discipline.

The use of corporal punishment has been declining in U.S. schools because of waning public acceptance, increased litigation against school boards and educators, and legal bans.

Corporal punishment is a technique that can easily be abused and can lead to physical injuries. Evidence indicates that corporal punishment negatively affects the social, psychological, and educational development of students and contributes to the cycle of child abuse and pro-violence attitudes of youth.

Effective discipline includes programs and strategies for changing student behavior, for changing school or classroom environments, and for educating and supporting teachers and parents.

Alternatives for changing student behavior include

- helping students achieve academic success by identifying academic and behavioral problems and strengths
- behavioral contracting
- positive reinforcement of appropriate behavior
- individual and group counseling
- disciplinary consequences that are meaningful to students and have an instructional component
- social skills training

corpus callosum The broad, thick band of neural fibers that connect the left and right hemispheres of the brain, thus allowing both hemispheres to work together on complex functions. Because the callosum exchanges information between the two hemispheres, it allows the brain to be more efficient. The two hemispheres can develop their own specialized functions, yet still take advantage of each other's benefits through the callosum. The right side senses input, checks with the left side to see if there are rules to deal with this pattern of input, integrates the stored information, and reacts in a modified way. Damage to any of these systems causes very poor, inappropriate responses. For example, if the corpus callosum can't access the appropriate information quickly enough (or at all), then reaction to stimuli will be completely spontaneous, impulsive, and based solely on instinct.

Research suggests that the corpus callosum may be smaller in children with ADHD, and that both ADHD and dyslexia may be linked to abnormalities in this part of the brain.

In the 18th century, the corpus callosum was considered the site of the soul, but by the early 20th century experts thought it existed merely to prevent the cerebral hemispheres from collapsing onto each other. It was not until the 1950s that scientists began to understand that the corpus callosum served to help transfer information between the two hemispheres. This was followed by the development in the early 1960s of a surgical intervention aimed at reducing the interhemispheric transmission of abnormal electrical discharges in epileptic patients.

corrective reading Supplemental, selective instruction for minor reading problems that is more specific than developmental reading but less intensive than remedial reading. Corrective reading instruction is often provided within a regular classroom by the regular teacher, aide, or a peer tutor.

criterion-referenced test A test that measures how thoroughly a student has mastered a specific skill or area of knowledge. It is based on the comparison of a student's specific knowledge to a predetermined level of mastery, rather than to another student's scores. The scores have meaning in terms of what the student knows or can do, rather than the relation to scores made by some external reference group. Such tests usually cover relatively small amounts of information and are closely related to instruction. Typically, a criterion-referenced test is subjective and relies on someone to observe and rate student work. Performance assessments are criterion-referenced tests.

Often, this type of assessment is used to evaluate the acquisition of skills or knowledge based on a set of objectives or learning goals determined by a teacher or school system. It can also be used to evaluate a specific program of instruction or a system by examining the progress of individual students and then developing statistical profiles based on specified outcomes.

The opposite of a criterion-referenced test is a NORM-REFERENCED TEST, which is a type of assessment that compares scores of students in one school with a reference group. This reference group is usually other students in the same grade, called the "norm group."

cross-categorical　A system for grouping students with disabilities. Cross-categorical grouping places students with different kinds of disabilities into the same instructional setting at the same time.

cross dominance　Also known as mixed dominance or mixed laterality, this is a condition in which an individual prefers one side of the body for some activities and the other side for other activities. For example, a person who has cross dominance might be right-footed and right-eyed but left-handed.

cued speech　The use of hand gestures in conjunction with lip reading to distinguish between specific sounds. This method of communication was developed in 1966 as a speechreading support system that in English uses eight hand configurations and four hand positions near the mouth to supplement visible speech. The hand cue signals a visual difference between sounds that look alike on the lips, such as "p" and "b." These cues enable a deaf or hard-of-hearing person to see the phonetic equivalent of what others hear.

The hand configurations and locations are called "cues," not "cued speech" itself, which is the combination of the cues with speech. The cues are not readable alone.

It was developed primarily because some congenitally deaf people don't become good readers because they don't have an easy way to learn spoken language as young deaf children. Proponents of the system believe cued speech makes spoken language visually clear and solves the communication problem, and also helps youngsters learn a spoken language more easily. It is most successful when used consistently from childhood.

See also CUEING.

cueing　Providing additional verbal or nonverbal signals in order to assist an individual in retrieving, decoding, or articulating words. It may also be used as a study strategy, through the development of mnemonic devices or study cards, to help provide prompts or cues for remembering and retrieving information or specific language.

See also CUED SPEECH.

cultural determinant　A factor arising from racial, ethnic, or socioeconomic background that may systematically influence test performance on a specific assessment instrument.

cumulative file　In public education, a cumulative file is the general file containing all the educational records and information maintained for any child enrolled in the school. Parents have a legal right to inspect the file and have copies of any information contained in it.

cursive writing　A form of handwriting (sometimes called "script") in which letters are joined together in each word. Cursive writing may be useful for individuals with perceptual difficulties who frequently reverse letters. Cursive writing is typically introduced in third grade.

Cylert (pemoline)　A stimulant medication sometimes used to treat ADHD, but not typically a first choice. Because of its association with life-threatening liver failure, Cylert is not ordinarily considered as first-line drug therapy for ADHD, and it was withdrawn from sale in Canada in September 1999 because of complications.

Since Cylert's debut in 1975, 13 cases of acute hepatic failure have been reported to the FDA. While the number of reported cases isn't large, the rate of reporting ranges from four to 17 times the rate expected in the general population. This estimate may be conservative because of underreporting and because of the long latency between the beginning of Cylert treatment and the occurrence of liver failure. Of the 13 cases, 11 ended in death or liver transplantation, usually within four weeks of the onset of signs and symptoms of liver failure.

Unlike Ritalin and Dexedrine, which can take effect within an hour, Cylert takes from two to four weeks to become effective. It is used by children and adults and is usually prescribed as part of a treatment plan that includes behavioral or educational interventions. Stimulant medications like Cylert are generally taken for as long a period of time as is helpful.

Although experts aren't sure how Cylert works, they believe it boosts the production of a neurotransmitter called dopamine.

Side Effects

In addition to the serious liver problems, common side effects include sleep problems and loss of appetite. It may decrease growth rate in children, so its use should be monitored carefully by a physician.

D

decoding Understanding language through listening and reading. Decoding most frequently refers to the ability to recognize letter and word patterns and link them to the corresponding sounds. Decoding is different from comprehension, which implies an understanding of the material read.

Reading is a twofold process; decoding is the first step, but then students must be able to comprehend what the words mean once they have accurately decoded them from the text. Slow, single-word reading is the biggest predictor of low reading comprehension skills.

Recent research on how children learn to read identifies decoding as a core problem for individuals with reading disorders. If a child has trouble learning sound-symbol relationships, there is a good chance that child will have a reading disability if not given early explicit PHONEMIC AWARENESS training.

Symptoms of poor decoding skills include slow, labored sounding out of words, frequent misidentification of familiar words (what/that or and/not), hesitant, stop-and-start reading, and frequent mispronunciations of words. An informal assessment of decoding skills can be performed by having an individual read aloud. Decoding skills are also assessed by having students read nonsense words such as *dat, smop, thinkle.*

dementia The significant impairment of memory, reasoning, personality, and intellect. Dementia is caused by brain injury or disease, including progressive forms of dementia such as Alzheimer's disease and some forms of Parkinson's disease. Generally, dementia involves some degree of language impairment, and in the case of progressive forms of dementia these impairments inevitably become more severe over time.

depression A mood disorder characterized by sadness, hopelessness, low self-esteem, fatigue, or agitation. Clinical depression is a serious disorder that responds well to medication and therapy. People with ATTENTION DEFICIT/HYPERACTIVITY DISORDER (ADHD) are at higher risk for developing depression because of the frustrations that go along with having ADHD.

Because it is not unusual for individuals with learning problems to feel despair and a loss of self-confidence, and because depression frequently co-exists with disorders such as ADHD, it is essential that symptoms of depression be recognized and evaluated if they are persistent or severe.

Symptoms

Major depression is almost always characterized by feelings of general sadness and total loss of pleasure for at least two weeks. There are a wide range of typical symptoms related to a clinical depression, including at least three of the following:

- deep sadness or crying jags
- gain or loss of weight
- chronic insomnia or excessive sleepiness
- outbursts of shouting and anger
- lost interest in hobbies and pleasure activities

- loss of interest in sex
- feelings of worthlessness, unattractiveness, guilt
- problems with concentration
- muddy, foggy thoughts
- anxiety, phobias, delusions, or fears
- restlessness
- slowed body movements
- suicidal thoughts

Treatment

Depression can be successfully treated and responds best to a combination of therapy and medication with antidepressants. Today there are a wide range of antidepressants on the market, including the selective serotonin reuptake inhibitors (Prozac, Zoloft, and others), tricyclic antidepressants, MAO inhibitors, and structurally unrelated drugs. Doctors may need to try several antidepressants before finding one that is effective in alleviating depression.

developmental arithmetic disorder See DYSCALCULIA.

developmental articulation disorder A condition in which a child may have trouble controlling the rate of speech, or may lag behind classmates in learning to make speech sounds.

Developmental articulation disorders are common, appearing in at least 10 percent of children younger than age eight. Fortunately, articulation disorders are often outgrown or successfully treated with speech therapy.

developmental disability Technically, this term refers to any significant disability acquired before the age of 22. In actuality, however, "developmental disability" has also begun to replace the term MENTAL RETARDATION to describe the condition of individuals with severely impaired intellectual functioning from birth.

The term brings the description of this particular spectrum of disability more into line with the general language used to define various types of difficulties, and its focus on development rather than retardation provides a more accurate way of describing the actual nature of these difficulties.

However, the term also has a legal definition as it appears in the Developmental Disabilities Assistance and Bill of Rights Act of 1990, Public Law 101-496, Section 102. In this law, the term "developmental disabilities" means severe, chronic disabilities of a person five years of age or older, which

- are caused by a mental or physical impairment
- occur before age 22
- are likely to continue indefinitely
- result in substantial functional limitations in at least three areas of self-care, language, learning, mobility, self-direction, ability to live independently, and economic self-sufficiency
- reflect the person's need for special long-term services

developmental expressive language disorder A condition in which a child with language impairments has problems using speech. This disorder can take many forms. For example, a four-year-old who speaks only in two-word phrases and a six-year-old who can't answer simple questions both have an expressive language disorder.

developmental lag A delay in some aspect of physical or mental development. For example, a student with a developmental lag in reading might be in the sixth grade but read like a third grader. If the student has the skills of a good third grade reader, the situation would be referred to as developmental lag, since there are no core issues like the ones a dyslexic student would have.

developmentally appropriate practice (DAP)
A set of guidelines ensuring that educational programs are appropriate for each child's age and developmental stage. The guidelines were recommended by the National Association for the Education of Young Children (NAEYC) in the early 1990s, requiring that early education programs be child centered and child directed with little effort to explicitly teach specific skills.

Developmentally appropriate practice has been debated by special educators who feel that early intervention and direct skill instruction are essential for children with learning disabilities to help them address their learning needs.

developmental reading disorder See
DYSLEXIA.

developmental receptive language disorder
A condition in which a child has trouble understanding certain aspects of speech. For example, a toddler who doesn't respond to his name or a first grader who consistently can't follow simple directions has a developmental receptive language disorder. Their hearing is fine, but they can't make sense of certain sounds, words, or sentences they hear. They may seem as if they aren't paying attention, but in fact they simply can't understand certain types of speech. Because using and understanding speech are strongly related, many people with receptive language disorders also have EXPRESSIVE LANGUAGE DISORDERS.

developmental speech and language disorders
People with developmental speech and language disorders have trouble producing speech sounds, using spoken language to communicate, or understanding what other people say. Speech and language problems are often the earliest indicators of a LEARNING DISABILITY. These speech and language disorders include DEVELOPMENTAL ARTICULATION DISORDER, DEVELOPMENTAL EXPRESSIVE LANGUAGE DISORDER, and DEVELOPMENTAL RECEPTIVE LANGUAGE DISORDER.

With a developmental articulation disorder, children may have trouble controlling their rate of speech, or they may lag behind their friends in learning to make speech sounds. These disorders are common, appearing in at least 10 percent of children younger than age eight. Fortunately, articulation disorders can often be outgrown or successfully treated with speech therapy.

Some children with developmental expressive language disorder have problems expressing themselves in speech—calling objects by the wrong names, speaking only in two-word phrases, or being unable to answer simple questions.

Some people have trouble understanding certain aspects of speech; this is developmental receptive language disorder. This explains the toddler who doesn't respond to his name or the worker who consistently can't follow simple directions. While hearing is normal, these individuals can't make sense of certain sounds, words, or sentences. Because using and understanding speech are strongly related, many people with receptive language disorders also have an expressive language disability.

Of course, some misuse of sounds, words, or grammar is a normal part of learning to speak. It's only when these problems persist that there is any cause for concern.

developmental spelling disorder
A significant difficulty in learning to spell. This occurs in the absence of reading or other written language difficulties.

developmental writing disorder
A condition in which a child with a writing disability, especially an EXPRESSIVE LANGUAGE DISORDER, may be unable to write complete, grammatical sentences. This problem involves several brain areas and functions that control vocabulary, grammar, hand movement, and memory.

Dexedrine (dextroamphetamine) A STIMU-LANT MEDICATION used to treat ADHD in children and adults as a part of a treatment program that includes behavioral and psychosocial interventions.

It takes about three to four weeks to feel the full effects, and the drug works better for some people than others, depending on dosage and individual differences. The short-acting form of this medication reaches maximum effect in about two hours; the extended release form reaches peak effectiveness in about 10 hours.

Side Effects

Typical side effects may include nervousness, insomnia, and loss of appetite. Prolonged or excessive use can lead to dependence. Physicians may recommend periods of time when the medication is stopped temporarily so behavior can be evaluated.

Drug Interactions

Dexedrine and the class of antidepressants called MAO inhibitors can cause serious or fatal interactions when taken together; at least 14 days must pass after stopping one of these drugs before taking the other. Acidifying agents such as guanethidine, reserpine, and fruit juices can lower the absorption of Dexedrine, and drugs such as Diamox (acetazolamide) increase absorption of amphetamines. The effects of tricyclic antidepressants and norepinephrine may become more concentrated when taken with Dexedrine. Thorazine (chlorpromazine), lithium, and Haldol (haloperidol) can blunt the effects of Dexedrine (dextroamphetamine).

dextroamphetamine See DEXEDRINE.

diagnosis The outcome of a clinical assessment. A diagnosis generally involves providing a specific label to a set of symptoms or phenomena exhibited by an individual, based on some standard diagnostic criteria, such as in the DIAGNOSTIC AND STATISTICAL MANUAL IV (DSM-IV).

Typically, a clinical diagnosis is reached after examining a range of factors, including performance on STANDARDIZED TESTS, reports of performance in classroom or home settings, and case history information derived from clinical interviews. Diagnostic criteria may vary and may change over time as new information develops through scientific research regarding specific disorders.

A diagnosis of learning disabilities can be reached in a variety of ways, due to the range of disabilities and deficits that can arise. Learning disabilities can be suspected very early on in a child's development if there are significant deficits or a DEVELOPMENTAL LAG. In the primary years, a two-year delay in skills acquisition is considered significant. For some older children, learning disabilities may be suspected only after a considerable length of time in which the child has experienced progressive difficulty in school. In other words, the deficits may be subtle and not indicative of the gap between the child's performance and his or her potential for achievement.

Formal diagnosis of learning disabilities is made by a qualified educational psychologist using standardized tests that compare ability to what is considered normal for an individual of that age and intelligence.

Diagnostic and Statistical Manual IVTR (DSM-IV-TR)

The primary manual of psychiatric classification, published by the American Psychiatric Association, that is used by a majority of practicing clinicians in the United States. Organized by categories of disorders (such as anxiety disorders or LEARNING DISORDERS), the text also provides diagnostic criteria and associated disorders for each listing.

The first edition was published in 1952; the fourth edition was published in 1994, significantly updating and adding listings from previous editions. It was followed by the most recent revision known as DSM-IV-TR.

In order for a diagnosis to be made, the individual's behavior must match the criteria listed for a specific disorder in DSM-IV. One criticism of the DSM is that there are no separate categories or criteria for the diagnosis of children. While the behavior may be slightly different, which is typically noted, children are essentially diagnosed using the same criteria as is used with adults. In addition, because a diagnosis from the DSM is typically required for health insurance coverage, some critics suggest that individuals, particularly children, may be prematurely diagnosed with serious disorders.

The DSM-IV can be used for two purposes: as a source of diagnostic information to enhance clinical practice, research, and education; and to communicate diagnostic information to others.

Each revision of the DSM is the end result of a systematic, comprehensive review of the psychiatric literature, and contains the most up-to-date information available to assist the clinician in making a differential diagnosis.

The APA continues to update the DSM about every decade. The most recent update is the DSM-IV-TR (text revision); in this update, the most important material remains exactly the same. The only things that have changed substantially are the text accompanying the diagnoses and some parts of the introduction and appendices.

diagnostic teaching An instructional method of teaching that adapts lesson plans based on a student's specific needs and learning styles. While specific goals and objectives are first developed, diagnostic teaching focuses on determining the breakdown point of skills and providing appropriate instruction to individual students. In general the focus is on a teacher's own understanding of a student's strengths and difficulties within the classroom context.

A diagnostic approach to instruction is important for students with learning disabilities, who may acquire information and skills at a different rate from their peers, and who also may display unexpected patterns of strength and weakness that require careful adaptation of basic instruc-

tional plans. The errors displayed by individuals with learning disabilities on specific academic tasks may be caused by a wide range of underlying issues; for instruction to be effective, it must take into account the nature of these factors through a process of error analysis and comparison of performance on different types of academic tasks.

diagnostic test Tests that provide information that will help reveal a student's particular learning style or disability. This type of evaluation is different from other forms of assessment because the goal is diagnosis, rather than solely the measurement of ability or of acquired knowledge.

See DIAGNOSTIC TEACHING; EVALUATION.

diet and ADHD One of the more controversial treatments for ATTENTION DEFICIT/HYPERACTIVITY DISORDER is an additive-free diet (the most popular of which is the Feingold Diet). Proponents of this diet, which promotes the elimination of most additives from food, assert that the plan will improve most (if not all) children's learning and attention problems.

In the past 15 years, many studies published in peer-reviewed journals have consistently failed to find support for the Feingold Diet. While a few studies have reported some limited success with this approach, at best this suggests that there may be a very small group of children who are responsive to additive-free diets.

At this time, it has not been shown that dietary intervention offers significant help to children with learning and attention problems.

differential diagnosis An assessment that can differentiate between two different disorders or conditions. A differential diagnosis is required in any case where specific symptoms might be caused by more than one underlying condition, such as ATTENTION DEFICIT/HYPERACTIVITY DISORDER or a LEARNING DISABILITY. A differential diagnosis is especially important in the case of symptoms that may be linked to ADHD because these symptoms may also be associated with other psychological problems.

direct instruction The explicit teaching of specific tasks, including the teaching of rules and strategies, teacher modeling, and explicit practice of the steps involved in learning the skill. Clear and consistent feedback and error analysis is important.

Proponents of direct instruction believe that the approach requires teacher training, a highly structured learning environment, and explicit preparation for each lesson. Teachers must monitor student progress and plan lessons so that errors are corrected quickly.

For students with learning disabilities, direct instruction is one important approach that focuses on a drill and reward system that can help the student learn basic skills. Because children with learning disabilities can have a range of educational problems, no one approach is likely to meet the needs of all students, but strategies that emphasize planning, organizing, and reviewing work are helpful.

directionality Sense of direction. The development of a sense of direction is an essential component of early childhood development. Directionality involves being able to distinguish left from right, as well as the ability to use visual cues to determine location and to find one's way to a familiar place. Difficulties in developing directionality are sometimes associated with learning disorders.

discrepancy In the context of learning disabilities and special education, discrepancy refers to the traditional approach of identifying a specific LEARNING DISABILITY by looking at a gap between performance on aptitude and achievement measures. In most states, a statistically significant discrepancy between ability and performance indicates a learning disability.

The discrepancy model has been questioned in recent years by research that focuses primarily on disability, such as phonological processing problems as the underlying factor in reading disabilities. Some experts argue that the discrepancy approach is not as effective a way of identifying learning disabilities as testing for underlying cognitive deficits. However, discrepancy formulas for determining learning disabilities are still deeply entrenched in law and in the procedures and regulations of state school systems, and are likely to continue to be a primary method for identifying schoolchildren who should receive special education services.

disinhibition Lack of restraint in responding to a situation. A child exhibiting disinhibition reacts impulsively and often inappropriately. An individual who has problems with disinhibition may daydream during lectures, or respond impulsively rather than thoughtfully to a social cue. Problems with disinhibition may also have an affect on a person's ability to use effective strategies to perform a task. In general, behaviors and ideation related to disinhibition may be traceable to general difficulties in impulse control that are a large element in ADHD.

distractibility The shifting of attention from the task at hand to sounds or sights that normally occur in the environment. Distractibility is closely linked to DISINHIBITION because it relates to a person's difficulty in controlling impulses to unimportant distractions. A distractible person may not be able to filter out or ignore external distractions, such as random sounds. Distractibility primarily refers to a problem with controlling the focus of attention, which may shift to unimportant information such as a picture on a wall or a noise from outside a room.

Certain BEHAVIORAL RATING SCALES can measure distractibility, which can be an important way of determining whether an attention disorder is present.

dominant hemisphere   Also known as cerebral dominance, this term refers to the side (or hemisphere) of the brain that usually controls a particular function.

Since language and logic are particularly important, the hemisphere that organizes and controls language is referred to as the dominant hemisphere. For most (99 percent) right-handed people, the left hemisphere is dominant. About 60 percent of left-handed people also process language and logic in the left hemisphere.

dopamine   A chemical in the brain that has been linked to ATTENTION DEFICIT/HYPERACTIVITY DISORDER. It appears that certain receptors in the brain that normally respond to the neurotransmitter called dopamine are not working properly. Most likely, dopamine is not being produced at normal levels in the brain.

Recent studies with adults who have ADHD point to a defect in an enzyme called dopa decarboxylase, which helps produce dopamine. This defect in dopamine production occurs in the anterior frontal cortex, an area associated with cognitive processes such as focusing and attention.

Current treatments use stimulants to enhance dopamine production throughout the brain, but these drugs can also cause such adverse effects as irritability, insomnia, and depression.

Down syndrome   A congenital form of mental retardation caused by an extra chromosome, characterized by distinct physical features as well as developmental disabilities. Down syndrome affects people of all ages, races, and economic levels, occurring once in about every 800 to 1,000 live births. More than 350,000 people in the United States alone have Down syndrome. The condition was first described in 1959 by French physician Jerome Lejeune, who discovered that instead of the usual 46 chromosomes present in each cell, there were 47 in the cells of individuals with Down syndrome. Because 95 percent of all cases of Down syndrome are caused by three copies of the 21st chromosome, it is referred to as "trisomy 21."

While Down syndrome is usually caused by an error in cell division, two other types of chromosomal abnormalities (mosaicism and translocation) are also implicated in Down syndrome. Regardless of the type of Down syndrome which a person may have, all people with Down syndrome have an extra portion of the number 21 chromosome present in some of their cells. This additional genetic material alters the course of development and causes the characteristics associated with the syndrome.

Women age 35 and older have a significantly increased risk of having a child with Down syndrome: a 35-year-old woman has a one in 400 chance of conceiving a child with Down syndrome and this chance increases gradually to one in 110 by age 40. At age 45 the incidence is about one in 35. Since many couples are postponing parenting until later in life, the incidence of Down syndrome conceptions is expected to increase. Therefore, genetic counseling for parents is important.

Maternal Diagnosis

Pregnant women have access to both screening and diagnostic tests to find out if their unborn child has Down syndrome. Screening tests estimate the risk of the fetus having Down syndrome, whereas diagnostic tests tell whether or not the fetus actually has the condition.

Screening tests are typically offered between 15 and 20 weeks of gestation, and they can accurately detect only about 60 percent of cases. Many women who undergo these tests will be given false-positive readings, and some women will be given false-negative readings. Prenatal diagnosis of Down syndrome is by chorionic villus sampling (CVS), amniocentesis, and percutaneous umbilical blood sampling (PUBS).

Each of these procedures carries a small risk of miscarriage as tissue is extracted from the placenta or the umbilical cord to examine the fetus's chromosomes, but the procedures are about 98 to 99 percent accurate in the detection of Down syndrome. Amniocentesis is usually performed between 12 and 20 weeks of gestation, CVS between eight and 12 weeks, and PUBS after 20 weeks.

Diagnosis of Child

The diagnosis of Down syndrome is usually suspected after birth as a result of the baby's appearance. Among the most common traits are low muscle tone, a flat facial profile, an upward slant to the eyes, an abnormal ear shape, a single deep crease across the center of the palm, and an excessive ability to extend the joints. Other common symptoms include a fifth finger with one furrow instead of two, small skin folds on the inner corner of the eyes, too much space between large and second toe, and an enlarged tongue compared to the size of the mouth.

Most people with Down syndrome have some level of mental retardation ranging from mild to moderate, but most children with Down syndrome learn to sit, walk, talk, play, toilet train, and do most other activities. Because speech is often delayed, careful attention should be paid to the child's hearing, as retention of fluid in the inner ear is a very common cause of hearing and speech difficulties.

Treatment

Early intervention services should begin shortly after birth to help children with Down syndrome develop to their full potential. These programs offer parents special instruction in teaching their child language, cognitive, self-help, and social skills, and specific exercises for gross and fine motor development. Research has shown that stimulation during early developmental stages improves the child's chances of developing to his or her fullest potential. Continuing education, positive public attitudes, and a stimulating home environment have also been found to promote the child's overall development. Quality educational programs and good medical care enable people with Down syndrome to become contributing members of their families and communities.

Because people with Down syndrome respond well to their environment, those who receive good medical care and are included in community activities can attend school, make friends, find work, participate in decisions that affect them, and make a positive contribution to society.

Over the past few decades, beginning with Section 504 of the REHABILITATION ACT OF 1973, continuing with the EDUCATION FOR ALL HANDICAPPED CHILDREN ACT OF 1975, and culminating with the passage of the AMERICANS WITH DISABILITIES ACT in 1991, people with Down syndrome have been granted equal protections under federal law.

Just as in the normal population, there is a wide variation in mental abilities, behavior, and developmental progress in individuals with Down syndrome. Their level of retardation may range from mild to severe, with the majority functioning in the mild to moderate range. Due to these individual differences, it is impossible to predict future achievements of children with Down syndrome.

Because of the range of ability in children with Down syndrome it is important for families and all members of the school's education team to place few limitations on potential capabilities. It may be effective to emphasize concrete concepts rather than abstract ideas. Teaching tasks in a step-by-step manner with frequent reinforcement and consistent feedback has been proven successful. Improved public acceptance of persons with disabilities, along with increased opportunities for adults with disabilities to live and work independently in the community, have expanded goals for individuals with Down syndrome. Independent Living Centers, group shared and supervised apartments, and support services in the community have proven to be important resources for persons with disabilities.

due process hearing   A remedy provided in the INDIVIDUALS WITH DISABILITIES ACT (IDEA) in which parents can protest decisions that have been made about special education services for their child.

The first type of due process hearing occurs at the local level, where all parties present their arguments and a specially trained hearing officer makes a decision about the disagreement. For example, if parents believe their child needs an interpreter who will sign instruction, but the school district representatives don't agree to provide one, the hearing officer could rule in two ways. He or she could agree with the school district and rule that the student isn't entitled to an interpreter, or side with the parents and require the school district to provide one.

After the local hearing officer has rendered a decision, the losing party may appeal the decision in a state-level due process hearing. At this hearing, a state hearing officer follows the same procedures as in the local hearing and renders a decision regarding the dispute. After the state-level hearing officer has rendered a decision, the losing party has the option to seek a legal remedy through the courts.

dysarthria A speech problem caused by damage to or disease of the muscles controlling the voice apparatus. Unlike APHASIA, patients with this condition have no problems with the speech center of the brain. They can select and write out words and sentences; they simply can't form vocal expressions.

The condition is a common characteristic of a wide range of degenerative diseases such as multiple sclerosis, Parkinson's disease, and Huntington's disease. It may be caused by a stroke, brain tumor, or damage to a particular nerve controlling the structures of speech.

There is no specific treatment, although medication or surgery may restore the ability to speak by treating the underlying disease. Speech therapy also may be of help.

dyscalculia A significant learning disability involving mathematics that affects between 2 percent and 6 percent of elementary school-age children in the United States. Dyscalculia is a medical term associated with brain dysfunction that is presumably present at birth. Many students identified as having a specific LEARNING DISABILITY or attention disorder may have associated problems with learning or applying mathematical concepts, functions, and procedures.

It may relate to a variety of more basic disorders such as confusion or deficits in perception, spatial skills, sequencing, and so on. It is sometimes referred to as ACALCULIA, which is technically a total inability to do arithmetic.

Because problems with arithmetic and mathematics may arise from widely varying causes, it is important to understand the underlying sources of the learning difficulty in this area before deciding what educational remedies to choose.

Symptoms

There are a variety of symptoms with this condition, including normal or advanced language and other skills and often good visual memory for the printed word. This is accompanied by poor mental math ability, often with problems in using money (such as balancing a checkbook, making change, and tipping). This may develop into an actual fear of money and its transactions.

In addition, a person with dyscalculia has problems with math processes such as addition, subtraction, or multiplication, as well as with math concepts (such as sequencing numbers). The student may have trouble retaining and retrieving concepts, or have problems grasping math rules.

This is combined with a poor sense of direction, as well as trouble reading maps, telling time, and grappling with mechanical processes. There is difficulty with abstract concepts of time and direction, schedules, keeping track of time, and the sequence of past and future events.

Common mistakes in working with numbers include number substitutions, reversals, and omissions. Students also may have trouble learning musical concepts, following directions in sports that demand sequencing or rules, and keeping track of scores and players during games such as cards and board games.

Treatment

Individuals with dyscalculia need help in organizing and processing information related to numbers and mathematical concepts. Since math is essentially a form of language using numbers instead of words as symbols, it is important to communicate frequently and clearly with a child as to what is needed to do a mathematical problem. While the condition is lifelong, performance can be improved with intensive intervention. The child should have real-life exposure to how to use math as a part of everyday life, counting ingredients in a cake, how to make change, and so on.

Parents and teachers should work together to determine helpful strategies, such as using graph paper to help with alignment on a page or a calculator to check work. Textbooks, workbooks, or computer programs may give students more opportunities to practice skills. A tutor or a learning center may provide additional enrichment opportunities.

dysfluency Difficulties in processing oral or written language fluently, in a continuous and consistent sequence. Dysfluency may occur in reading, speaking, or writing. It may arise from a range of potential sources, and is primarily a descriptive term for specific behaviors that arise from other learning problems, rather than a specific category of learning difficulty in itself.

dysgraphia A medical term for a brain condition that causes poor handwriting or problems performing the physical aspects of writing (such as an awkward pencil grip or bad handwriting), spelling, or putting thoughts on paper. The disorder causes a person's writing to be distorted or incorrect.

In children, the disorder generally appears when they are first introduced to writing, as they make inappropriately sized and spaced letters, or write wrong or misspelled words. The term may also be used to categorize more general writing problems, although in many cases these issues may be more clearly attributable to a more pervasive learning problem such as ADHD or specific reading disability. Children with the disorder may have other learning disabilities, but they usually have no social or other academic problems.

Cases of dysgraphia in adults generally occur after an injury or trauma. In addition to poor handwriting, dysgraphia is characterized by wrong or odd spelling, and production of words that are not correct (such as using "boy" for "child"). The cause of the disorder is unknown.

Symptoms

A problem with dysgraphia may be suspected if the person has difficulty putting together a written document (such as using an outline), bad or illegible handwriting, awkward or cramped pencil grip, or avoids tasks that involve writing. The person may have problems in fleshing out ideas on paper or writing the minimum (or less) that the assignment requires in contrast to the person's ability to discuss such ideas verbally. There may be an inconsistency in the way letters and words look, or problems with writing within the margins or line spacing and inconsistent spacing between words.

Treatment

Treatment may include therapy for motor disorders to help control writing movements. Other treatments may address memory or other neurological problems. Many people with dysgraphia benefit from explicit instruction in the skills required to produce a written work. Checklists that outline all the steps involved in a writing process may help. For example, a student could be taught several different ways to create an outline and use a checklist to make sure all the steps in creating an outline have been used.

Some teachers may allow students with a disorder in written expression to use other methods, such as an oral report, to assess their understanding of a subject instead of asking them to write a paper or take a written test.

Computers can help many students with dysgraphia. Spell check, grammar check, and other programs may help individuals with dysgraphia. A tape recorder or creating a drawing to capture ideas before putting them on paper may help as well.

Although some individuals with dysgraphia can improve their writing ability, others struggle with the problem throughout their lives.

dyslexia A specific learning difficulty, usually with spelling and writing, and sometimes with reading and numbers. It is characterized by problems in coping with written symbols, despite normal intelligence. Dyslexic children and adults may have problems putting things in order, following instructions, and may confuse left and right. The word *dyslexia* comes from the Greek meaning "difficulty with words."

Experts estimate that dyslexia is estimated to occur in about 8 percent of the population. It is a permanent disability that is often accompanied by strengths in areas such as creativity or physical coordination. Each dyslexic person's difficulties are different and vary from slight to very severe disruption of the learning process.

Its cause has not been fully established, but the effect creates neurological anomalies in the brain. These anomalies trigger varying degrees of difficulty in learning when using words and sometimes symbols. Children or students who are dyslexic have trouble sorting out the sounds within words, which is why they have problems with reading, writing, and spelling. Most children with dyslexia have difficulty with text, memory, and basic mathematics.

Children are either born with dyslexia or acquire the difficulty during early childhood, but it is when they begin to learn using words and sometimes other symbols that it becomes a noticeable problem.

Symptoms

Dyslexia may include a variety of reading problems, such as

- lack of understanding what is read
- lack of awareness of sounds that make up words, often including a difficulty with blending sounds to make words
- problems with spelling
- problems with the order of letters in words
- trouble rhyming words
- difficulty with pronouncing words
- delay in speaking
- delay in learning the alphabet, numbers, days of the week, months, colors, shapes, and other basic information
- difficulty understanding subtleties of language such as jokes or slang

Cause

Modern experts believe dyslexia may be caused by differences in brain structure and function present since birth, with a strong genetic component. A number of studies have indicated a strong heritability for dyslexia, predominantly among boys within a family. In general, the ratio of males to females identified with dyslexia is about four to one. Because of this, the role of the hormone testosterone before birth is being investigated as a possible cause of inherited dyslexia.

The reading difficulties associated with dyslexia aren't related to intelligence or motivation; students often possess unusual talents, especially in areas that require visual, spatial, and motor skills. This disorder is not due to a physical disability, such as a visual problem. Instead, it is a problem in how the brain processes the information as the individual is reading.

Traditional definitions of dyslexia have relied on an unexpected gap between learning aptitude and achievement in school, particularly in the area of reading. However, contemporary research has indicated that difficulties or delays in developing awareness of sounds and processing abilities play a primary factor in the development of the reading problems associated with dyslexia. Word-finding difficulties are a second factor in the case of some individuals with severe reading difficulties.

Some research links it to low levels of the brain chemical dopamine.

Treatment

Although dyslexia is a lifelong condition, with appropriate instruction individuals with dyslexia may largely overcome their reading difficulties. Individuals with a reading disability most often benefit from a language program that provides direct instruction in understanding the letter-sound system. The earlier this instruction is given, the greater the chance the person will become a fluent reader.

Typically, the more senses that can be used when learning something, the better the person will learn. For individuals with reading disabilities, it is important to learn as much as possible by seeing, hearing, writing, and speaking. For example, a teacher of students with this disability can provide a written outline of the day's lecture in addition to giving the lecture itself. Books on tape can help someone access literature with all of its benefits, including vocabulary and ideas.

Parents of children with reading disabilities can encourage their children to read by providing reading materials on subjects in which they have an interest. Several decades of teacher-based and clinical research support the need for a multisensory, sequential, phonetic-based approach to reading instruction as the essential foundation for the development of reading skills. For example, a student learning the consonant blend "bl" might listen to the sound while looking at the letters, then say it aloud while tracing the two letters on a rough-board. This method of instruction increases the chance that the information will be stored and retained in long-term memory.

There is no total cure, but the effects can be eased by skilled, specialist teaching of phonics, sequencing, and techniques to raise the person's self-esteem. Given proper support, dyslexic students are able to go on to college and pursue successful careers.

See also LEARNING DISABILITY; APPENDIX A.

dysnomia A specific form of APHASIA that involves problems in finding words as a result of the inability to recall and express the names of objects or concepts. Individuals with this condition may substitute a general term like "thing" for a word that they cannot recall, substitute another word in place of the target word, or use circumlocution—talking around the word that they are trying to remember and express. The condition is not as severe as ANOMIA (the complete loss of the ability to recall words, as the names of objects, persons, activities).

Dysnomia rarely occurs by itself, but is associated with other difficulties, including expressive-language disorders and, in some cases, attention disorders. It often occurs with a language or learning disability.

dysphasia A term for a disorder of communication that may result from damage to the brain due to stroke, head injury, or disease. Dysphasia may potentially affect understanding, speaking, reading, or writing.

dysphonetic A subtype of DYSLEXIA characterized by specific reading-spelling error patterns. Dysphonetic readers typically have a functional albeit limited sight word vocabulary, but they lack phonic word analysis skills. Their most striking error is the substitution of a word similar in meaning to the original word but unlike it phonetically (such as "sheet" for "quilt").

Their misspellings are phonetically inaccurate and include such errors as extra letters, omitted syllables, reversed syllables, letter-order errors, and other sequencing mistakes.

dyspraxia A general term used to describe a range of different conditions involving difficulty with learned patterns of movement without any muscle or nerve damage. In some cases, dyspraxia is used to describe coordination problems and gross-motor and fine-motor body movements. It causes an underdevelopment of the brain in which messages aren't properly transmitted to the body, producing a number of problems in physical and thinking areas. It affects at least 2 percent of the population in varying degrees; 70 percent of those affected are male. Dyspraxia can be subtle or more pronounced, and often a person's disability is not readily apparent.

The term is also commonly used in the field of speech-language therapy to describe the condition of developmental verbal dyspraxia, in which a child has significant problems in producing speech sounds and sequencing sounds into words. This condition may also be accompanied by a difficulty in making and coordinating the physical movements required to produce speech (oral dyspraxia). There are many other types of dyspraxia, including

- ideomotor: inability to perform single motor tasks, such as combing hair or waving goodbye
- ideational: difficulty with multilevel tasks, such as taking the proper sequence of steps for brushing teeth
- dressing: problems with dressing and putting clothes on in order
- constructional: difficulty with spatial relations
- verbal: problems and delay with expressive language

Symptoms

Dyspraxia causes a range of symptoms such as coordination problems (awkwardness, clumsiness, trouble with hopping, skipping, throwing and catching a ball, or riding a bike). There may be confusion about which hand to use for tasks, problems with holding a pen or pencil properly, and sensitivity to touch (the child may find some clothes uncomfortable; there may be an intolerance to having hair or teeth brushed, or nails and hair cut). In addition, there may be problems with short-term memory, trouble with reading and writing, poor sense of direction, speech problems, phobias, or obsessive behavior.

While older children may be verbally adept, they may not develop the social skills to get along with their peers. While children with dyspraxia can be of average or above average intelligence, they often have immature behavior. Logic and reasoning may be challenging.

Treatment

There is no cure for dyspraxia, but the earlier a child is treated, the greater the chance of improvement. Occupational therapists, physiotherapists, and accommodations at school can all help a child to cope with the condition. A child with dyspraxia wants to communicate, but often can't, so pressuring such a child will lead only to further inhibition. Repetitive verbal activities can help develop language skills, including songs, poems, nursery rhymes, and so on. A child who has trouble communicating can use sign language or a communication board to supplement speech temporarily. To improve motor function, the child should practice tasks to learn the correct sequence of movements that must be followed. Physical activities should be encouraged to strengthen a child's overall performance and coordination, beginning with simple physical tasks and leading up to more complicated tasks involving multiple steps.

dyssemia Difficulty in using and understanding nonverbal signs and signals; a nonverbal communication deficit.

dystaxia Difficulty controlling voluntary movements.

See also ATAXIA.

early childhood assessment Testing that identifies early developmental and learning problems in preschool and primary grade children. Early childhood assessment practices allow for accurate and fair identification of the developmental needs of infants, preschoolers, and young children.

Sound early childhood assessment should involve a multidisciplinary team, including school psychologists with specialized training in the assessment of the young child, and who view behavior and development from a longitudinal perspective.

Early assessment of potential problems is essential because of a child's broad and rapid development. Intervention services for any psychological and developmental problems are essential and cost-effective.

Standardized assessment procedures should be used with great caution in educational decision-making because such tools are inherently less accurate when used with young children. Multidisciplinary team assessments must include multiple sources of information, multiple approaches to assessment, and multiple settings in order to yield a comprehensive understanding of children's skills and needs. Therefore, assessments should center on the child in the family system and home environment, both substantial influences on the development of young children.

early intervention program A program designed to identify and provide intervention for infants and young children who are developmentally delayed and at high risk for school fail-ure. The purpose of this type of program is to help prevent problems as the child matures.

These programs address the needs of young children from birth to the beginning of school with a collaborative effort from parents and medical, social services, and educational professionals. The pre-academic skills that may need help include self-concept, fine and gross motor skills, awareness of sounds, visual discrimination, communication and language development, thinking skills, and social skills. Nationally recognized early intervention programs include Project Head Start and Reading Recovery.

See also INDIVIDUALIZED FAMILY SERVICE PROGRAM.

educable mentally handicapped (EMH) See MILD MENTAL RETARDATION.

educational consultant A term used to describe a range of individuals with varying backgrounds and areas of expertise. For example, some educational consultants may specialize in college placement, while others may provide testing and specialize in primary or secondary school placement or consultation. An educational consultant may or may not have a background in LEARNING DISABILITY. Consultants who specialize in special education should have a background in assessment.

An educational consultant may provide counseling to help student and family choose a school, college, or other program that will foster academic and social growth. Educational consultants can provide a student and family with individual attention, firsthand knowledge of hundreds of educational opportunities, and the time to explore all of the options. Consultants may specialize in college admission, boarding school, summer programs, troubled teens, international students, or learning disabilities.

See also INDEPENDENT EDUCATIONAL CONSULTANT ASSOCIATION.

educational evaluation An educational evaluation is typically part of the process of defining an INDIVIDUALIZED EDUCATION PROGRAM (IEP). Educational evaluation may involve administration of standardized academic tests, assessment of performance in different academic classes, and observation of classroom performance. To be effective, evaluation should encompass a number of different types of measures, and involve the entire range of academic skill areas.

See also INDEPENDENT EDUCATION EVALUATION.

educational therapist A professional who evaluates and treats learning problems in young children, adolescents, and adults. These problems may include DYSLEXIA; attention deficit disorder; reading, writing, language, or math problems; academic SELF-ESTEEM and motivation; social skills; and organizational and study skills.

An educational therapist is skilled in

- formal and informal education assessment
- synthesis of information from other specialists and parents
- development and implementation of appropriate remedial programs for school-related learning and behavioral problems
- strategies for addressing social and emotional aspects of learning problems
- forming supportive relationships with the client and those involved in the client's educational development
- improving communication between the client, family, school, and other professionals

In a remediation session, the educational therapist works with a client on activities chosen especially for that person based on results from formal and informal testing. The educational therapist, who keeps extensive notes on each session, provides activities with an appropriate level of challenge and watches the client's response to those activities to assess their approach to the task and how they process information. This is a key element of progress during treatment.

Educational therapists plan and carry out treatment using educational situations, equipment, and methods to rehabilitate patients. Some educational therapists participate in the rehabilitation of blind patients. Educational therapists try to diminish emotional stress of clients, provide a sense of achievement, and channel energies into acceptable forms of behavior.

Education Department General Administrative Regulations (EDGAR) Regulations for managing projects funded by grants awarded by the Department of Education. As is generally the case with the Code of Federal Regulations, specific regulations falling within EDGAR define, specify, and provide the framework for implementing laws about education.

Education for All Handicapped Children Act of 1975 (PL 94–142) This significant legislation, renamed the INDIVIDUALS WITH DISABILITIES EDUCATION ACT in 1990, requires the provision of a free and appropriate public education to children with disabilities.

elaboration The process of discussing or going over new information in order to form connections with familiar information, a process that helps memory and affects depth of processing. There is a great deal of evidence in support of the idea that the more details are processed and repeated, the more likely they are to be retrieved from long-term memory.

electroencephalogram (EEG) A graphic record of the electrical activity at the surface of the brain obtained by attaching small electrodes to the scalp. This allows the regular electrical potential of the brain to be amplified and recorded on an oscillograph in wave patterns. It can be recorded in graphic form by an electroencephalograph.

Characteristic changes in type and frequency of the waves can provide different information about the brain and how it is functioning. These wave patterns can be used to diagnose specific disorders, diseases, and injuries.

eligibility The criteria for whether or not a student is eligible for special education services is determined by the INDIVIDUALIZED EDUCATION PROGRAM team. The team should consider qualitative and quantitative information from the assessment process.

Many states continue to determine eligibility by a DISCREPANCY formula, which is a mathematical equation that shows a significant discrepancy between a student's achievement (ACHIEVEMENT TEST scores) and potential (IQ score).

However, recent studies discourage the practice of determining eligibility solely on discrepancy of test scores, and encourage the consideration of other significant factors such as the observations and experiences of teachers and parents.

See also INTELLIGENCE QUOTIENT.

eligibility committee See MULTIDISCIPLINARY TEAM.

emotional and behavioral disorder A condition in which behavioral or emotional responses of a student interfere with performance in self-care, social relationships, personal adjustment, academic progress, classroom behavior, or work adjustment. Therefore, early identification and intervention for students with emotional and/or behavioral problems is essential.

EBD is more than a transient, expected response to stress in the child's environment; the problem persists even with individualized interventions, such as feedback, consultation with parents, and modification of the educational environment.

Assessment

EBD must be exhibited in at least two different settings, at least one of which is school related. It can coexist with other handicapping conditions, such as schizophrenia, affective disorders, anxiety disorders, or other disturbances.

It is important that the assessment identify both the strengths and needs of the individual and those with whom the student interacts. The assessment should ensure that the child's difficulties are not primarily due to transient developmental or environmental variables, cultural or linguistic differences, or influences of other handicapping conditions. Referral for special services should not be used as a disciplinary action or an effort to resolve conflicts.

The results of the assessment should provide information about

- environmental factors: the relationship between the instructional, social, and community environment and the student's specific problems
- strengths: identify the resources of the student, family, teacher(s), and school setting
- history: duration of the difficulties, their relationship to specific developmental or situational stressors and previous attempts to resolve the difficulties
- intensity: how severe the problems are in affecting school achievement, social skills, or interpersonal relationships within the school setting
- pervasiveness: the number of settings in which difficulties occur in the school, family, or community
- persistence: the extent to which difficulties have continued despite the use of well-

planned, empirically based and individualized intervention strategies provided within lesser restrictive environments

- developmental/cultural data: the extent to which the student's behavior is different from the behavior expected for children of the same age, culture, and ethnic background. Information should be obtained from a variety of sources that can provide data about the child's difficulties across various settings

The assessment should gather information about a child's behavioral and emotional functioning, developmental history, areas of significant impairment in school adaptive behavior and achievement, impairment outside the school setting in areas such as vocational skills, and social skills or interpersonal relationships. Because biological and neurological factors may contribute to, cause, or trigger problem behaviors, consultation with medical care providers and consideration of relevant student and family medical history is important.

Formal methods for gathering information may include behavior checklists, standardized self-reports, structured interviews, rating scales, and other appropriate assessment techniques. Informal methods, such as behavior observation and analysis of work samples, can also be useful.

Treatment

Eligibility for services under the category of emotional/behavioral disorders should not automatically imply placement in a categorical special education program. Since emotional and behavioral disorders have many influences, interventions for children with these disorders must be comprehensive. Interventions should be planned by a team that includes the parent, the child, the school psychologist and other teachers, administrators, and community service providers. Intervention plans should take into account the strengths of the child, the family, the child's teachers, and the school.

Most schools exist primarily as an educational setting rather than a treatment setting, so children with significant emotional or behavioral disorders may need treatment outside school.

Individualized academic and curricular interventions Children with emotional or behavioral problems frequently achieve below-grade expectations in academic areas. Academic problems often seem less important than a student's behavioral difficulties. Students may benefit from adaptations to the curriculum, alteration of the pace of delivery, improvements to the instructional and organizational ecology, and instruction in learning and study skills.

Consultation with teachers Teachers may benefit from a discussion of the needs to the student and the most effective strategies to help the child improve behavior. Teachers will also benefit from the psychosocial support component of consultation in dealing with the frustration and isolation that often are present when working with children with significant problems.

Consultation and partnership with parents Parents will benefit from consultation directed at understanding their child's difficulties, developing and implementing effective behavior management strategies, and working collaboratively with other caregivers. The parent may also need assistance with negotiating the array of services available in the community.

Individual and group counseling Counseling may help the student more readily improve social skills and school adjustment. Students often need help in dealing with the stress in their environment, and understanding responsibility and self-directedness.

Social skills training Students with emotional and behavioral disorders often have problems with social skills, so social skills training in the child's multiple environments is often helpful.

Crisis planning and management Crises should be anticipated and plans for dealing with crises should be a part of the student's intervention plan.

Specialized educational settings By law, children must be provided services in the least restrictive environment that meets the student's academic, psychological, and social needs. Many students' needs can be effectively addressed through consultation with teachers and parents, short-term counseling, and interventions in the regular classroom setting.

Job and transitional planning Career exploration, pre-vocational and vocational skills development, and transition to the after-high school world should be included for all adolescents with emotional and behavioral disorders.

emotional/behavioral tests A psychological test that measures how parents, teachers, and the child rate the child's behavior, attitude, and feelings at home and at school. They include

- Behavior Assessment System for Children
- Connor's Behavior Rating Scales, Revised
- Achenbach
- Reynolds Child Depression Scale
- Piers Harris Self-Concept Scales
- Differential Test of Conduct and Emotional Problems
- Assessment of Interpersonal Relationships
- Depression and Anxiety in Youth Scale
- Multidimension Depression Inventory

emotional disturbance Emotional, behavioral, or mental disorders that can interfere with a child's ability to learn. Emotional disturbance is defined under the INDIVIDUALS WITH DISABILITIES EDUCATION ACT.

Experts aren't sure what causes emotional disturbance, but various factors such as heredity, brain disorder, diet, stress, and family functioning have been suggested as possible causes. More than 463,172 children and youth with a serious emotional disturbance were provided services in the public schools in 1998.

Symptoms
Many children who don't have emotional disturbances may act out occasionally, but when children have serious emotional disturbances

these behaviors continue over long periods of time. Some of the characteristics and behaviors seen in children who have emotional disturbances include

- short attention span, impulsiveness
- acting out, fighting
- withdrawal, excessive fear or anxiety
- immaturity (inappropriate crying, temper tantrums, poor coping skills)
- learning difficulties (academically performing below grade level)

Children with the most serious emotional disturbances may experience distorted thinking, excessive anxiety, bizarre behavior, or abnormal mood swings.

Diagnosis
Emotional disturbance is a condition exhibiting one or more of the following characteristics over a long period of time and to a severe degree:

- an inability to learn that cannot be explained by intellectual, sensory, or health factors
- an inability to build or maintain satisfactory relationships with other children and teachers
- inappropriate types of behavior or feelings under normal circumstances
- a general unhappiness or depression
- a tendency to develop physical symptoms or fears associated with personal or school problems

The federal government is currently reviewing the way in which serious emotional disturbance is defined; the definition may be revised.

Education
Educational programs for students with a serious emotional disturbance need to include attention to mastering academics, developing social skills, and increasing self-awareness, self-esteem, and self-control. Career education (both academic

and vocational programs) is also a major part of secondary education and should be a part of every adolescent's transition plan in the INDIVID-UALIZED EDUCATION PROGRAM (IEP).

Students eligible for special education services under the category of "serious emotional disturbance" may have IEPs that include psychological or counseling services as a related service. These must be provided by a qualified social worker, psychologist, or guidance counselor.

encoding   The process of expressing messages through speaking or writing.

English as a Second Language (ESL) Instruction in which individuals are taught English with minimal emphasis on their native language. (Adult English for Speakers of Other Languages, or adult ESOL, is alternately used in various parts of the United States.) As the number of ESL students in regular classrooms increases, instruction of these students has become more controversial. While some promote a bilingual approach to instruction for individuals for whom English is a second language, others suggest an immersion approach is more efficient.

Adult ESL programs vary in scope and content. Some programs, especially those for recent arrivals, including refugees, emphasize survival or life skills in the curriculum and focus on improving listening and speaking abilities. Others stress work-related topics, citizenship and civics education, family literacy, or academic or GED preparation. Learners who lack literacy skills in their native language and those who are new to the Roman alphabet may be placed in classes that focus on developing basic literacy skills. Classes are provided by local educational agencies, community colleges, local businesses and unions, community-based organizations, volunteer groups, churches, and for-profit language schools.

ESL teachers use a variety of approaches to teach adult learners to speak, read, and write English. Some approaches focus on language functions such as asking for assistance and expressing likes and dislikes, still others focus on the knowledge and skills needed to function in the United States, such as giving and following directions on the job. Some approaches focus on discussing and writing about issues in the learners' lives. Finally, some emphasize teaching the grammar rules of the language. However, a mix of approaches is usually necessary to effectively teach English as a second language.

Some techniques developed for use with second language learners have been useful for teaching individuals with learning disabilities, such as the use of manipulatives.

See also BILINGUAL APPROACH.

Enright Diagnostic Inventory of Basic Arithmetic Skills   This test, designed for elementary and middle school grades, provides a task analysis of the student's computation errors using whole numbers, fractions, and decimals. It also identifies areas in which the student demonstrates mastery.

environmental factors   Factors that impact normal development of children, such as parental substance abuse, extreme poverty, disturbed parent-child interaction, and neglect. For a student to be identified with a LEARNING DISABILITY, it must be first determined that environmental factors are not the primary cause of the learning problems.

environmental toxins   Some environmental toxins may lead to a LEARNING DISABILITY, possibly by disrupting childhood brain development or brain processes.

Cadmium and lead, both prevalent in the environment, are becoming a leading focus of neurological research. Cadmium (used in making some steel products) can leach into the soil and then into food.

Lead was once common in paint and gasoline, and is still present in some water pipes.

A study of animals sponsored by the National Institutes of Health showed a connection between exposure to lead and learning difficulties. In the study, rats exposed to lead experienced changes in their brainwaves, slowing their ability to learn. The learning problems lasted for weeks, long after the rats were no longer exposed to lead.

epilepsy A chronic condition of the nervous system marked primarily by recurrent seizures. Epilepsy may express itself in major (*grand mal*) seizures causing unconsciousness, or in minor (*petit mal*) seizures. It is sometimes associated with other conditions, including specific LEARNING DISABILITIES or attention disorders.

Symptoms

Seizures may include convulsions, brief stares, muscle spasms, odd sensations, or episodes of automatic behavior and altered consciousness.

Diagnosis

A doctor can diagnose epilepsy from a number of different tests. Which tests are ordered may vary, depending on how much each test reveals, but they may include

- a detailed medical history
- a thorough physical examination, especially of the nervous system
- blood tests
- electroencephalogram (EEG)
- brain scans (magnetic resonance imaging [MRI]) and/or computed tomography (CT) scans

Treatment

Epilepsy is a lifelong condition that is usually controllable with medication. More than 20 medications are available to treat epilepsy. If medicines aren't able to prevent seizures, other methods may be tried, including surgery, a special diet, or vagus nerve stimulation (VNS). The goal of all epilepsy treatment is to prevent further seizures, avoid side effects, and make it possible for the patient to lead a normal, active life.

Most epilepsy medicines are taken by mouth in the form of tablets, capsules, sprinkles, or syrup. They may include

- carbamazepine (brand names: Tegretol, Tegretol-XR, Carbatrol)
- clonazepam (Klonopin)
- ethosuximide (Zarontin)
- phenobarbital
- phenytoin (Dilantin)
- primidone (Mysoline)
- valproic acid (Depakene)
- divalproex sodium (Depakote)

Newer drugs, which are also prescribed for epilepsy, include felbamate (Felbatol); gabapentin (Neurontin); lamotrigine (Lamictal); levetiracetam (Keppra); oxcarbazepine (Trileptal); tiagabine (Gabitril); topiramate (Topamax); and zonisamide (Zonegran). Other new drugs are in development. A rectal gel form of diazepam (Diastat) may be prescribed to stop cluster seizures or prolonged seizures. Some doctors may prescribe pills of diazepam (Valium), lorazepam (Ativan), or clonazepam (Klonopin) for the same purpose. A steroid drug (ACTH) may be injected to treat children with a type of epilepsy called infantile spasms, or for severe seizures that can't be controlled with other drugs. It is usually given by a doctor who has had special training in using this medicine for epilepsy.

The particular drug that is prescribed depends on what kind of seizure a person is having, since different drugs control different types of seizures. People also react to these medicines in different ways. Some experience side effects, others may not. Some people's bodies break down medicines at a faster or slower rate than the average person. Some people's seizures will respond well to a particular drug while someone else will have seizures that continue. This is why it may take some time to find exactly the right dose of the right drug for each person who has a seizure disorder.

In addition to medications, brain surgery can be a successful way of treating epilepsy. Surgery is most likely to be considered when someone with epilepsy has already tried the standard medicines without success (or has bad reactions to them), has seizures that always start in just one part of the brain, and has seizures in a part of the brain that can be removed without damaging important things like speech, memory, or eyesight.

Surgery for epilepsy is a delicate, complicated operation that must be performed by an experienced surgical team. In addition to operations that remove a small part of the brain where seizures begin, other procedures may be done to interrupt the spread of electrical energy in the brain.

episodic memory That part of MEMORY that stores the events an individual experiences in life. Episodic memory enables a person to remember personal experiences, to be consciously aware of an earlier experience in a certain situation at a certain time. According to some psychologists, there are at least five major human memory systems for which evidence is now available. They include episodic, semantic, procedural, perceptual representation, and short-term memory.

Episodic memory operates together with SEMANTIC MEMORY, which stores concepts about the world in the broadest sense, and makes it available for retrieval. Remembering the contents of a dinner consumed last evening would require episodic memory. Remembering that a foot has 12 inches or that the Sun is at the center of the solar system involves semantic memory.

Episodic memory is more easily impaired than semantic memory, perhaps because rehearsal or repetition tends to be minimal.

error analysis An approach to assessment that goes beyond test performance to examine the nature of the errors and to discern patterns in types of errors. Error analysis may be used either with formal tests or in informal academic settings, for example, as when a teacher examines a written composition to identify specific patterns of mechanical or grammatical errors.

Analyzing errors of decoding performance is an important first step to defining appropriate educational interventions. Determining which sound-symbol patterns are involved in specific patterns of reading mistakes provides a starting point for reading instruction.

evaluation Testing of an individual for the purpose of diagnosis or treatment. In educational settings, an evaluation is a required part of a plan for special education services, usually called an INDIVIDUALIZED EDUCATION PROGRAM (IEP). For the evaluation of a DEVELOPMENTAL DISABILITY or LEARNING DISABILITY, multiple assessments are required, including intelligence and achievement tests.

A parent can ask the school to test a child, or the school may ask parents for permission to do an evaluation. If the school thinks a child may have a disability and may need special education and related services, it must evaluate the child before providing these services. This evaluation is free to the family.

Step 1: Checking What's Already Known

An evaluation will tell the parents and the school if a child has a disability—and what kind of special help the child needs in school. The evaluation will be done by a group of people, including parents, who will begin by checking the child's school file and recent test scores and interviews with parents and teachers. This initial survey will provide information to decide if a child has a disability and what kind of special help may be needed. However, if a child is being evaluated for the first time, the initial review may not provide enough information.

Step 2. Collecting More Information

Before the school can conduct additional testing, staffers must ask the parents for permission, and describe what tests will be used and any other ways in which the school will collect information about the child.

The group involved in a child's evaluation will include

- at least one of the child's regular education teachers
- at least one of the child's special education teachers or service providers
- parents
- a school administrator expert in special education policies, children with disabilities, the general curriculum, and available resources
- an expert who can interpret the evaluation results and talk about what instruction may be necessary
- individuals (invited by parents or the school) with knowledge or special expertise about the child
- the child, if appropriate
- representatives from other agencies responsible for paying for or providing transition services
- other qualified professionals such as a school psychologist, occupational therapist, speech therapist, physical therapist, medical specialists

Although tests are an important part of an evaluation, they are only part of the process. The evaluation should also include the observations of professionals who have worked with the child, the child's relevant medical history, and the parents' ideas about the child's experiences, abilities, needs, and behavior.

It's important that the school evaluate a child in all areas of possible disability. For example, the tests should evaluate

- language skills (speaking and understanding)
- thoughts and behavior
- adaptability to change
- school achievement
- intelligence
- movement, thinking, learning, seeing, and hearing function
- job-related and other post-school interests and abilities

Tests must be given in the child's native language or by other means of communication (for example, sign language, if the child is deaf). Tests must not be biased, and the tests must be given correctly. Evaluation results will be used to decide if a child is a "child with a disability" and to determine what kind of educational program is needed. These decisions can't be made based on only one procedure, such as a single test.

Step 3. Assessing Eligibility

The next step in the evaluation process is to decide if the child is eligible for special education. This decision will be based on the results of the child's evaluation and local policies about eligibility for these special services. Based on the evaluation results, the committee will decide if the child is eligible for special education and related services. Under the IDEA, parents have the right to be part of any group that decides a child's eligibility for special education and related services.

The IDEA lists 13 different disability categories under which a child may be eligible for services:

- autism
- deaf-blindness
- deafness
- hearing impairment
- mental retardation
- multiple disabilities
- orthopedic impairment
- other health impairment (such as having limited strength, vitality, or alertness that affects a child's educational performance)

- serious emotional disturbance
- specific learning disability
- speech or language impairment
- traumatic brain injury
- visual impairment, including blindness

Parents have the right to receive a copy of the evaluation report and to receive a copy of the paperwork about the child's eligibility for special education.

Step 4. Developing an IEP

If the child is eligible for special education and related services (such as speech therapy), parents then meet with the school to discuss special educational needs and to create an individualized education program for the child. The IEP is a written document that parents and school personnel develop together to describe a child's educational program, including special services.

Not eligible If a child is not eligible for special education and related services, the school must inform parents in writing and must provide information about an appeal if the parents disagree with this decision. Parents have the right to disagree with the eligibility decision.

executive functions Mental activities associated with self-control, attention, focus, or concentration that allow an individual to achieve specific goals. Problems in executive function are associated with dysfunction of the frontal part of the brain. Mild or nonspecific deficits of executive functions are common in the general population. Executive functions may also be impaired by injury to the brain, fatigue, depression, schizophrenia, Alzheimer's, anxiety, and various psychological disorders, including LEARNING DISABILITY, depression, anxiety, and ADHD.

Problems with attention, self-regulation, planning, and impulse control may be connected to differences in the processing of neurotransmitters, particularly dopamine, in the brain.

Executive functions control four kinds of mental activities. *Working memory* is essential to the problem-solving process. Information must be held in mind and internalized while a task is being completed. *Internalized* or *private speech* allows people to use complex sets of rules in problem solving. These include rules for using sets of rules. Third is the *control of emotions and impulses,* which allows an individual to remain focused and to continually return to a path of progress toward a desired goal. This allows an individual to set aside the attraction of immediate gratification. The achievement of deferred greater gratification is the product of this kind of self-regulation. Fourth is *reconstitution,* a process of observing behaviors and then synthesizing components of what has been observed into new combinations. This function is essential to problem solving and survival in a complicated world.

Individuals with ADHD and learning disabilities may have problems in reading long assignments or completing writing projects, since these tasks require executive functions. These difficulties may be connected to differences in the way certain brain chemicals are processed in the prefrontal lobes.

Some individuals with executive function difficulties are also very impulsive, having a hard time considering alternatives and consequences before they act. In solving problems, they are likely to select the first alternative without weighing other possibilities. They often speak out without thinking of the consequences of their statements. Some students with these problems get so fidgety that it is hard for them to sit through a 50- or 90-minute class session.

Many individuals with executive function difficulties experience problems with time. Understanding the passage of time and planning for the future or the completion of a task by a particular point in time, can be a challenge. These individuals may frequently arrive late to appointments or classes. Long-term academic projects are among the greatest challenges for students who have executive function difficulties.

experiential learning Learning based on experiences rather than lectures or reading. Experiential learning, also referred to as hands-on learning, can be especially helpful to students with LEARNING DISABILITY since it allows them to learn without being hindered by difficulties in reading or writing. An experiential approach to education and learning is based on the belief that students are more motivated and will remember concepts better when they have a direct physical experience.

Experiential learning also may have a strong basis in the nature of memory, especially for individuals with learning disabilities or attention deficit disorders. For many students, learning techniques that incorporate sight and touch are much easier for them to remember and retrieve. Evidence suggests that many individuals with learning disabilities or ADHD have a hard time remembering concepts, rules, and verbal information (semantic memory), while finding it much easier to remember events, people, places, and experiences (episodic memory).

To some degree, experiential learning activities may provide a means for bridging these two basic forms of memory, and for enabling individuals to use strengths in one area to compensate for weaknesses in the other.

explicit direct instruction Structured, sequential, and cumulative instruction that is presented in a way that follows a logical sequence, without assuming any prior skills or language knowledge.

explicit memory Type of memory used to reorganize or recall presented materials.

expository writing A term that refers to informational writing typically given during the first year of college to prepare first-year students for academic writing. Generally, entering first-year students will take at least one semester of expository writing. Some colleges require a two-semester sequence of expository writing courses.

In some cases, students with writing problems may be required to complete developmental or basic writing courses before they can enter the expository writing course.

Expository writing includes description, comparison/contrast, definition, classification, argument, process analysis, and cause-and-effect. These types of writing or rhetorical strategies may be taught using models and examples, and as ends in themselves, or as strategies to use within informational essays that include a number of different patterns.

In general, the goal of teaching these types of writing patterns is to provide a foundation for the kinds of text-based writing required in specific academic disciplines.

Expository writing may be contrasted with expressive writing or the personal essay, in which students are allowed to focus on their own experience, perceptions, and memories. Much more than expressive writing, expository writing may pose problems for individuals with LEARNING DISABILITY who may find it difficult to organize ideas, support main ideas with details, or apply paragraph and essay structures.

See also RHETORICAL PATTERNS.

expressive language A type of communication involving speaking and writing. (Listening and reading are considered to be RECEPTIVE LANGUAGE.) The process of producing spoken language is called *oral expressive language.*

expressive language disorders An impairment in the ability to express ideas through language; characterized by problems with vocabulary, grammatical structures, word order, and overall language development. Expressive language disorders may have a severe impact on an individual's ability to generate spoken language and may be associated with other language-based learning disorders, such as reading disability or written expression disorder. Three to 10 percent of all school-age children have expressive language disorder.

There are a number of disorders relating to expressive language. DYSNOMIA refers to the inability to remember and express specific words. Individuals with dysnomia may "talk around" a word in order to express an idea without finding the appropriate words. For example, someone with dysnomia might say "that thing you eat that is yellow and long" when attempting to say "banana."

Expressive language disorders also include those patients who can remember the word they want to say, but can't physically manipulate their speech muscles to produce the word. This disorder is called APRAXIA. Disorders in oral expressive language are called expressive APHASIA. Students would be considered aphasic if they have problems expressing themselves orally but have no difficulty understanding language spoken to them and are successful with nonverbal tasks.

Cause

Although the cause of this disorder is unknown, brain damage and malnutrition have been associated as underlying factors. The condition can be present at birth or acquired at a later time, if brain damage or a medical condition affects otherwise normal development.

Diagnosis

Expressive language disorders are diagnosed by tests of discrepancy between verbal performance and nonverbal and receptive measures of potential performance. Because of a general cultural bias toward associating intelligence with communication, individuals with an expressive-language disorder may often be seen by others as less capable and intelligent than they actually are, even when nonverbal measures indicate extremely high intellectual potential.

Treatment

Expressive language disorders are treated by speech-language pathologists.

externalization The attribution of specific behaviors or feelings to causes outside the self. Externalization is common in school settings when students experience repeated failure and have poor self-esteem. In these cases, many will blame these problems on teachers or institutions, rather than on their own actions or lack of ability.

extrinsic phonics PHONICS taught as a supplemental learning aid rather than as an integral part of the program of reading instruction, often in separate workbooks during special time periods.

eye and foot coordination The ability to control and direct movements of hands (and arms) and feet (and legs) in accordance with visual stimuli. Examples of eye-foot coordinated activities are operating a kick- or foot-drive potter's wheel and driving a car.

eye-hand coordination A combination of fine motor skills of the hand and visual skills. Eye-hand coordination is required for many daily activities such as handwriting, drawing, typing on a keyboard, and many sports such as basketball, baseball, and javelin. Individuals with DYSGRAPHIA often have poor eye-hand coordination, resulting in poor control of handwriting.

See also VISUAL MOTOR SKILLS; FINE MOTOR SKILLS.

Family Educational Rights and Privacy Act (FERPA)   This act, also known as the Buckley Amendment, outlines procedures and guidelines for maintaining and disclosing student records.

Under this law, parents and students over 18 years of age have the right to review education records within 45 days of their application, and to request a change of records that the parent or student believe to be inaccurate or misleading.

Individuals also have the right to request disclosure of records that contain personally identifiable information.

Under the act, such information may also be disclosed without consent to school officials with a legitimate educational interest. (The definition of "school official" includes individuals employed by a school district as an administrator, supervisor, teacher, or support staff member, and may also include other individuals performing official functions, such as school board members.)

FERPA is important legislation for parents of children with learning disabilities who seek services under IDEA because it governs the circumstances under which information related to a child's academic performance and learning needs may be made available to others.

family history   An important component of a thorough assessment. A family history will identify developmental factors that may have had an impact on the individual, together with family events, trends, and other conditions. A family history may point toward potential genetic links between an individual's condition and that of parents or other family members, and it may also discern factors in the family dynamic that have an impact on an individual's case.

family therapy   A type of behavioral therapy that involves the entire family in treatment. In many cases, behavioral problems affect the entire family as well as the person with a learning disability. In family therapy, the child with a learning disability, together with parents and siblings, is supported emotionally and guided to find better ways to handle disruptive behaviors and to promote change.

far point copying   The ability to see and copy from a distance, typically used in the context of being able to read from a chalk or whiteboard and to copy the written or diagrammed information.

Federal Register   A daily publication of the U.S. government that contains amendments to federal regulations and other legal and legislative information.

Feingold diet   See DIET AND ADHD.

fetal alcohol effect   A combination of mild effects of prenatal alcohol intake; less severe than FETAL ALCOHOL SYNDROME. Symptoms include LEARNING DISABILITIES and other brain differences that do not become evident until well after birth.

While individuals with this condition may lack the outward physical appearance of alcohol damage and generally have higher IQs, the internal damage to the brain and other organs can be just as serious as in FAS. Because FAE individuals "look normal," they are expected to perform normally. These issues lead to secondary disabilities—those that develop as a result of failure to properly deal with the primary disabilities.

fetal alcohol syndrome (FAS)   A condition that describes the physical and mental birth defects in a child caused by the mother's consumption of alcohol during pregnancy. Maternal use of alcohol during pregnancy may have been a factor for a substantial number of children receiving special education services.

More than 10 percent of children have been exposed to high levels of alcohol before birth, which may cause effects ranging from mild learning disabilities to major physical, mental, and intellectual impairment. It takes very little alcohol to cause serious damage; research has shown that even a single exposure to high levels of alcohol can cause significant brain damage in an unborn child.

Cause

Alcohol in a pregnant woman's bloodstream circulates to the fetus by crossing the placenta. There, the alcohol interferes with the ability of the fetus to receive enough oxygen and nourishment for normal cell development in the brain and other body organs.

Symptoms

A variety of problems are typically associated with FAS, including

- growth deficiencies: small body size and weight, slower than normal development, and failure to catch up
- skeletal deformities: deformed ribs and sternum; curved spine; hip dislocations; bent, fused, webbed, or missing fingers or toes; limited movement of joints; small head

- facial abnormalities: small eye openings; skin webbing between eyes and base of nose; drooping eyelids; nearsightedness; failure of eyes to move in same direction; short upturned nose; sunken nasal bridge; flat or absent groove between nose and upper lip; thin upper lip; opening in roof of mouth; small jaw; low-set or poorly formed ears
- organ deformities: heart defects; heart murmurs; genital malformations; kidney and urinary defects
- central nervous system problems: small brain; faulty arrangement of brain cells and connective tissue; mental retardation, usually mild to moderate but occasionally severe; LEARNING DISABILITY; short attention span; irritability in infancy; hyperactivity in childhood; poor body, hand, and finger coordination.

Diagnosis

Early diagnosis can help prevent secondary disabilities such as mental health problems, dropping out of school, trouble with the law, and substance abuse. After diagnosis, parents often find that their ability to cope with the child's behavior changes dramatically when they understand that the problems are most likely based on organic brain damage, rather than the child's choice to be inattentive or uncooperative.

Treatment

FAS is a lifetime disability with no cure; a child will not outgrow the problem. However, early and intensive intervention can make an enormous difference in the prognosis for a child. Up to about age 10 or 12 is the best time to intervene, since this is the period of greatest development of fixed neural pathways.

Prevention

FAS is preventable if women refrain from alcohol use during pregnancy. Studies suggest that drinking a large amount of alcohol at any one time may be more dangerous to the fetus than drinking small amounts more often. The fetus is most vulnerable to various types of injuries, depending on the stage of development in which alcohol is encountered.

Because a safe amount of drinking during pregnancy has not been determined, all major authorities agree that women should not drink at all during pregnancy. Unfortunately, women sometimes wait until a pregnancy is confirmed before they stop drinking. By then, the embryo has gone through several weeks of critical development, a period during which exposure to alcohol can be very damaging. Therefore, experts urge women who are pregnant or anticipating a pregnancy to abstain from drinking alcoholic beverages.

figurative language   Forms of communication that use nonliteral ways of conveying meaning, such as comparisons, analogies, and exaggeration. Common forms of figurative language are metaphors (such as "the moon was a ghostly galleon") or similes ("my love is like a red, red rose"). Figurative language is common in literature, but it is also used in everyday speech: "I could eat a horse." Difficulty with understanding or using figurative language may cause significant problems for an individual.

figure-ground deficits   Difficulty telling the difference between foreground and background images or sounds. Individuals with this deficit may have trouble with printed words on a page; identifying important visual information in pictures, photographs, graphs, or charts; or following conversation in a crowded room.

See also FIGURE-GROUND DISCRIMINATION.

figure-ground discrimination   The ability to visually distinguish between foreground and background. Individuals with deficits in this area can't easily identify the predominant image or design in a picture from other objects and background. Figure-ground discrimination can also refer to the auditory discrimination involved in understanding what a person is saying when

there are other sounds, including other people speaking in the same room.

See also FIGURE-GROUND DEFICITS.

fine motor skills   The use of small muscle groups for specific tasks such as handwriting. Fine motor abilities are developmental, with children generally improving in their ability to use writing or drawing implements as they enter elementary school and are introduced to the concept of writing and copying. Deficits in fine motor function can have a detrimental effect on the development of writing skills.

finger agnosia   The inability to recognize and interpret sensory impressions with fingers (usually the finger tips); caused by an impairment in the brain.

fluoxetine   See PROZAC.

fluency   Fluid or unrestricted movements or abilities. Often, fluency refers to learned or practiced ability in oral language. Individuals are said to be fluent in a language when they can speak in an uninterrupted fashion and convey meaning easily.

Individuals with speech difficulties such as stuttering are said to have *dysfluent* language abilities.

In reading development, fluency refers to the development of an automatic reading process in which words are effortlessly decoded and understood.

fluent aphasia   A language disorder characterized by clear articulation, normal rhythm, long phrases having nonsensical content, and incorrect words or sounds. This type of aphasia includes Wernicke's aphasia and anomic aphasias.

formal operational stage   The fourth and final stage in psychologist Jean Piaget's stage theory of cognitive development that occurs some time after the age of 11. Preadolescents gradually become capable of abstract logic and hypothetical reasoning, and become able to generate many possible solutions to problems. They can use deduction to draw conclusions based on observations, and can debate moral dilemmas and detect inconsistencies in the behavior of others. All these cognitive abilities have important social consequences as children become adolescents.

fragile X syndrome   Also called Martin-Bell syndrome, marker X syndrome, and Escalante syndrome; a genetic condition causing moderate mental retardation (mostly in boys). Children with this condition tend to have a long, narrow face with thick features, a prominent jaw, blue eyes, and large body size; later in life, large testicles also develop. This is an X-linked disorder with a fragile site on the long arm of the X chromosome.

The 30 percent of female carriers appear to be more mildly affected, and experience shyness, anxiety, and panic attacks. A carrier female has a 38 percent risk of producing a son with mental retardation and a 16 percent chance of producing a daughter with mental retardation.

The syndrome accounts for approximately 5 percent of mental retardation in males, but has also been linked to LEARNING DISABILITIES, autism, speech and language disorders, and mathematics and motor disabilities.

free appropriate public education   Special education and related services—provided at public expense, under public supervision and direction, and without charge—that meet the standards of the state's department of education and are based on an INDIVIDUALIZED EDUCATION PROGRAM.

Under Public Law 94–142 and IDEA (the INDIVIDUALS WITH DISABILITIES EDUCATION ACT), chil-

dren with disabilities who fall under the act must be provided with "a free appropriate public education which emphasizes special education and related services. . . ."

Under the act, states are required to provide the minimum services that assure equal access to educational services, but are not expected to provide all of the services that may be required for students to reach their full potential.

See also EDUCATION FOR ALL HANDICAPPED CHILDREN ACT OF 1975 (Public Law 94–142).

frontal lobe   One of four major areas of the cerebral cortex in the brain that lie just behind the forehead and extend back to the central fissure. This area includes the prefrontal lobes and the motor cortex. It is involved in producing speech, voluntary movement, making plans and judgments, and memory. The prefrontal area involves the ability to concentrate and pay attention and provide elaboration of thought. It is considered to be the seat of judgment, inhibition, personality, and emotional traits.

Damage to the frontal lobes can impair a person's ability to plan and organize, and can cause problems with impulsivity and motor control. Damage also can impair recent memory, and lead to inattentiveness, an inability to concentrate, behavior disorders, difficulty in learning new information, inappropriate social or sexual behavior, a lack of emotion, and expressive APHASIA.

Experts believe that physiological differences in this area of the brain also account for much of the normal individual variation in fine motor skills.

full inclusion   A placement in which a special education student receives instruction within the regular classroom setting for the entire school day.

Gall, Franz Joseph (1758–1828)   One of the founders of phrenology, Gall was born in Baden, now a part of Germany, on March 9, 1758. He is best known for identifying a set of organs in the brain that he associated with 35 affective and intellectual faculties, believing that the size of these organs in the brain could be detected by cranial bumps. This idea was widely popular at the turn of the 19th century and had many advocates.

Gall studied medicine in Vienna, Austria, where he became a renowned neuroanatomist, physiologist, and pioneer in the study of the localization of mental functions in the brain.

At the turn of the 19th century, he developed "cranioscopy," which was a method to divine the personality and development of mental and moral faculties on the basis of the external shape of the skull. Cranioscopy was later renamed "phrenology" (*phrenos,* "mind," and *logos,* "study") by his followers.

IIis revolutionary concepts on brain localization offended religious leaders and scientists alike. The church considered his theory blasphemous (they did not approve of the idea that the mind, which was created by God, should have a physical seat in the brain). Established science also condemned him for a variety of reasons, including the fact that Gall couldn't provide scientific proof of his theory.

Because of this disapproval, Gall was forced to leave Austria in 1805 and go to France, where his theories were likewise pronounced invalid by politicians and scientists alike. Despite all this, Gall was able to live comfortably from his phrenological theories and practices. They were best accepted in England, where the ruling class used his beliefs to justify the so-called inferiority of colonial subjects, including the Irish. Phrenology also became very popular in the United States from 1820 to 1850.

Despite his misguided theories, he also made many true scientific contributions, such as his discovery that the gray matter of the brain contained cell bodies (neurons) and the white matter contained fibers (axons). Gall's most important contribution involved his discovery of the localization of specific behaviors to areas in the brain. His ideas led to further study in attempts to correlate specific intellectual or psychological deficits to areas in the brain through the examination of diseased brains.

Gall died in Paris, on August 22, 1828.

Gallistel-Ellis Test of Coding Skills (G-E Test)   This assessment for grades two through six is designed to test a child's ability to decode and spell the basic phonetic patterns in the English language. Reading and spelling of irregular patterns are also tested. G-E Test results can be helpful in planning reading remediation.

gender differences   Statistics from schools and research show that boys are diagnosed with LEARNING DISABILITY up to four times more often than are girls, although recent research suggests that there may be as many girls with learning disabilities as boys. Many factors, such as biological and cultural reasons, may explain the prevalence of identifying boys with learning disabilities. Biological research indicates boys may be more vulnerable to learning disabilities. Other studies show that boys are referred for special education more frequently because they exhibit more disruptive behaviors. Yet some other studies attribute the disproportionate number of identified boys to increased academic pressure, making boys more likely to buckle under stress.

general education Regular instruction provided to most students. Placing special education students in general education classes is considered the LEAST RESTRICTIVE ENVIRONMENT, but special considerations must be made to ensure students are able to achieve academically and socially in this environment.

genetic factors In both DYSLEXIA and ATTENTION DEFICIT/HYPERACTIVITY DISORDER (ADHD), research has identified genetic factors that appear to make an individual more predisposed to having the condition.

Genetic factors have mainly been identified through family studies that identify groups of family members who have experienced similar conditions. In addition, some genetic research has begun to identify specific genes and chromosomes that may be involved in the genetic transmission of dyslexia or ADHD. Research that indicates a genetic component or genetic factors underlying these two disorders also supports a neurological basis for understanding their nature and underlying factors.

Gerstmann's syndrome A condition characterized by DYSLEXIA, difficulty locating body parts in space (FINGER AGNOSIA), difficulty with mathematics (DYSCALCULIA), right-left confusion, and difficulty in writing (DYSGRAPHIA). It is not the same as the Gerstmann-Sträussler-Scheinker syndrome, a type of spongiform encephalopathy similar to Creutzfeldt-Jakob syndrome.

Although the four main diagnostic features are the same, there are differences between the Gerstmann's syndrome that occurs in adults and the syndrome (often called developmental Gerstmann's syndrome) that is exhibited in children.

gifted and talented The definition and assessment of giftedness varies from state to state and even from school district to school district. Most definitions of giftedness include characteristics such as extraordinary inquisitiveness, creativity, spontaneity, and emotionality. Many of these characteristics can be found in students with a LEARNING DISABILITY; therefore, students with learning disabilities may also be gifted in certain areas.

Both types of learners require stimulation. When a gifted student's learning needs are not met, the student may display disruptive behaviors or signs of depression.

Academic accommodations for the gifted may range from supplementing regular education programs with acceleration and enrichment activities, to self-contained programs. Suggested features of such programs would include teaching thinking skills and independent projects. The identification of gifted students and implementation of special services largely depend on how the school defines giftedness.

Gillingham, Anna (1878–1963) A gifted psychologist and educator with a superb mastery of language; well known in the field of LANGUAGE DISABILITIES. Together with neuropsychiatrist Samuel Orton, she helped develop techniques for remediating reading and language processing problems in children with DYSLEXIA, helped train teachers in the method, and compiled and published instructional materials.

Over the past 50 years, the ORTON-GILLINGHAM APPROACH has been the most influential, widely used, and respected program for teaching reading, and is still in use today.

See also ORTON, SAMUEL.

global aphasia   Loss of all language function.

grade equivalent   A score that expresses a student's performance as the average performance for a particular grade. These scores are expressed in grades and tenths of grades (for example, 6.4 is grade six and four months).

Grade-level equivalent scores are determined by giving a test that is developed for a particular grade to students in other grades. For instance, test designers establish grade-equivalents for a fourth grade test by giving that same test to students who are in the sixth and the second grades.

Grade-level equivalent scores are often misunderstood. If a fourth grader received a seventh grade equivalent score on a fourth grade reading achievement test, the child is not ready for seventh grade material. Actually, the score means that the child reads fourth grade material as well as the average seventh grader.

grapheme   The written letter symbol that represents a sound (phoneme). For example, the grapheme "c" represents the sounds "k" and "s."

graphic organizer   A device that helps an individual understand and recall concepts by visually displaying how ideas are connected. Venn diagrams, flow charts, and mind maps are all examples of visual organizers. Using graphic organizers is a useful strategy with learning disabled students because it makes related ideas more meaningful by utilizing vision, which can aid in recall.

Research has shown that using visual organizers has increased reading comprehension by mapping out main ideas and details. In the context of writing, visual organizers can be useful in generating and organizing ideas.

graphomotor ability   Handwriting skills or drawing figures in replication of models or in response to specific prompts. Graphomotor ability is linked to fine motor skills but can be distinguished from them because of the role that memory plays—for example, memory for the forms of letters, which must be called into play in various ways in copying tasks, writing from dictation, and in independent writing.

Problems with graphomotor skills may exist by themselves, but they are also frequently linked to attention disorders or learning disabilities.

graphophonemic knowledge   The understanding that words are made of sounds and sounds are written with letters in the right order. Students who understand this can blend sounds associated with letters into words and can separate words into component sounds for spelling and writing.

Students should be assessed to determine if they can hear sounds in spoken language prior to letter-sound instruction.

Gray Oral Reading Test-Diagnostic   The GORT-D measures a child's speed and accuracy when reading out loud, comprehension, ability to sound out and blend nonsense words that follow English structural patterns, ability to find smaller words within larger words, word identification and comprehension skill, and the ability to deal with compound words, contractions, and inflectional endings. Because many of the subtests don't use traditional formats, the score may not reflect a student's classroom performance.

gross motor skills   Skills in which the large muscles are used in the neck, torso, and arms and legs. The development of gross motor skills involves activities such as rolling over, crawling, sitting, walking, running, catching, and jumping.

Early development of gross motor skills appears to be largely inbred, while later gross-motor abilities (used for such skills as swimming, bicycling, skiing, and so on) are largely learned.

There is little relationship between gross motor abilities and INTELLIGENCE.

guided reading   Reading instruction in which the teacher provides the structure and purpose for reading and for responding to the materials read. Most basic reading programs have guided reading lessons.

hand-eye coordination Ability of the hand and eye to perform together.

handicap A term that refers to a disadvantage or impairment based on a disabling condition. Federal legislation, such as Public Law 94–142: the EDUCATION FOR ALL HANDICAPPED CHILDREN ACT OF 1975, uses "handicap" to identify the disadvantageous status of an individual with specific impairments as compared to others without such impairments.

However, the term "handicapped" is no longer used to mean disability or disorder, as it places an emphasis on social status or on defining an individual, rather than suggesting a particular difference. In the same manner that many individuals challenge the use of the word "disability" because it by definition focuses on a negative condition, "handicap" is best used in a legal context rather than in a social one.

haptic sense A person's sense of touch. Haptic recognition tests involve blindfolded subjects feeling geometric shapes, then choosing the picture corresponding to the shape from a limited set. Many people with language-based disabilities have a difficult time with these tasks.

hard neurological signs Physical signs of brain injury that can be identified medically.

See also SOFT NEUROLOGICAL SIGNS.

Head Start An EARLY INTERVENTION PROGRAM established under the Economic Opportunity Act of 1964 in order to provide preschool educational opportunities to disadvantaged children. In 1972, Project Head Start was amended to include children with disabilities. This program has proven to be the most influential national early childhood program; it allowed comprehensive studies to be done on the effect of early intervention and school success.

Project Head Start was established by Congress in 1965, part of President Lyndon B. Johnson's War on Poverty and the 1964 Economic Opportunity Act. Head Start is the only national program of its kind to use a comprehensive service approach to early childhood education. First established as a summer program for low-income preschool children and their families, Head Start has grown to include full-day, full-year programming and services for children from birth to three years of age, their families, and pregnant women.

Head Start has received strong bipartisan support through 35 years of presidential administrations and has been consistently acknowledged for its effectiveness in helping children become successful in school and later life. The program's hallmark has been its strong emphasis on families, recognizing that parents are the first and primary educators, nurturers, and advocates of their children.

For 35 years, Head Start has also taken a strong community advocacy approach, recognizing that communities must be supportive for healthy families and children.

It provides comprehensive prekindergarten experiences (education, health care, nutrition, and social services) to almost 18 million of the nation's poorest children. Research demonstrates that Head Start can help children build the confidence and skills they need to succeed in school and to become the leaders, taxpayers, and productive citizens of the future.

A national review of 36 studies on the long-term impact of early childhood education programs found that low-income children who participated in such programs were less likely to be held back in school or to be placed in special education classes, more likely to succeed in school and to graduate, and more likely to be rated as behaving well in class and being better adjusted in school.

The typical child completing Head Start has the knowledge and skills in early literacy and numbers and the skills that signify a readiness to learn more in kindergarten, such as listening and comprehension skills. Children also acquire a variety of social skills important for kindergarten, such as following the teacher's directions, using free time in acceptable ways, and helping put work materials away.

Head Start children perform higher on cognitive tests than children from other low-income families who have not attended center-based preschool programs, according to a comparison between the results of the Head Start study and earlier studies. In 1999, Head Start served more than 835,000 children at a cost of $4.66 billion.

hearing problems "Hearing impairment" and "deafness" are two of the categories under which children with disabilities may be eligible for special education and related services under the INDIVIDUALS WITH DISABILITIES EDUCATION ACT (IDEA).

While the term "hearing impairment" is often used to describe a wide range of hearing losses, including deafness, the regulations for IDEA define hearing loss and deafness separately.

Hearing impairment is defined by IDEA as "an impairment in hearing, whether permanent or fluctuating, that adversely affects a child's educational performance." Deafness is defined as "a hearing impairment that is so severe that the child is impaired in processing linguistic information through hearing, with or without amplification." Thus, deafness may be viewed as a condition that prevents an individual from receiving sound in all or most of its forms. In contrast, a child with a hearing loss can generally respond to auditory stimuli, including speech.

Hearing loss and deafness affect individuals of all ages and may occur at any time from infancy through old age. More than 70,000 students aged 6 to 21 (or 1.3 percent of all students with disabilities) received special education services under the category of "hearing impairment" during 1998. However, the number of children with hearing loss and deafness is undoubtedly higher, since many of these students may have other disabilities as well.

Hearing problems can exist in only one ear or in both ears, and may be described as slight, mild, moderate, severe, or profound, depending upon how well a person can hear the intensities or frequencies associated with speech. Generally, only children whose hearing loss is greater than 90 decibels (dB) are considered deaf for the purposes of educational placement.

There are four types of hearing loss: *conductive* hearing loss is caused by diseases or obstructions in the outer or middle ear. A person with a conductive hearing loss usually is able to use a hearing aid well or can be helped medically or surgically. *Sensorineural* hearing loss is caused by damage to the delicate sensory hair cells of the inner ear or the nerves that supply it. These hearing losses can range from mild to profound, so that a hearing aid may not help. A *mixed* hearing loss refers to a combination of conductive and sensorineural loss and means that a problem occurs in both the outer or middle and the inner ear. A *central* hearing loss is caused by damage to the nerves of the central nervous system, either in the pathways to the brain or in the brain itself.

Education

Hearing loss or deafness does not affect a person's intellect or ability to learn, but children who are either hard of hearing or deaf generally require some form of special education services, including

- regular speech, language, and auditory training from a specialist
- amplification systems
- services of an interpreter for those students who use manual communication
- favorable seating in the class to facilitate speechreading
- captioned films/videos
- assistance of a notetaker, who takes notes
- instruction for the teacher and other students in alternate communication methods such as sign language
- counseling

Children who are hard of hearing may find it harder to learn vocabulary, grammar, word order, idiomatic expressions of verbal communication. For children who are deaf or have severe hearing losses, early, consistent, and conscious use of visible communication modes such as sign language or fingerspelling—or oral training—can help reduce this language delay.

By age four or five, most children who are deaf are enrolled in school on a full-day basis and do special work on communication and language development.

higher cognitive functions   A term that usually refers to complex thinking skills such as judgment, abstraction, problem-solving, and planning.

See also HIGHER ORDER THINKING.

higher order thinking   Advanced intellectual abilities that go beyond basic information processing. Higher order thinking involves such abilities as concept formation, understanding rules, problem-solving skills, and the ability to look at information from multiple perspectives.

Students exercise their higher order thinking abilities when they analyze, synthesize, and evaluate materials to which they have been exposed. The construction or creation of new material also requires higher order thinking.

In general, abilities in the area of higher order thinking are closely linked to intellectual capacity. However, individuals with learning disabilities who have underlying information-processing deficits may appear to have difficulties with higher order activities. This may be especially true with higher order tasks involving a verbal component for students with language-based learning problems.

holistic assessment   An approach to assessment of academic skills and performance using a variety of methods, with an emphasis on the quality of the information rather than the quantity.

Methods of holistic assessment include

- observing the student in various settings
- interviewing parents, teachers, and the student
- academic, developmental, and medical history of the student
- educational testing and writing samples

hyperactivity   Constant and excessive movement and activity. A child with hyperactivity may not be able to stop an action when directed to, or to sit still for any period of time. Hyperactivity often occurs with inattentiveness and impulsivity. An affected child might have trouble sitting still, fidgets excessively, and moves about excessively even during sleep. Onset occurs before the age of seven years. Behaviors are chronic (present throughout the child's life), present throughout the child's day, and are not due to other factors such as anxiety or depression.

In older children, symptoms of hyperactivity may be more subtle, displaying themselves in restlessness, fidgeting, a tendency to interrupt in class, or in conflict-seeking behaviors with peers and family members.

See also ATTENTION DEFICIT/HYPERACTIVITY DISORDER; HYPERKINESIS.

hyperkinesis   A condition of abnormally increased muscle movement; often associated with ATTENTION DEFICIT/HYPERACTIVITY DISORDER (ADHD) in children. It is often used interchangeably with HYPERACTIVITY.

hyperlexia   A complex condition that includes an ability to read words at a far earlier developmental stage than is typical, and often an intense fascination with symbols such as letters and numbers. These word-calling skills are high in the presence of poor reading comprehension. It also involves a significant difficulty in understanding verbal language and problems with social skills, including difficulty interacting appropriately with peers and family members.

In addition, some children with hyperlexia may also develop expressive language skills in unusual ways, echoing what they hear without understanding the meaning, and failing to develop the ability to initiate conversations. They often exhibit a powerful need to maintain routines and ritualistic patterns of behavior, and have trouble with transitions and handling external sensory stimuli.

Children with hyperlexia often display very strong auditory and VISUAL MEMORY, but may have trouble understanding and reasoning in abstract rather than concrete and literal terms. Often, their approach to listening to others may be highly selective, and they can appear to be deaf.

The term hyperlexia was first used in 1967, although the condition was described in the 1940s. There is no consensus concerning either the cause or significance of the condition. Hyperlexia has been reported in populations of children with varying cognitive abilities, including some with severe mental retardation. Intellec-

tual level by itself does not therefore seem to be a definitive factor in the condition. Hyperlexia is considered by some researchers to be a unique type of language disorder and a condition occurring with another reading disability. Others report that children with hyperlexia demonstrate a profile opposite from that shown by children with classic dyslexia on certain tests.

Hyperlexia shares similar characteristics with AUTISM, behavior disorders, language disorders, emotional disorders, attention deficit disorder, hearing impairment, giftedness, and paradoxically, MENTAL RETARDATION.

Diagnosis
To develop effective teaching strategies and more typical childhood development, it is important to differentiate hyperlexia from other disorders. A thorough assessment by a speech and language pathologist who is familiar with hyperlexia is the first step. Psychological tests that emphasize visual processes rather than verbal skills can also help identify hyperlexia. Hearing, neurological, psychiatric, blood chemistry, and genetic evaluations can be performed to rule out other disorders, but are not needed to identify hyperlexia.

Treatment
The future of a hyperlexic child depends on developing language expression and comprehension skills. Intensive speech and language therapy and early intervention programs can help. The child's reading skills should be used as a primary means of developing language.

It is also important to teach the child appropriate social skills by providing opportunities for the child to interact with others whose behavior is more socially appropriate. Parent, teachers, and other professionals should work together to develop programs for each child.

hypoactivity   A medical term for lethargy. Some individuals with a LEARNING DISABILITY, attention disorders, or other conditions affecting learning may suffer from hypoactivity, making it more difficult to complete school work.

ideation   A mental representation of thoughts or visual images, or a combination of linguistic and visual representations.

illiteracy   The inability to read or write a language. The 1988 UNESCO proclamation stated that "widespread illiteracy is . . . a gross violation of the basic human right to learn, know, and communicate."

illiterate   Unable to read and write.
See also ILLITERACY.

implicit memory   MEMORY without awareness, which occurs when information that was encoded is subsequently expressed without conscious recollection.

impulse control   Current research suggests that lack of impulse control is a major underlying factor in attention disorders. The onset of the ability to control impulses is a significant element of child development. Individuals with impulse control problems also may have trouble sustaining a train of thought.

Individuals with impulse control disorders suffer from recurrent failure to resist impulsive behaviors that may be harmful to themselves or others. The disorders include intermittent explosive disorder, explosive disorder, kleptomania, pathological gambling, pyromania (setting fires), and trichotillomania (pulling out one's hair).

impulsivity   Difficulty in controlling or monitoring speech or actions, often a primary element in ADHD (ATTENTION DEFICIT/HYPERACTIVITY DISORDER). An individual who has problems with impulsivity may blurt out responses without thinking, make take excessive risks, or may act in socially inappropriate ways.

Impulsivity may also affect school performance in more subtle ways. For example, a student may respond impulsively to questions on a multiple-choice test, choosing answers before considering all alternatives. Likewise, an impulsive individual might answer an essay question before having thought through a response.

Impulsivity is often poorly understood in school, and may be judged harshly in social or interpersonal contexts, rather than seen as arising from underlying difficulties in IMPULSE CONTROL.

inattention   Difficulty in focusing on important information in the immediate environment. It is a major constituent in attention disorders, and may have a pervasive negative effect on academic or social functioning.

Independent Educational Consultant Association   A nonprofit, international professional association representing full-time, experienced, independent EDUCATIONAL CONSULTANTS. Chartered in 1976, the association's headquarters is located in the Washington, D.C., area. IECA sponsors professional training institutes, workshops, and conferences, publishes a directory of qualified consultants, offers information to students and their families regarding school selection issues, and works to ensure that those in the profession adhere to the highest ethical and business standards.

IECA has developed a strict set of ethical guidelines that govern the actions of consultants in their relationships with students and families, schools and colleges, and with colleagues. These include a responsibility to understand each student's special strengths, values, and needs, while striving to include all family members in the educational planning process. An IECA member does not accept any compensation from educational institutions for placement of a child.

IECA also established the Independent Educational Consultants Association Foundation. The foundation supports projects that will benefit those involved in the process of making educational choices, including students, families, educational consultants, and other professionals.

Contact: 3251 Old Lee Highway, Suite 510, Fairfax, VA 22030–1504; phone: (703) 591–4850; website: http://www.educationalconsulting.org

independent education evaluation   An evaluation of a student conducted by a qualified examiner who doesn't work for the school district. According to Public Law 94–142 (amended to the INDIVIDUALS WITH DISABILITIES EDUCATION ACT), parents have the right to have their child independently tested either to seek a more comprehensive assessment than is sometimes provided in a school setting, or because they fear a school-based evaluation is biased or inaccurate.

An IEE would include the same elements as a school-mandated evaluation, focusing on measures of aptitude and achievement. Parents may obtain an evaluation at school district expense if they disagree with the evaluation arranged for by the school district.

If the parent wants the school district to pay for the tests, the district may ask (but not require) the parents to explain the reason why they object to the district's evaluation. The

school district also may ask for an impartial hearing to show that its evaluation is appropriate. If the impartial hearing officer finds that the district evaluation is appropriate, parents still have the right to obtain an IEE—but the district doesn't have to pay for it. The school district may not unreasonably delay either providing the test or calling an impartial hearing to defend the district's own evaluation.

Individualized Education Program (IEP)   A written educational prescription developed for each child with a LEARNING DISABILITY, describing what special education the child needs and what will be done to address those needs. School districts are required by law to develop these programs, sometimes called an Individualized Education Plan, in cooperation with parents. An IEP must be created for each exceptional child, according to the INDIVIDUALS WITH DISABILITIES EDUCATION ACT (IDEA, formerly PL 94–142).

An IEP is prepared by a team including parents, the child, the child's teacher, educational specialists, and a representative of the public agency that oversees special education.

An IEP includes information about the child's current level of academic performance; annual goals and short-term educational objectives; specific educational services to be provided; a definition of the extent to which the student will take part in regular educational programs; and a timetable for providing services. The IEP also defines procedures for measuring how well the educational objectives are being met.

An IEP must contain

- the child's present levels of educational performance
- annual and short-term educational goals
- the specific special education program and related services that will be provided
- the extent to which the child will participate in regular education programs with non-handicapped children

- a statement of when services will begin and how long they will last

- provisions for evaluating the effectiveness of the program and the student's performance at least once a year

- statement of transition services for students 14 years of age or older

Individualized Education Program Committee
A group of people who meet to create an INDIVIDUAL EDUCATION PROGRAM for a child who has been identified as learning disabled by a multidisciplinary team.

The committee should include a representative of the public school, the student's teacher, one or both parents, the student (when appropriate), and any other individuals deemed relevant by the school or parents such as an educational psychologist, speech teacher, legal expert, or adviser.

Individualized Family Service Program
A written plan developed with teachers and parents to outline special services to be provided to children of preschool age.

As stated in Public Law 99–457, Part H, families play a crucial part in a child's development from birth to age two; therefore, the individualized family services program is written to address the special needs of the child and the family.

According to the INDIVIDUALS WITH DISABILITIES EDUCATION ACT (IDEA), an IFSP must include

- present levels of the child's development (cognitive, physical, language/speech, psychosocial, and self-help)

- family resources and concerns regarding the child's development

- expected outcomes for the family and child, including criteria, timelines, and assessment procedures

- specific intervention services necessary to meet the needs of the family and child

- projected start and end dates of services

- name of case manager

- steps needed for smooth transition from early intervention program to preschool program

See also EARLY INTERVENTION PROGRAM.

individualized reading
An approach to reading instruction developed in the 1950s as an alternative to basic reading programs; emphasizes student selection of reading materials and self-pacing in reading. With this method, the teacher adjusts instruction to student needs during small-group work and in individual conferences.

Individuals with Disabilities Education Act (IDEA), The
A law that provides children with disabilities access to a free, appropriate public education, and to improve the educational experience of such children. IDEA was first enacted as the Education for All Handicapped Children Act of 1975 (Public Law 94–142), renamed in 1990 (Public Law 101–476) and amended (Public Law 102–119) in 1991. Under the IDEA, money is given to local school systems to educate children up to age 22; local schools are required to comply with the act as a condition of receiving funds.

Prior to IDEA's implementation in 1975, approximately a million children with disabilities were shut out of schools and hundreds of thousands more were denied appropriate services. Since then, IDEA has changed the lives of these children. Many are learning and achieving at levels previously thought impossible, graduating from high school, going to college, and entering the workforce as productive citizens in unprecedented numbers. Previously, 90 percent of children with developmental disabilities were housed in state institutions; today, they are no longer institutionalized. Today three times as many young people with disabilities are enrolled in colleges or universities, and twice as many of today's 20-year-olds with disabilities are working.

The IDEA covers students with a specific LEARNING DISABILITY as defined within the act. Both DYSLEXIA and ATTENTION DEFICIT/HYPERACTIVITY DISORDER are covered by the IDEA. IDEA also is for students who have mental retardation; hearing, vision, orthopedic, speech, or language impairments; serious emotional disturbance, autism, traumatic brain injury, or other health impairments.

The IDEA provides that children covered by the act have access to a FREE APPROPRIATE PUBLIC EDUCATION. In general, students receiving services under the IDEA will take part in regular educational programs to some degree, and also receive special education services as described in their INDIVIDUALIZED EDUCATION PROGRAM (IEP).

Most students who fall under the IDEA are served within their own public school system, although in some cases students may attend a private educational institution, with the school district assuming the cost.

inferential thinking

inferential thinking A primary element in high order thinking and an essential factor in academic success, involving the ability to examine factual information and make predictions. These predictions might involve estimating likely behavior based on the characteristics of a figure in a story or film, deducing expected outcomes, or determining the nature or meaning of an event from an analysis of surface elements.

Some individuals with a LEARNING DISABILITY may struggle with inferential thinking, especially if such reasoning processes require the ability to reason verbally or understand texts. At the same time, with appropriate support, individuals with learning disabilities may demonstrate strength in this area of cognitive performance.

information processing disorders A problem in any of the ways in which an individual processes information: VISUAL DISCRIMINATION, visual figure-ground discrimination, VISUAL MEMORY, VISUAL MOTOR COORDINATION, visual closure, understanding spatial relationships, AUDITORY DISCRIMINATION, AUDITORY FIGURE-GROUND DISCRIMINATION, and AUDITORY MEMORY.

A person's senses of sight, smell, hearing, taste, and touch are constantly providing information, which is stored in short- and long-term memory. For each of the hundreds of things people do each day, they need to quickly decide what information to use to complete the task. Managing all of the stored information and using it effectively is called "information processing."

A child with an information processing disorder may have trouble with one or more of the information processing skills, which interferes with using information efficiently, solving problems, or completing tasks. The inability to process information efficiently often causes frustration and learning failure.

Visual Discrimination

The ability to visually compare the features of different items to distinguish one from another. Children with this condition may find it hard to notice the small differences between some letters and numbers, certain colors, or between similar shapes and patterns.

Visual Figure-Ground Discrimination

The ability to separate a shape or printed character from its background. Children with problems in this area may find it hard to find the specific bit of information they need from a printed page or computer screen filled with words and numbers.

Visual Memory

Long-term visual memory is the ability to recall something seen a long time ago, while short-term visual memory is the ability to remember something seen very recently. Visual memory often depends upon the nature of the information being processed. For example, most people find it easier to remember what an object looked like four weeks ago if the object is associated with a special event. Children with problems in this area may find it hard to describe a place they've visited, remember the spelling of a familiar but irregularly spelled word, dial a telephone number without looking carefully at each of the numbers and letters on the telephone, or use a calculator, typewriter, or computer keyboard with speed and accuracy.

Visual Motor Processing

The kind of thinking needed to use feedback from the eyes to coordinate the movement of other parts of the body. For example, eyes and hands need to work together to write with a pen or pencil. Children with problems in this area may find it difficult to write neatly or stay within the margins or on the lines of a page, use scissors, sew, move around without bumping into things, place objects on surfaces so they won't fall off, participate in sports that require well-timed and precise movements in space.

Visual Closure

The ability to know what an object is when only parts of it are visible. Children with problems in this area may find it difficult to recognize a picture of a familiar object missing some parts, or to identify a word when a letter is missing.

Spatial Relationships

How objects are positioned in the space. People use their ability to recognize and understand spatial relationships as they interact with their surroundings and also when they look at objects on paper. The ability to recognize and understand spatial relationships helps people understand whether objects are near or far, on our left or right, or over or under other objects. This skill is needed to learn to read, write, count, and think about numbers. Children with problems in this area may find it hard to find their way from one place to another, or write intelligibly.

Auditory Discrimination

The ability to notice, compare, and distinguish the distinct and separate sounds in words. In order to read efficiently, students must be able to isolate sounds, especially those that match letters in the alphabet. Children with problems in this area may find it difficult to learn to read or understand spoken language, follow directions, and remember details.

Auditory Figure-Ground Discrimination

The ability to pick out important sounds from a noisy background. Children with problems in this area may find it hard to separate meaningful sounds from background noise.

Auditory Memory

Like visual memory, there are two kinds of auditory memory. Long-term auditory memory is the ability to recall something heard long ago, whereas short-term auditory memory is the ability to remember something heard very recently. Children with problems in this area may find it difficult to remember people's names, memorize and recall telephone numbers, follow multistep spoken directions, recall stories they have been told, or remember lines from songs.

Treatment

There are things that can be done to help someone make it easier to process information. These include:

- simplify directions
- maintain eye contact while speaking
- speak slowly, especially when providing new information
- ask for repetitions

People with learning disabilities often have strong preferences for one type of information processing over another. These preferences are sometimes referred to as learning or working styles. Something as simple as giving instructions both orally and in writing can be of enormous help to some individuals with learning disabilities.

information-processing model   A theory of learning and MEMORY that examines the way people take in, store, and retrieve information based on a computer model. This theory can be reduced to a three-step process:

1. Input or encoding (taking in information)
2. Storage (transferring information into long-term memory)
3. Retrieval (taking information out of long-term memory and expressing it)

A person's senses of sight, smell, hearing, taste, and touch are constantly providing information, which is stored in short- and long-term memory. For each of the hundreds of things people do each day, they need to quickly decide what information to use to complete the task. Managing all of the stored information and using it effectively is called "information processing."

See also INFORMATION PROCESSING DISORDERS.

inhibition   The ability to defer responses to unimportant distractions. The ability to control inappropriate responses or strategies while developing more effective or appropriate ones is essential to success in both academic and social settings.

Individuals with ADHD often have difficulty with inhibition, and because of this may express themselves in ways that are impulsive or inappropriate, or may experience difficulty with internal distractibility.

See also DISINHIBITION.

initial blend   The joining of two or more consonant sounds, represented by letters, without losing the identity of the sounds, as in the "bl" sound in *black*. An initial blend also involves the joining of the first consonant and vowel sounds in a word, as "b" and "a" in *baby*. Many experts believe this process is a crucial step in learning phonics.

insertions   Words or letters that an individual incorrectly includes in a sentence when reading orally. An example might be reading "blank" for

"bank" or, instead of reading "It was night," reading "It was a dark night."

instructional reading level   The reading ability or grade level of material that is challenging, but not frustrating, for the student to read successfully with normal classroom instruction and support. Although this may vary, a student should score better than 95 percent word-identification accuracy and better than 75 percent comprehension in order to be considered as reading at this level.

intelligence   As commonly used, intelligence refers to the level of intellectual functioning and capacity of an individual—the ability to learn or understand.

Recently some experts have suggested that intelligence is not a single phenomenon, but that there exist "multiple intelligences"—a number of discrete "intelligences"—and that an individual will possess a unique pattern of strengths and abilities across this range of intellectual functions.

In the context of a LEARNING DISABILITY, the concept of intelligence is important for two reasons. First, there can often be significant discrepancies between intellectual ability and academic performance. Second, learning disabilities have often been misunderstood as a sign of lower intelligence despite extensive research and the achievement of many notable individuals with learning disabilities, such as Albert Einstein, Thomas Edison, and Nelson Rockefeller.

Intelligence is measured by intelligence tests, which provide an INTELLIGENCE QUOTIENT (IQ), a measure of intellectual development that is the ratio of a child's mental age to his chronological age, multiplied by 100.

intelligence quotient (IQ)   A measurement of intelligence based on performance on intelligence tests. Use of intelligence testing remains controversial because of the limitations of testing for specific abilities and knowledge, and because of possible cultural bias in the design of tests.

Nonetheless, IQ is used in educational and psychological settings in combination with other types of tests in order to evaluate an individual's mental capacity and to recommend appropriate remediation or treatment.

For individuals with LEARNING DISABILITY, IQ scores can demonstrate superior intelligence despite weak language skills or poor academic performance. Conversely, poor performance on intelligence tests can inaccurately reflect true ability and potential, with many capable individuals outperforming the level of achievement their IQ scores might have predicted.

IQ is generally based on a mean of 100, with scores ranging in classification from mentally retarded at the low end to very superior at the high end.

The concept of intelligence has existed for centuries, but it wasn't until this century that scientists began testing it—and debating whether or not they should. Intelligence testing was developed in the late 19th century as France's Alfred Binet began work on tests of individual differences, which led him to study "subnormal" children in Paris schools. Several years later, Binet and Paris physician Theodore Simon recommended that an accurate diagnosis of intelligence be established for schoolchildren. The result was the Simon-Binet test of intelligence, which first appeared in 1905 and was revised in 1908.

Binet thought of the test as a tool for selecting students who needed special remedial teaching, not as a measure of absolute and innate ability. The test was translated into English for the American audience in 1908 by Henry H. Goddard and revised several times, but it was not until 1916 that the test was standardized with the revision by Lewis M. Terman in the form known as the Stanford-Binet test.

In 1911, William Stern developed the idea of relating mental age to chronological age with his formulation of the Intelligence Quotient. This simple formulation of IQ = MA/CA x 100 gave a number to stand for the performance of the child. This allowed the IQ to be manipulated within statistical tests and to be used for prediction of later performance.

During World War I, the first massive use of psychological tests of intelligence was begun with the testing of military recruits. Hundreds of psychologists and graduate students in psychology were recruited to administer the tests to recruits. After the war, critics were outraged to find that the army test suggested that southern and eastern Europeans were inferior to northern Europeans, and that blacks were inferior to whites. Some believe it was these test results that prompted restrictive immigration policies in America in 1924 and fanned the flames of racial prejudice against blacks and other minorities.

David Wechsler developed his tests in response to many of the criticisms of the Binet tests. In 1939, he introduced his Wechsler Adult Intelligence Scale (WAIS), the first of a stable of tests still much in use.

Since that time there have been many intelligence tests produced, some specifically aimed at reducing cultural and background effects on pencil-and-paper tests. In 1969, the debate about the inherent versus the environmental bases of intelligence exploded with an article by psychologist Arthur Jensen in which he argued for the inheritance of racial differences in intelligence. The debate continued into the last decade of the 20th century in response to further controversial work on intelligence and class structure in American life. In recent years, influential books by psychologist Howard Gardner and others have supported multiple intelligences over a single global factor in intelligence.

interim alternative educational setting (IAES)

Because students with disabilities must not be suspended for longer than 10 days, when such a student needs to be disciplined, an IAES is an alternative to suspension.

Most students with disabilities are disciplined as are any other students, but in certain extraordinary circumstances, a suspension longer than 10 days would require education in an IAES. School officials may place students with disabilities in an alternative educational setting with or without parental consent. The interim alternative educational setting is determined by the INDIVIDUALIZED EDUCATION PROGRAM COMMITTEE and allows the student to continue to participate in general educational programs and receive special services as outlined on the IEP. If suspension is necessary for a longer period, an IAES must be put into place for up to 45 days.

internalization   The incorporation of external information within an individual's thought processes, emotions, and behavior. Internalization may be positive, such as when an individual internalizes positive feedback and forms a more positive self-image. Internalization may also be used to denote the process of acquiring specific skills or strategies, such as keeping a daily schedule or automatically proofreading written work.

Often, however, internalization refers to taking in negative feedback and self-images, as when a student who struggles to succeed in school internalizes the notion that academic failure is inevitable and lies beyond his or her control.

intervention   See EARLY INTERVENTION PROGRAM.

invented spelling   An attempt to spell an unknown word based on a child's knowledge of the spelling system and how it works. Invented spellings are often used as an instructional strategy in beginning writing, as the child moves toward controlled use of conventional spelling of words. For example, invented spelling for the word "because" may look like: bekuz, bcus, or beekuz.

The concept of invented spelling is controversial, however. Proponents believe invented

spelling is a natural development of writing, and that by encouraging students to use invented spelling, they are freed from the burden of perfection so they can express their thoughts more easily. Critics believe invented spelling should not be encouraged because it may interfere with learning proper spelling from reading, or with learning specific spelling rules.

inversion   A confusion in the directionality of letters or numbers. For example: "m" for "w" or "6" for "9," in reading, spelling, or mathematics.

IQ   See INTELLIGENCE QUOTIENT.

itinerant teacher   A SPECIAL EDUCATION teacher who works in several schools within an area or district. It is not an uncommon practice for special services to be spread across a district, especially when part-time personnel are employed. For small schools, itinerant teachers may include district music, art, and physical education teachers, who may visit each school once a week.

For students with special learning needs, special educators are an important part of the child's INDIVIDUAL EDUCATION PROGRAM (IEP). Special services are mandated by the local and federal agencies, and must be reevaluated periodically. This creates fluctuations in staffing and the services provided in each school on an annual basis.

While itinerant teachers can provide the necessary special instruction for each student, it is more difficult for children to develop ongoing relationships with such teachers, depending on the contact hours, if the teachers are not available more informally. This type of service provision can also make children more self-conscious about their learning differences, as it calls attention to their need for special instruction by teachers who visit the school for the sole purpose of providing direct services and participating in IEP conferences.

Kaufman Test of Educational Achievement
This test for children in grades one through 12 measures decoding of letters and individual words, spelling, reading comprehension, math computation, and the ability to answer math reasoning questions. The K-TEA is most useful in students beyond first grade, since there are too few lower level questions to adequately assess a first grader with poor skills.

Key Math Diagnostic Arithmetic Test–Revised This test is designed for students from age five through 15 years, 11 months, to assess their knowledge of basic mathematical concepts such as numbers, fractions, decimals, percentages, geometric shapes, principles, addition, subtraction, multiplication, division, mental computation, measurement, time and money estimation, interpretation, and problem solving.

kinesthetic One of the body's senses that refers to the acquisition of information from body movements. Like other forms of learning, kinesthetic learning involves the input of stimuli to specific channels in the brain, in this case through the motion of joints and muscles. Kinesthetic learning is best understood through movements that have been made automatic through practice and repetition, or made unconscious and automatic, such as throwing a baseball or driving a car.

For individuals with strengths in kinesthetic learning, reinforcement of learning in basic skill areas might be supplemented with a kinesthetic approach, such as walking or dancing move-ments used to represent concepts or steps in a sequence, to aid recall.

Kurzweil reading machine A device that provides both sound and visual presentation of scanned text and images on a computer screen; considered to be the world's first consumer product to successfully incorporate artificial intelligence technology. Text can be imported into the program by scanning or typing directly into the machine. Once text is in the program, users can adjust features such as reading speed, reading units, highlighting, and voices to preferred settings.

Additional study features such as highlighters, note creation, and built-in dictionary make the device a powerful active reading tool.

The first Kurzweil Reading Machine, which was introduced in 1976, was basically a scanner that contained a camera that could move in both vertical and horizontal directions. As the camera automatically moved back and forth scanning each line of print, it transmitted the image electronically to a minicomputer in a separate cabinet. The minicomputer recognized the characters, grouped them into words and computed the pronunciation of each word. To accomplish this last task, several hundred pronunciation rules were programmed in, along with several thousand exceptions. The resulting string of sounds (phonemes) was sent to a speech synthesizer, which articulated each word.

Subsequent models of the KRM were substantially improved, but they are organized in a similar way.

Today, the user simply places a document face down on the machine, presses start, and listens. The KRM can control the movement of the scanner, back it up, make it reread sections or spell out words, and provide a variety of other functions.

Within 10 years, the technology is expected to improve so that a full print-to-speech reading machine will be produced that can fit in a pocket. The device will simply be held over the page to be scanned, and snap a picture of the page. All of the electronics and computation will be inside this small camera-sized device. The student can then listen to the text being read from a small speaker or earphone.

It should also be possible to snap a picture and read a poster on a wall, street sign, soup can, an ID badge, or an appliance LCD display—and many other examples of real-world text. This reading machine should cost less than a thousand dollars and will ultimately come down to a few hundred dollars.

language An organized system of symbols that represents objects, actions, feelings, processes, and relationships. Every language has rules that govern how that language is used.

language delay A lag in the development of communication skills, progressing more slowly than would be expected based on age, environment, or specific deprivation or disease. Children with a LEARNING DISABILITY are likely to have LANGUAGE delays. Language delay includes the diagnostic subgroups of language disorder, language and learning disability, MENTAL RETARDATION, and AUTISM.

language development Changes in the features of a LANGUAGE over time because of contact with other languages or technological advancements, as the growth of technical terms in English after the Industrial Revolution.

language disabilities A range of deficits in linguistics, whether related to expressive language, written or oral, receptive language, or auditory processing, the processing of sounds and meaning.

language disorder A developmental disorder involving disabilities of reception, integration, recall, and/or production of language. Language disorders may be spoken, written, or both.

See also LEARNING DISABILITY.

language processing disabilities The most common type of LEARNING DISABILITY; children with this problem may have trouble with any aspect of language, such as:

• hearing words correctly
• remembering verbal material
• understanding the meaning of words
• communicating clearly

Children with this problem have trouble with the spoken word, which usually interferes with reading and writing when these children first start school. This learning problem may range from mild to extremely severe—so difficult that these children may find that coping with reading and writing is like learning a foreign language. They may be slow in learning to speak, and speak in brief sentences, and their memory for verbal directions may be poor.

Many children with this problem may speak in a garbled fashion because their brains may have trouble sorting out the right sounds; these children may pronounce "elephant" as "efelunt." They may have a poor grasp of grammar and trouble with word sequencing in a sentence, and may confuse words that sound alike. These types of errors usually get worse if they must speak in public or before an authority figure.

laterality The awareness of both sides of one's body.

See also LATERAL PREFERENCE.

lateral preference The development of a preference for one side of the body, also sometimes called "lateral dominance" or "lateralization." This preference develops very early in life, and is expressed most prominently in "handedness" (the dominant hand that a child uses for activities such as writing or throwing a ball).

In some cases, lateralization is not clear, and an individual will express a mixed lateral preference—writing with one hand, for example, and throwing a ball with the other.

lead poisoning One of the most common preventable diseases in the United States. Repeated exposure to low levels of lead can lead to a LEARNING DISABILITY. The brain is most sensitive to lead during the first six years of life, when the brain cells are rapidly developing. Nearly one million U.S. children have lead levels in their blood that are high enough to cause irreversible damage to their health.

Lead can be ingested from dust, soil, and lead-based paint flecks in old homes. In fact, more than 80 percent of homes built before 1978 have lead paint, and the older the house, the more likely it is to contain lead-based paint. In public playgrounds and in yards, the dirt where children play may contain high lead levels. For decades, peeling exterior building paint, air emissions from leaded car exhaust, and pollution from smelters and other industries have been significant sources. The highest levels of lead in soil usually are found close to foundations of homes painted with exterior leaded paint.

In addition, lead is still found in low levels in some drinking water as a result of a lead-based solder on old water pipes. The Environmental Protection Agency estimates that drinking water is the source of about 20 percent of Americans' lead exposure. Even after lead pipes were banned, leaded solder was legal for use on drinking water lines until the 1980s and is still for sale in hardware stores. Faucets and plumbing fittings may legally contain up to 8 percent lead.

The greatest risk is to infants using formula mixed with contaminated water.

Lead-glazed pottery that hasn't been properly fired also can allow lead to leach into whatever comes into contact with it, and lead can be found in some folk remedies, "health foods," and cosmetics.

Because young children are often crawling and mouthing objects, they are more likely to ingest lead; moreover, a child's smaller body size means a higher dose of lead per exposure. At the same time, a child is not as capable of clearing lead from the body, so the body's concentration builds up.

While the symptoms of severe lead poisoning are obvious, repeated exposures to small amounts can also cause poisoning but may not be as easily detectable. There may be no visible symptoms of lead poisoning in this instance that would alert parents to seek medical care.

There is new evidence that lead poisoning is harmful at blood levels once thought safe. Lower IQ scores, slower development, and more attention problems have been observed in children with lead levels as low as 10 micrograms per deciliter. (Micrograms per deciliter, written µg/dL, indicate the amount of lead in a deciliter of blood.)

The symptoms of low levels of lead poisoning are low IQ scores, decreased attention span, poor hearing, speech delays, and other developmental problems.

Screening

The Centers for Disease Control and Prevention (CDC) recommends testing every child at 12 months of age and, if resources allow, at 24 months. Screening should start at six months if the child is at risk of lead exposure (for example, if the child lives in an older home built before 1960, which has peeling or chipping paint). Decisions about further testing should be based on previous blood-lead test results, and the child's risk of lead exposure. In some states, more frequent lead screening is required by law. The Centers for Disease Control and

Prevention in 1991 identified a number of reasons for testing a child for lead poisoning, including

- child lives or regularly visits a house built before 1960 and being renovated, or that has peeling, chipped paint
- sibling or classmate is being treated for lead poisoning
- child lives with someone whose hobby or work includes exposure to lead, such as making pottery or stained glass and working in auto repair or bridge or highway construction
- child lives near industry likely to release lead
- child received treatment for foreign object in ear, nose, or stomach
- child often swallows nonfood items
- any child under six with unexplained developmental delays, hearing problem, irritability, severe attention deficit, violent tantrums, or unexplained anemia

The test will identify how many micrograms of lead are found in one deciliter of the child's blood. Based on what is known today, children should have under 10 micrograms per deciliter (10 µg/dL) of blood lead concentration. If higher levels are found, there are certain steps that can be taken.

At 10–19 µg/dL, a child has mild lead poisoning and should be retested in a few months. The home and all the places the child spends time should be checked for lead sources, and identified lead hazards should be controlled. Frequent wet cleaning and handwashing will help reduce lead dust. Good nutrition can help the child fight lead.

A blood lead level between 20 and 44 means the child has moderate lead poisoning. Sources of lead in the child's environment must be removed, and the child may need chelation therapy to remove lead from the body. Chelation therapy means the child is given a drug capable of binding lead and reducing its acute toxicity.

All drugs have potential side effects and must be used with caution.

A blood lead concentration of 45 to 69 is severe lead poisoning. A child with this concentration needs both medical treatment and lead removed from the environment.

A blood lead level over 70 is an acute medical emergency. The child may stay in the hospital for treatment and not be released until he or she can return to a lead-free, safe home.

Treatments

If a thumb-prick blood test reveals a high lead level, a blood sample taken from a vein must be tested before chelation therapy begins.

Prevention

To prevent further lead poisoning, parents should keep children away from peeling or chipping paint and chewable surfaces painted with lead-based paint, especially windows, window sills, and window wells. Parents should wet mop and wet wipe hard surfaces, using trisodium phosphate detergent (found at hardware stores) or automatic dishwasher soap and water. Hard surfaces should not be vacuumed because this is believed to scatter dust. If inspection shows a house has lead-based paint, the family should not renovate or attempt to remove the paint themselves. Work should be done by someone who knows how to protect workers, the family, and the environment. The family should not be in the home during renovations or paint removal.

Parents should wash children's hands and faces before meals and wash toys and pacifiers frequently. Children should eat regular nutritious meals, since more lead is absorbed on an empty stomach. Children's diets should contain plenty of iron, such as liver, fortified cereal, cooked beans, spinach, and raisins. Calcium is also important (including foods like milk, yogurt, cheese, and cooked greens).

If soil around the home is likely to be contaminated (if a home was built before 1960 or near a major highway), parents should plant grass or other ground cover. If lead-based paint is the source of soil contamination, most lead will be near painted surfaces such as exterior walls. In such cases, parents should plant bushes next to the house to keep children away. If the soil is contaminated with lead, parents should provide a sandbox with a solid bottom and top cover, and clean sand for children to play and dig in.

If the lead content of tap water in the home is higher than the drinking water standard, parents should let the water run for several minutes (until the temperature changes) before using. Only fully flushed water from the cold-water tap should be used for drinking and cooking. To conserve water, parents should collect drinking water in bottles at night after water has been fully flushed from the tap. This procedure will help if the source of lead is from the home's plumbing, but it won't help if the city water supply is contaminated.

Parents should not store food in open cans (especially imported cans), nor in pottery that is meant for decorative use, or in lead crystal or china.

If members of the family work with lead, they should make sure children aren't exposed to any lead-contaminated clothing or scrap material brought home.

learned helplessness   A conditioned response that creates problems in thinking, motivation, and emotions in children with learning disabilities. The theory of learned helplessness was developed in the 1960s after researchers observed the phenomenon in dogs. During their research, scientists used electric shocks when the dogs tried to leave their cage. Later, when the dogs were provided a way out, they made no effort to escape. This "giving up" after a period of negative consequences was termed "learned helplessness."

Many studies have suggested that children with a LEARNING DISABILITY develop learned helplessness in academic settings as a result of continual failure in school. This failure also leads to withdrawal, unwillingness to approach new tasks, depression, and a lack of persistence. Like the dogs in the study, students who have developed learned helplessness may apply this maladaptive behavior to new situations where they should be capable of academic success, but instead believe their efforts are useless. Learned-helpless children see failure as permanent—it is caused by lack of ability, about which they can do nothing. They also believe failure is present in everything they do.

Other factors have been shown to contribute to this learned academic helplessness:

- grouping students with a variety of disabilities under one teacher
- too much external reinforcement
- lack of early identification of learning disabilities
- belief that intelligence can't be changed
- lack of reward for individual effort

The concept of learned helplessness is tied to the idea of control. Individuals who may be defined as having learned helplessness essentially believe that their performance is outside their control—that no matter what they do, they will fail. As a result of continual academic failure, some students with learning disabilities come to expect failure regardless of their effort. This expectation can erode motivation. Often, students who exhibit learned helplessness also tend to believe that the responsibility for learning rests entirely with the teacher.

The cure for learned helplessness is not the rediscovery of the power of positive thinking; positive statements alone, without first dealing with underlying negative beliefs, will have little effect. If a student is to conquer learned helplessness, the individual must change the destructive things he says to himself when he fails.

Treatment

It is what the child thinks about his failure and its cause that leads to learned helplessness. In other words, it's not just the failure, but the way the child sees the failure, that is important. This is one of the reasons why it is possible to treat learned helplessness.

Cognitive behavioral training teaches a child to recognize his automatic negative thoughts and then to change these thoughts by gathering evidence to the contrary. The child should be taught to

- make different explanations (reattributions) and use them to dispute automatic thoughts
- distract himself from the thoughts that depress him
- change unrealistic, demanding assumptions to realistic, flexible ones

Research has shown that the most productive learners are those who believe intelligence can be changed and that effort is just as powerful as ability in achieving success.

learning centers An instructional part of a classroom organized by tables, in which a teacher arranges learning materials such as worksheets or games. Learning centers are also known as "teaching stations" or "instructional stations." Children can complete these activities on their own to supplement their other classroom learning experiences.

Learning Disabilities Association National nonprofit membership organization dedicated to enhancing the quality of life for everyone with a LEARNING DISABILITY and their families, and offers advocacy, education, research, and services.

Formerly known as the Association for Children and Adults with Learning Disabilities, LDA was formed in 1964 by a group of concerned parents on behalf of children with learning disabilities. LDA is the only national organization devoted to defining and finding solutions for the broad spectrum of these problems.

Contact: 4156 Library Road, Pittsburgh, PA 15234-1349; phone: (412) 341-1515; website: http://www.ldanatl.org.

learning disability A neurobiological disorder in which a person's brain works or is structured differently, affecting one or more of the basic processes involved in understanding or using spoken or written LANGUAGE. Such a disability may result in a problem with listening, thinking, speaking, reading, writing, spelling, or doing mathematical calculations. Experts believe that children with learning disabilities have a problem with the way the brain handles information, which in turn hinders the normal learning process.

Learning disabilities affect one in seven people, and represent a national problem of enormous proportions. Every year, 120,000 additional students are diagnosed with learning disabilities, a diagnosis now shared by 2.4 million schoolchildren in the United States. Many thousands more are never properly diagnosed or treated, or don't get treatment because they are not considered eligible for services.

The most common learning disability is difficulty with language and reading. A recent National Institutes of Health study showed that 67 percent of young students identified as being at risk for reading difficulties were able to achieve average or above-average reading ability when they received help early.

All children learn in highly individual ways. Children with learning disabilities simply process information differently, but they are generally of normal or above-average intelligence.

Sometimes overlooked as "hidden handicaps," learning disabilities are often not easily recognized, accepted, or considered serious once detected. The impact of the disability, which often runs in families, ranges from relatively mild to severe. Learning disabilities can be lifelong conditions that, in some cases, affect many parts of a person's life: school or work, daily routines, friendships, and family life. In some people, many overlapping learning disabilities may be apparent, while others may have a single, isolated learning problem that has little impact on other areas of their lives.

Learning disabilities are not the same as MENTAL RETARDATION, AUTISM, deafness, blindness, or behavioral disorders. Nor are learning disabilities caused by poverty, environmental factors, or cultural differences. Learning disabilities are not curable, but individuals can learn to compensate for and even overcome areas of weakness. Attention deficits and hyperactivity sometimes appear with learning disabilities, but not always.

Common learning disabilities include:

- dyslexia: a language-based disability in which a person has trouble understanding words, sentences, or paragraphs.
- dyscalculia: a mathematical disability in which a person has a very difficult time solving arithmetic problems and grasping math concepts.
- dysgraphia: a writing disability in which a person finds it hard to form letters correctly or write within a defined space.
- auditory and visual processing disabilities: a sensory disability in which a person has difficulty understanding language despite normal hearing and vision.

More than one in six children will experience a problem learning to read during the first three years in school, according to the U.S. Department of Education. Currently, more than 2.8 million school-age children receive SPECIAL EDUCATION services as students with learning disabilities, which represents about 5 percent of all children in public schools. However, these statistics don't include the tens of thousands of students who attend private and religious schools, nor do they include the scores of students who may have serious problems with learning, but who may not meet the criteria established by school districts to receive special education services.

Symptoms

The earlier a learning disability is detected, the better chance a child will have of succeeding in school and in life. Parents are encouraged to understand the warning signs of a learning disability from as early as preschool, since the first years in school are especially crucial for a young child.

However, the very definition of "learning disability" hinders its identification with young children. The crucial element in identifying learning disabilities is their effect on academic performance, but the problems learning disabilities cause aren't apparent until the child goes to school. How can a learning disability in reading be identified when a child is too young to be taught to read? With young children, the range of what is "normal" is so wide that it is extremely difficult in most cases, and impossible in others, to tell the difference between simple developmental immaturity and a learning disability.

There is no one indication of learning disabilities. Although most children have an occasional problem with learning or behavior, a consistent pattern of the following problems may suggest the need for further testing:

Preschool

If the child has problems

- learning the alphabet
- rhyming words
- connecting sounds and letters
- counting or learning numbers
- being understood when speaking to a stranger
- using scissors, crayons, or paint
- reacting too much or too little to touch
- using words or using phrases
- pronunciation
- walking up and down stairs
- talking (identified as a "late talker")
- remembering names of colors
- dressing

Elementary School

Does the child have trouble with

- learning new vocabulary
- speaking in full sentences
- understanding conversation rules
- retelling stories
- remembering information
- playing with peers
- moving from one activity to another
- expressing thoughts
- holding a pencil
- handwriting
- handling math problems
- following directions
- self-esteem
- remembering routines
- learning
- reading comprehension
- drawing or copying shapes
- deciding what information presented in class is important
- modulating voice
- neatness and organization
- meeting deadlines
- playing age-appropriate board games

Adulthood

Does the adult have trouble with

- remembering new information
- organization
- reading comprehension
- getting along with peers or coworkers
- finding or keeping a job
- sense of direction
- understanding subtle jokes
- making appropriate remarks

- self-expression
- following directions
- reading, writing, spelling, and math
- self-esteem
- using proper grammar
- meeting deadlines

Symptoms may appear in only one skill area, such as reading or writing, in many people with learning disabilities. The following is a brief outline of warning signs for possible learning disabilities in specific skill areas:

Attention
- has short attention span
- is impulsive
- has difficulty conforming to routines
- is easily distracted

Auditory
- doesn't respond to sounds of spoken language
- consistently misunderstands what is being said
- overly sensitive to sound
- has trouble differentiating simultaneous sounds

Language
- can explain things orally but not in writing
- has trouble telling or understanding jokes or stories
- misinterprets language
- doesn't understand what is said
- responds in an inappropriate manner, unrelated to what is said
- responds only partially to what is said

Math
- problems with arithmetic, math language, and math concepts
- reverses numbers

- problems with time, sequencing, or problem solving

Memory
- learns information presented one way but not another
- trouble memorizing information
- unable to repeat what has just been said

Movement
- performs similar tasks differently each day
- has trouble dialing phone numbers or holding a pencil
- has poor coordination, is clumsy
- is unaware of physical surroundings
- has a tendency to self-injury

Organization
- has trouble following a schedule
- is often late
- has trouble learning about time
- has difficulty organizing belongings

Reading
- poor reading ability or poor comprehension
- may misread information
- problems with syntax or grammar
- confuse or reverse similar letters or numbers
- problems reading addresses, small print, and/or columns

Social
- has trouble with social skills
- misinterprets nonverbal social cues
- experiences social isolation
- doesn't use appropriate eye contact

Thinking Skills
- acquires new skills slowly
- has trouble following directions

- confuses right/left, up/down, under/over, behind/between
- gets lost in large buildings
- seems unaware of time or sequence of events

Writing
- problems writing down ideas
- problems organizing thoughts on paper
- reverses or omits letters, words, or phrases when writing
- problems with sentence structure, writing mechanics
- may spell the same word differently in a single paper
- may read well but not write well (or vice versa)

It's important to remember most people have one or more of the above warning signs and experts aren't worried if a child has one or two of these symptoms. Experts get more concerned if a child has many of these symptoms, especially if the child is older or symptoms are severe.

What Isn't LD

It's also important to understand what isn't included in the LD category. For example, although attention deficit disorder and ATTENTION DEFICIT/HYPERACTIVITY DISORDER are not learning disabilities themselves, there is a 20 percent probability that someone with ADD or ADHD also has one or more learning disabilities. Other conditions that are not considered to be learning disabilities themselves include autism, blindness and deafness, emotional problems, hyperactivity, illiteracy, mental retardation, "slow learner," or physical disability.

Diagnosis

"LD" is a broad term that covers a range of possible causes, symptoms, and treatments. Partly because learning disabilities can show up in so many forms, it is difficult to diagnose or to pinpoint the causes. And since a diagnosis depends on the classification used, (IDEA vs. *Diagnostic and Statistical Manual of Mental Disorders*), a child may be identified as learning disabled under one system but not another.

Not all learning problems are necessarily learning disabilities; many children are simply slow to develop certain skills. Because children show natural differences in their rate of development, sometimes what seems to be a learning disability may simply be a delay in maturation or a difference in learning style. To be diagnosed as a learning disability, specific criteria must be met. These criteria appear in the *Diagnostic and Statistical Manual of Mental Disorders* (DSM) and IDEA. DSM divides learning disorders into three broad categories: developmental speech and language disorders, academic skills disorders, and "other," a term that includes certain coordination disorders and learning handicaps not covered by the other terms. Each of these categories includes a number of more specific disorders.

IDEA uses a slightly different classification system that specifies seven areas of learning disability:

- basic reading skill
- reading comprehension
- mathematics calculation
- mathematics reasoning
- written expression
- oral expression
- listening comprehension

Under IDEA, each area of learning disability is divided by the "severe discrepancy between potential and achievement" the law requires.

Developmental Speech and Language Disorders

Speech and language problems are often the earliest indicators of a learning disability. While not classified as learning disabilities themselves, they often accompany learning disabilities. People with developmental speech and language disorders have trouble producing speech sounds, using spoken language to communicate, or understanding what other people say. Depending on the problem, the specific diagnosis may be:

- developmental articulation disorder
- developmental expressive language disorder
- developmental receptive language disorder

With a *developmental articulation disorder,* children may have trouble controlling their rate of speech, or they may lag behind their friends in learning to make speech sounds. These disorders are common, appearing in at least 10 percent of children younger than age eight. Fortunately, articulation disorders can often be outgrown or successfully treated with speech therapy.

Some children with *developmental expressive language disorder* have problems expressing themselves in speech, such as calling objects by the wrong names, speaking only in two-word phrases, or not being able to answer simple questions.

Some people have trouble understanding certain aspects of speech; this is *developmental receptive language disorder.* This explains the toddler who doesn't respond to his name or the worker who consistently can't follow simple directions. While hearing is normal, these individuals can't make sense of certain sounds, words, or sentences. Because using and understanding speech are strongly related, many people with receptive language disorders also have an expressive language disability.

Of course, some misuse of sounds, words, or grammar is a normal part of learning to speak. It's only when these problems persist that there is any cause for concern.

Academic Skills Disorders

Students with academic skills disorders often lag far behind their classmates in developing reading, writing, or arithmetic skills. The diagnoses in this category include:

- developmental reading disorder
- developmental writing disorder
- developmental arithmetic disorder

Developmental reading disorder (also known as dyslexia) is quite widespread, affecting between 2 percent and 8 percent of elementary school children. The ability to read requires a rich, intact network of nerve cells that connect the brain's centers of vision, language, and memory. While a person can have problems in any of the tasks involved in reading, scientists have found that a significant number of people with dyslexia share an inability to distinguish or separate the sounds in spoken words. For example, a child might not be able to identify the word "cat" by sounding out the individual letters, c-a-t, or to play rhyming games. Fortunately, remedial reading specialists have developed techniques that can help many children with dyslexia acquire these skills. However, there is more to reading than recognizing words. If the brain can't form images or relate new ideas to those stored in memory, the reader won't be able to understand or remember the new concepts. This is why other types of reading disabilities can appear in the upper grades when the focus of reading shifts from word identification to comprehension.

Writing, too, involves several brain areas and functions. The brain networks for vocabulary, grammar, hand movement, and memory must all work well if the child is to be able to write well. A *developmental writing disorder* may be caused by problems in any of these areas. A child with a writing disability, particularly an expressive language disorder, might be unable to compose complete, grammatical sentences.

Arithmetic involves recognizing numbers and symbols, memorizing facts such as the multiplication table, aligning numbers, and understanding abstract concepts like place value and fractions. Any of these may be difficult for children with *developmental arithmetic disorders*. Problems with numbers or basic concepts are likely to show up early, whereas problems that appear in the later grades are more often tied to problems in reasoning.

Many aspects of speaking, listening, reading, writing, and arithmetic overlap and build on the same brain capabilities. So it's not surprising that people can be diagnosed as having more than one area of learning disability. For example, the ability to understand language underlies the ability to learn to speak. Therefore, any disorder that interferes with the ability to understand language will also interfere with the development of speech, which in turn hinders learning to read and write. A single problem in the brain's operation can disrupt many types of activity.

"Other" Learning Disabilities

There are additional categories of learning disabilities, such as "motor skills disorders" and "specific developmental disorders not otherwise specified." These diagnoses include delays in acquiring language, academic, and motor skills that can affect the ability to learn but do not meet the criteria for a specific learning disability. Also included are coordination disorders that can lead to poor penmanship, as well as certain spelling and memory disorders.

Attention Disorders

Nearly 4 million school-age children have learning disabilities; of these, at least 20 percent also have a type of disorder that leaves them unable to focus their attention. Some children and adults who have attention disorders are easily distracted or appear to daydream constantly. Children with this problem may have a number of learning difficulties.

In a large proportion of affected children (mostly boys) the attention deficit is accompanied by hyperactivity, running into traffic, or toppling desks. Hyperactive children can't sit still: they blurt out answers, they interrupt, they can't wait their turn. Because of their constant motion and explosive energy, hyperactive children often get into trouble with parents, teachers, and peers. By adolescence, physical hyperactivity usually subsides into fidgeting and restlessness, but the problems with attention and concentration often continue into adulthood.

At work, adults with ADHD often have trouble organizing tasks or completing their work. They don't seem to listen to or follow directions. Their work may be messy and appear careless.

Attention disorders (with or without hyperactivity) aren't considered learning disabilities in themselves, but, because attention problems can seriously interfere with school performance, they often accompany academic skills disorders.

Causes

Experts don't know exactly what causes learning disabilities, but they are assumed to be disorders of the central nervous system triggered by many different factors. These may include heredity, problems during pregnancy or birth, and incidents after birth.

The fact that learning disabilities tend to run in families indicates that there may be a genetic link. For example, children who lack some of the skills needed for reading, such as hearing the separate sounds of words, are likely to have a parent with a related problem. However, a parent's learning disability may take a slightly different form in the child. A parent who has a writing disorder may have a child with an expressive language disorder. For this reason, it seems unlikely that specific learning disorders are inherited directly. Instead, what is inherited might be a subtle brain dysfunction that can lead to a learning disability.

There may be an alternative explanation for why LD might seem to run in families. Some learning difficulties may actually stem from the family environment. For example, parents who have expressive language disorders might talk less to their children, or the language they use may be distorted. In such cases, the child lacks a good model for acquiring language and, therefore, may seem to be learning disabled.

LD problems also may be caused by illness or injury during or before birth, or by the use of drugs and alcohol during pregnancy, untreated Rh incompatibility with the mother, premature or prolonged labor, or lack of oxygen or low weight at birth.

Throughout pregnancy, the fetal brain develops from a few cells into a complex organ made of billions of specialized, interconnected nerve cells called neurons. During this process, things can go wrong that may alter how the neurons form or interconnect.

In the early stages of pregnancy, the brain stem forms the part of the brain that controls basic functions such as breathing and digestion. Later, a deep ridge divides the cerebrum (the thinking part of the brain) into two halves, a right and left hemisphere. Finally, the areas involved with processing sight, sound, and other senses develop, as well as the areas associated with attention, thinking, and emotion.

As new cells form, they move into place to create various brain structures. Nerve cells rapidly grow to form networks with other parts of the brain. These networks allow information to be shared among various regions of the brain.

Throughout pregnancy, this brain development is vulnerable to disruptions. If the disruption occurs early, the fetus may die or the infant may be born with widespread disabilities and possibly mental retardation. If the disruption occurs later, when the cells are becoming specialized and moving into place, it may leave errors in the cell makeup, location, or connections. Some scientists believe that these errors may later show up as learning disorders.

Scientists have found that mothers who smoke during pregnancy may be more likely to bear smaller babies, who tend to be at risk for a variety of problems, including learning disorders. Alcohol also may be dangerous to the fetus's developing brain, distorting the developing neurons. Heavy alcohol use during pregnancy has been linked to FETAL ALCOHOL SYNDROME, a condition that can lead to low birth weight, intellectual impairment, HYPERACTIVITY, and certain physical defects. Any alcohol use during pregnancy may influence the child's development and lead to problems with learning, attention, memory, or problem solving. Drugs such as cocaine (especially crack cocaine) seem to affect the normal development of brain receptors that help to transmit incoming signals from skin, eyes, and ears. Because children with certain learning disabilities have trouble understanding speech sounds or letters, some researchers believe that learning disabilities (as well as ADHD) may be related to faulty receptors. Current research points to drug abuse as a possible cause of receptor damage. Other research indicates that mothers exposed to toxins such as pesticides and even substances normally considered harmless (such as caffeine) can interfere with fetal development. Children born to these mothers have a higher frequency of learning problems. This area of research is highly controversial.

After birth, learning disabilities may be caused by head injuries, nutritional deprivation, poisonous substances, or child abuse. New brain cells and neural networks continue to be produced for a year or so after the child is born, and these cells are vulnerable to certain disruptions, too.

Some environmental toxins may lead to learning disabilities, possibly by disrupting childhood brain development or brain processes. Cadmium and lead, both prevalent in the environment, are becoming a leading focus of neurological research. Cadmium, used in making some steel products, can get into the soil, then into food. Lead was once common in paint and gasoline, and is still present in some water pipes. A study of animals sponsored by the National Institutes of Health showed a connection between exposure to lead and learning difficulties. In the study, rats exposed to lead experienced changes in their brainwaves, slowing their ability to learn. The learning problems lasted for weeks, long after the rats were no longer exposed to lead.

In addition, there is growing evidence that learning problems may develop in children with cancer who had been treated with chemotherapy or radiation at an early age. This seems particularly true of children with brain tumors who received radiation to the skull.

Treatment

By law, a learning disability is defined as a significant gap between a person's intelligence and the skills the person has achieved at each age. This means that a severely retarded 10-year-old who speaks like a six-year-old probably doesn't have a language or speech disability. He has mastered language up to the limits of his intelligence. On the other hand, a fifth grader with an IQ of 100 who can't write a simple sentence probably does have a learning disability.

Learning disorders may be informally flagged by observing significant delays in the child's skill development. Psychologists generally determine delays in the development of academic skills by comparing the statistical relationship between the IQ and achievement tests. If this statistical relationship is not known, psychologists must resort to less reliable ways of comparing potential and actual achievement. One alternative procedure is to simply compare IQ scores with the standard scores children obtain on achievement scales. The problem with this procedure is that directly comparing IQ and achievement test standard scores does not take into account how strongly the IQ and achievement test may be related. If a child's IQ is 85, for example, the predicted standard score in basic reading may be 90 on one test and 94 on another. Using a direct comparison of IQ and standard scores assumes that all IQ tests are related to all achievement tests to the same degree.

Parents and professionals should each gather information and discuss concerns about a child who is struggling with learning problems. The child's parents should arrange for a comprehensive psychoeducational evaluation, which can take place only with the parent's written consent. Evaluations can help identify the child's relative strengths and difficulties, and help determine whether the student is eligible for special assistance in school.

When parents and school staff agree, the public school system must provide an evaluation to determine if a student is entitled to special education services. Evaluations can be arranged for free through the school system, or through private clinics, private evaluators, hospital clinics, or university clinics. However, some school districts may not automatically accept test results from outside sources. Parents should check with their school district before seeking evaluation services from private facilities.

The actual diagnosis of learning disabilities is made using standardized tests that compare the child's level of ability to what is considered normal development for a person of that age and intelligence. Test outcomes depend not only on the child's actual abilities, but also on the reliability of the test and the child's ability to pay attention and understand the questions.

Each type of LD is diagnosed in slightly different ways. To diagnose speech and language disorders, a speech therapist tests the child's pronunciation, vocabulary, and grammar and compares them to the developmental abilities seen in most children that age. A psychologist tests the child's intelligence. A physician checks for any ear infections, and an audiologist may be consulted to rule out auditory problems. If the problem involves articulation, a doctor examines the child's vocal cords and throat. In the case of academic skills disorders, academic development in reading, writing, and math is evaluated using individually administered standardized tests. In addition, vision and hearing are tested to be sure the student can see words clearly and can hear adequately. The specialist also checks if the child has missed much school. It's important to rule out these other possible factors. After all, treatment for a learning disability is very different from the remedy for poor vision or missing school.

ADHD is diagnosed by checking for the long-term presence of specific behaviors, such as considerable fidgeting, losing things, interrupting, and talking excessively, and by ruling out medical factors that may sometimes cause the same behavioral symptoms. Other signs include an inability to remain seated, stay on task, or take turns. A diagnosis of ADHD is made only if the child shows such behaviors substantially more than other children of the same age.

If the school fails to notice a learning delay, parents can request an outside evaluation. Federal law requires school districts to maintain lists of sources for outside evaluations that can be obtained at public expense. Parents are also free to seek private evaluations by qualified individuals. By federal law, school districts must consider the results of any outside evaluation, although they may challenge the validity of those results, the qualifications of the examiner, or the appropriateness of the conclusions reached by the evaluator. After confirming the diagnosis, the public school is obligated to provide an appropriate educational program.

Parents should stay abreast of each step of the school's evaluation, and they may appeal the school's decision if they disagree with the findings of the diagnostic team. Parents always have the option of getting a second opinion. However, even when parents decide to obtain an outside evaluation, school districts must follow the same procedures required by federal law before they place a child in special education. For example, school districts must try to intervene with a child's learning problems for a reasonable period of time and document that their strategies for overcoming the problems aren't working. An outside evaluator's recommendation for immediate placement can't take precedence over such requirements. In addition, even if parents get an outside evaluation, the decision to classify or not classify a child as "learning disabled" rests with the placement team, to which the parents belong. Parents are free to appeal the decision to classify or to not classify and, if they lose, they may take court action. But contrary to the common perception, a private evaluator may not dictate classification and placement to the placement team.

Remediation

Although a diagnosis is important, even more important is creating a plan for getting the right help. Schools typically provide special education programs either in a separate all-day ("self-contained") classroom or as a special education class that the student attends for several hours each week ("resource classes"). Some parents hire trained tutors to work with their child after school. If the problems are severe, some parents choose to place their child in a special school for the learning disabled. However, a child's school district is not obligated to pay for this placement unless the district agrees to the placement, or they are directed to pay as the result of a due process hearing or court action. Parents can't simply decide on their own to place their child into a facility and expect reimbursement from their local school district.

Planning a special education program begins with systematically identifying what the student can and can't do. The specialist looks for patterns in the child's gaps, such as the failure to hear the separate sounds in words or other sound discrimination problems. Special education teachers also identify the types of tasks the child can do and the senses that function well. By using the senses that are intact and bypassing the disabilities, many children can develop needed skills. These strengths offer alternative ways in which the child can learn.

After assessing the child's strengths and weaknesses, the special education teacher designs an INDIVIDUALIZED EDUCATION PROGRAM (IEP). The IEP outlines the specific skills the child needs to develop as well as appropriate learning activities that build on the child's strengths. Many effective learning activities engage several skills and senses. For example, in learning to spell and recognize words, a student may be asked to see, say, write, and spell each new word. The student may also write the words in sand, which engages the sense of touch. Many experts believe that the more senses children use in learning a skill, the more likely they are to retain it.

An individualized, skill-based approach often succeeds in helping where regular classroom instruction fails. Therapy for speech and language disorders focuses on providing a stimulating but structured environment for hearing and practicing language patterns. For example, the therapist may help a child who has an articulation disorder to produce specific speech sounds. During an engaging activity, the therapist may talk about the toys, then encourage the child to use the same sounds or words. In addition, the child may watch the therapist make the sound, feel the vibration in the therapist's throat, then practice making the sounds before a mirror.

Assistive Technology

Learning disabilities can't be cured, but with the help of certain tools a child with a learning disability can work around difficulties with reading, writing, numbers, spelling, organization, or memory. Complex, high-tech tools and devices, called ASSISTIVE TECHNOLOGY, can help people work around specific deficits.

Tools for people with learning disabilities can be as simple as highlighters, color coding files or drawers, books on tape, tape recorders, calculators, or a different paper color or background color on a computer screen. Sometimes standard technologies (such as voice recognition systems) can be adapted or designed to help people with learning disabilities perform everyday tasks. Complex assistive technology includes talking computers that help people with reading and writing difficulties, speech recognition systems that translate oral language into written text, talking calculators that assist people with math difficulties, and software that suggests spelling for people with spelling difficulties.

Researchers are also investigating nonstandard teaching methods. Some create artificial learning conditions that may help the brain receive information in nonstandard ways. For example, in some language disorders, the brain seems abnormally slow to process verbal information. Scientists are testing whether computers that talk can help teach children to process spoken sounds more quickly. The computer starts slowly, pronouncing one sound at a time. As the child gets better at recognizing the sounds and hearing them as words, the sounds are gradually speeded up to a normal rate of speech.

History

Early in the 20th century, certain children had come to the attention of a British physician, eye surgeon James Hinshelwood, M.D., who tried to correlate his knowledge of patients who had received head injury from disease or trauma with the similar symptoms he saw in children with reading problems. In 1917 he published research in which he used "word blindness" to refer to dyslexia.

In the early 1930s, American psychiatrist Samuel Orton, M.D., refused to accept the belief that emotional difficulties were behind learning problems. He noted, for example, that children with learning problems often displayed "mixed laterality," and suggested that the failure of one hemisphere of the brain to become dominant caused the disorder. Today, factors around hemispheric dominance are still considered important in the field of learning disabilities.

After World War I, an encephalitis epidemic left a number of cases of brain damage, which lead to the description of the disorganized and erratic behavior associated with hyperactivity. In 1947, German neurologist and psychiatrist Alfred Strauss described this syndrome in children, noting both perceptual and abstract reasoning problems. Although for a time hyperactivity was described as "Strauss syndrome," the terms "brain damaged" and "brain injured" became common.

In 1959, noting perceptual and learning similarities in patients with cerebral palsy and other neurological handicaps, researchers in the field proposed the term "cerebral dysfunction" to include cerebral palsy, mental retardation, and what was then called "hyperkinetic behavior disorder," characterized by irritability, short attention span, purposeless activity, and poor school work in reading, arithmetic, and handwriting.

In 1963, American experts began planning a series of task forces to investigate learning disabilities, in part because of parental pressure.

Certainly since 1968 the field of learning disabilities has been characterized by conflict and confusion, as the original focus and the term "learning disability" stretched to include all children who were underachieving for any reason. On the other hand, it is very possible that this "exclusion clause" has had the effect of excluding from appropriate programs children with learning disabilities who have come from disadvantaged backgrounds. Often the learning problems of such children would be diagnosed only in terms of their deprived environment, and not looked at in the real context of physiological causes. Thus, learning disabilities have tended to become a middle-class phenomenon—while the child of the middle class would be diagnosed as having a learning disability, a child of the slums would automatically be considered deprived. Unfortunate also has been the designation of learning disabilities as solely an educational problem and not a medical or health problem.

In 1981, a position paper on the definition was prepared by the National Joint Committee for Learning Disabilities (NJCLD), composed of five major and concerned organizations in the United States. The NJCLD urged that the disorders represented by the collective term "learning disabilities" be understood as intrinsic to the individual, and that the basis of the disorders be presumed to be due to central nervous system dysfunction.

Controversy

The term "learning disability" was coined by psychologist Samuel A. Kirk in 1963 to describe children who experience difficulty acquiring academic skills despite normal intelligence. He proposed this term because of his discomfort with the widespread use in an educational setting of medically oriented terms such as DYSLEXIA, congenital word blindness, reading and math retardation, and MINIMAL BRAIN DYSFUNCTION. Although the term has become widely accepted, there has been a great deal of controversy about the exact definition and methods of assessment and identification of the condition.

The term has provided a focal point for legislation and advocacy that has resulted in far-reaching changes in the nature of public and postsecondary education in the United States. At the same time, the term "learning disabilities," the range of potential learning problems that it includes, and the broad and rapidly changing field that it describes, continue to be controversial. In fact, there is still no consensus on the definition of learning disabilities or on what the category should include or exclude, and the coming years are likely to see continuing debate on the fundamental issues of definition, classification, diagnosis, and treatment.

According to the National Joint Committee on Learning Disabilities (NJCLD), the term refers to a group of disorders marked by significant difficulties in listening, speaking, reading, writing, reasoning, or mathematical abilities. These disorders are presumed to be caused by central nervous system dysfunction, and may occur at any time. Although learning disabilities may appear at the same time as other handicapping conditions (such as deafness, blindness, mental retardation, or serious emotional disturbance), they aren't caused by these conditions.

The primary legal definition of a learning disability, according to Public Law 94–142 (as amended by Public Law 101–76), indicates a disorder in one or more of the basic psychological processes involved in understanding or in using spoken or written language. This may include an imperfect ability to listen, think, speak, read, write, spell, or to do mathematical calculations. The term includes such conditions as perceptual handicaps, brain injury, minimal brain dysfunction, dyslexia, and developmental aphasia. The term does not include children who have problems primarily caused by visual, hearing, or motor disabilities, or by mental retardation, emotional disturbance, or by environmental, cultural, or economic disadvantage.

Most definitions suggest that learning disabilities are permanent, affect a range of language and mathematics functions, and are caused at least in part from problems within the central nervous system. In addition, definitions of LD have generally focused on two key identifying factors: discrepancy and exclusion.

"Discrepancy" means that a child with a learning disability exhibits a significant gap between aptitude and performance. In many states, a diagnosis of a learning disability depends on a very strict statistical measurement of this discrepancy between achievement and aptitude.

Unfortunately, Congress has never provided any guidance as to what it meant by the requirement of "a severe discrepancy between potential and achievement," which has led to widely differing practices for making such a determination.

"Exclusion" means that a learning disability is not caused by some other handicapping condition, such as physical impairment or social status. A child who struggles to learn because she can't see, or because he comes from a background of poverty and disadvantage, is not considered to have a learning disability if these are the primary factors in the learning problems.

Both the discrepancy formulation for learning disabilities, and the role that exclusion of other conditions plays, have become subjects for increasing debate in recent years. Many researchers have proposed redefining the concept of learning disabilities to focus on specific language and thought processing problems that may be identified by appropriate testing, without necessarily involving the question of aptitude or intellectual potential.

Some experts have argued that the exclusionary element in definitions of LD has led to the under-identification or misdiagnosis of individuals who come from poverty or from minority cultural, racial, or ethnic backgrounds. They argue that the difficulties such children have in learning are more likely to be caused by their backgrounds and upbringing than to a potential learning disability, and that approaches to diagnosis that depend on aptitude/achievement discrepancies are also likely to underrepresent such individuals.

A third major area of controversy has to do with excluding social and behavioral disabilities from standard definitions of learning disabilities, and to excluding ADHD from this general category. This debate is highlighted by the difference between the NJCLD definition quoted above and the following definition from the National Institute of Mental Health:

> Learning Disabilities (LD) is a disorder that affects people's ability to either interpret what they see and hear or to link information from different parts of the brain. These limitations can show up in many ways—as specific difficulties with spoken and written language, coordination, self-control, or attention. Such difficulties extend to schoolwork and can impede learning to read or write, or to do math.
>
> Learning disabilities can be lifelong conditions that, in some cases, affect many parts of a person's life: school or work, daily routines, family life, and sometimes even friendships and play. In some people, many overlapping learning disabilities may be apparent. Other people may have a single, isolated learning problem that has little impact on other areas of their lives.

The continuing controversy and debate that surrounds the concept of learning disabilities is complicated by different disciplines and theoretical perspectives, as well as the advocacy of parents, economic pressures on school districts, and political and legal developments. These controversies are likely to continue in the years to come.

Treatment for learning disabilities is extremely important if the child is to be successful. In fact, 35 percent of students with untreated learning disabilities don't finish high school, and drop out before they receive transitional vocational services to help them get a job. Most students with learning disabilities weren't fully employed one year after graduating from high school. Adolescents with untreated learning disabilities are at higher risk for drug and alcohol abuse. One study showed that up to 60 percent of adolescents in treatment for substance abuse had learning disabilities.

Even though learning disabilities can't be cured, there is still cause for hope. Because certain learning problems reflect delayed development, many children do eventually catch up.

Of the speech and language disorders, children who have an articulation or an expressive language disorder are the least likely to have long-term problems. Despite initial delays, most children do learn to speak. For people with dyslexia, the outlook is mixed. But an appropriate remedial reading program can help learners make great strides. With age, and appropriate help from parents and clinicians, children with ADHD become better able to suppress their hyperactivity and to channel it into more socially acceptable behaviors.

Federal Protection

As of 1981, people with learning disabilities were included under the protection of laws originally designed to protect the rights of people with mobility handicaps. More recent federal laws specifically guarantee equal opportunity and raise the level of services to people with disabilities. Once a learning disability is identified, children are guaranteed a free public education specifically designed around their individual needs. Adolescents with disabilities can receive practical assistance and extra training to help make the transition to jobs and independent living. Adults have access to job training and technology that open new doors of opportunity.

The INDIVIDUALS WITH DISABILITIES EDUCATION ACT of 1990 assures a public education to school-age children with diagnosed learning disabilities. Under this act, public schools are required to design and implement an individualized education program tailored to each child's specific needs. The 1991 IDEA extended services to developmentally delayed children as young as five. This law makes it possible for young children to receive help even before they begin school.

The AMERICANS WITH DISABILITIES ACT of 1990 guarantees equal employment opportunity for people with learning disabilities and protects disabled workers against job discrimination. Employers may not consider the learning disability when selecting among job applicants, and must make "reasonable accommodations" to help workers who have handicaps do their job. Such accommodations may include shifting job responsibilities, modifying equipment, or adjusting work schedules.

By law, public colleges and universities must remove barriers that keep out disabled students. As a result, many colleges now recruit students with learning disabilities. Depending on the student's areas of difficulty, the school may offer help including recorded books and lectures, providing an isolated area to take tests, or allowing a student to tape rather than write reports. Students with learning disabilities can arrange to take college entrance exams orally or in isolated rooms free from distraction. Many colleges are creating special programs to specifically accommodate these students.

Local school districts can help parents identify the requirements and the process for getting special education services for their child. If parents don't get the answers here, they can contact their state department of public instruction. Other agencies serve disabled infants and preschool children, while still others offer mental health and counseling services. The National Information Center for Children and Youth can provide referrals to appropriate local resources and state agencies.

Counselors at each state department of vocational rehabilitation serve the employment needs of adolescents and adults with learning disabilities. They can refer adults to free or subsidized health care, counseling, and high school equivalence (GED) programs. They can assist in arranging for job training that sidesteps the disability. State departments of vocational rehabilitation can also assist in finding special equipment that can make it possible for disabled individuals to receive training, retain a job, or live on their own.

Finally, state-run protection and advocacy agencies and client assistance programs serve to protect these rights. As experts on the laws, they offer legal assistance, as well as information about local health, housing, and social services. School districts must maintain lists of agencies and organizations that parents can contact for help in obtaining services for a child suspected of having a handicap.

Consequences

People with learning disabilities who have not been diagnosed or properly treated, experience serious, lifelong negative consequences including low self-esteem, delinquency, and illiteracy. Thirty-five percent of students identified with learning disabilities drop out of high school (this doesn't include students who drop out without being identified as having learning disabilities). Fifty to 80 percent of adults with severe literacy problems have undetected or untreated learning disabilities. Fifty percent of young criminal offenders tested were found to have previously undetected learning disabilities; when offered educational services that addressed their learning disability, the recidivism rates of these young offenders dropped to below 2 percent.

learning disorder   A more specific term than LEARNING DISABILITY, but without the same legal weight. A learning disorder may include any of a broad spectrum of dysfunctions in the ability to learn, including some syndromes and difficulties that are not generally grouped under the category of learning disabilities.

Learning disorders refer to the specific mental processes involved in learning problems. For example, the inability to remember information that the student hears in a specific order (referred to as a disorder in auditory-sequential memory) would be referred to as a learning disorder.

learning modalities   The way in which information is received and expressed, such as visual, tactile, auditory, or kinesthetic. Generally, individuals have strengths in a certain modality and learn better when information is presented through that channel. For example, an individual whose strongest learning modality is visual will have difficulty learning information given by lecture alone, with no visual aids such as notes on the board.

Research shows that since people have different learning strengths, it is better to design lessons that use more than one modality, such as a combination of visual and auditory. This allows all learners, including those with learning disabilities, to access information using their strongest learning modality.

learning strategies   The idea that *how* an individual learns is more important than *what* he or she learns. This is an especially useful approach with individuals who have a LEARNING DISABILITY and who may not learn efficiently.

Learning strategies include the cognitive (thinking) aspect of learning as well as the behavioral (actions) aspect of learning to help individuals in planning, executing, and evaluating a learning task. Components of teaching learning strategies would include teaching individuals to be active participants in their learning, encouraging collaborative learning, and utilizing questioning to aid in comprehension.

learning style   An individual's behavior, temperament, and attitude in a learning situation. Some of the best-known learning styles are visual, auditory, or kinesthetic. Some experts argue that it is important to match an individual's learning style with the style of instruction to make learning easier. For example, an individual with a strong visual learning style should be taught to read with an emphasis on the shapes of words.

There are many different learning styles, but none are either "right" or "wrong." Although a student may prefer one style over another, pref-

erences develop like muscles: the more they are used, the stronger they become. Successful students have flexible and integrated learning styles. No one uses one of the styles exclusively, and there is usually significant overlap in learning styles.

Visual learners relate most effectively to written information, notes, diagrams, and pictures. Typically they will be unhappy with a presentation where they can't take detailed notes. To a degree, information does not exist for a visual learner unless it has been seen written down. This is why some visual learners take notes even when they have printed notes in front of them. Visual learners will tend to be most effective in written communication. They make up about 65 percent of the population.

Auditory learners relate most effectively to the spoken word. They tend to listen to a lecture and then take notes afterward, or rely on printed notes. Because written information will often have little meaning until it's heard, it may help auditory learners to read written information out loud. Auditory learners may be sophisticated speakers, and may specialize in subjects like law or politics. Auditory learners make up about 30 percent of the population.

Kinesthetic learners learn best through touch, movement, and space, and learn skills by imitation and practice. Kinesthetic learners can appear slow, because information is usually not presented in a style that suits their learning methods. Kinesthetic learners make up around 5 percent of the population.

learning style inventory   A test or questionnaire that tries to assess the way a person learns (LEARNING STYLE). Understanding a person's learning style can help a teacher develop appropriate ways to teach.

There are many learning style inventories available, such as the Myers-Briggs Personality Type Indicator, based on Carl Jung's theories of conscious functioning, or the Grasha-Riechmann Student Learning Style Scales, developed by Anthony Grasha and Sheryl Riechmann, who designed a test to assess adolescent differences by focusing on how students interact with teachers and colleagues with respect to their learning processes.

Interest in learning style inventories has increased since the growth in popularity of a multiple intelligences perspective to learning.

least restrictive environment (LRE)   The setting where a pupil with a disability can be educated with no more segregation than is absolutely necessary. Students with disabilities should have the opportunity to participate as fully as possible in school and school activities with classmates who aren't disabled.

The concept of "least restrictive environment" is one of the most confusing and controversial in education for children with disabilities. As originally formulated in Public Law 94–142, children with disabilities were to be guaranteed a "free appropriate public education" in the "least restrictive environment," but it was not clear what that meant.

The concept was more fully described in the INDIVIDUALS WITH DISABILITIES EDUCATION ACT (IDEA), which required that learning disabled students be placed, when appropriate, in settings with regular (non-special education) students to provide maximum opportunities to learn in the least restrictive environment. The IEP team must make these decisions of placement when writing the IEP (INDIVIDUALIZED EDUCATION PROGRAM). Settings in regular education programs are considered less restrictive than in special programs/schools.

Generally, there is a presumption that a child with a disability should be served in the regular classroom with as much interaction with non-handicapped classmates as possible, although some disagree. According to current federal law, a child with a disability may be removed from the regular classroom only when the nature or severity of the disability is such that the education in regular classes cannot be achieved satis-factorily, even with the use of supplementary aids and services.

However, for specific areas of intensive training or if a child's handicap makes him disruptive to others, it is appropriate to remove a child from the regular classroom. For example, a child with a reading disability may appropriately be educated in most academic areas in the regular classroom with assistance in note taking and test taking, but it may be necessary to remove the child from the classroom to work in a small group or one-on-one, specifically in the area of reading. The child's placement and services depend on the child's individual needs, not on administrative convenience.

Before a student's least restrictive environment is determined, the student's educational needs must be identified. This is the job of the CHILD STUDY COMMITTEE, made up of the student's parents, teacher, school administrator, and others who know the student. After the team determines the student's educational strengths and needs, it develops annual program goals and objectives, which are part of the individualized education program (IEP). Only after the IEP is developed does the team consider the placement options. In fact, the IEP drives all aspects of the child's educational program.

There must be compelling educational reasons, based on the individual student's educational needs, for removing the student from the regular classroom. Those reasons must be listed on the IEP.

legally blind   A legal term that is used to determine eligibility for services. Many individuals who are legally blind are not totally blind, but have—and use—some vision.

legal rights/protection   See INDIVIDUALS WITH DISABILITIES EDUCATION ACT; REHABILITATION ACT OF 1973.

letter formation problems   See DYSGRAPHIA.

letter recognition The ability to recognize all letters in the alphabet, the building blocks of words and sentences. Early readers and individuals with learning disabilities may confuse visually similar letters such as "b" and "d" or "m" and "n." Letter recognition is an important pre-reading skill that leads to word recognition in the decoding process. It is generally introduced in preschool or kindergarten.

As young children master the alphabet song and recite their ABCs, they must also learn to identify the shapes that represent those sounds. Children are often quick to recognize the letters in their names, but other letters may be less familiar.

lifetime education A philosophy of education that suggests learning needn't be restricted to a certain period of a person's life. Instead, people should engage in learning activities throughout their lives.

limbic system A combination of neural structures folded around the top of the brainstem that is linked to the development of learning disabilities. It is involved in the production of emotional responses connected to fear and aggression, and is also associated with interest in food, drink, and sex. It includes the hippocampus, the amygdala, and the hypothalamus.

linguistic approach A method of teaching reading and spelling that uses similar word patterns (word families). The linguistic approach emphasizes the predictability and regularity of English word patterns by incorporating them in sentences and stories such as "The fat cat sat on the big mat."

linguistics The formal study of language, including the sound system, development, and function of human languages. Linguistic theory and the understanding of natural language processing provided by linguistics are essential to understanding how language processing may differ for individuals with language-based learning disabilities.

listening comprehension level The highest grade level of material that can be understood well when it is read aloud to a student. Listening comprehension level, measured by reading successively more difficult passages to a student, is useful in estimating the student's potential silent reading level. Although the suggested criteria vary, better than 75 percent comprehension is often used as a standard in judging whether a student understands material at this level.

listening vocabulary The number of words a person understands when they are heard in speech; also, hearing vocabulary, sometimes called "receptive vocabulary."

literacy The ability to read and write in a person's native language. The development of literacy is fairly recent in terms of human history; the first literate cultures appeared about 5,000 years ago. The development of literacy made possible the transmission of culture and scientific knowledge, historical chronicles, and stories and poetry, across generations in a relatively stable form. Many of the advances of global civilization are indebted in major ways to the role of literacy.

Before the rise of literacy, the transmission of culture was by word of mouth. Many famous texts such as the Homeric epics and the Bible first existed and were transmitted in oral form before they were written down. Until the most recent century, literacy was primarily limited to those within the socioeconomic elite of various cultures. Even today, the illiteracy rate is very high in many Third World countries and among disadvantaged individuals in industrialized nations.

The rise of universal public education in Western industrial nations during the 1800s set the stage for a much broader literacy within the general population. It is not surprising that it was during this period that reading problems among some schoolchildren were first described. These early investigations were the first steps toward understanding the nature of dyslexia and learning disabilities.

Illiteracy continues to be a major social problem in the United States, and is the focus of many contemporary movements toward reform in public school systems. However, the causes of illiteracy are complex, relating to social, economic, and cultural factors that schools are not capable of addressing independently. The role that undiagnosed learning disabilities play in the rate of illiteracy is most likely significant.

Local Education Agency (LEA) A formal term for a designated school district, as differentiated from the state education agency (SEA).

locus of control A motivational term related to that source to which people attribute their successes or failures. People with an internal locus of control believe they are responsible for their own successes and failures, whereas people with an external locus of control would most often blame (or thank) fate, destiny, luck, society, or some other force beyond their control. Locus of control has great influence on a person's motivation, expectations, self-esteem, risk-taking behavior, and even on the actual outcome of actions. Determining a person's locus of control is important in helping to address the individual's problems.

Children's motivation at school is linked to their belief in whether they have control over personal successes and failures. Children won't try hard if they believe they have no control over the outcome of the situation.

That influence extends to students with high ability as well as to students with low ability. For example, students with high ability but with an external locus of control attribute their early successes in school to fixed inborn ability.

These students come to believe that they can coast on their inborn ability and that they will never make low grades because of that inborn ability. These students sometimes begin to earn drastically lower grades in middle school and high school than they did in elementary school because middle and high school grades are more performance-based, and because they don't feel any obligation to put forth strong effort.

Many children will fall between these two extremes of internal and external locus of control, and possess characteristics of each type. A child's locus of control tells a lot about his behavior, actions, and motivations. An internalizer will do much better at school and in life than an externalizer, while an externalizer will think mistakes at school are caused by work that's too hard. Believing nothing can be done, this child will not try hard. Externalizers develop lower expectations, choose easier challenges, and give up quickly. These feelings of helplessness will extend to other situations and influence the child's outlook, attitudes, and motivation toward all activities.

Without a feeling of control or influence on what other people think, these children won't contact new people or try to repair friendships when problems occur.

An internalizer will expect to do well as a result of hard work, and will easily initiate conversations and play with other children. Internalizers will take the lead in solving problems and learning to share, reciprocate, and get along with others. An internalizer will excel at school and do better than other children of equal intelligence.

Whether a child is an internalizer or externalizer is partly due to the parents' attitudes. A child's locus of control begins to develop at infancy, when they start to learn if they have control over the world around them. The more a child's crying is ignored during the first years, the more likely a child will feel powerless. As the child grows, parents should continue to nurture the child's locus of control. Encouraging independence will go a long way toward making your child an internalizer. Children who are allowed to make decisions, go places, and are given time to solve everyday problems tend to become internalizers. Children who are not granted these privileges usually become externalizers.

Externalizers will often have a dominating mother and father who make all the necessary decisions for them.

long-term memory The long-range storage of information in memory on a relatively permanent basis. A person can store an indefinite number of chunks of information in long-term memory in interconnected semantic networks.

What a person chooses to store in long-term memory is probably closely tied to the emotions. In fact, the LIMBIC SYSTEM, which mediates emotion in the brain, is highly involved in memory function. Because humans generally seek pleasure and shun pain, we tend to repeat something that is rewarding (remember it) and avoid what is painful (forget it).

Researchers divide long-term memory into three types: procedural, semantic, and episodic. Procedural memory is the ability to remember how to do something (such as ride a horse or write a letter). Semantic memory involves remembering factual information, such as the capital of Oregon or the multiplication tables. It has no connection to where or when we learned the information. Episodic memory involves remembering personal events, such as a first kiss or where one learned to ride a bike.

Long-term memory differs from short-term memory in more than the length of time that a memory is able to be retrieved. The nerve changes involved in long-term memory may be different; the process is not easily disrupted and its capacity is virtually unlimited. Retrieval from short-term memory is virtually automatic, but retrieval in long-term memory is not easy or always automatic.

M

mainstreaming The placement of disabled students in the regular education classroom, or in activities such as sports, field trips, or school programs, with nonhandicapped students. Mainstreaming was introduced in the 1970s as a result of PUBLIC LAW 94–142, which mandated that special needs children be placed in the LEAST RESTRICTIVE ENVIRONMENT. Until the approval of PL 94–142 in 1975, most special needs children (from mildly to severely disabled) were educated in self-contained settings.

The philosophy of mainstreaming disabled children into the regular classroom comes from the idea that, since most individuals will be "mainstreamed" into society, the integration of regular and special needs students should begin at an early age. It was also believed that school resources could be used more efficiently if special needs students were placed in the regular classroom. Mainstreaming also required regular educators to share the responsibility for disabled students with special educators. Conversely, mainstreaming benefits regular education students by increasing their understanding and tolerance of students with differences.

Longitudinal studies of mainstreaming over the past two decades indicate that mainstreaming is defined differently depending on the school and school district. In most school systems, mainstreaming involves placing a special needs student in the regular classroom setting for one subject area or a portion of the day depending on what is best for the student. According to research, mainstreaming can be a valid alternative to self-contained classrooms, but it is not an appropriate practice for all special needs students. A delicate balance must be struck among the student's need, teacher training, attitudes toward mainstreaming, and cost factors.

Most students with learning disabilities are educated in the regular classroom while receiving support services. Although parents sometimes worry that their children's needs will not be met in a regular classroom setting, mainstreaming does not mean that special-education students are "dumped" into classes indiscriminately. Rather, students are placed in a regular classroom with support services so they can perform adequately. The concept of mainstreaming is a response to the fact that students can benefit from regular classroom placement if they get additional assistance at the same time. Forms of assistance might be an aide, modification of instruction, more instruction time, and communication with the regular classroom teacher.

Parents of nondisabled children often complain that the disabled child might disrupt the class or take up too much of the teacher's time. Both are legitimate concerns, and if any child is so disruptive he interferes with the functioning of the class, then intervention is necessary. In fact, recent court decisions have established the school's right to remove disruptive students to more restrictive settings if they are preventing others from learning.

Considerable time, energy, and planning go into every successful mainstreaming experience. Parents must be advocates for their children and provide input about the type and amount of mainstreaming that takes place, and they need to forge positive relationships with school personnel. This should be done during the development and implementation of the individualized education program.

Mainstreaming works when

- parents and teachers work together
- specific mainstreaming experiences are recorded in the child's IEP
- special education teachers meet with regular classroom teachers in the mainstreamed setting
- mainstream teachers get information on the special education student's strengths, needs, and techniques considered helpful for the student's particular learning disability
- mainstream teachers have time to consult with special education teachers to discuss student progress
- regular students are given information to better understand students with special needs

manic depression   See BIPOLAR DISORDER.

mapping   In educational terms, a strategy for displaying related ideas in a visual format. Mapping may refer to flow charts, diagrams, or using color-coding to draw connections and help recall information. One important example of mapping is "mind-mapping" (also called clustering), which is used in the process of writing to generate and organize ideas and information that can eventually be translated into a linear outline.

A mind map might consist of a core topic at the center of the page, with major subtopics spreading outward from it, and relevant details attached to each subtopic. Such an approach may be especially helpful for individuals who have difficulty with sequencing information but are strong in the area of visual-spatial reasoning.

Likewise, a GRAPHIC ORGANIZER for representing information may help a student who has trouble with reading comprehension because of problems organizing and identifying key information and relationships between concepts and supporting evidence.

margin notes   Notes placed in the margins of texts in order to paraphrase main ideas or important details in the reader's words. Margin noting is an effective way to become an active reader. By condensing information in the reader's own words, margin notes serve to enhance comprehension, boost recall, and simplify reviewing.

mastery   Learning a skill to the point where an individual uses the skill automatically, consistently, and without cuing, in a variety of contexts. Mastery of a specific skill can be measured in a number of ways. One such measurement may be a mastery test, which is designed to assess the application of a specific skill.

In order to master material, children need to be appropriately placed and given adequate instruction. The following four criteria should be used to place children appropriately in an instructional setting:

1. A child should understand material taught with 70 percent correctness.
2. A child should score 90 percent on material previously taught and reviewed.
3. Children should complete material in a "lesson" in the anticipated amount of time and shouldn't need more practice.
4. Children should completely understand material presented at the end of each lesson.

These criteria are rarely met in a school setting in which classes are heterogeneous, with children of varying abilities, and when individual instruction time may be limited. Proponents of DIRECT INSTRUCTION suggest that rote drill and practice is required for mastery of basic skills. Nonetheless, children often are moved from one grade level to the next without mastering skills or course content.

mathematics disorder A disorder in which mathematical ability, as measured by individually administered standardized tests, is substantially below what is expected given the child's chronological age, intelligence, and education level. The disorder significantly interferes with academic achievement and with activities of daily living that require mathematical ability.

math facts Basic addition, subtraction, and multiplication, the automatic recall of which helps speed up computation.

math manipulatives Objects such as blocks, coins, or buttons that students can use to help them learn math.

math phobia A fear or anxiety about learning mathematics.

math skills Mathematics is a core academic curriculum, which typically is taught sequentially through each grade level. The sequence of math skills starts from simple and concrete (counting and classification in kindergarten) to more complex and abstract skills (scientific notation in middle school).

Sound math instruction should include teaching concepts, skills, and problem solving rather than an accumulation of computation skills. Math skill development requires opportunities for practice and review, learning to generalize skills to a variety of situations, and understanding math vocabulary.

To master arithmetic, children must understand numbers (that is, the quantity that each number represents), counting, the conceptual (such as understanding the base-10 number system) and procedural (such as borrowing from one column to the next) features involved in solving simple and complex arithmetic problems.

Just when and how children acquire these skills is fairly theoretical, although most current research supports Jean Piaget's theory that youngsters develop math concepts in four stages. Although recent research has revised Piaget's timeline, the sequence remains the same. Piaget's stages are

1. sensorimotor: birth to two years (manipulates objects, uses trial and error, thinks through solutions mentally)
2. preoperational: two to four years (uses reason, but not logic)
3. concrete operational: seven to 11 years (solves concrete problems, can reverse thought process, develops classification skills, learns to sort by category, understands serial order)
4. formal operations: 11 to 15 years and up (uses abstract reasoning, applies logic, solves verbal problems and problems dealing with the future, develops capacity to think scientifically

A learning disability in math can result from problems in learning any one or any combination of these more basic skills. To complicate matters further, it is possible that different children have different patterns of strength and weakness when it comes to understanding and learning these basic skills.

maturation Developmental growth based on chronological aging. Theories based on maturation and development generally suggest that individuals will perform in certain ways at certain stages of development. However, if interpreted or applied too narrowly, such approaches may fail to recognize the wide range in individual development over time.

maturation lag A delay in normal development exists as a core feature of many learning disorders. In general, maturation lag refers to any developmental difficulty in which an element of an individual's intellectual, cognitive, social, or behavioral functioning lags behind that predicted by normal development.

meaning-based instruction   Instruction that is directed toward purposeful reading and writing with an emphasis on comprehension and composition.

mean score   The average score in a grouping of scores. To identify the mean, all scores in a group are added together and then divided by the number of individual scores. For example, a grouping of scores includes the following: 10, 16, 13, 12, 3, 6. These scores are added together for a sum of 60. This sum is then divided by the total number of test scores, in this case six. The mean is said to be 10.

megavitamins and ADHD   The use of very high doses of vitamins and minerals to treat ATTENTION DEFICIT/HYPERACTIVITY DISORDER is based on the theory that some people have a genetic abnormality that requires higher levels of vitamins and minerals.

However, there is a complete lack of supporting scientific evidence for megavitamin treatment for learning disabilities, and there are no well-controlled studies supporting these claims. Both the American Psychiatric Association and the American Academy of Pediatrics have concluded that the use of megavitamins to treat behavioral and learning problems is not justified.

memory   A general term that covers a wide range of cognitive functions related to taking in, processing, storing, and retrieving information. Memory is closely tied to attention, and may also be profoundly influenced by linguistic, auditory, or visual-spatial processing abilities.

In general, types of memory can be categorized in two fashions: first, by the stage in the sequence of processes involved in taking in, storing, and recalling information; and second, by the sensory modality involved in the initial stage of memory input (such as auditory, visual, kinesthetic, and so on).

In terms of stages or types of the cognitive processes involved in memory, present theory identifies three major types of memory: short-term memory, active working memory, and long-term memory. Short-term memory involves immediate storage and processing of information, as a prelude to direct response or manipulating the information in some fashion, or to moving the information into long-term memory, or to shifting attention and forgetting the information. Short-term memory may be auditory or visual in form depending on the nature of the input, or may involve other perceptual systems as well. The capacity of short-term memory is very limited, and the duration in which information is held in short-term memory is brief and measured in seconds.

Active working memory refers to the capacity to hold information in mind, either temporarily storing it while referring to more immediate tasks or information, or focusing on it in reflection, consideration, or some other form of mental manipulation. Active working memory has to do with concentration or focus, and is closely linked to attention. Information sustained and processed in working memory may be verbal or nonverbal in nature. The role of active working memory in a broad range of academic, social, and personal domains is extremely important. It is a fundamental component in the process of writing or reading, for example, and it is active working memory that enables reflection on past behavior or helps us note the passing of time. Current theories regarding attention disorders see the impact that deficits in impulse control have on working memory as a core factor in the symptoms of ADHD.

Long-term memory refers to storage of information in memory on a relatively permanent basis, operating over an extended period of time. In academic settings, success in many areas depends on the ability to recognize and remember salient information, and to transfer this information into long-term memory in a fashion that will enable effective recall on demand, as in a testing situation. In general, long-term memory is not affected directly by learning disabilities or attention disorders. However, the dual ability to move information from short-term memory into long-term memory—and to retrieve information stored in long-term memory—may be significantly affected by a wide range of learning disorders.

memory, active working A type of short-term MEMORY that enables a person to hold information in mind while manipulating or using it. For example, when adding several numbers together, a person might hold the amount "carried" in active working memory while adding a new row of numbers. When learning this skill, children typically are taught to write the "carried" amount above the next number, because they will not yet be able to perform this operation mentally.

Research suggests that remembering gets easier with age because using these processes becomes more automatic after extended use and practice. Active working memory also allows a person to return to earlier steps in a problem-solving sequence so the process can be integrated. Because it has a limited capacity, this kind of memory is linked to attention.

Active working memory is critical to success at school, at home, and in personal relationships, and it's a fundamental component in the process of reading and writing. It enables reflection on past events and helps monitor the passing of time. Individuals who have ADHD or a learning disability that includes difficulties with impulsivity and attention may find it difficult to use active working memory effectively.

mental age A score that equates performance on an intelligence test with the expected mental development for individuals at a specific age. In other words, the individual receives the same number of correct answers on a standardized IQ test as the average person of that age in the sample population.

Saying that an older person with mental retardation is like a person of a younger age, or that a 30-year-old person with mental retardation "has the mental age of a 6-year-old," is not a correct usage of "mental age."

The mental age refers only to the intelligence test score. It does not describe the level and nature of the person's experience and functioning in aspects of community life.

Most intelligence tests have questions that become increasingly challenging and are rated for a specific age. When a child achieves a mental age score of 12, he or she is said to be performing at the level of 12 years of age for the skills measured by the specific test, regardless of actual chronological age.

mental retardation Below-average intellectual functioning abilities as determined by intelligence quotient (IQ) testing, and low adaptive functioning at home or in a work environment. An individual is considered to have mental retardation if IQ is below 70–75; there are significant limitations in two or more adaptive skill areas; and if the condition is present from childhood.

Between 6.2 and 7.5 million people have mental retardation, which is 10 times more common than cerebral palsy and 28 times more prevalent than neural tube defects such as spina bifida. Mental retardation cuts across the lines of racial, ethnic, educational, social, and economic backgrounds; one out of 10 American families is directly affected by mental retardation.

Intelligence testing alone is only one measure of functioning ability. A person with limits in intellectual functioning who does not have limits in adaptive skill areas may not be diagnosed as having mental retardation. "Adaptive skill areas" are those daily living skills needed to live, work, and play in the community. They include communication, self-care, home living, social skills, leisure, health and safety, self-direction, functional academics (reading, writing, basic math), community use, and work. Adaptive skills are assessed in the person's typical environment across all aspects of an individual's life. Psychologists and educators assess adaptive behavior by interviews with people who know the client as well as by scales completed by people who know the client. For example, parents, caregivers, house supervisors, and others who know the client will rate the individual on the Vineland Social Maturity Scales. The Vineland asks many questions regarding the client's abilities in communication, socialization, daily living skills, and (for children 5 and below) motor function.

Many individuals have been diagnosed with mental retardation, particularly at a young age, who are later diagnosed with profound learning disabilities but with average or above-average intelligence. This was much more common before states and federal agencies began to require that the evaluations to identify individuals as mentally retarded use multiple measures, including not only IQ testing but assessment of adaptive behavior.

The effects of mental retardation vary considerably among people, just as the range of abilities varies considerably among people who do not have mental retardation. About 87 percent will be mildly affected and will be only a little slower than average in learning new information and skills. As children, their mental retardation is not easy to see, and may not be identified until school age. As adults, many individuals with mental retardation will be able to lead independent lives in the community.

The remaining 13 percent of people with mental retardation (those with IQs under 50) will have serious limits in function. However, with early intervention, a good education, and appropriate supports as an adult, all can lead satisfying lives in the community.

People with mental retardation may have trouble communicating, interacting with others, and being independent. There may also be concerns with regard to understanding health and safety issues. Not all skills are necessarily impaired, and individuals with mental retardation may learn to function independently in many areas. However, education programs, providing skilled assistance and ongoing support, are necessary for determining appropriate living and work environments.

While the term "mental retardation" still exists as a clinical diagnosis, contemporary usage is moving toward terms such as "developmental disabilities," which some believe do not carry the same negative connotations or misuse. In the past, those who were retarded were traditionally divided by IQ scores into *educable, trainable,* and *custodial;* today, the more commonly used terms include *mild, moderate, severe,* or *profound* categories, based on the level of functioning and IQ. Individuals with mental retardation are not a homogenous group, but have widely differing levels of functioning.

Mild retardation This classification is used to specify an individual whose IQ test scores lie between 55 and 68 or 69, and correspond to an educators' label of "educable retarded." The individual is capable of learning basic academic subjects. Many people with mild retardation are able to live and work independently.

Moderate retardation This classification is used to specify an individual whose IQ test scores are between 40 and 55; it corresponds to the earlier label of trainable retarded. These individuals can usually learn functional academics and vocational skills. They often achieve coached employment goals and live with limited assistance.

Severe and profound mental retardation This classification applies to individuals with IQ scores below 25. These are the most seriously impaired of the mentally retarded, often characterized by physical and sensory impairment as well as mental retardation. They can sometimes achieve supported employment goals; more typically they can function at the level of sheltered employment. They generally require significant assistance with daily living skills.

Diagnosis

Mental retardation is diagnosed primarily on the basis of intelligence testing, but affected individuals often demonstrate other brain problems such as attention deficits, movement problems, and perceptual difficulties. Dexterity and coordination may also be limited.

The first step is to administer standardized intelligence tests and a standardized adaptive skills scale. Next, an expert should describe the person's strengths and weaknesses in intellectual and adaptive behavior skills, emotions, physical health, and environment. These skills can be assessed by formal testing, observations, interviews, and interacting with the person in daily life.

Cause

Mental retardation can be caused by any condition that impairs development of the brain before birth, during birth, or in the childhood years. Several hundred causes have been discovered, but about a third of the time, the cause remains unknown. Mild mental retardation with no known cause occurs often in some families. This is called "cultural-familial" mental retardation. The three major known causes of mental retardation are DOWN SYNDROME, FETAL ALCOHOL SYNDROME, and FRAGILE X SYNDROME.

Genetic conditions These conditions are caused by abnormal genes or from other disorders of the genes caused during pregnancy by infections, overexposure to X rays and other factors. More than 500 genetic diseases are associated with mental retardation, such as

- PKU (PHENYLKETONURIA): a single gene disorder caused by a defective enzyme
- Down syndrome: a chromosomal disorder that happens sporadically, caused by too many or too few chromosomes, or by a change in structure of a chromosome
- fragile X syndrome: a single gene disorder located on the X chromosome that is the leading inherited cause of mental retardation

Problems during pregnancy Alcohol, drugs, or smoking during pregnancy can cause mental retardation. Other risks include malnutrition, certain environmental contaminants, and illnesses of the mother during pregnancy, such as toxoplasmosis, cytomegalovirus, rubella, and syphilis. Pregnant women who are infected with HIV may pass the virus to their child, leading to future neurological damage.

Problems at birth Although any unusual stress during birth may injure the infant's brain, prematurity and low birth weight are more likely to predict serious problems than any other conditions.

Problems after birth Childhood diseases such as whooping cough, chicken pox, measles, and Hib disease (which may lead to meningitis and encephalitis) can damage the brain, as can accidents such as a blow to the head or near drowning. Lead, mercury, and other environmental toxins can cause irreparable damage to the brain and nervous system.

Poverty and cultural deprivation Children in poor families may become mentally retarded because of malnutrition, disease-producing conditions, inadequate medical care, and environmental health hazards. Also, children in disadvantaged areas may be deprived of many common cultural and day-to-day experiences provided to other youngsters. Research suggests that such understimulation can result in irreversible damage and can serve as a cause of mental retardation.

Prevention

It is possible to prevent some forms of mental retardation. During the past 30 years, significant advances in research have prevented many cases of mental retardation. For example, every year in the United States, about 250 cases of mental retardation due to PKU are prevented by newborn screening and dietary treatment. Newborn screening and thyroid hormone replacement therapy prevent 1,000 cases of mental retardation a year due to congenital hypothyroidism; and more than 1,000 cases of mental retardation from Rh disease and severe jaundice are prevented by using anti-Rh immune globulin to prevent Rh disease. The Hib vaccine prevents another 5,000 cases of mental retardation caused by Hib diseases, and 4,000 cases of mental retardation due to measles encephalitis can be prevented because of the measles vaccine. Countless numbers of cases of mental retardation caused by rubella during pregnancy are prevented thanks to the rubella vaccine.

Removing lead from the environment reduces brain damage in children, and child safety seats and bicycle helmets reduce head trauma. Early intervention programs with high-risk infants and children have shown remarkable results in reducing the predicted incidence of subnormal intellectual functioning.

Finally, early prenatal care and preventive measures before and during pregnancy increase a woman's chances of preventing mental retardation. Pediatric AIDS is being reduced by AZT treatment of the mother during pregnancy; and dietary supplementation with folic acid reduces the risk of neural tube defects. Research continues on new ways to prevent mental retardation, including research on the development and function of the nervous system, a wide variety of fetal treatments, and gene therapy to correct the abnormality produced by defective genes.

metacognition The awareness and knowledge of an individual's own mental processes; the ability to think about thinking. Metacognition refers to one's understanding of what strategies are available for learning and what strategies are best used in which situations. It involves the ability to select and manage cognitive strategies effectively. Ordinarily these abilities develop in childhood; children learn that mental activities go along with decision-making. They know when they know something and when they don't.

Metacognition skills are directly related to reading, writing, problem solving, and any process that requires error monitoring. Students must be able to examine how they learn best and what resources they can draw upon in order to set and achieve academic goals.

One of the reasons individuals with learning disabilities tend to have academic difficulties is a lack of skills in selecting and managing task-appropriate strategies. Many theorists and educators believe that these skills can be intentionally taught and developed.

metacognitive awareness In reading, when a child knows that what she is reading makes sense, by monitoring and controlling her own comprehension.

metacognitive learning Knowledge of strategies to enhance an individual's learning. Metacognitive learners know their strengths and weaknesses and can direct their learning accordingly.

Individuals with learning disabilities often lack metacognitive skills, but can greatly benefit from being explicitly taught such skills. Metacognitive learning skills would include the ability to classify, self-monitor, evaluate, and predict their own learning.

Beyond monitoring progress, evaluating how well a person has performed is a metacognitive skill. Because metacognitive learners are aware of their limitations, they can also predict their learning.

methylphenidate hydrochloride See RITALIN.

micro-uniting Breaking a large task into smaller steps. For many learners, especially learning-disabled learners, completing assignments or projects on time can be a challenge. Micro-uniting assignments can make an overwhelming project become manageable by outlining the subtasks necessary and creating a timeline to complete each task.

mild mental retardation Mental retardation in which the IQ level is between 50 and 70. Adults with mild mental retardation typically achieve functional literacy and are able to live independently (or with minimal assistance) in the community.

minimal brain dysfunction (MBD)   A general term used to describe a young child who shows behavioral, cognitive, and affective signs of brain injury. The term is usually used for cases in which the pattern of thought and action would typically be caused by organic abnormality, but none is apparent.

Historically, MBD was the term used to define and classify learning and behavioral difficulties now classified under the category of ATTENTION DEFICIT/HYPERACTIVITY DISORDER. It generally includes HYPERACTIVITY, impulsivity, various neurological soft signs, and any of a number of learning and language disabilities such as DYSLEXIA and DYSCALCULIA.

The term is often used as though there were an identifiable MBD syndrome, a collection of fairly specific disorders that could be taken as hallmarks of some underlying neurological cause. Although the issue is far from settled, the evidence to support a single MBD syndrome is largely unconvincing.

minimum competency testing   An assessment that tries to establish the minimum level of achievement. At least 36 states now require some type of minimum competency, which may be tied in with the ability to graduate.

There is a great deal of controversy about minimum competency tests. Critics worry that the blame for a poor school program may be shifted to the students. While the goal of minimum competency testing is to improve overall achievement, critics worry that the tests will in fact depress some students' achievement levels. There is also concern about the impact of such tests on minority achievement.

Students with an identified LEARNING DISABIL-ITY can waive the tests, although some schools suggest that these students take the tests anyway in the freshman year. If the student fails the entire test, he could then take it again with modifications as stipulated in his individual education program. A student with learning disabilities as a senior can sometimes waive the tests.

miscue analysis   A type of reading assessment in which the errors (miscues) that students make in reading provide a diagnostic window into the underlying language processes that caused the mistakes. Miscue analysis focuses on the differences between a student's oral reading performance and the printed text.

Miscue analysis does not look at problems solely with single sounds and their written symbols. It also focuses closely on the ways in which patterns and structures in a student's underlying language differ from those of the text.

mixed dominance   See CROSS DOMINANCE.

mixed receptive-expressive language disorder   A language disability causing problems in both understanding and expressing language. The condition was formerly called "developmental receptive language disorder." Today, it is generally understood that receptive language deficits don't occur all by themselves, but appear together with problems expressing language.

Three percent to 5 percent of all children have both receptive and expressive language disorder. The cause of this disorder is unknown, but problems with receptive skills begin before the age of four. Difficulty understanding and using language can cause problems with social interaction, and make it difficult to function independently as an adult.

Symptoms

There are a number of symptoms that indicate this condition, including problems in

- language comprehension
- language expression
- articulation
- recalling early visual or auditory memories

Diagnosis

Parents who are concerned about their child's acquisition of language should have the child tested, since early intervention offers the best possible outcome. Standardized receptive and expressive language tests can be given to any child suspected of having this disorder. An audiogram should also be given to rule out the possibility of deafness.

Treatment

Speech and language therapy are the best way to treat this type of language disorder. Psychotherapy is also recommended for children because of the possibility of emotional or behavioral problems.

See also EXPRESSIVE LANGUAGE DISORDERS; COMMUNICATION DISORDER.

mnemonic strategies   MEMORY aids devised to help an individual remember information. Mnemonic strategies include rhymes, nonsense words or sentences, anagrams, and images.

A common mnemonic for remembering the colors of the rainbow is *Roy G. Biv* in which each letter represents the colors in order: Red, Orange, Yellow, Green, Blue, Indigo, and Violet. The well-known poem that starts "Thirty days hath September . . ." is often the only way in which adults can remember how many days are in a particular month.

Most mnemonic strategies don't have any inherent connection with the material to be learned, but they impose meaning on material that is otherwise disorganized. In general, these strategies usually involve adding something to the material to be learned to make it easier to remember.

Individuals with LEARNING DISABILITY who have trouble remembering information often find using mnemonic strategies helpful. Mnemonics can be especially useful in remembering unrelated information that is not connected to anything meaningful.

modality   The CHANNEL or mode through which information is taken in and processed. The most common examples are visual (sight), auditory (hearing), tactile (touch), and kinesthetic (movement).

modified self-contained classroom   A self-contained program in which the students receive instruction from a regular education teacher for some part of the school day.

morpheme   The smallest unit of meaning in a language. There are two types of morpheme, free and bound. Morphemes that stand alone and have a meaning by themselves are called "free morphemes"; these include words such as *house, create, talk.* "Bound" morphemes are the prefixes and suffixes that don't have meaning as independent words. Individuals with learning disabilities can enhance their vocabularies by improving their awareness of the smallest unit of meaning in a language through explicit training in prefixes, roots, and suffixes.

For example, psychology can be broken into two morphemes: *psych,* meaning "mind," and *ology,* meaning "the study of." When an individual becomes aware of meaningful word parts such as *psych,* dozens of other words (such as psychedelic, psychometric, psychic) become understandable.

morphological awareness   An explicit awareness that words are composed of base forms, roots, prefixes, and suffixes and that those parts affect the word's meaning. For example, an individual who has acquired morphological awareness can see how the following words are similar: unforgivable, forgave, forgiving, and give.

Recent research has shown that morphological awareness has a significant impact on spelling, vocabulary development, and reading comprehension. The more skilled in morphological awareness individuals are, the better they are at spelling. Individuals with learning disabilities don't perform as well as their normal peers with spelling words that change phonologically (such as run/ran or diving/dove).

Vocabulary development is also related to morphological awareness. Children who are taught about parts of words tend to have more developed vocabularies than children without such instruction. Young children with language difficulties in particular benefit from explicit instruction on how words work.

Reading comprehension also improves with an awareness of how words are put together. Research has shown that teaching morphological awareness before learning to read can predict how well a student comprehends by grade two. Explicit instruction in elementary grades on prefixes, roots, and suffixes provides morphological awareness. Older students benefit from learning the origins of words for vocabulary and spelling enrichment. Teaching vocabulary using word families helps individuals with learning difficulties negotiate between spelling and phonological shifts (such as democracy/democrat/hypocrisy/technocrat).

morphology The study of how words are constructed. For individuals with a LEARNING DISABILITY, studying how words are composed is an important way to boost language competence.

See also MORPHEME; MORPHOLOGICAL AWARENESS.

motivation The internal process that causes an individual to move toward the completion of a goal or to back away from a negative situation or stimulus. Motivation is frequently discussed in relation to learners. Various theories exist that attempt to explain what motivates individuals to act or to strive to complete difficult tasks.

See also LEARNED HELPLESSNESS; LOCUS OF CONTROL.

Motor Free Visual Perception Test (MVPT)
A test of visual perception designed for children aged four through eight years, 11 months that should be used in combination with a copying measure such as the BENDER VISUAL-MOTOR GESTALT TEST or the developmental test of visual-motor integration.

In this test, the child selects the correct figure during tasks involving spatial relationships, visual discrimination, figure-ground relationships, visual closure, and visual memory.

motor planning Thinking about a desired result and judging what motor activities or strategies will produce that result. For example, motor planning would be involved in determining how hard to throw a ball in order to reach another person.

motor sequencing Determining an appropriate sequence of movements to fulfill a task or produce a desired outcome. Movements are ordered both in terms of what is done first and next (temporal sequence) and in terms of what movements are performed simultaneously.

For example, in cutting with scissors, the hand holding the scissors alternates in temporal sequence opening and closing the hand; when the hand holding the scissors is in open position, the forearm concurrently moves the hand forward, so that the cutting advances. In describing the sequencing involved in an activity process, in addition to observing what is the sequence, it's possible to note whether the sequencing is simple, moderate, or complex. Many different movements would result in complex motor sequencing.

motor skills A wide range of capabilities involved in movement, such as the use and regulation of muscles and muscle groups with appropriate timing and sequencing, the ability to recall through motor memory the muscular steps used to perform a task in the past, and the use of ongoing sensory feedback to regulate muscular responses and activities.

motor tics Movements that a person can't control. Motor tics can include eye blinking, rolling the eyes, grimacing, or shrugging the shoulders.

multicategorical classroom A classroom that mixes together children with a variety of disabilities or handicapping conditions, under the instruction of a single special education teacher.

multicultural assessment Assessment that takes into account the specific environmental and sociocultural factors that may be involved in determining ability and potential.

See also SOCIOCULTURAL PERSPECTIVE.

multidisciplinary team A group of specialists who work together to meet students' needs. This type of team combines members' varied expertise to gather information and make decisions about students' eligibility for special services. Members of the team may include a LEARNING DISABILITY specialist, school nurse, teacher, social worker, school psychologist, speech and language pathologist, and parents. Amendments to the INDIVIDUALS WITH DISABILITIES EDUCATION ACT (IDEA) in 1997 included general teachers on the multidisciplinary team.

multifactored evaluation An assessment of more than one area of a child's functioning so that no one factor may contribute to a misdiagnosis.

multimodal See LEARNING MODALITIES.

multiple disabilities A child with a combination of two or more disabilities, such as deafness, blindness, mental retardation, or speech and language problems. Children with multiple disabilities usually have many problems with socialization, communication, and adaptation. Placement in a program designed for just one of the disabilities may not work, so children are usually placed in a program designed to handle all their problems.

ADHD often appears in children with multiple disabilities, but it is not always diagnosed. Because these problems are often complex, it can be quite challenging to identify the primary obstacle to learning.

multiple intelligences Recent advances in cognitive science, developmental psychology, and neuroscience suggest that each person's level of intelligence, as it has been traditionally considered, is actually made up of a number of faculties that can work individually or together with other abilities. Harvard professor Howard Gardner originally identified eight such types of intelligences, including verbal/linguistic, logical/mathematic, visual/spatial, musical/rhythmic, body/kinesthetic, interpersonal, intrapersonal, and naturalistic. Each of these eight types represents abilities within a specific area of human functioning.

Gardner believed that the forms of intelligence that are measured by most intelligence tests correspond to verbal/linguistic, logical/mathematic, and visual/spatial intelligences, meaning that traditional measures of intelligence overlook or fail to recognize abilities and gifts in other areas.

Although not based on or validated by research Gardner's theories have become increasingly influential. However, standard measures of intelligence continue to focus on verbal and nonverbal reasoning measures that depend heavily on linguistic, logical, and visual-spatial abilities, and the common understanding of intelligence continues to be mostly closely linked to verbal capabilities.

Many school curricula narrowly emphasize linguistic and mathematical intelligences, which can be the weakest areas for learning-disabled students. Often individuals with learning disabilities have talents that are not valued in academic settings. The theory of multiple intelligences emphasizes the need to acknowledge and cultivate different kinds of thinking and different abilities.

Musical Intelligence

Child prodigies such as Menuhin, Mozart, Saint-Saens, Boulez, and others experience music "naturally." The ability to perform and compose music has been scientifically pinpointed in certain areas of the brain. Indeed, cases of autistic and other impaired children who can perform brilliantly but are unable to talk or interact with others illustrate this.

Each individual has a different musical ability, and there are even people who are totally amusical, yet continue to have very normal and successful lives. Although musical intelligence may not seem as obvious a form of intellect as mathematical or logical ability, from a neurological point of view the ability to perform and comprehend musically appears to work independently from other forms of intelligence.

Body/Kinesthetic

One of the most controversial of Gardner's intelligences is the idea of body-kinesthetic intelligence. In Gardner's theory, each person possesses a certain control of movements, balance, agility, and grace. For some extraordinary individuals, such Michael Jordan or Jackie Joyner Kersey, strength in body-kinesthetic intelligence appeared even before they began formal training. Super athletes all seem to have a natural sense of how their body should act and react in a demanding physical situation. It is also long known that each hemisphere of the brain controls the opposite side of the body's movements; in APRAXIA or other conditions, some people lack the ability to voluntarily control muscles, though they continue to move involuntarily.

Some people, however, argue that physical control does not constitute a designation as a form of intelligence. But Gardner and other multiple intelligences researchers maintain that body-kinesthetic ability does indeed deserve such a recognition.

Logical/Mathematic

The most easily understood cognitive faculty is logical-mathematic intelligence—the ability to mentally process logical problems and equations—the type most often found on multiple-choice standardized tests. Logical-mathematic intelligence often doesn't require verbal articulation. Individuals who have good logical-mathematic abilities are able to process logical questions at an unusually rapid rate.

Before the advent of the theory of multiple intelligences, logical-mathematic intelligence was considered a pseudonym for intelligence itself, the "raw intellect" that Western culture revered. Although the theory of multiple intelligences agrees that logical-mathematic intelligence is indeed a key section of the intellect, it is by no means the only one that should be developed.

Linguistic

Everyone possesses the ability to use language; although some can master only basic levels of communication, others can speak many languages with grace and ease. For years, researchers have recognized the connection between language and the brain. Damage to one portion of the brain (BROCA'S AREA) will affect the ability to express clear grammatical sentences, although a person's understanding of vocabulary and syntax remains intact. As Howard Gardner notes, even young children and deaf individuals will begin to develop their own unique language if they aren't offered an alternative. A person's ability to construct and comprehend language may vary, but as a cognitive trait it is still universal.

Spatial

Spatial intelligence involves the ability to comprehend shapes and images in three dimensions. Whether trying to put together a puzzle or create a sculpture, we use our spatial intelligence to interpret what we may or may not physically see. Advances in neuroscience have now provided researchers with clear-cut proof of the role of spatial intelligence in the right hemisphere of the brain.

In rare instances, for example, certain brain injuries can cause people to lose the ability to recognize their closest relatives. Though they may see the other person perfectly well, they are unable to comprehend who they see.

And yet a blind person may feel a shape and identify it with ease, although she is unable to see it. Because most people use spatial intelligence in conjunction with sight, its existence as an autonomous cognitive attribute may not seem obvious, but recent research suggests that it is an independent portion of the intellect.

Interpersonal

Humans are social animals who thrive when involved with others. This ability to interact with others, understand them, and interpret their behavior is called interpersonal intelligence. According to Gardner, individuals' interpersonal intelligence allows them to notice the moods, temperaments, motivations, and intentions of others.

From a psychological and neurological point of view, the connection between interpersonal intelligence and the brain has been explored for generations; if the frontal lobe is damaged, that person's personality and ability to interact well with others is destroyed. Interpersonal intelligence allows us to affect others by understanding others; without it, an individual loses the ability to exist socially.

Intrapersonal

Related to interpersonal intelligence, intrapersonal intelligence is the cognitive ability to understand and sense the "self." Intrapersonal intelligence allows individuals to tap into internal feelings and thoughts. A strong intrapersonal intelligence can lead to self-esteem, self-enhancement, and a strength of character that can be used to solve internal problems.

On the other hand, a weak intrapersonal intelligence (such as with autistic children) prevents a person from recognizing the self as separate from the surrounding environment.

Intrapersonal intelligence often is not recognized from the outside unless it is expressed in some form, such as rage or joy.

Naturalistic

Recently added to the original list of seven multiple intelligences, naturalistic intelligence is a person's ability to identify and classify patterns in nature. During our prehistory, hunter-gatherers would rely on naturalistic intelligence to identify what plants or animals were edible and which weren't. Today, naturalistic intelligence may be seen in the way we relate to our surroundings. People who are sensitive to changes in weather patterns or are adept at distinguishing nuances among large numbers of similar objects may be expressing naturalistic intelligence abilities.

Impact on Schools

If the theory of multiple intelligences is true, it means that the most common form of assessment in the United States may not be the best. This type of assessment involves multiple-choice or fill-in-the-blank questions that have been developed from a given set of information that has been deemed worthy of being "necessary knowledge." Correct answers on this type of test do little to help students understand the subject. Though some can demonstrate their knowledge of the "facts," many can't truly explain the context of the knowledge and the ramification of the facts. Limited response assessment gives educators and politicians an efficient means of ranking students as successful or not, but does very little for the student in terms of understanding the subject.

multisensory   Learning that involves more than one sense, including visual, auditory, kinesthetic, and tactile, to help reinforce learning.

See also LEARNING MODALITIES; VAKT.

National Association of School Psychologists

A professional organization for school psychologists that promotes educationally and psychologically healthy environments for all children. NASP supports state-of-the-art research and training, advocacy, ongoing program evaluation, and caring professional service.

With more than 21,000 members, the National Association of School Psychologists is the largest association of school psychologists in the world. NASP members work in educational settings, from preschool through higher education. NASP exists as an alternative to the American Psychological Association (APA), especially for subdoctoral, associate-level evaluators. There has been some conflict in recent years between NASP and APA about whether subdoctoral, associate-level evaluators are competent to work without supervision.

The APA believes only a person with a doctorate can work unsupervised, while NASP supports licensure of subdoctoral evaluators for unsupervised practice.

The APA supports identification of psychologists as psychologists first, with specializations including school psychology, whereas the NASP supports the existence of school psychology as a separate profession from psychology.

Contact: 4340 East West Highway, Suite 402, Bethesda, MD 20814; phone: (301) 657–0270; website: http://www.naspweb.org.

National Association of Social Workers (NASW), The

The largest membership organization of professional SOCIAL WORKERS in the world, with more than 150,000 members. NASW works to enhance the professional growth and development of its members, to create and maintain professional standards, and to advance sound social policies.

National Center for Learning Disabilities

A nonprofit organization that seeks to raise public awareness and understanding of learning disabilities, provide information and referrals, and arrange educational programs and legislative advocacy. NCLD provides educational tools to heighten understanding of learning disabilities, including the annual publication called *Their World,* quarterly newsletters, articles, specific state-by-state resource listings, and videos about learning disabilities.

Founded in 1977, NCLD's mission is to increase opportunities for all individuals with learning disabilities to achieve their potential.

Contact: 381 Park Avenue South, Suite 1401, New York, NY 10016; phone: (212) 545–7510; toll free (888) 575–7373; website: http://www. ncld.org.

National Head Start Association (NHSA), The

A private not-for-profit membership organization representing Head Start programs, staff, and the children they serve. NHSA provides a national forum for the enhancement of Head Start services for poor children up to age five and their families. It is the only national organization dedicated exclusively to the concerns of the Head Start community.

Over the past 25 years, NHSA's mission has changed from simply defending Head Start in

Congress to actively expanding and improving the program. From planning massive annual training conferences to publishing a vast array of publications, the National Head Start Association continually strives to improve the quality of Head Start's comprehensive services for America's children and families.

Contact: 1651 Prince Street, Alexandria, VA 22314; phone: (703) 739–0875; website: http://www.nhsa.org

National Information Center for Children and Youth with Disabilities This national information and referral center provides information on disabilities and disability-related issues for families, educators, and other professionals with a special focus on children from birth to age 22. The association provides information on specific disabilities, early intervention, special education and related services, individualized education programs, family issues, disability organizations, professional associations, education rights, and transition to adult life, among other topics. The group also offers referrals, information service, and materials in English and Spanish.

Contact: PO Box 1492, Washington, DC 20013; phone: (800) 695–0285; website: http://www.nichcy.org

National Parent Network on Disabilities A nonprofit organization dedicated to empowering parents of children with disabilities. Located in Washington, D.C., NPND provides up-to-date information on the activities of all three branches of government that affect individuals with disabilities and their families. NPND's primary activities include advocating for and supporting the development and implementation of legislation that will improve the lives and protect the rights of children, youth, and adults with disabilities. Members include individuals and family members, as well as national, state, and local organizations that represent the interests of individuals with disabilities.

The network was formally established in December 1988, but traces its origins to a much earlier time when pioneer parent leaders sought a structured national presence representing the interests and needs of all parents of children with disabilities and special health care needs.

In 1976, five parent center coalitions were established with federal funding to provide information, training, and support to parents of children with disabilities. The initial parent center coalitions were effective, and by 1983, the federal government had expanded the program. As of 1995, there were 76 Parent Training and Information Centers (PTIs) located in all states and jurisdictions, serving more than 750,000 parents and their families. In 1989, the NPND established its first office in Washington, D.C.

Contact: 1130 17th Street, NW, Suite 400, Washington, DC 20036; phone: (202) 463–2299; website: http://www.npnd.org.

near-point copying The ability to copy when text or other visual information is close at hand.

near-point deficits The ability to see material close at hand is an essential factor in reading well. It has to do with the ability to see forms and letters clearly at a distance of about 16 inches, the standard distance used in reading.

An individual with near-point deficits has a problem with vision itself rather than with the visual-perceptual system, and may require corrective lenses or other treatment.

needs assessment In education, a broad-based appraisal of objectives and conditions in an attempt to relate goals to existing strengths and weaknesses. A needs assessment may examine the goals, assets, and so on of a particular school system and may lead to specific recommendations for improvement.

negative reinforcement Reinforcement that is used to increase a certain behavior. Contrary to popular belief, it is not the same as punishment, which is used to decrease a certain behavior. For example, in the classroom a child may be sent to time-out (negative experience) for an inappropriate behavior, but once the child has maintained appropriate behavior, she may return from time-out, encouraging better behavior in the future.

neurobiology   The biological makeup of the brain, including brain structure and functions, as well as biochemical processes.

neurological assessment   Testing based on a neurological examination, providing information about the ways in which dysfunctions or differences in brain function may affect function of movement, thought, or social, emotional, psychological, or behavioral activities.

neurological disorders   A spectrum of potential effects on human development, performance, and behavior ranging from profound disorders that may affect every aspect of human functioning, to minimal dysfunctions that create little impairment in the ability to learn and perform effectively. In all cases, neurological disorders or dysfunctions involve impairments in neurological functioning that are based in the biochemistry and structure of the brain.

neurological examination   A test that may typically involve two elements, a conventional assessment of neurological functioning, and an examination of "soft" (subtle) neurological signs if a learning disability is suspected.

A conventional assessment will include a family and medical history, as well as physical examination of specific neurological functions, such as cranial nerves, reflexes, and other motor functions. In some cases a neurological examination may also involve more specialized procedures such as an EEG to measure electrical activity in the brain, X rays, CAT scans, or other brain-imaging techniques, or biochemical, endocrinologic, or genetic studies.

Examination of soft neurological signs may include a variety of tasks designed to identify more subtle gross-motor, visual-motor, or fine-motor difficulties. Such tasks are relatively informal, involving activities such as copying forms, hopping or standing on one foot, or testing finger dexterity.

neurological impress method   An approach to reading instruction for students with significant reading disabilities. With this method, the teacher and student read the same material aloud, rapidly and at the same time, as the teacher directs his voice into the ear of the student at close range. The theory behind this system is that the auditory feedback will help the student develop reading fluency.

neurologist   A physician specializing in brain function. Neurologists can assess and treat with medication a variety of neurological conditions and disorders.

neurology   The branch of medicine that focuses on the study of diseases and disorders of the nervous system.

neuropsychological examination   Testing that brings together psychological and neurological examination, exploring a number of broad areas in brain and behavioral functioning. These include intellectual functioning, attention, memory, language, sensorimotor functions, executive functions, social and emotional functions, and learning abilities.

A neuropsychological examination typically involves administration of a complex battery of tests designed to identify levels of functioning within specific areas and to compare abilities and problems in all areas.

neuropsychologist A psychologist who focuses on the relationship between behavior and neurological functions.

See also NEUROPSYCHOLOGY.

neuropsychology The study of the relationship between brain function and behavior. This field includes neuropsychologists who work in experimental and clinical settings; experimental neuropsychologists, who work with both human and animal models; and clinical neuropsychologists, who look for procedures that will help people with neurologically based disorders by studying brain and behavior relationships.

neurotransmitter A chemical messenger in the brain that is released from the ends of a brain cell to carry information across the gap between cells, where it arrives at specific sites on a receiving cell.

Examples of neurotransmitters include acetylcholine, dopamine, epinephrine, serotonin, and various neuropeptides.

Treatment for attention disorders involving medications focuses primarily on regulating the action of neurotransmitters.

See also ATTENTION DEFICIT/HYPERACTIVITY DISORDER.

noncategorical An approach to grouping children in a classroom without reference to any diagnostic label or category.

nonfluent aphasia A language disorder characterized by little speech and poor articulation in which a person uses primarily nouns and verbs; automatic phrases, such as "yes" and "no," prevail. This condition is also called BROCA'S APHASIA.

nonphonetic word In teaching, a word whose pronunciation may not be accurately predicted from its spelling.

nonsense words See PSEUDOWORD DECODING.

nonverbal learning disabilities A form of LEARNING DISABILITY that primarily affects social functioning in areas such as interpersonal skills, social perception, and interaction. Also called "right-hemisphere learning disorders," this problem often goes unrecognized for a large part of a child's schooling. Since abnormalities of the right hemisphere interfere with understanding and adaptive learning, experts believe that nonverbal learning disabilities are more debilitating than verbal disabilities.

Experts suspect that nonverbal learning disabilities are caused by a problem in the right hemisphere of the brain, either from brain injury or damage before birth. The damage primarily affects visual-spatial perception, processing, and reasoning. Individuals with NLD often display significant strengths in verbal areas and may develop reading and speaking skills earlier than their peers; consequently, their nonverbal learning difficulties may be overlooked. Both parents and teachers will often suspect that something is wrong early on, but they can't quite figure out what it is.

Nonverbal learning disorders remain predominantly misunderstood and largely unrecognized. Although NLD syndrome was discovered in the early 1970s, even today education professionals are largely unfamiliar with nonverbal learning disorders. Typically, parents are assured that everything is fine and that their child is "just a perfectionist," or is immature, bored, or a bit clumsy. Rarely are a parent or teacher's concerns accepted until the child reaches a point in school where he is no longer able to function. These children are often labeled "behavior problems" or "emotionally disturbed" because of their frequent inappropriate and unexpected conduct, despite the fact that NLD has a neurological rather than an emotional origin.

It is especially important to identify children with nonverbal learning disorders because overestimates of the child's abilities and unrealistic demands made by parents and teachers can lead to ongoing emotional problems. Unfortunately, there are few resources available for the child with NLD syndrome through schools or private agencies, and it's hard to find a professional who understands nonverbal learning disabilities.

Nonverbal learning disorders are much less common than language-based learning disorders (affecting only between .1 percent to 1 percent of the general population). Unlike language-based learning disabilities, the NLD syndrome affects girls as often as boys. Although there aren't many people with NLD, experts suspect that as school assessment procedures improve, a higher proportion of children will be identified with NLD.

Symptoms

Individuals with NLD may experience significant difficulties in perceiving and understanding the subtle visual cues important to nonverbal communication that form the basis of social interaction and interpersonal relations. They may misread overt signals of impatience, annoyance, or the desire to end an interaction, and consequently may respond in ways that are perceived by others as inappropriate.

A person with NLD syndrome may have trouble adapting to new situations, or accurately reading nonverbal signals and cues. Although these students make progress in school, they have trouble "producing" in situations where speed and adaptability are required.

There are three categories of dysfunction:

- lack of coordination, severe balance problems, or difficulties with fine motor skills

- poor visual recall, faulty spatial perceptions, or difficulties with spatial relations

- lack of ability to comprehend nonverbal communication, trouble adjusting to new situations, or significant problems with social judgment and social interaction

Children with nonverbal learning disorders commonly appear awkward and uncoordinated

in both fine and gross motor skills. They may have had extreme difficulty learning to ride a bike or to kick a soccer ball. Fine motor skills, such as cutting with scissors or tying shoe laces, seem to be impossible for them. Young children with NLD are less likely to explore their environment because they can't rely on their own perceptions. These children don't learn much from experience or repetition and can't generalize information.

In the early years, children may appear confused much of the time despite a high intelligence and high scores on receptive and expressive language measures. Closer observation will reveal a social ineptness due to misinterpretations of body language and tone of voice. These children don't perceive subtle cues in their environment, such as the idea of personal space, the facial expressions of others, or nonverbal displays of pleasure or displeasure. These are all social skills that are normally grasped intuitively through observation, not directly taught.

Instead, these children cope by relying on language as their principal means of social relating, gathering information, and relieving anxiety. They often develop an exceptional memory for rote material. Since the nonverbal processing area of the brain isn't giving automatic feedback, they rely solely on memory of past experiences, each of which they labeled verbally to guide them in future situations. This, of course, is less effective and less reliable than being able to sense and interpret another person's social cues. Normal conversational "give and take" seems impossible for these children.

It's hard for these children to change from one activity to another or to move from one place to another. A child with NLD needs to concentrate merely to get through a room. Owing to the inability to handle such information processing demands, these children will instinctively avoid any kind of novelty.

Problems with NLD grow more apparent and more profound during the latter stages of childhood development and into adolescence and adulthood, as pressures on social interaction increase and the requirements for appropriate social performance become more subtle and complex.

Cause

Language-based learning disorders are believed to be inherited, but a specific genetic problem has not yet been discovered. Nonverbal learning disabilities involve the performance processes that originate in the right cerebral hemisphere of the brain, which specializes in nonverbal processing. Brain scans of individuals with NLD often reveal mild abnormalities of the right cerebral hemisphere. A number of children suffering from NLD have at some time early in their development

- sustained a moderate to severe head injury
- received repeated radiation treatments on or near their heads over a prolonged period of time
- had a congenital absence of the corpus callosum
- been treated for hydrocephalus
- had brain tissue removed from the right hemisphere

All of this damage listed above would involve significant destruction of white matter connections in the right hemisphere. Current evidence suggests that a contributing cause of the NLD syndrome involves early damage of the right cerebral hemisphere, or white matter disease that forces the left hemisphere system to function on its own.

Prognosis

How well these children progress seems to depend on early identification and accommodation. Typically, the NLD child is regularly punished for circumstances he can't help, without ever really understanding why, and is often left with little hope that the situation will ever improve. As a result, these children tend to have

serious forms of depression, withdrawal, anxiety, and in some cases, will contemplate or commit suicide.

Diagnosis

Whereas language-based disabilities are usually obvious to parents and educators, nonverbal learning disorders routinely go unrecognized. Many of the early symptoms of nonverbal learning disabilities—the language-based accomplishments—make parents and teachers proud.

This child may speak like an adult at two or three years of age, and during early childhood, he is usually considered "gifted" by his parents and teachers. Sometimes the NLD child has a history of rote reading at a very young age. This child is generally an eager, enthusiastic learner who quickly memorizes rote material.

Extraordinary early speech and vocabulary development are not often suspected to be a coping strategy, used by a child with problems in the right-hemisphere brain system and limited access to nonverbal processing abilities. The NLD child is also likely to acquire an unusual aptitude for spelling, but few adults will consider this to be a reflection of the overdependence on auditory perceptions.

Likewise, remarkable rote memory skills, attention to detail, and a natural facility for decoding, encoding, and early reading development aren't generally causes for alarm. Yet these are some of the important early indicators that a child is having trouble relating to and functioning in the nonverbal world.

Dysfunctions associated with NLD are less apparent at the age of seven to eight years than at 10 to 14 years, and they become progressively more apparent and more debilitating with each year. During late elementary school, the child will begin to not turn in, or not complete, written assignments. The child produces limited written output and the process is always slow and laborious. By the time the problem is revealed, the child may have already shut down in response to impossible academic pressures and performance demands.

Treatment

Parents and the school should not underestimate the gravity of this disability. The main problem in the painstaking approach to teaching the child is the caregiver's faulty impression that the child is much more adept than he is. Everyone tends to overestimate the intelligence of NLD adolescents. The child should be shielded from teasing, persecution, and other sources of anxiety.

Independence should be introduced gradually, in controlled, nonthreatening situations. The more completely the strengths and weaknesses of the child are understood, the better prepared the care providers will be to promote the child's independence. These children should never be left to their own devices in new activities or situations that lack sufficient structure. Goals and expectations must be attainable.

Occupational therapy is a good idea for the younger child. Use of a computer word processor can help, since the spatial and fine motor skills needed for typing aren't as complicated as those involved in handwriting. Tasks requiring folding, cutting with scissors, or arranging material (maps, graphs, mobiles) will require considerable help. Timed assignments will need to be modified or eliminated.

Adults need to check often that the child understands, and that information is presented clearly. All expectations need to be direct and explicit, and the student's schedule needs to be as predictable as possible. He should be prepared in advance for changes in routine, such as: assemblies, field trips, minimum days, vacation days, finals, and so on.

This type of child needs to be assigned to one case manager at school who will oversee progress and can make sure all of the school staff are making the necessary accommodations and modifications. In-service training and orientation for all school staff that promotes tolerance and acceptance is a vital part of the overall plan for success, as everyone must be familiar with and supportive of the child's academic and social needs.

This child needs to be in a learning environment that provides daily, nonthreatening contact with nondisabled peers—not a "special" or alternative program—in order to boost social development. This child will benefit from cooperative learning situations when grouped with good role models.

Transitions will always be difficult for this child, so he will need time during the school day to collect his thoughts before "switching gears."

Teachers will need to present strategies for conversation skills, how and when to change the subject, tone and expression of voice, and nonverbal body language (facial expressions, correct social distance).

Isolation, deprivation, and punishment are not effective methods to change the behavior of a child who is already trying his best to conform, but who misinterprets nonverbal cues. If inappropriate behavior causes problems at school, a behavioral intervention plan detailing a course of action may need to be a part of this child's IEP or 504 plan.

nonverbal memory   Memory for figures, spatial relationships, and so on. Nonverbal memory is assumed to be based in the deep structures of the right temporal lobe.

normalization   The procedure of placing handicapped individuals in situations as close to normal ones as possible, such as placing a retarded person in a group home rather than in an institution.

norm-referenced test   An assessment that compares a person's score against the typical scores of a specified sample of people who have already taken the same exam, called the "norm group." The norm defined by this group represents the distribution of test scores among them. An example of a norm group might be a nationwide sample of ninth graders, or a sample identified by gender, age, and ethnic background.

Most standardized achievement tests are norm-referenced. Norm-referenced testing is different from criterion-referenced testing, and doesn't serve the same purposes or share the same characteristics.

Commercial, national, norm-referenced achievement tests include the California Achievement Test (CAT); Comprehensive Test of Basic Skills (CTBS) (which includes the Terra Nova), Iowa Test of Basic Skills (ITBS), and Tests of Academic Proficiency (TAP); Metropolitan Achievement Test (MAT); and Stanford Achievement Test (SAT, not to be confused with the college admissions SAT). IQ, cognitive ability, school readiness, and developmental screening tests are also NRTs.

NRTs are designed to compare students' scores. A commercial norm-referenced test does not compare all the students who take the test in a given year; instead; test makers select a sample from the target student population (say, ninth graders). The test is "normed" on this sample, which is supposed to fairly represent the entire target population (all ninth graders in the nation). Students' scores are then reported in relation to the scores of this norm group.

To make comparing easier, test makers create exams in which the results are designed to resemble a bell-shaped curve: most students will score near the middle, and only a few will score low or high.

Scores are usually reported as percentile ranks. The scores range from 1st to 99th percentile, with the average student score set at the 50th percentile. If Jake scored at the 83rd percentile, it means he scored higher than 83 percent of the test takers in the norm group. Scores also can be reported as "grade equivalents," "stanines," and "normal curve equivalents."

One more question right or wrong can cause a big change in a student's score. In fact, having one more correct answer can sometimes cause a student's percentile score to jump more than 10 points.

In making an NRT, it is often more important to choose questions that sort people along the curve than it is to make sure that the content covered by the test is adequate; thus, tests sometimes emphasize small and meaningless differences among test takers. Since the tests are made to sort students, most of the things everyone knows aren't tested. Questions may be obscure or tricky, in order to help rank the test-takers.

In addition, tests can be biased, favoring one kind of student or another for reasons that have nothing to do with the subject area being tested. For example, knowledge that is more commonly learned by middle- or upper-class children outside of school is often included in tests. To help make the bell curve, test makers usually eliminate questions that students with low overall scores might get right, but those with high overall scores get wrong. Thus, most questions that favor minority groups are eliminated.

NRTs usually have to be completed in a time limit. Some students don't finish, even if they know the material. This can be especially unfair to students with a LEARNING DISABILITY or whose first language is not English. This is another way in which test makers sort people out.

No test is perfectly reliable, and all tests have a "measurement error." A score that appears as an absolute number—say, Jake's 83—really is an estimate. For example, Jake's real score is probably between 76 and 90, but it could be even further off; therefore, results may be reported in "score bands," which indicate the range within which the true score probably lies. Subscores on tests are even less precise, usually because there are often very few items on this portion. A score band for Sally's math subtest might show that her score is between the 45th and 99th percentile because only a handful of questions were asked.

Measurement error may be due to the fact that a student may not feel well, and test-taking conditions aren't the same from place to place. Moreover, scores for young children are much less reliable because their moods and attention are more varied. Also, young children develop quickly and unevenly, so a score that is accurate today could be completely wrong next month.

If a child or a school's score goes up on a norm-referenced test, that may or may not mean the child knows more or the school has improved. Schools cannot teach everything. They teach some facts, some procedures, some concepts, some skills—but not others. Often, schools focus most on what is tested and stop teaching many things that are not tested. When scores go up, it does not mean the students know more, it means they know more of what is on that test.

Teaching to the test explains why scores usually go down when a new test is used. A district usually uses an NRT for five to 10 years. Each year, the score goes up as teachers become familiar with what is on the test, but when a new test is introduced, the scores suddenly drop. The students don't know less; it is just that different things are now being tested.

It's often easier to use a norm-referenced test to compare students because they were created to rank test takers. These tests provide a quick snapshot of some of the things most people expect students to learn. They are relatively cheap and easy to administer.

Unfortunately, politicians often call for all students to score above the national average. Since NRTs are constructed so that half the population is always below the midpoint, it's impossible to have all students score above the 50th percentile.

If they were used only as one additional piece of information and not much importance was put on them, they would not be much of a problem. Many mistakes can be made by relying on test scores to make educational decisions. Every major maker of NRTs tells schools not to use them as the basis for making decisions about retention, graduation, or replacement. The test makers know that their tests are not designed to be used that way. According to the Standards for Educational and Psychological Measurement, in elementary or secondary education, a

decision or characterization that will have a major impact on a test taker should not automatically be made on the basis of a single test score.

Any one test can measure only a limited part of a subject area or a limited range of important human abilities. A reading test may measure only some particular reading skills, not a full range of the ability to understand and use texts. Multiple-choice math tests can measure skill in computation or solving routine problems, but they are not good for testing whether students can reason mathematically and apply their knowledge to real-world problems.

Most NRTs focus too heavily on memorization and routine procedures. Multiple-choice and short-answer questions don't measure most knowledge that students need to do well in college, qualify for good jobs, or be active and informed citizens. Tests like these can't show whether a student can write a research paper, understand current events or the impact of science on society, or debate important issues. They don't test problem-solving, decision-making, judgment, or social skills.

Tests often force teachers to overemphasize memorization over thinking and knowledge application. Since the tests are very limited, teaching just what's on the test weakens a curriculum. Defining "improvement" in a school district as a rise in test scores often leads to test coaching. Linking teacher raises to test scores is almost a guarantee that test coaching will occur.

Norm-referenced tests also can lower academic expectations. NRTs support the idea that learning or intelligence fits a bell curve. If educators believe it, they are more likely to have low expectations of students who score below average.

Norm-referenced tests are the opposite of criterion-referenced tests, which determine whether each student has achieved specific skills or concepts. Unlike NRTs, CRTs are used to find out how much students know before instruction begins and after it has finished. They measure specific skills that make up a designated curriculum and compare each individual with a preset standard for acceptable achievement. The performance of others is irrelevant.

norms   The typical distribution of scores on a given test among a specific norm group.

objective left-right discrimination A higher level of discrimination in which an individual can consistently and accurately be aware of the relation of left and right sides of the body on another person as well as himself. The client can imitate in a mirror fashion the movements of another; later he can reverse the sides, imitating the action of another so that his right hand is truly performing what another person's right hand is doing. Naming the sides of the self and in other objects and in pictures is a conceptual skill and might be considered at the lower level of cognitive function.

obsessive-compulsive disorder (OCD) An anxiety disorder characterized by severe obsessions and/or compulsions. People with obsessive-compulsive disorder (OCD) suffer intensely from recurrent, unwanted thoughts (obsessions) or rituals (compulsions), which they feel they can't control. Rituals such as handwashing, counting, checking, or cleaning are often performed as a way of preventing obsessive thoughts or making them go away. Performing these rituals, however, provides only temporary relief, and not performing them markedly increases anxiety. Left untreated, obsessions and the need to perform rituals can take over a person's life. OCD is often a chronic, relapsing illness.

OCD is often linked with other anxiety disorders, major depression, and Tourette's syndrome. While OCD can coexist with ATTENTION DEFICIT/HYPERACTIVITY DISORDER, it is not yet clear how that link occurs.

Many healthy people have some of the symptoms of OCD, such as checking the stove several times before leaving the house. But the disorder is diagnosed only when such activities consume at least an hour a day, are very distressing, and interfere with daily life. Most adults with this condition know that what they're doing is senseless, but they can't stop. However, children with OCD may not realize that their behavior is unusual.

OCD strikes men and women in about the same number, affecting about one in 50 people. It can appear in childhood, adolescence, or adulthood, but usually first appears in the teens or early adulthood. One-third of adults with OCD experienced their first symptoms as children.

The symptoms may come and go, may get better over time, or they can grow progressively worse. Evidence suggests that OCD might run in families. Often, people with OCD may avoid situations in which they might have to confront their obsessions, or they may try unsuccessfully to use alcohol or drugs to calm themselves. Severe OCD can keep someone from working or from carrying out normal responsibilities at home, but more often it doesn't develop to those extremes.

Cause

There is growing evidence that OCD is caused by a physical problem in the brain, not because of family problems, or attitudes learned in childhood, such as an emphasis on cleanliness, or a belief that certain thoughts are dangerous or unacceptable.

Brain scans using positron emission tomography (PET) have found that those with OCD have different patterns of brain activity from people with other mental illnesses or people with no mental illness at all. In addition, PET scans show that in patients with OCD, both behavioral therapy and medication produce changes in a part of the brain called the caudate nucleus. This is graphic evidence that both psychotherapy and medication affect the brain.

Treatment

A combination of the two treatments is often helpful for most patients; some individuals respond best to one therapy, some to another. Medications that are effective are the antidepressants fluvoxamine, paroxetine, sertraline, clomipramine, and fluoxetine. Others are showing promise and may soon be available. Behavioral therapy (specifically "exposure and response prevention") is also helpful in treating OCD. This type of therapy involves exposing the person to whatever triggers the problem and then helping the person avoid the usual ritual. This might involve having the patient touch something dirty and then not wash his hands. This therapy is often successful in patients who complete a behavioral therapy program, although results have been less favorable in some people who have both OCD and depression.

Another therapy favored by many specialists involves cognitive therapy. Cognitive therapists treat what they consider to be the unproductive self-statements (such as "If I don't wash my hands, it will be horrible") that they believe are responsible for the discomfort that people with OCD experience.

The most popular type of cognitive therapy is rational-emotive therapy (RET) developed by psychologist Albert Ellis. In RET, the therapist emphasizes replacing unproductive self-statements such as, "If I don't wash may hands I will die," with more productive self-statements such as "If I don't wash my hands, I may be uncomfortable, and I may feel an urge to wash my hands, but I will not die." Through extensive practice in rephrasing self-statements, RET therapists believe, the person eventually overcomes the discomfort they have experienced and are able to change the rituals and obsessions that have made their (and the people around them) miserable.

occipital lobe   One of four major pairs of lobes of the cerebral cortex that include the center of the visual perception system. Although protected from injury because of their location at the back of the brain, any significant trauma could produce subtle changes to the visual-perceptual system, such as visual field defects.

The occipital lobe is involved in visual-spatial processing, discrimination of movement, and color discrimination. Damage to one side of the occipital lobe causes loss of vision. Disorders of the occipital lobe can cause visual hallucinations and illusions. Lesions in the parietal-temporal-occipital association area can cause word blindness, ALEXIA and AGRAPHIA.

occupational therapists   Professionals who work directly with individuals with impaired physical or motor functions caused by disease, injury, or surgical or other medical interventions. They work with individuals who have conditions that are mentally, physically, developmentally, or emotionally disabling, and help them to develop, recover, or maintain daily living and work skills. They help clients not only to improve basic motor functions and reasoning abilities, but also to compensate for permanent loss of function. Their goal is to help clients have independent, productive, and satisfying lives.

Occupational therapists may work exclusively with individuals in a particular age group, or with particular disabilities. In schools, for example, they evaluate children's abilities, recommend and provide therapy, modify classroom equipment, and in general, help children participate as fully as possible in school programs and activities.

Occupational therapists assist clients in performing activities of all types, such as using a computer. Physical exercises may be used to increase strength and dexterity, while paper and pencil exercises may be chosen to improve visual acuity and the ability to discern patterns. A client with short-term memory loss, for instance, might be encouraged to make lists to aid recall. One with coordination problems might be assigned exercises to improve hand-eye coordination. Occupational therapists also use computer programs to help clients improve decision making, abstract reasoning, problem solving, and perceptual skills, as well as memory, sequencing, and coordination—all of which are important for independent living.

In mental health settings, they may treat mentally retarded individuals, choosing activities that help people learn to cope with daily life, such as time management skills, budgeting, shopping, homemaking, and use of public transportation. They may also work with individuals who are dealing with alcoholism, drug abuse, depression, eating disorders, or stress-related disorders.

Occupational therapists must have at least a bachelor's degree in occupational therapy, and the profession is regulated in all states. To obtain a license, applicants must graduate from an accredited educational program and pass a national certification examination. Those who pass the test are called "registered occupational therapists." Occupational therapy coursework includes physical, biological, and behavioral sciences, and the application of occupational therapy theory and skills. Completion of six months of supervised fieldwork is also required.

Office for Civil Rights The government office that ensures equal access to education and promotes educational excellence throughout the nation through vigorous enforcement of civil rights.

Part of the Department of Education, this office is responsible for monitoring the scope of laws and regulations regarding civil rights in educational contexts.

The Office for Civil Rights enforces five federal laws that prohibit discrimination in education programs and activities that receive federal financial assistance. Discrimination on the basis of race, color, and national origin is prohibited by Title VI of the Civil Rights Act of 1964: sex discrimination is prohibited by Title IX of the Education Amendments of 1972; discrimination on the basis of disability is prohibited by Section 504 of the REHABILITATION ACT OF 1973; and age discrimination is prohibited by the Age Discrimination Act of 1975. The Department of Justice also has delegated OCR responsibility for enforcing Title II of the AMERICANS WITH DISABILITIES ACT of 1990.

The civil rights laws enforced by OCR include all state education agencies, elementary and secondary school systems, colleges and universities, vocational school, proprietary schools, state vocational rehabilitation agencies, libraries, and museums that receive U.S. Department of Education funds.

A complaint of discrimination can be filed by anyone who believes that a school that receives federal financial assistance has discriminated against someone on the basis of race, color, national origin, sex, disability, or age. The person or organization filing the complaint need not be a victim, but may complain on behalf of another person.

Most of OCR's activities are conducted by its 12 enforcement offices throughout the country involved in preventing, identifying, ending, and remedying discrimination against America's students.

Contact: U.S. Department of Education, Office for Civil Rights Customer Service Team, Mary E. Switzer Building, 330 C Street, SW, Washington, DC 20202; phone: (800) 421–3481; email: OCR@ed.gov; website: http://www.ed.gov/offices/OCR.

Office of Special Education Programs A component of the Office of Special Education and Rehabilitative Services (OSERS), which is one of the principal components of the U.S. Department of Education. The office's mission and organization focus on the free appropriate public education of children and youth with disabilities from birth through age 21.

They are the primary administrative agency for the implementation of the INDIVIDUALS WITH DISABILITIES EDUCATION ACT (IDEA). While many matters relating to IDEA legislation are typically handled at the state level, the OSEP has the authority to investigate complaints, withhold funds, and review individual state plans pertaining to compliance.

OSEP currently funds more than 1,200 projects in 18 programs authorized by federal legislation.

oppositional behavior   Behavior that is negative, hostile, and defiant in nature. Some degree of oppositional behavior is normal in childhood and adolescence, and represents one method by which a child separates from parental or social expectations in order to define individual identity.

In some cases, an unusual degree of oppositional behavior may accompany an attention disorder or self-esteem or self-concept difficulties arising from learning problems in school.

A significant and ongoing pattern of oppositional behavior may indicate the presence of OPPOSITIONAL DEFIANT DISORDER, a condition that frequently occurs along with attention disorders.

oppositional defiant disorder (ODD)   A psychological disorder characterized by angry, hostile, and impulsive behavior in opposition to authority figures. This antisocial disorder of early to middle childhood may evolve into a CONDUCT DISORDER, usually diagnosed before the age of 12; children with oppositional defiant disorder defy adult rules, are angry, and often lose their tempers.

ODD is considered less severe than conduct disorder, and may involve behaviors that include overt resistance to rules and instructions, lying,

and violations of other social norms. ODD can occur together with ATTENTION DEFICIT/HYPERACTIVITY DISORDER (ADHD). Indeed, many behavioral problems associated with ADHD may in fact be symptoms of ODD.

This is the most common psychiatric problem in children, which affects more than 5 percent of all children. In younger children it is more common in boys than in girls, but as they grow older, the rate is the same in both.

ODD and ADHD

It is extremely rare for a physician to see a child with only ODD; usually, the child has another psychiatric disorder—often ADHD. A child with ADHD has a 30 percent to 40 percent risk of also having ODD.

ODD is characterized by aggressiveness, but not impulsiveness. In ODD, individuals annoy others on purpose, while it is usually not so purposeful in ADHD. ODD signs and symptoms are much more difficult to live with than ADHD. ADHD sometimes goes away, but ODD rarely does. Unlike ADHD, ODD is not characterized by poor social skills, and children with ODD can sit still.

Children and adolescents with ADHD alone do things without thinking, but they are not necessarily aggressive. An ADHD child may impulsively push someone too hard on a swing or knock a child down, but she would probably be sorry afterward. A child with ODD plus ADHD might push the child out of the swing and then deny it, bragging about it to her friends later. Children with ADHD and ODD often get in a lot of trouble as their impulsiveness and hyperactivity often lead to fights, rough play, and huge temper tantrums.

Children with ODD develop signs of mood disorders or anxiety as they get older; by the time these children reach the end of elementary school, about 25 percent will have disabling mood or anxiety problems. When ODD is present with ADHD, depression, TOURETTE'S SYNDROME, anxiety disorders, or other disorders, it makes life with that child far more difficult.

Diagnosis

The criteria for ODD include a pattern of negative, hostile, defiant behavior lasting at least six months. The disturbance in behavior causes significant problems with social, school, or job functioning. At least four of the following symptoms must be present. The individual *often*

- loses temper
- argues with adults
- actively defies or refuses to comply with adults' requests or rules
- deliberately annoys people
- blames others for mistakes or misbehavior
- is touchy or easily annoyed by others
- is angry and resentful
- is spiteful and vindictive

All of the criteria above include the word "often"—this may mean different things to different people. After all, these behaviors occur to a varying degree in all normal children. Researchers have found that "often" is best solved by the following criteria:

At least four times a week the child is angry and resentful and deliberately annoys people.

At least twice a week the child is touchy or easily annoyed by others, loses his temper, argues with adults, and actively defies or refuses to comply with adults' requests or rules.

In the last three months, the child is spiteful and vindictive, and blames others for his or her mistakes or misbehavior.

The problems usually begin between ages one and three, and appears to run in families. If a parent is alcoholic and has been in trouble with the law, their children are almost three times as likely to have ODD.

oral language   Speaking and listening. Development of good oral language in young children is important for the development of good reading and writing skills later. Difficulties in early oral language development in sounds, word meanings, and sentence structure can be a warning sign for possible LANGUAGE DISORDER.

Language includes four dimensions, which are developed in children in the following order: listening, speaking, reading, and writing. Thus, oral language plays an important role in the normal development of reading and writing.

oral reading   Reading out loud. Oral reading is used to measure an individual's reading skills, which are usually recorded as "grade level." For example, a child's oral reading rate of 3.4 means he is reading material at a third grade, fourth month level.

Recording an individual's oral reading errors can be used to diagnose reading problems. By looking for reading patterns, it's possible to design a remediation program accordingly.

organicity   A term used to refer to unusual or abnormal behavior that is likely to have a biological basis.

organizational strategies   Individuals with a LEARNING DISABILITY often have trouble with organizational skills, and can benefit from learning to use strategies to help them manage their time, materials, and information. There are countless organizational strategies available.

For school-age students, teachers can provide clear routines and structures in the classroom. Students can be taught to prepare a notebook for each class and keep materials neat. Keeping a daily planner can help map out assignment due dates, appointments, and daily schedules. Teaching strategies such as active reading and note-taking skills are also useful for organizing information, which can often be overwhelming for learning-disabled individuals.

orthographic awareness   An individual's command of the sound-letter relationship. As children learn to write, their approaches to spelling change as they become more aware of sounds and letters. In the beginning, children often spell very simply (such as "bt" for "boat"). As they get older they may apply conventions of spelling but still misspell ("bote" for "boat").

With more exposure to written language, as they become more proficient readers and learn specific spelling patterns, young writers begin to apply more sophisticated spelling patterns ("boat" for "boat"). Learning-disabled individuals who have underdeveloped orthographic awareness often have problems with spelling.

orthography   The formal name for spelling—the system of representing spoken language in written form. The spelling of English can be difficult to learn due to many irregular spelling patterns. For example, "do," "due," and "dew" are all pronounced the same way. English has 44 sounds, but it has only 26 letters.

The letter-sound correspondence is essential for reading, as is the sound-letter correspondence for correct spelling. Difficulties in these relationships can result in language disabilities.

Orton, Samuel Torrey (1879–1948)   A neuropsychiatrist and pathologist who was a pioneer in reading failure and related language processing difficulties; first to identify DYSLEXIA. Orton first identified dyslexia as *strephosymbolia* (twisted symbols), after noting the letter reversals that some dyslexics demonstrate in their writing. Although transposing letters also occurs in the writing of most young children, and reversals aren't necessary for a diagnosis of dyslexia or reading disability, it remains as a common stereotype of the disorder.

A professor of neuropsychiatry and neuropathology at the Neurological Institute of Columbia University, Orton was a pioneer in focusing attention on language differences by bringing together neuropsychiatric information and principals of remediation. As early as 1925 he had identified the syndrome of developmental reading disability, separated it from mental

defect and brain damage, and offered a physiological explanation with a favorable prognosis.

As early as the 1920s, Orton had extensively studied children with the kind of language processing difficulties now commonly associated with dyslexia and had formulated a set of teaching principles and practices for such children. During his lifetime, Orton directed many research projects dealing with developmental reading disabilities. It was during one of these projects that he met Anna Gillingham (1878–1963), a teacher and psychologist in the field of language disabilities. Together, they developed procedures and comprehensive materials for early identification and remediation of dyslexic children. Their program is known today as the ORTON-GILLINGHAM APPROACH to reading instruction. Their manual, published first in 1936, is now in its seventh edition.

Modern research has continued to confirm Orton's theories about the physiological differences experienced by dyslexics. Although early remediation is most effective, these methods have been successfully adapted for use with older students and adults.

See also GILLINGHAM, ANNA.

Orton-Gillingham approach   A multisensory approach to reading, writing, and spelling born of a theory of reading disabilities devised by Samuel Orton, Anna Gillingham, and Bessie Stillman in the 1930s. Their approach was based on the idea that the brain stores information in both hemispheres; when the connection between the two hemispheres isn't fully developed, individuals may read words in reverse.

Dyslexics have the potential to be accomplished readers and adequate spellers. The ability to achieve this potential depends on two variables: the instructional approach and the amount of practice. The Orton-Gillingham approach to reading and spelling ensures success by developing multisensory techniques for memory and retrieval. This practical teaching technique emphasizes the reading-decoding process.

The teacher introduces the elements of the language systematically, and students are taught letter-sound relationships using all senses: seeing the letter (visual), saying the letter (auditory), and writing the letter (kinesthetic). In this respect. Orton-Gillingham differs from traditional phonics instruction. Once letters are mastered, letters are grouped into blends, and short, structured passages are used for reading and dictation. Infinitely flexible, it is a philosophy rather than a system. The student learns the elements of language-consonants, digraphs, blends, and diphthongs in an orderly fashion.

As students learn new material, they continue to review old material until it becomes automatic. The teacher addresses vocabulary, sentence structure, composition, and reading comprehension in a similar structured, sequential, and cumulative manner.

At best, the teacher tries to understand how an individual learns and to devise appropriate teaching strategies. In every lesson, the student experiences success and gains confidence as well as skill. Learning becomes a happy experience. The Orton-Gillingham approach is appropriate for teaching individuals, small groups, and classrooms. It is appropriate for teaching in the primary, elementary, and intermediate grades, and at the secondary and college level, as well as for adults.

An Orton-Gillingham approach, while not the only program available, is probably the best known for helping children with dyslexia learn to read. The fundamental principles on which it is based, including developing phonemic awareness, and using a multisensory approach, are considered essential components in reading instruction today.

The Orton-Gillingham approach has proven successful with students who have struggled in learning to read and spell through traditional classroom methods, despite normal intelligence, hearing, and vision. It is the program most recommended by experts in the field of dyslexia.

Modern research has continued to confirm Dr. Orton's theories about the physiological differences experienced by dyslexics. Early remediation is most effective; however, these methods have been successfully adapted for use with older students and adults. The result is the development of lifelong language skills and the wonderful feeling of success in the world of written language.

See also GILLINGHAM, ANNA; ORTON, SAMUEL TORREY.

outcomes assessment   The assessment of student attainment or mastery of specific learning objectives. While the term may be used in relation to assessment of an individual student's program and performance, it is more commonly used in the context of overall institutional research and evaluation. This allows a school to see whether student performance meets the educational goals defined by the school, and helps the school evaluate the effectiveness of those goals.

The nature and focus of outcomes assessment varies according to the nature of a school and its mission. For example, outcomes assessment for a high school might focus on the percentage of students in specific grades who meet established standards for competency in reading, writing, and critical skills.

While outcomes assessment typically focuses on academic accomplishments, it may also take into account social and emotional development. In the past decade, outcomes assessment has become an increasingly important activity for educational institutions, both public and private, as a primary means of demonstrating institutional effectiveness and justifying their use of federal, state, and local funds.

parapnasias   Use of incorrect words or word combinations.

parenting skills training   A type of behavioral therapy that can be helpful in dealing with children with a LEARNING DISABILITY. Rearing children under the best of circumstances is challenging, but when one or more of a parent's children have a learning disability, special discipline techniques may be necessary to help modify behavior. For instance, many therapists recommend consistent use of "time outs" when a child loses control. Other techniques include rewards and penalties or stress-reduction methods, such as meditation. Parents are further encouraged to spend "quality time" each day with the child; read a book together, toss a football, or play a board game, for example. Since children with learning disabilities tend to receive more than an average share of negative feedback, parents can balance that out by praising good behavior and good deeds, large and small, and pointing out the child's strengths and abilities.

parietal lobes   One of four major pairs of lobes of the cerebral cortex. It is an area located at the upper middle part of the head above the temporal lobes, and includes the sensory cortex and the association areas involved in processing information about body sensation, touch, and spatial organization. The association areas in the parietal lobes are also involved in secondary language and visual processing.

Lesions in association areas in the parietal lobe can cause difficulties in learning tasks that require an understanding of spatial perception and the body's position in space. GERSTMANN'S SYNDROME is associated with damage to these areas; this syndrome may include left to right confusion, difficulty naming fingers when specific fingers are touched (FINGER AGNOSIA), problems in writing (DYSGRAPHIA), and problems with mathematics (DYSCALCULIA).

pattern recognition   The ability to remember and recognize patterns is a key component of learning. Pattern recognition is an important element in reading development, in which an effective reader will increasingly come to recognize that certain patterns (such as specific consonant clusters like *th* or *st*) represent stable sounds, or that certain prefixes and suffixes (such as *re-* or *-ing*) convey specific meanings.

The ability to recognize and remember patterns is essential in developing mathematical and writing abilities, and also plays an essential role in developing higher order cognitive abilities such as critical thinking, analysis, and problem solving.

Pattern recognition may be a significant difficulty for individuals with a LEARNING DISABILITY or attention disorders.

Peabody Picture Vocabulary Test–Third Edition (PPVT-III)   A developmental test of language assessment that measures receptive vocabulary (that is, vocabulary a person understands when he hears it used by someone else) by having a student point to the correct picture that depicts a dictated word from among a group of four pictures. Children who have poor visual comprehension of pictures, or who tend to respond impulsively, may have a low score on the PPVT-III, even though they have adequate language skills.

Because this test looks at only one aspect of language development, it should be used together with other tests that measure other aspects of language ability, such as oral communication skills and comprehension of grammatical structures. Receptive vocabulary is only a small subset of cognitive ability and should never be confused with intelligence.

pedagogy   The study of teaching methods, including the educational goals and objectives and the means of achieving such goals. Pedagogy encompasses educational psychology and theories of learning.

pemoline   See CYLERT.

percentile   A value on a scale of 100 that indicates the percent of a distribution that is equal to or below it. It is the point on a distribution of NORMS in a standardized test below which a certain percentage of the scores fall. For example, if 50 percent of the scores fall below a raw score of 80 on a test, then the score of 80 is the 50th percentile.

perception   The process through which sensory information (hearing, sight, touch, movement, taste, smell) is recognized and interpreted.

Perception involves both the intake of information through the senses, and processing and making sense of that information within cognition. While sensory experience itself is largely automatic for humans, perception also involves learned behavior and intellectual capacity.

perceptual disorder   A disorder involving the perception of stimuli from one or more of the senses. Unlike visual or hearing problems, perceptual disorders involve the processing of information received through a sense, either in perception or understanding.

A number of distinct brain problems are caused by defects in visual, sensory, and hearing perception that represent fundamental defects in perception rather than complex problems of memory, reasoning, or motor function. They usually involve only parts of the brain.

perceptual handicap   See PERCEPTUAL DISORDER.

perceptual learning disabilities   See PERCEPTUAL DISORDER.

perceptual-motor skills   In everything children do, they look, listen, and touch, and then make a perceptual judgment about the things they see, hear, and feel. It is this perceptual judgment that dictates the way they react to their world (what is seen, what is heard, and what is felt). When perceptions are well developed, then reactions are more likely to be appropriate for each given situation.

There are six perceptual systems that take in information from the environment: visual (sight), auditory (sound), tactile (touch), kinesthetic (muscle feeling), olfactory (smell), and gustatory (taste). Perceptual-motor skills or behavior generally will involve perceptual input through more than one of these systems, and a complex sequence of motor activities.

Motor learning is an important part of childhood development. There is a natural developmental sequence of perceptual motor skill development, beginning very early with skills such as rolling over and sitting up, and proceeding to activities such as crawling, standing, walking, running, and jumping. As development progresses, the requirements for integration of perceptual systems and motor behavior grow steadily more subtle and complex.

Delays in the development of age-appropriate perceptual-motor skills may have significant and sometimes pervasive effects on school and social performance.

perceptual processing   The systems and processes by which raw data from the surrounding environment is taken in through the perceptual system and interpreted by the brain. In general, visual processing and auditory processing are the most commonly referred to areas of perceptual processing, when addressing issues of learning and learning problems in clinical or educational settings.

perfectionism   A set of self-defeating thoughts and behaviors aimed at reaching excessively high and unrealistic goals. Many people who have trouble with writing or finishing school projects have problems with perfectionism, which may be closely related to anxiety or to OBSESSIVE-COMPULSIVE DISORDER. Individuals diagnosed with ATTENTION DEFICIT/HYPERACTIVITY DISORDER (ADHD) frequently have perfectionist tendencies, particularly in areas they feel are important. One key factor in perfectionism that is often characteristic of both learning-disabled students and those with ADHD is the inability to differentiate between important and unimportant information. For example, a perfectionistic student may spend hours on a homework assignment because she repeatedly crumples up her paper and tosses it in the trash when some of the letters are not the same size as others, or because she keeps changing pencils to obtain a certain color of lead. In such cases, perfectionism is another manifestation of the social imperception that so often characterizes students with learning disabilities and ADHD.

The issue of perfectionism may seem to be linked to a failure to understand the nature of a task's requirements. However, it appears equally likely that perfectionist behavior may arise from deeper underlying factors, and may best be addressed through a combination of behavioral and cognitive treatments.

Perfectionism is often mistakenly seen as desirable or even necessary for success. However, recent studies have shown that perfectionistic attitudes actually interfere with success. The desire to be perfect can both deprive an individual of a sense of personal satisfaction and cause that person to fail to achieve as much as those with more realistic goals.

Most perfectionists learned early in life that they were valued because of how much they achieved. As a result, they learned to value themselves only on the basis of other people's approval, so that self-esteem came to be based primarily on external standards. This can leave people vulnerable and excessively sensitive to the opinions and criticism of others. In attempting to protect themselves from criticism, these individuals may decide that being perfect is their only defense.

A number of negative feelings, thoughts, and beliefs may be associated with perfectionism, including

- fear of failure: perfectionists often equate failure to achieve their goals with a lack of personal worth or value

- fear of making mistakes: perfectionists often equate mistakes with failure. In orienting their lives around avoiding mistakes, perfectionists miss opportunities to learn and grow

- fear of disapproval: if they let others see their flaws, perfectionists often fear that they won't be accepted. Trying to be perfect is a way of trying to protect themselves from criticism, rejection, and disapproval

- all-or-nothing thinking: perfectionists often think they are worthless if their accomplishments aren't perfect, and they have trouble putting things in perspective. For example, a straight-A student who gets a "B" might think he is "a total failure"

- the "shoulds": the lives of perfectionists are often structured by an endless list of rigid rules about how their lives must be led. With such an overemphasis on shoulds, perfectionists rarely take into account their own desires

- others' success: perfectionists tend to perceive others as achieving success with a minimum of effort, few errors, little emotional stress, and maximum self-confidence, whereas their own efforts are inadequate

Perfectionists are often trapped in a vicious cycle in which they set unreachable goals and then fail to meet them because the goals were impossible to begin with. Failure was thus inevitable. The constant pressure to achieve perfection and the inevitable chronic failure lessen productivity and effectiveness. As perfectionists become more self-critical, their self-esteem suffers, which may also lead to anxiety and depression. At this point perfectionists may give up completely on their goals and set different unrealistic goals, but this thinking sets the entire cycle in motion again.

Perfectionists need to understand that perfectionism is undesirable, and they must challenge the self-defeating thoughts and behaviors that fuel perfectionism. Cognitive therapy is often helpful in achieving this.

perseveration   Persistent repetition of a behavior or activity regardless of the result, or having trouble switching from one activity to another. Extreme examples of perseveration may be seen in individuals with a DEVELOPMENTAL DISABILITY or AUTISM, for whom repetitive hand motions, rocking, or other movements are common characteristics. More typical examples in childhood might involve singing a song from a video again and again.

In a school setting, perseveration can be used to describe the fixation on a specific element in a broader task, such as spending all of the time of an exam on a single essay question. Psychologists often encounter perseveration in students they evaluate for learning disabilities. For example, if a student is told to copy six small circles in a straight row, the student may make the circles all the way across the width of the page, draw-

ing 30 or more. Teachers and parents often report perseverative behaviors among students with learning disabilities and ADHD. For example, if they ask the student to hop four times on the left foot, the student may hop 20 or more times or until he loses his balance.

This type of behavior may be caused by inflexible strategies and problems in shifting from one task to another.

personality test   A type of test that is meant to assess a broad range of personality traits and characteristics, and provide a spectrum of potential information, from indications of personal styles or patterns to evidence of significant personality disorders or other psychological difficulties. Personality tests are often administered as part of a comprehensive assessment battery in order to assure an accurate diagnosis of complex symptoms.

The oldest, most-studied personality test is the Minnesota Multiphasic Personality Inventory (MMPI), a true/false test with 567 questions. It's used by psychologists in hospitals, clinics, and in private practice, to help diagnose the possible existence of mental disorders. The MMPI was first published in 1943, and was restandardized with updated language in 1989 as the MMPI-2. An adolescent version of the MMPI-2 (the MMPI-A) is also available.

The Millon Clinical Multiaxial Inventory (MCMI) is another personality test recently updated as the MCMI-III. It was written by Dr. Theodore Millon (founding editor of the *Journal of Personality Disorders*) to specifically assess personality disorders, as opposed to the MMPI, which screens for a broad range of psychological problems. An adolescent version of this test also exists.

A third widely used personality test is called the Sixteen Primary Factor Inventory (also known as the 16PF or the Cattell 16PF), which is a more positive test that evaluates personality traits and identifies the test taker's strengths. Developed by Raymond Cattell, it is used primarily for job seekers and to assess relationship strengths and weaknesses. A children's version of the 16PF (the Children's Personality Questionnaire, or CPQ) and an adolescent version (the High School Personality Questionnaire) are also available.

phenylketonuria (PKU)   An inherited metabolic disease (one of the inborn errors of metabolism) that leads to MENTAL RETARDATION and other developmental disabilities if untreated in infancy. In this condition, an amino acid called phenylalanine builds up in the bloodstream, causing brain damage. Infants with untreated PKU appear to develop typically for the first few months of life, but by 12 months of age most babies will have a significant developmental delay and will be diagnosed with mental retardation.

PKU is inherited as a single-gene disorder, which is a condition caused by a mutant or abnormal gene. It is an autosomal recessive disorder, which means that each parent of a child with PKU carries one defective gene for the disorder and one normal gene. In a recessive condition, an individual must have two defective genes in order to have the disorder. Individuals with only one copy of a defective gene are called "carriers," show no symptoms of having the disease, and usually remain unaware of their status until they have an affected child. In order for a child to inherit PKU, both parents must be PKU carriers. When this occurs, there is a one in four chance of their producing an affected child with each pregnancy. Boys and girls are equally at risk of inheriting this disorder.

Diagnosis

Before the 1960s, most infants born with PKU developed mental retardation and cerebral palsy. Although treatment for PKU using a low phenylalanine diet was first described in the 1950s, the inability to detect PKU early in the child's life limited effective treatment. The first newborn screening test was developed by Dr. Robert Guthrie in 1959 specifically to test for PKU. This simple yet effective and economical test was developed to screen newborn infants for PKU before leaving the hospital. Today, all states routinely screen newborns for PKU. The American Academy of Pediatrics recommends that infants receiving the test during the first 24 hours of life be retested at two to three weeks of age during their first postnatal pediatric visit.

To test for PKU, a few drops of blood are taken from the infant's heel, and then tested in a state laboratory for abnormal amounts of phenylalanine. The normal phenylalanine level is less than 2 milligrams per deciliter (mg/dl). Those with phenylalanine levels of 20.0 mg/dl or higher are considered likely to have "classical" PKU. Infants with these high levels are further tested to confirm the diagnosis before treatment is started.

Some infants with slightly higher levels of phenylalanine have "mild hyperphenylalanemia." Today many clinicians believe that any child with a phenylalanine level greater than 6 or 8 mg/dl should be treated with a modified phenylalanine-restricted diet.

Treatment

Although PKU is not preventable, its symptoms can often be treated successfully through the use of a carefully regimented diet with a restricted phenylalanine content. Babies are given a special formula that contains very low phenylalanine levels; then they gradually progress to eating certain vegetables and other foods that are low in phenylalanine. Affected children must have their blood tested regularly to ensure the presence of the correct level of phenylalanine. Foods recommended for those affected by PKU contain small amounts of protein, such as fruits and vegetables, limited amounts of cereal and grain products, and special low-protein products.

High-protein foods such as meat, fish, eggs, poultry, dairy products, nuts, peanut butter, legumes, soy products, and products containing Nutrasweet should be avoided. The food program used to treat those with PKU is quite expensive, typically costing up to $10,000 a year or more. Although health departments may pay for the formula in some states and mandated insurance coverage may cover the cost in other states, most insurance companies do not cover the cost of treatment for those with PKU because it is considered nutritional rather than medical therapy.

While phenylalanine restricted diets have proven to be highly effective in preventing mental retardation, it is now recognized that there may still be subtle cognitive deficits. Usually the individual has a normal IQ, but the incidence of ATTENTION DEFICIT/HYPERACTIVITY DISORDER (ADHD) and learning disabilities is higher compared to those children who do not have PKU.

Recent studies have found that children with PKU who stopped the diet in early childhood did not develop as rapidly as children who remained on the diet, and had more learning disabilities, behavioral problems, and other neurological problems. Thus, until research provides alternative treatments, everyone with PKU should remain on a restricted diet indefinitely in order to maintain a safe level of phenylalanine (believed to be in the range of 2–6 mg/dl).

Pregnancy and PKU

Pregnant women with PKU who aren't receiving dietary therapy have high levels of phenylalanine that can damage their unborn child, causing mental retardation and other congenital defects. High levels of phenylalanine are extremely toxic to the brain of a fetus. Although the child doesn't have PKU, there will be brain damage from the toxic effects of phenylalanine in the womb. This is known as maternal PKU.

More than 90 percent of infants born to women with PKU who are not on a specialized diet will have mental retardation, and may also have small head size, heart defects, and low birth weight. These infants cannot be treated with a special diet since they do not have PKU. Therefore, women who have PKU should be on a phenylalanine-restricted diet at least one year before pregnancy and should stay on the diet while breast-feeding to increase the chance of having a healthy child.

phoneme A single sound. English has 44 phonemes, which are represented by 26 letters (GRAPHEMES).

phonemic awareness The awareness of the sounds (PHONEMES) that make up whole words. A person who has weak phonemic awareness will have trouble judging sounds within words. This causes students to omit, substitute, or reverse sounds and letters within words, and can make learning a second language quite difficult. Individuals with weak phonological processing can't judge whether what they say matches what they see. Although phonemic awareness is not necessary for understanding spoken language, the ability to break apart and manipulate the sounds in a written word is a crucial skill when learning to read and write.

For example, when an individual hears the word "sat," the ear hears one continuous sound. When children develop phonemic awareness, they can break the word into three phonemes—/s/-/a/-/t/—making it possible to read and spell correctly. When children have developed phonological awareness, they can isolate sounds, rhyme, blend sounds, and manipulate the sounds of language.

Research indicates phonemic awareness is often underdeveloped for individuals with a LEARNING DISABILITY. Brain scans identify that the brains of learning-disabled individuals can't segment words and syllables into phonemes nor can they blend sounds into words.

Since poor phonemic awareness is known to be a core deficit in learning-disabled individuals, explicit and systematic instruction in a phonics approach has significant benefits to children with reading problems from kindergarten to sixth grade.

The benefits of explicit phonics instructions, which improve phonemic awareness, are overwhelmingly supported by research done by the National Institute of Child Health and Human Development (NICHD), which endorses this method for regular classroom reading instruction.

Many children have trouble judging sounds within words. Although they see letters correctly, they can't detect and correct their errors in reading and spelling. This causes problems with decoding, spelling, and pronunciation. A child with this problem might read "seep" for "sleep," spell words like "girl" as "gril," and mispronounce common words.

Individuals who don't develop phonemic awareness in preschool often have trouble learning to read and spell. Therefore, it's important to measure phonemic awareness as children enter first grade. There are informal and formal means of assessing phonemic awareness. Some informal tests would include the following:

- asking an individual to add, delete, or change the sounds in a word
- matching rhyming words
- matching initial, middle, or final sounds of words
- asking an individual to tap on the table for each sound they hear in a given word

When children have trouble with such tasks, more formal assessment of phonemic awareness may be required. There are many formal tests available to assess phonemic awareness, such as the Lindamood Auditory Conceptualization Test or the Test of Phonological Awareness.

phonics An approach to teaching reading and spelling that emphasizes symbol-sound relationships; used especially in beginning or remedial instruction. Being able to discriminate sounds is an essential element in reading and communicating well.

Phonics programs published by major educational publishers have been used to teach reading for decades. These programs offer books, workbooks, computer software, and other teaching materials that introduce letter and word patterns in a systematic and structured way.

There are two phonics approaches: synthetic and analytic. *Synthetic phonics* is a method where individuals are taught single letters and their sounds. Once the letters are mastered, individuals are taught to synthesize the letters into whole words. *Analytic phonics* teaches whole word families (cat, fat, mat, hat) and then teaches individuals to analyze the phonemic elements of the words. Traditionally, reading was taught in U.S. schools using phonics instruction, with its emphasis on developing word-recognition skills.

However, the phonics approach to learning was criticized in the 1980s when many schools changed direction and embraced the WHOLE LANGUAGE APPROACH, a more holistic and content-driven approach to teaching reading. This method attempts to get students to read right away, using high-quality children's literature, and emphasizes using contextual cues to aid comprehension.

As national reading scores declined, the movement toward whole language began to change again. Studies comparing whole language and phonics showed that children who are explicitly taught phonics in a direct and systematic way achieve higher scores on reading tests.

Today, most schools use a combination of both approaches. A growing body of research suggests that contextual cues cannot replace word recognition. Good readers don't skip words or rely on context but read virtually every word and see all letters. In fact, studies demonstrate that only poor readers rely on contextual cues for word identification. Teaching children to guess the meaning of words by context actually decreases the odds that they will learn to read well.

Children who don't understand what they read usually have poor word-recognition skills. Because these children have to devote so much attention to slowly and carefully figuring out the words, they focus less attention on what the text means. Children who recognize words more readily can focus more attention on meaning.

Many experts in education today agree that word-recognition skills as taught in phonics are the critical building blocks for reading success. Still, research also demonstrates that phonics alone is less effective than phonics combined with whole language. An average child needs to read a word four to eight times before word-recognition becomes automatic.

Therefore, the process of reading strengthens the child's ability to perceive sounds in both verbal and written language. Moreover, for practice to be most effective, children need to read stories that are at their reading level; in other words, they should be able to recognize most of the words.

While the trends of teaching reading shift from year to year in general education, the field of learning disabilities has consistently found a phonics approach most effective to teach children with learning disabilities.

phonological processing   The ability to hear speech sounds (phonemes) and words and identify different sound segments.

See also PHONICS.

phonology   The sound system of a language. PHONICS comes from this word. A PHONEME (sound) is the smallest unit of language; different languages and dialects use different phonemes.

PKU   See PHENYLKETONURIA.

PL 94–142   See EDUCATION FOR ALL HANDICAPPED CHILDREN ACT OF 1975.

portfolio assessment   A representative collection of a student's work that was completed over a period of time. Sometimes referred to as authentic assessment, the collection is used to assess progress and achievement in writing, art, reading, or mathematics. Portfolio assessment is a much more useful means of checking the progress of students with a LEARNING DISABILITY than traditional paper/pencil tests, which often are not true reflections of the student's progress.

However, assessment of portfolios can present problems due to their subjective nature. Many educators have developed effective ways to identify progress in specific skill areas. Materials collected in portfolios may include writing samples, science projects, spelling tests, behavioral checklists, teacher observation notes, videotapes of performances, and/or math projects.

positive reinforcement   A method of promoting certain behavior by providing a positive stimulus. When the desired behavior is produced, the stimulus is presented. For example, teachers frequently use stickers or gold stars (positive stimulus) when a child has completed an assignment correctly (desired behavior).

As the positive reinforcement is repeated, the desired behavior is reinforced.

See also NEGATIVE REINFORCEMENT.

Prader-Willi syndrome   A complex genetic disorder that includes short stature, MENTAL RETARDATION or a LEARNING DISABILITY, incomplete sexual development, characteristic behavior problems, low muscle tone, and an involuntary urge to eat constantly. This, coupled with a reduced need for calories, leads to obesity.

PWS is found in people of both sexes and all races, and in about one in 14,000 people in the United States. Prader-Willi syndrome is one of the 10 most common conditions seen in genetics clinics and is the most common genetic cause of obesity that has been identified.

Although PWS is associated with an abnormality of chromosome 15, it's generally considered not to be an inherited condition, but rather a spontaneous genetic birth defect that occurs at or near the time of conception. The faulty chromosome affects functioning of the hypothalamus.

Newborns with PWS are "floppy" and, because of poor muscle tone, can't suck well enough to get sufficient nutrients. Often they must be fed through a tube for several months after birth until muscle control improves. Sometime in the following years, usually by preschool age, children with PWS develop an increased interest in food and quickly gain excessive weight if calories aren't restricted.

In addition to sometimes extreme attempts to obtain food, people with PWS are prone to temper outbursts, stubbornness, rigidity, argumentativeness, and repetitive thoughts and behaviors. Strategies to deal with these problems usually include structuring the person's environment, implementing behavioral management techniques, and, occasionally, drug therapy.

People with PWS can attend school, enjoy community activities, get jobs, and even move away from home, although they need a lot of help. Schoolchildren with PWS are likely to need SPECIAL EDUCATION and related services, such as speech and occupational therapy. In community, work, and residential settings, adolescents and adults often need special assistance to learn and carry out responsibilities and to get along with others. Always, people with PWS need around-the-clock food supervision. As adults, most affected individuals do best in a special group home for people with PWS, where food access can be restricted without interfering with those who don't need such restriction. Although in the past many patients died in adolescence or young adulthood, preventing obesity will allow a person with PWS to live a normal lifespan.

Diagnosis

Early diagnosis of Prader-Willi syndrome gives parents an opportunity to manage their child's diet and avoid obesity and its related problems from the start. Since infants and young children with PWS typically have developmental delays in all areas, diagnosis may facilitate a family's access to critical early intervention services and help identify areas of need or risk. Diagnosis also makes it possible for families to get information and support from professionals and other families who are dealing with the syndrome.

Many doctors will refer a suspected patient to a medical geneticist who specializes in diagnosing and testing for genetic conditions such as PWS. After taking a history and doing a physical examination, the diagnostician will arrange for specialized genetic testing to be done on a blood sample to evaluate for the genetic abnormality found in people with PWS.

For more information, contact the Prader-Willi Syndrome Association (USA). It has a toll-free number and is organized to answer questions and help individuals deal with the problems associated with PWS. PWSA (USA) provides a newsletter and other publications, an annual national conference, and chapters throughout the country to provide family support and advocacy. One can also call a local genetics unit to ask for information on PWS.

See also PRADER-WILLI SYNDROME ASSOCIATION.

Prader-Willi Syndrome Association   A nonprofit organization that provides a newsletter and other publications, an annual national conference, and chapters throughout the country to provide family support and advocacy.

Contact: Suite 220, 2510 South Brentwood Boulevard, St. Louis, MO 63144; phone: (800) 926–4797 or (314) 962–7644; website: http://www.pwsausa.org.

pragmatic language   Verbal and nonverbal language that includes tone of voice, posture, gestures, and facial expression used in social interaction.

pragmatic skills   The social element of language usage. Pragmatic skills include taking turns in conversation, asking relevant questions, staying on topic, and engaging in active listening. Individuals with LEARNING DISABILITY often have problems in processing or responding to pragmatic cues; this can cause poor social skills and problems in communication.

praxia Knowing or recognizing objects; dependent on an intact parietal lobe.

praxis Also known as motor planning, this is the ability to integrate input from the senses and to formulate and execute a sequence of unfamiliar actions.

prefrontal lobes A part of the brain also known as the prefrontal cortex; found under the forehead. This part of the brain is the center for executive functions and higher order thinking, and supports self-control, sequencing behaviors, planning, and the ability to modulate motor responses. The prefrontal lobes are also thought to be involved in the monitoring of internal emotional states. It is one of the largest cortical sub-regions of the brain and plays an important role in human problem solving.

preoperational stage The second of four stages in Jean Piaget's theory of cognitive development, which he theorized occurred from about age two to six. During this period of time, the child learns to use language but lacks logic, relying instead on immediate experience. Recent research has suggested that children reach cognitive milestones, such as the ability to sequence and categorize, at ages younger than Piaget estimated.

The most important advancement during this stage is the ability to use language and symbols. Children of this age have the ability to pretend and they get great joy from it as they practice this new ability. They can pretend that sticks are boats and swords, and in their play they take on roles in complicated games. They pretend to be heroes and villains, mothers and fathers, and characters from the stories they hear.

Children tend to be egocentric during this stage, unable to see things from any perspective but their own. During this period, they reason by moving from particular to particular—for example, children might explain that the car

goes because the radio is on or that it gets dark at night because they go to sleep. They don't understand the idea that objects remain the same in terms of mass or number when shape or arrangement changes.

pre-referral process Strategies a teacher uses when a student is obviously having trouble in class but has not yet been officially referred for a multidisciplinary team evaluation. In the pre-referral stage, a teacher informally collects data concerning the area of difficulty.

There are several pre-referral models of intervention used to avoid the lengthy and involved process of referral. In the consultation model, the teacher brings data to a child study team or identified school consultant. Another popular model is peer collaboration, in which a teacher meets with a colleague to share data.

In all pre-referral models the teacher develops a statement of the concern, shares data, and brainstorms interventions with colleagues. The pre-referral process is important because intervention on an informal level may effectively address the difficulty. If intervention strategies fail, the student will most likely be formally referred to the school's child study committee/team.

pretest A test given in a specific skill area before instruction or remediation has taken place. Typically it is followed by a posttest given after instruction to measure progress.

print disabilities A range of visual, perceptual, or physical impairments that may prevent a person from reading standard print. Examples of print disabilities include blindness, visual impairment, DYSLEXIA, and other types of LEARNING DISABILITY.

printing instruction While computer keyboarding skills are becoming more and more a part of writing, printing remains an essential skill. Printing instruction begins in kindergarten where children are taught to write the letters of the alphabet, and continues through third grade until CURSIVE WRITING is introduced. Problems in forming letters accurately may be caused by poor visual and motor skills. Extreme printing difficulties are called DYSGRAPHIA.

problem solving   In relation to schoolwork, problem solving refers to finding the answer to mathematical word problems. It requires a type of thinking in which an individual must analyze and interpret information and then make decisions about how to find a solution. The complexity in problem solving can be particularly difficult for individuals with language disorders, since it requires one to combine language and thinking before applying the appropriate mathematical computation in a variety of settings.

problem-solving skill   The ability to consider the probable factors that can influence the outcome of each of various solutions to a problem, and to select the best solution. Patients with deficits in this skill may become "immobilized" when faced with such a problem. By being unable to think of possible solutions, they respond by doing nothing.

program specialist   A specialist who works within an educational system and provides consultation and assessment in special needs areas.

proofreading   The process in which an individual reviews a completed piece of work for mistakes. For many individuals with a LEARNING DISABILITY, finding errors can be difficult. Unlike most students, who check over their work for accuracy, many students with learning disabilities and ADHD never bother with proofreading unless they receive specific practice in it. Such students do not understand the proofreading process and must be taught the specific skills involved in proofreading in detail.

New software programs and computer tools may make proofreading easier by identifying grammatical and/or spelling errors. People with learning disabilities may find it helpful to proofread for one skill at a time. For example, an individual may read over a homework essay to be sure sentence structure is cohesive, followed by a second reading for spelling errors. Another proofreading strategy is to let time lapse between writing and proofreading.

proprioceptive system   A person's sensory system that uses receptors in joints, muscles, and tendons to help an individual perceive his position in space.

prosody   The inflections and intonations of speech.

Prozac (fluoxetine)   An antidepressant medication that is sometimes used to treat ATTENTION DEFICIT/HYPERACTIVITY DISORDER in patients who are also depressed, both alone and in conjunction with RITALIN (methylphenidate). Results of trials with this medication suggest that Prozac may be helpful in the treatment of ADHD, although the first-line therapy for ADHD is still Ritalin or DEXEDRINE (dextroamphetamine).

Introduced in 1988, Prozac was the first of a new class of antidepressants known as selective serotonin reuptake inhibitors (SSRIs), which increase the levels of a neurotransmitter called serotonin. Many people who are depressed have low levels of this chemical, and therefore improve when serotonin levels rise.

Like other pharmaceutical interventions for ADHD, Prozac is usually prescribed as part of a treatment plan that includes educational and psychosocial interventions. Prozac and other antidepressant medications in the SSRI class (such as Zoloft) are sometimes prescribed when individuals with ADHD don't respond to stimulant medication, or when they have other coexisting conditions such as depression or obsessive-compulsive disorder.

Like all antidepressants, Prozac takes one to three weeks to achieve its full effect.

Studies suggest that younger people respond to Prozac with very small doses, and that a sizable portion of young people who don't respond to other antidepressants do respond to Prozac.

Side Effects

All antidepressants carry side effects, but Prozac and the other SSRIs cause fewer, less uncomfortable problems than older antidepressants. Most common side effects include (in the order of frequency) sexual problems, nausea, headache, insomnia, diarrhea, nervousness, and anxiety. Less common side effects include dry mouth, appetite loss, tremor, upper respiratory infection, and dizziness.

Studies suggest that younger people experience slightly different side effects, including restlessness and sweating as the most common complaints, followed by drowsiness, dry mouth, and tremors.

pseudoword decoding   A type of phonological awareness test in which individuals are asked to decode nonsense words such as "pid," "frap," "theap," and "phing." Nonsense word decoding is often a subtest on achievement tests or reading tests.

The task is useful because it differentiates the skill of decoding (sound-symbol relationship) from sight word recognition (in which an individual may simply have remembered the shape of a word).

When used effectively, a great deal can be learned diagnostically about what letter patterns an individual has not yet mastered, so that remediation can be designed accordingly.

Other than for the purpose of assessing decoding skills, pseudoword decoding—the ability to read nonsense words—is not a particularly useful skill.

psychiatrist   A psychiatrist is a physician who specializes in the diagnosis, treatment, and prevention of mental illnesses and substance use disorders. Typically, either a psychiatrist or a pediatrician will be involved when medication for attention deficit disorders are prescribed.

It takes many years of education and training to become a psychiatrist, beginning with graduation from college and then medical school, followed by four years of residency training in the field of psychiatry. Many psychiatrists undergo additional training so that they can further specialize in such areas as child and adolescent psychiatry, geriatric psychiatry, forensic psychiatry, psychopharmacology, and/or psychoanalysis. This extensive medical training enables the psychiatrist to understand the body's functions, and the complex relationship between emotional illness and other medical illnesses.

psychological evaluation   A set of procedures that is sometimes used as part of a general assessment of an individual's learning difficulties, especially when there are other significant behavioral, social, or emotional elements involved. A psychological evaluation is necessary to determine whether psychological or emotional factors may be involved in an individual's performance or behavior, or to rule out such possible conditions as depression, obsessive-compulsive disorder, or a personality disorder in cases where symptoms or behavior might indicate the presence of a significant psychological problem.

A psychological evaluation will involve the administration of multiple psychological measures, gathering of anecdotal information about the child, and any other information about the child's psychological functioning. Psychological ethics as well as the Standards for Educational and Psychological Testing state that no single test or procedure constitutes a complete psychological evaluation.

psychologist   A mental health expert who specializes in the diagnosis and treatment of mental or emotional problems. Clinical psychologists often use a range of assessment tools, including intelligence testing, to assess, diagnose, and treat patients. Psychologists can treat learning disabilities by helping the person explore upsetting thoughts and feelings so as to help find more positive ways to channel emotions.

A psychologist usually holds a doctoral degree (Ph.D., Psy.D., or Ed.D.) from a university or professional school. Generally, a psychologist in clinical practice will have a degree in clinical psychology (although it might be in counseling psychology). The American Psychological Association (APA), the largest organization representing psychologists in the world and which accredits doctoral training programs in psychology, has adopted the "scientist-practitioner" model of psychological training. That is, all psychologists trained under this model are expert in the theoretical issues and practical applications of psychology. With the exception of the Psy.D. (a purely clinical degree), all psychologists have had extensive training in research, having completed a doctoral dissertation as a major part of the training. In fact, the psychologist's training in research is what most distinguishes a psychologist from other providers of mental health treatment. In addition to research training, the psychologist will have completed one or more clinical internships.

A psychologist studies and understands brain and behavior processes from a scientific viewpoint and applies this knowledge to help people understand, explain, and change behavior. Psychologists study the biological and social principles of learning, behavior, emotion, and human development and their interaction with environmental and biochemical/genetic factors to answer research questions about how people respond in various facets of their lives.

Psychologists develop standardized assessment tools to measure behavior and therapeutic interventions to help people improve their ability to function as individuals and in groups.

The APA believes that psychologists must be trained first in the core knowledge of psychology, including a comprehensive set of psychological ethics and practices. Only after they have been trained in the core knowledge of psychology do they specialize. Although there are many subspecialties within psychology, APA advocates licensure in four major psychological specialties and provides training and practice guidelines in each: clinical psychology; counseling psychology; school psychology; and industrial psychology.

psychologist, educational A Ph.D.-level mental health expert who specializes in assessment and consultation relating to educational issues, including the assessment of learning disabilities. Educational psychologists use a range of assessment tools, including intelligence and academic achievement testing.

Special educational needs, learning difficulties, DYSLEXIA, behavior problems, and gifted children all fall within the scope of the educational psychologist's expertise. The educational psychologist is qualified to give advice based upon expert assessment and observation of the child's strengths and weaknesses, drawing upon a knowledge of child psychology, child development, and education.

Psychologists use a range of techniques to put together a picture of the child's strengths and difficulties and identify important factors affecting the child's learning and behavior. Individual tests of intelligence will give a profile of the child's verbal and nonverbal thinking skills and may identify specific areas of strength and weakness that need to be taken into account. Tests of reading, spelling, and number are used to measure the child's achievement against expectations and potential. Information is also gathered through structured classroom observation, and interviews with teachers and parents. Getting an objective picture helps understanding and provides a framework for discussing solutions to problems.

psychologist, school   A professionally trained PSYCHOLOGIST who specializes in working with preschool and school-aged children, adolescents, their teachers and families to help make education for students a positive and rewarding experience.

School psychologists address many issues, such as crisis intervention, social skills training, behavioral management techniques, self-esteem, attention deficit disorders, post-traumatic stress disorders, and special education regulations. A school psychologist is also trained in counseling and crisis intervention and is often involved in one-on-one counseling and in group counseling with elementary and high school students.

In addition, school psychologists administer and interpret intelligence tests and achievement tests, and complete social-emotional assessments such as tests of personality or depression. They are primarily responsible in helping schools make an educational diagnosis of a LEARNING DISABILITY such as attention deficit disorder. One of the main roles of the school psychologist is to administer a variety of psychoeducational tests to students who are experiencing academic or behavioral problems in the classroom. Based on these test results and information collected from the student's teachers and parents, the school psychologist helps the schools determine if a student is eligible for special education services.

School psychologists work with students who have vastly different educational problems and needs, including learning disabilities, traumatic brain injuries, emotional and behavioral disorders, AUTISM, intellectual disabilities, and developmental delays.

There are several differences between a school psychologist and a school counselor. There is an ongoing controversy surrounding the nature and degree of training a person must have to be a school psychologist. At a bare minimum, school psychologists must have a specialist degree (that is, masters degree plus 30 graduate hours, advocated by NASP) or a doc-

toral degree (advocated by APA). Most school counselors, in contrast, have earned a bachelor's degree and a few have a master's. In addition, counselors are not trained or qualified to administer and interpret psychological and social-emotional assessments, nor are they able to make educational diagnoses of handicapping conditions as required by federal law. Many counselors spend their school day doing guidance in the classrooms.

School psychologists earn a bachelor's degree followed by an advanced degree—usually a master's degree plus 30 graduate credits. Many school psychology programs across the country offer a specialist degree as well, which is a master's degree plus 30 credits. The specialist degree is an intermediary degree between a master's and a Ph.D. In fact, most states require a specialist degree (or its equivalent) in order to become certified as a school psychologist. Certification allows the practitioner to work in a public school setting but is insufficient in most states to qualify the person for a license for private practice. Licensure for private practice in psychology, including school psychology, requires at minimum a doctorate in most states, although a few states allow a restricted form of licensure for associate-level school psychologists. Training focuses on mental health, child development, learning, and motivation.

School psychologists must be certified to work in the schools or licensed for private practice or to work as a supervising psychologist in most other settings in the state in which services are to be provided. The National Psychology Certification Board (NPCB) and the National Association of School Psychologists (NASP) are trying to establish a national certification in school psychology. However, the training requirements for this certification only requires associate-level training, not the doctoral training advocated by APA. Hence, doctoral-level school psychologists, many of whom were trained under and support the APA model, don't support the current national certification because the training requirements are lower than those advocated by the APA. Each state has different requirements for certification to work in the schools, although most follow the APA guidelines for licensure as professional school psychologists.

Public Law 94–142   See EDUCATION FOR ALL HANDICAPPED CHILDREN ACT OF 1975 (PL 94–142).

raw score The number of correct responses on a NORM-REFERENCED TEST, a test that compares the performance of the test taker to the performance of a preselected group of children whose performance on the test becomes the standard against which test companies compare all other children's performances.

Generally, raw scores are converted into more precise quantitative measurements based on various factors. In themselves, raw scores provide only partial information and should not be used to determine a diagnosis or educational intervention.

readability A measure of how easy it is to comprehend a text depending on a number of variables. These include vocabulary, sentence complexity, format, writing style, and topic, plus the reading comprehension level, interest, background information, and decoding skills of the reader.

Some methods of predicting the readability of a text are used to gauge whether an individual can successfully read and comprehend a passage. One such method is to read a section of a passage and count the number of words that are unfamiliar to the reader. If, for example, the reader encounters more than three unfamiliar words, the readability may be too difficult.

In educational settings, a text's readability is often measured in grade level. For example, a history textbook with a readability of 9.3 means an average ninth grade, third month student should be able to read and comprehend it.

readiness The degree to which an individual is prepared developmentally to learn a new skill. Readiness is a term often used in early education to describe a child's acquisition of prerequisite emotional, social, and cognitive skills for academic learning.

For example, reading readiness would include pre-reading skills such as letter identification, print awareness, and rhyming. When a child has demonstrated mastery of such skills, that child would be ready to learn to read.

However, the concept of readiness can be applied to any stage of learning. For example, readiness for algebra must mean an individual has mastered certain mathematical computations.

Normal three- to six-year-olds acquire academic and social readiness skills naturally when brought up in a literate environment, but developmentally delayed, learning disabled, or environmentally deprived children may need extra training or early intervention to prepare them for learning. Early school failure or unnecessary referrals can be prevented with some extra attention in early education to bolster children's readiness for school.

See also EARLY INTERVENTION PROGRAM.

readiness tests Tests that measure whether an individual has achieved a level of development or acquired the skills and information required to begin a new level of educational activity. For example, children are often given a reading readiness test that assesses whether they have reached a stage where it is appropriate for formal reading instruction to begin.

Readiness tests are tests administered individually or in groups, usually at the end of kindergarten or the beginning of first grade, to determine which children are prepared for academic learning and which need time to develop pre-academic skills. There are many types of readiness skills that vary from informal requests such as "draw a person" or "write the alphabet", to commercial inventories and examinations. The goals of these tests are to assess various skills deemed necessary for school success.

reading Students learn to read by knowing the sounds of letters and knowing the meanings of words (vocabulary), word parts, and groups of words (overall meaning, or semantics). To build this foundation, children need effective reading instruction.

The two main approaches to teaching reading today are WHOLE LANGUAGE and PHONICS. The "whole language" approach focuses on comprehension and is based on the understanding that reading is about finding the meaning in written language. Children learn meanings of words by multiple experiences with words, both written and spoken. A whole language approach to teaching reading can include teaching reading and writing throughout the day in the context of the lesson topics and also emphasizing storybooks rather than worksheets. Many writing opportunities are also important in the whole language approach.

In contrast, phonics focuses on the sounds of letters and words. A phonics approach focuses instruction on learning to associate printed letters and combinations of letters with their corresponding sounds. Phonics instruction gives students strategies to unlock or decode words.

A phonics approach to teaching reading can include "sounding out" words as a way of figuring out new words. For example, in a phonics lesson, the word "cat" would be sounded out as "cc-aa-tt." Practice worksheets or exercises focus on letter sounds, matching pictures with spoken words, short vowel/long vowel, or "letter of the week."

Many schools combine both approaches because of a decade of research suggesting that there is no one best way to build students' literacy skills. A balanced approach to teaching reading combines a strong foundation in phonics with whole language methods. Only through more than one kind of instruction can students gain the skills to recognize and manipulate the sounds of letters and words and the skills to understand what they read. Since all children learn differently, only a balanced approach to teaching reading can give all children the skills they need to read well.

Students learn to read in a certain order: first they must understand that words are made up of different sounds, then associate those sounds with written words, and finally decode words and read groups of words. Students who have trouble learning to read need to be specifically taught the relationships of letters, words, and sounds, since being aware of letter/sound relationships is the main tool good readers use to decode unfamiliar words.

Each child needs practice to be a fluent reader. Research at the National Institutes of Health has found that phonics instruction should be taught as part of a comprehensive, literature-based reading program. Many opportunities for children to read at their own reading level help them to learn to read for meaning and enjoy reading. Highly trained teachers can help children develop good, overall literacy skills, with good vocabularies, knowledge of correct syntax and spelling, reasoning and questioning skills.

Children with a language-based LEARNING DISABILITY have a harder time learning to read because they have a harder time with sounds of letters and words than other children. Research indicates that because phonics instruction focuses on recognizing and manipulating sounds of letters and words, more intense phonics instruction may be helpful for children with learning disabilities.

The ability to read is a fundamental skill for success in life. Reading research has found compelling evidence that children who have a poor start in reading have trouble catching up and develop negative attitudes toward reading, poor vocabulary growth, and missed opportunities for development of reading comprehension strategies.

Most children who are poor readers experience early and continuing difficulties in learning how to accurately identify printed words. These students have problems with "sounding out" unfamiliar words, and with developing "sight vocabulary" of words they are able to read fluently and automatically. The ability to develop these skills is necessary for fluent reading and good reading comprehension.

Diagnostic tests can predict with a high degree of accuracy which students in kindergarten and first grade will have difficulty learning to read. These tests can distinguish, with 92 percent accuracy, those children who will read below the 20th percentile at the end of second grade. These tests take as little as 10 to 15 minutes per child, and can be administered by classroom teachers. Prediction of reading disabilities from tests given at the beginning of first grade are more accurate than those administered during the first semester of kindergarten. The results from these objective tests can be supplemented by teacher ratings of behavior and attention.

Experts suggest a combination of types of tests to identify students who will experience reading problems—knowledge of letter names or sounds, and understanding of sounds (phonemic awareness).

Letter name and sound knowledge Knowledge of letter name (a test better suited to kindergarten) is measured by asking for the name of each letter presented in uppercase type on a single card. Letter sound knowledge is measured by presenting all letters in lowercase type and asking for the "sound the letter makes in words." If a consonant letter can represent two different sounds (such as "c" or "g"), then the tester probes for the second sound and asks for the short and long pronunciation of each vowel. This test is better suited for children in first grade.

Understanding of sounds A test to measure phonemic awareness (the ability to identify, think about, or manipulate the individual sounds in words) comes in a variety of measures divided into three broad categories:

Sound comparison This test includes tasks that require a child to make comparisons between the sounds in different words (such as "which word begins with the same first sound as *can: bag, cat, or fish?*"). The test also includes tasks that require children to generate words that have the same first and last sound as a target word.

Phoneme segmentation This test includes tasks that involve counting, pronouncing, deleting, adding, or reversing the individual sound in words (such as "say 'card' without the 'd' sound or say the sounds in 'hat' one at a time).

Phoneme blending In this test, the tester pronounces a series of sounds in isolation and asks the child to blend them together to make a word ("What word do these sounds make /c/-/a/-/t/?").

A number of tests can be used for early screening purposes, including:

- Phonological Awareness Test: five different measures of phonemic awareness plus a measure of sensitivity to rhyme. This test is nationally normed on children ages five through nine.

- Test of Phonological Awareness: a group-administered test for kindergarten and first grade children nationally normed on children ages five through seven

- Yopp-Singer Test of Phoneme Segmentation: a brief test of children's ability to isolate and pronounce the individual phonemes in words

- Letter identification subtest of the Woodcock Reading Mastery Test Revised

- Graphemes subtest of the Phonological Awareness Test: a comprehensive assessment of letter sound knowledge

Identifying reading difficulties early means children have more time to learn to be successful readers. Since reading is learned more easily and effectively during the early years, identifying language-based learning disabilities and providing appropriate interventions gives children more time to learn to read well.

A child identified as needing help will require careful and direct instruction in reading. An effective preventive program may involve several levels of instructional intensity ranging from small groups to one-on-one teaching, depending upon the severity of the difficulties for each child. In this way, a preventive program can be focused on the children who are most in need. Children with a reading disability/dyslexia will have a positive beginning to their education and a much greater chance for success. Up to 90 percent of poor readers can increase their skills to "average" with prevention and intervention programs that combine instruction in phonemic awareness, phonics spelling, reading fluency, and reading comprehension strategies provided by well trained teachers.

Kindergarten

In kindergarten, children begin to

- recognize some common words
- name uppercase and lowercase letters
- begin to associate letters and sounds
- recognize poetry
- distinguish reality from fantasy
- can match simple words to pictures
- aware of whether words begin or end with same sound
- beginning to be able to break words into syllables
- understand that reading goes from left to right and top to bottom on the page
- aware of time sequence in a story

First Grade

In first grade, children begin to

- read long and short vowels
- read word families (hat, bat, cat)
- follow simple written directions
- larger sight vocabulary
- aware of author, title, and table of contents
- recognize a play
- interpret maps and globes
- identify consonants in words
- can break dictated words into individual sounds
- aware of root words, endings, compound words, and contractions
- recognize main idea and cause/effect
- draw conclusions

Second Grade

In second grade, children begin to

- sound out unfamiliar words based on individual letter sounds
- identify words from contextual clues
- vary pitch and stress when reading aloud
- recognize character, setting, and motive of story
- use library for research
- interpret graphs
- use dictionary
- master harder phonetic skills
- understand root words and endings
- aware of syllabication

Third Grade

In third grade, children begin to

- increase sight vocabulary and word-analysis ability

- understand homophones
- increase reading speed
- develop silent reading skills
- distinguish fiction and nonfiction, fact versus opinion
- understand synonyms and antonyms
- recognize author's purpose
- use index
- use encyclopedia
- interpret diagrams

Fourth Grade

In fourth grade, children begin to

- develop different reading styles for different types of reading
- expand vocabulary
- understand plot and main idea
- summarize a book or article
- organize study materials
- understand different genres (biography, folk tales, science fiction, and so on)
- understand author's point of view
- read a newspaper

reading comprehension   The ability to understand what is read. Reading involves two processes: decoding (word recognition) and comprehension (understanding). In order to understand the text, an individual must be able to first recognize the words. Often, individuals with learning disabilities will be better at understanding than recognizing words. However, both skills are necessary for reading competency.

There is a relationship between vocabulary and comprehension—messages are composed of ideas, and ideas are expressed in words. Many studies have shown a close link between vocabulary knowledge and reading comprehension.

Good readers are active readers who have clear goals in mind for their reading, and they typically look over the text before they read, noting such things as the structure of the text and text sections that might be relevant to their goals. As they read, good readers frequently make predictions, reading selectively, continually making decisions about their reading—what to read carefully, what to read quickly, what not to read, what to reread, and so on. Good readers construct, revise, and question the meanings they make as they read. They draw upon, compare, and integrate their prior knowledge with material in the text. They think about the authors of the text, their style, beliefs, intentions, historical milieu, and so on. They monitor their understanding of the text, making adjustments in their reading as necessary. Good readers try to determine the meaning of unfamiliar words and concepts in the text, and deal with inconsistencies or gaps as needed. They evaluate the text's quality and value, and react to the text in a range of ways, both intellectual and emotional.

Moreover, good readers read different kinds of text differently. For example, when reading narrative, good readers attend closely to the setting and characters; when reading expository text these readers frequently construct and revise summaries of what they have read. Comprehension is a complex process, but one that for good readers is both satisfying and productive.

Research suggests that it's possible to help students learn the comprehension strategies used by good readers, and that this improves their overall comprehension of text, both the texts used to teach the strategies and texts they read on their own in the future.

Good comprehension instruction includes both explicit instruction in specific comprehension strategies and a great deal of time and opportunity for actual reading, writing, and discussion of text.

Good reading comprehension depends on many factors. Individuals with learning disabilities may have a weakness in one or more of the following six subskills of reading comprehension.

1. fluent decoding—the ability to accurately and quickly read each word in a passage
2. broad background knowledge—exposure to a wide variety of language experiences (stories, books, culture) often gained through reading and vocabulary development
3. oral vocabulary development—exposure to rich vocabulary
4. oral language comprehension—understanding oral syntax
5. knowledge of language conventions—can grasp main ideas, paraphrasing, topic sentences, dialogue, irony, and so on
6. reasoning skills—can make inferences, and predict, clarify, summarize information

Research has revealed information about good comprehension that contradicts many beliefs held by proponents of whole language instruction from the mid-1970s. Back then, experts believed that good readers made a lot of "guesses" while reading based on semantic and syntactic cues. However, there is very little guessing involved in good reading comprehension. Individuals with strong reading comprehension skills actually process every letter in a word, but they do so very quickly and effortlessly. Efficient readers depend on the sounds of the letters to read accurately, and they spend little energy rereading words.

recall   A term used to denote the ability to retrieve information from LONG-TERM MEMORY. Recall is involved in a broad range of tasks and specific tests, from remembering a phone number to calling up information for a school exam. While useful as a descriptive term, it does not refer to a specific area of cognitive function.

Difficulty recalling information may be caused by a number of different learning problems. This may include problems imprinting information during processing because of poor attention or short-term memory, as well as difficulty with rapid retrieval tasks that are typically found in expressive-language disorders.

receptive language   The forms of language that are received as input: from listening and reading. Listening and reading are receptive skills that involve feeding information into the brain, as opposed to speaking and writing, which are the expressive forms of language. Most individuals maintain a fairly similar set of receptive and expressive, oral and written language function, but those with learning problems may have specific deficits in one or more of these areas.

Individuals with DYSLEXIA or specific reading disabilities have problems with receptive language, involving deficits in both oral language and processing sounds (phonological processing), and significant problems in decoding and understanding texts. Some individuals with these problems still have relatively strong oral expression, although most will have problems with written expression due to problems with reading written language.

reciprocal reading/teaching   A situation in which teachers and students take turns in reading or discussing a written passage. Reciprocal reading is useful because teachers model good reading such as pausing at punctuation, using intonation, and tracking with a finger. Reciprocal teaching also can involve shared discussion where the teacher can model good comprehension and questioning strategies to promote critical thinking.

In reciprocal teaching and learning, teachers and students share in the process of a learning activity and teachers can also monitor and assess students while they try out new reading/thinking strategies.

Recording for the Blind & Dyslexic   A nonprofit organization devoted to providing educational materials such as textbooks and reference materials to people who can't effectively read standard print. Originally named Recording for the Blind, the organization was founded in 1948 by New York City philanthropist Anne T. Macdonald, a member of the women's auxiliary of the New York Public Library, in response to the plight of blinded GIs who couldn't read Braille but wanted to have access to books. She mobilized the efforts of the women's auxiliary, and began recording books in the attic of the library.

Believing that "education is a right, not a privilege," Macdonald transformed the attic of the New York Public Library into a studio, recording on what was then state-of-the-art technology: six-inch vinyl SoundScriber discs that played only 12 minutes of material per side on phonographs. Demand was so great that by 1951 the organization had incorporated as the nation's only nonprofit group to record textbooks. The following year, Macdonald established recording studios in seven new cities. Today, in addition to the national headquarters, the association has 32 recording studios across the United States.

Materials range from textbooks to literature and are available to all academic levels from kindergarten to postgraduate. In 1995, the organization's name added "and dyslexic" to reflect the use of the service by many individuals with a LEARNING DISABILITY. In fact, more than 70 percent of the group's 91,000 members (kindergarteners through graduate school, as well as working professionals) have learning disabilities. For those with a visual or reading disability, using taped books and other materials can be extremely helpful.

Today the organization serves more than 91,000 members around the world, distributing 238,543 titles in 2000. The SoundScriber discs were long ago replaced with high-fidelity, four-track cassettes; soon, digital audio technology will be introduced, allowing members access to more than 83,000 titles in the master library on CD-ROM (and eventually over the Internet). More than 5,700 volunteers added 4,300 titles to the master library in the year 2000.

Contact: 20 Roszel Road, Princeton, NJ 08540; phone: (800) 221–4792; website: www.rfbd.org.

See also PRINT DISABILITIES.

referral process When a teacher becomes concerned about a child struggling with daily schoolwork, he or she refers that student to the school's CHILD STUDY COMMITTEE for consideration of appropriate interventions. Frequently, the child study team's interventions will result in significant alleviation of the problems that brought the student to their attention. If, however, the interventions don't help, and the child still has significant difficulties, the committee may refer the student for a multidisciplinary evaluation. A referral to the child study team can be made by the student or a parent, teacher, or other professional. Schools frequently receive "prescriptions" from outside psychologists, reading tutors, and physicians demanding an immediate multidisciplinary evaluation. And many parents seek to bypass the child study team referral and demand that their child receive a referral without first trying to solve the problems by appropriate interventions. However, such demands cannot bypass the requirement that the child first be referred to the child study team for consideration of appropriate interventions before resorting to a multidisciplinary evaluation.

Once a referral has been made, school personnel must begin a process that begins with notifying the parents of the referral. Parents must give written permission for an evaluation to be carried out by the multidisciplinary team.

Strict federal and state laws outline what happens once a referral has been made. Once written permission has been received by the child's parents, the student is evaluated by a multidisciplinary team. The evaluation is then reviewed by the team, which must decide if the student is eligible for special services. Once the team has decided if services are needed, parents (and the student, when appropriate) are called to discuss the situation at a case conference. At this conference, the committee formulates the student's INDIVIDUALIZED EDUCATION PROGRAM (IEP), a document that summarizes a child's educational performance, plans the short-term educational goals, and outlines annual goals. It also gives methods for measuring progress.

If the child does not qualify for special education, it is still important for the parents to work with the teacher to create an informal program that meets the child's needs.

reflex test The testing of reflexes is necessary to ensure that a child's motor system is working properly. Tested reflexes are correlated with specific nerves in the spinal cord.

regular education Non–special education classes.

See also GENERAL EDUCATION.

Rehabilitation Act of 1973 (RA) (Public Law 93–112, Section 504) A major piece of legislation requiring that schools not discriminate against children with disabilities (including a LEARNING DISABILITY) and that they provide children with reasonable accommodations. Under some circumstances, these "reasonable accommodations" may include the provision of services.

While the INDIVIDUALS WITH DISABILITIES EDUCATION ACT (IDEA) focuses on "free appropriate public education" for children with disabilities, Section 504 of the Rehabilitation Act is intended to prohibit discrimination against individuals with handicaps in programs receiving federal financial assistance. The RA is more general in scope, and its definition of "disabled" is somewhat broader than that of "handicapped" in the IDEA.

Unlike the IDEA, which applies primarily to public elementary and secondary education for children with disabilities, the Rehabilitation Act also applies to postsecondary institutions that receive federal funds in any form. To fall under the protection of the RA, an individual must meet the definition of "disabled" in the act and be "otherwise qualified," and establish that he or she was denied employment or education "solely by reason" of the disability. In addition, the act requires that an employer or educational institution must make "reasonable accommodations" for the disability.

Eligibility
Eligibility for Section 504 is based on the existence of an identified physical or mental condition that substantially limits a major life activity. As learning is considered a major life activity, children diagnosed with ATTENTION DEFICIT/HYPERACTIVITY DISORDER (ADHD) are entitled to the protections of Section 504 if the disability is substantially limiting their ability to learn. Children who aren't eligible for special education may still be guaranteed access to related services if they meet the Section 504 eligibility criteria.

Evaluation
Although Section 504 requires nondiscriminatory testing, there are far fewer regulations placed on the testing procedure than are required for IDEA. In addition, unlike IDEA, Section 504 does not discuss the frequency of testing; the role outside evaluations may play; nor require parental consent for testing. It does require that an evaluation be conducted before a child receives a remediation plan and before any changes are made to the plan.

Section 504 Plan
If the child is eligible for services under Section 504, the school district must develop a "Section 504 plan." However, the regulations don't dictate the frequency of review of the 504 plan, and don't specify the right of parents to participate in its development.

In general, Section 504 provides a faster, more flexible and less stigmatizing procedure for obtaining some accommodations and services for children with disabilities. By virtue of the looser eligibility criteria, some children may receive protection who aren't eligible for services or protection under IDEA, and less information is needed to obtain eligibility. For example, a student with a broken leg who must ride an elevator to his third floor science class qualifies for a Section 504 plan until his leg has healed. Or, a student with a serious hearing loss who can participate in group standardized testing if there is an aide to sign instructions that the test proctor would ordinarily read out loud to the test takers will qualify for a Section 504 plan providing an interpreter. Thus, Section 504 can provide an efficient way to obtain limited assistance without the stigma and bureaucratic procedures attached to IDEA.

There are some benefits under IDEA, however:

- a wider range of service options
- procedures for parent participation and procedural safeguards that are far more extensive
- a degree of regulation far more specific than that found in Section 504
- a more stringent enforcement mechanism to ensure that the requirements of the law are met

If a child has behavioral problems that could lead to the possibility of excessive discipline, suspension, and expulsion, parents should be particularly aware of the less rigorous safeguards provided by Section 504.

reliability A statistical term that refers to the consistency of test scores in different contexts or with different populations. A judgment of a high degree of reliability indicates that a test is dependable and relatively free from random errors of measurement.

remedial programs Programs designed to address specific weaknesses for individuals who aren't achieving up to grade-level expectations. Remedial programs take place outside the regu-

lar or general classroom and are typically tailored to meet individual needs. Remedial programs can also take place in clinics or in private tutoring centers.

Remedial programs in public schools (such as resource room instruction) that are indicated on an INDIVIDUALIZED EDUCATION PROGRAM (IEP) are free. Remediation of skills through intensive instruction and practice occurs in remedial programs.

resource room An educational setting within a school that offers remedial instruction to students with a LEARNING DISABILITY or other handicaps. Students generally spend most of their day in general or regular education classes, but visit the resource room for a portion of their day (often 45–60 minutes) for individual or small-group instruction on specific areas outlined on the student's INDIVIDUALIZED EDUCATION PROGRAM (IEP).

The resource room teacher often supports the regular education curriculum while also providing remediation. Certain considerations must be taken into account when scheduling students in the resource room. For example, if a student excels in or enjoys physical education class, care should be taken to avoid pulling the student out of that class for his resource room time.

The resource room does not necessarily serve only students within a single class of handicap, such as an all-LD or an all–seriously emotionally disturbed class. Rather, many serve students with a mixture of handicaps such a few LD, a few with hearing problems, several with emotional disturbance, and so on.

One way most states distinguish a resource room from a self-contained placement is that students are considered to be in a resource room placement if they attend that SPECIAL EDUCATION class for at least one instructional period per day but attend special education classes for less than half of the day.

The different types of remedial instruction settings include

Consultative: The child never physically enters the special education class, but a special education teacher consults with the regular classroom teacher who actually provides the instruction.

Itinerant: The student attends less than one period of special education per day, such as one period once a week, half a period two days per week, and so on.

Resource: The student attends special education classes for at least one instructional period per day but less than half of the school day.

Self-Contained: The student attends special education classes for more than half of the school day, but the student remains in the same school he would attend if he were not handicapped.

Self-Contained With School Transfer: The student attends a self-contained class but must transfer to another school than she would attend if she were not handicapped. School districts frequently resort to this if there are not enough students in each school for that school to have its own self-contained class, but, pooled together, there are enough students to make a class if two or more schools combine their students who need that class.

Homebound: The child is sent home and receives one to five instructional periods per week from a special education teacher who visits the home. This arrangement occurs if there is some factor (such as severe medical fragility) that endangers the student if he attends school, or that endangers others (such as a student classified as handicapped but whose behavior consistently prevents others from learning or endangers others).

Segregated, Other Facility: The student is removed from the local school and placed in a facility educating only students with handicaps, but the student goes home each night. This is the type of program that many school districts provided prior to Public Law 94-142, which required that schools educate students with handicaps in the Least Restrictive Environment.

Institutional Placement: Placement in an institution such as a state mental hospital, used only in severe circumstances, such as severe medical disorders, psychoses that cause the student to be a danger to self or others, or when a student has been committed to a juvenile facility following criminal charges.

resource teacher A SPECIAL EDUCATION teacher who works with students with disabilities. Usually, these children spend part of their school day in a RESOURCE ROOM staffed with trained teachers in order to receive individualized attention.

reticular activating system (RASY) The part of the brain that filters out extraneous stimuli and helps a person stay focused. A network of nerve fibers (also known as the reticular formation) located in the brain stem moderates the level of central nervous system activity, controlling arousal, consciousness, and attention. It is also involved in breathing and cardiac functions, movement, awareness, and sleep. Many neurologists and neuropsychologists believe that a dysfunction in the RASY plays an important role in ADHD. Theoretically, the way that stimulant drugs such as Ritalin work to control the symptoms of ADHD is to stimulate the RASY to exert proper control over the individual's arousal, consciousness, and attention.

retrieval The searching and finding process that leads to recognition and recall, bringing information out of LONG-TERM MEMORY.

Rett syndrome A progressive neurological disorder in which individuals exhibit a LEARNING DISABILITY, poor muscle tone, autistic-like behavior, useless hand movements, lessened ability to express feelings, avoidance of eye contact, a lag in brain and head growth, walking abnormalities, and seizures. Loss of muscle tone is usually the first symptom.

The syndrome occurs in about one of every 10,000 to 15,000 live female births, with symptoms usually appearing in early childhood, between the ages of 6–18 months. Experts believe that while boys can get Rett syndrome, in boys the condition is fatal and they don't survive much past birth. This is because of the difference in sex chromosomes. Females have two X chromosomes, but only one is active in any particular cell. That means that only about half the cells in a girl's nervous system will actually be using the defective gene. Because boys have a single X chromosome, all of their cells are obliged to use the faulty version of the gene, which presumably results in fatal defects.

Rett syndrome follows a tragic and irreversible course. Although the child develops normally for the first six months to 18 months of life, she begins to gradually deteriorate mentally and physically. As the damage to the nervous system worsens, she loses the ability to speak, begins to have trouble walking or crawling, and is shaken by seizures. One of the most striking symptoms is loss of conscious control of the hands, leading to continual, compulsive hand-wringing. Though rarely fatal, Rett syndrome nevertheless leaves its victims permanently impaired.

Predicting the severity of Rett syndrome in any individual is difficult, but in spite of the severe impairments that characterize this disorder, most children with Rett syndrome survive at least into their 40s. Girls and women with Rett can continue to learn and enjoy family and friends well into middle age and beyond. They experience a full range of emotions and show engaging personalities as they take part in social, educational, and recreational activities at home and in the community. However, the risk of death increases with age, and sudden, unexplained death often occurs, possibly from brainstem problems that interfere with breathing.

First described by Dr. Andreas Rett, the condition received worldwide recognition after research by Bengt Hagberg and colleagues was published in 1983.

Symptoms

The child with Rett syndrome usually shows an early period of apparently normal or near-normal development until six months to 18 months of life. A period of temporary stagnation or regression follows during which the child loses communication skills and purposeful use of the hands. Soon, stereotyped hand movements, gait disturbances, and slowing of the rate of head growth become apparent.

Most girls don't crawl typically, but may "bottom scoot" without using their hands. Many girls begin independent walking within the normal age range, while others show significant delay or inability to walk independently. Some begin walking and lose this skill, while others continue to walk throughout life. Still others don't walk until late childhood or adolescence.

A girl's problems may include seizures, which can range from nonexistent to severe, but do tend to lessen in their intensity in later adolescence. Disorganized breathing patterns also may occur and tend to decrease with age. While scoliosis is a prominent feature of RS, it can range from mild to severe.

APRAXIA (dyspraxia), the inability to program the body to perform motor movements, is the most fundamental and severely handicapping aspect of the condition. It can interfere with every body movement, including eye gaze and speech, making it difficult for the child to do what she wants to do. Due to apraxia and lack of verbal communication skills, an accurate assessment of intelligence is difficult. Most traditional testing methods require use of the hands or speech, which may be impossible for the girl with Rett. Some children start to use single words and word combinations before they lose this ability.

Cause

Most researchers now agree that Rett syndrome is a developmental disorder rather than a progressive, degenerative disorder as once thought. In October 1999, scientists discovered a genetic mutation on the X chromosome that has been linked to Rett syndrome. This mutation has been found in up to 75 percent of typical and atypical cases of Rett. Continued research will focus on other still unidentified genetic factors that contribute to the condition. Researchers agree that its severity is probably not linked to the exact location of individual mutations on the gene, but to the X inactivation patterns in each affected girl.

The gene produces part of a switch that shuts off production of as yet unidentified proteins. Experts suspect that overproduction of some proteins might cause the nervous system deterioration characteristic of the disease. Discovery of the gene will enable the unraveling of the steps of the disease process and could eventually lead to drugs that will lessen the damage.

Diagnosis

Diagnosing the disorder before the child is four or five years old is often difficult. However, the discovery of the genetic mutation will lead to a genetic test to improve the accuracy of early diagnosis. If combined with an effective therapy, the test might allow doctors to forestall the drastic consequences of the disease.

The condition is most often misdiagnosed as AUTISM, CEREBRAL PALSY, or nonspecific developmental delay. While many health professionals may not be familiar with Rett syndrome, it is a relatively frequent cause of neurological dysfunction in females.

Treatment

There is no cure for Rett syndrome; however, there are several treatment options, including treatments for the learning disabilities and seizures that may occur. Some children may require special nutritional programs to maintain adequate weight.

Rett Syndrome Association (IRSA), International A support group for parents of children with RETT SYNDROME; founded by parents in early 1984. IRSA is a partnership of parents and professionals dedicated to better understanding Rett syndrome. Members include parents, relatives, doctors, therapists, researchers, and friends interested in providing a better future for girls with Rett syndrome.

IRSA supports medical research to determine the cause and find a cure for Rett syndrome; increases public awareness of the condition; and provides information and support to families of affected children.

Contact: 9121 Piscataway Road, Suite 2B, Clinton, MD 20735; phone: (301) 856–3334; (800) 818–RETT–7388; website: http://www.rettsyndrome.org.

Rett Syndrome Research Foundation (RSRF) A nonprofit foundation created in 1999 by six parents of girls with RETT SYNDROME that is dedicated to finding a treatment and cure.

Contact: 4600 Devitt Drive, Cincinnati, OH 45246; phone: (513) 874-3020; website: http://www.rsrf.org

reverbalization A strategy in which an individual restates a message out loud to enhance memorization and ensure understanding. Similar to paraphrasing, where individuals restate a message using their own words (usually in writing); in reverbalizing, the individual repeats information out loud to promote LONG-TERM MEMORY.

For individuals with short-term memory or AUDITORY PROCESSING difficulties, reverbalizing information can enhance learning through rehearsal.

Diagnostically, reverbalizing can be an effective way for instructors to monitor whether students have accurately received information.

reversals A reading or writing error in which similar-shaped letters or words are reversed. For example, a student would reverse "b" for "d" or "was" for "saw."

Reversal errors in emergent readers and writers are common and disappear with more experience; however, reversals that continue to interfere with a student's progress indicate a language processing difficulty that may require treatment.

Remediation for reversals could include using multimodal strategies such as tracing, color-coding, speaking, or using mnemonic devices.

rhetorical patterns   The way in which prose is organized, using six common structures:

- definition
- chronology
- compare-contrast
- cause-effect
- problem-solution
- enumeration

By recognizing a rhetorical pattern when reading, an individual may find it easier to comprehend the passage and predict what might happen next.

Recognizing rhetorical patterns is also important in writing because the patterns provide clear structures around which the writer can organize main ideas and details. Rhetorical patterns may be used alone or in combinations.

Ritalin (methylphenidate hydrochloride)   A medication prescribed for individuals (usually children) who have an abnormally high level of activity, or ATTENTION DEFICIT/HYPERACTIVITY DISORDER (ADHD). About 3 to 5 percent of the general population has the disorder, which is characterized by agitated behavior and an inability to focus on tasks.

This central nervous system stimulant has effects similar to, but more potent than, caffeine—but weaker than amphetamines. It has a notably calming effect on hyperactive children and a "focusing" effect on those with ADHD.

Scientists think ADHD occurs in part because certain receptors in the brain involved in focusing attention and reining in impulsiveness fail to respond to dopamine and norepinephrine, the brain's natural neurotransmitters. It is the interaction between these chemicals and the brain's receptors that helps most people stick with tedious chores, or rein in inappropriate impulses. Researchers think that drugs like Ritalin boost the level of these brain chemicals and stimulate the inhibitory receptors—which is why a stimulant drug can increase inhibition. The drugs enter the body quickly, curing nothing but helping a child focus on the important work of learning.

Although the drug clearly reduces the symptoms of ADHD, and many students have been taking the drug for years, no studies have continued long enough to see if it has a lasting effect on academic performance or social behavior. Moreover, a positive response to Ritalin doesn't automatically mean a child suffers from ADHD. Stimulants can temporarily sharpen almost anyone's focus. Ritalin has become one of the more widely sought-after drugs on the black market because of its attention-focusing effects. Many college students buy black market Ritalin to enhance their study skills.

However, while most experts agree that medication can help, it isn't the only solution—parents and teachers need to learn new ways (such as rewards and consequences) in which to teach their children how to focus and sit still.

Extensive research suggests a combination of stimulants and behavior management is the best way to treat ADHD. First introduced in the 1940s, Ritalin is usually prescribed as a part of a treatment plan that includes educational and psychosocial interventions for children with behavior characterized by

- moderate-to-severe distractibility
- short attention span

- hyperactivity
- emotional lability
- impulsivity

The widespread use of Ritalin in children is not without controversy. Some experts are vehemently opposed to medicating children who are deemed too inattentive or active for a "normal" classroom. However, there is no specific evidence that clearly establishes the mechanism by which Ritalin produces its mental and behavioral effects in children. Because a diagnosis of ADHD itself is not always straightforward, and because some doctors prescribe it after a brief conversation with concerned parents, without obtaining the proper diagnostic information, critics argue that far too many children who are simply extremely energetic are given a diagnosis of ADHD and medicated.

A doctor should prescribe Ritalin only after medical, psychological, behavioral, and educational assessments. The doctor or therapist should talk both to parents and the child, and get information from teachers before prescribing stimulants. Pediatric neurologists and developmental pediatricians warn that ADHD symptoms are often caused by other symptoms. The diagnosis should only be made after these conditions are ruled out.

Dosage

Closely monitored treatment with stimulants (Ritalin is one of four commonly prescribed, and its use has increased 700 percent in one decade) can erase enough symptoms of ADHD to eliminate the diagnosis for 82 to 85 percent of children. While most parents give their children a typical twice-daily dose, one recent government study suggests that three times a day works better, with a nighttime dose about half the size of the first two.

It may take up to one month for the medication to achieve its maximum effect in children, and 30 minutes to take effect in adults. Medications like Ritalin are usually taken for as long as it is helpful or necessary. While there has been

an increase in the number of stimulant prescriptions for children under age five, there is no evidence that these drugs are safe or effective when used on young children.

Risk of Abuse

Because of its stimulant properties, however, there have been reports of Ritalin abuse by adults who turn to the drug for its stimulant effects: appetite suppression, wakefulness, increased focus and attentiveness, and euphoria. When abused, the tablets are either taken orally or crushed, and snorted or smoked. Some abusers dissolve the tablets in water and inject the mixture, although this can cause problems if insoluble fillers in the tablets block small blood vessels.

Because stimulant medicines such as Ritalin have the potential for abuse, the U.S. Drug Enforcement Administration (DEA) has placed stringent, Schedule II controls on their manufacture, distribution, and prescription. For example, DEA requires special licenses for these activities, and prescription refills are not allowed. States may impose further regulations, such as limiting the number of dosage units per prescription.

Side Effects

Common side effects include decrease or loss of appetite, nervousness, sleep problems, weight loss, or dizziness. There is also evidence that brain growth slows in children who take Ritalin and other stimulants. However, once these children stop taking Ritalin, there is usually a substantial growth rebound, although the extent of the rebound varies.

Contraindications

Ritalin should not be used in children with anxiety, tension, agitation, irregular heart rhythms, severe angina pectoris, or glaucoma, or in anyone with motor tics or a family history or diagnosis of TOURETTE'S SYNDROME. Although a relationship has not been established, suppression of growth (such as weight gain and/or height) has been reported with the long-term use of stimulants in children. Therefore, patients who need long-term therapy should be carefully monitored; it may be a good idea to withhold the drug on weekends and during school holidays.

See also STIMULANT MEDICATIONS.

rule-governed behavior   The ways in which humans are able to use LANGUAGE or other symbolic stimuli to govern or control behavior. Language use is rule-governed behavior, rather than simply a skill.

Assessment of language problems must take into account the ways in which an individual may have failed to learn specific language rules, or may have substituted self-generated rules for the standard rules governing usage.

saliency The relevance of an item or phenomenon to a task or activity. For example, the homework assignment that a teacher writes on the blackboard is highly salient to a student in the class, while the sounds of an activity out in the hallway are nonsalient. Problems with determining saliency (what is relevant or important to a particular task) are a significant issue in individuals with attention disorders.

scale scores Scale scores provide a statistical method of giving relative meaning to a student's STANDARDIZED TEST scores. Scale score reporting systems have been used more and more often in recent years.

A scale used for a test score usually refers to numbers assigned to students based on how well they did on the test. The higher the number, the better their test performance. Therefore, a scale might be made up of a set of raw scores, in which each test item that is correctly answered adds one more point on the raw score scale. However, raw scores alone are very hard to interpret—a student's score on a raw score scale provides no hint of the child's relative performance. A raw score of "53" means nothing in itself. As a result, testing experts developed scales—like the scale score—to help interpret test results.

Scale scores are converted raw scores using an arbitrarily chosen scale that represents achievement (or ability). A scale-score system is created when a test manufacturer invents a new numerical scale; students' raw scores are then converted to this new scale. For example, in a test of 50 items, a student could achieve a raw score ranging from 0 to 50; a new converted scale of 500 to 1,000 is assigned to correspond to the raw scores. If a student achieves a perfect raw score of 50, the scale score will be 1,000.

One of the reasons that scale scores are used is because it may be necessary to test a student several times using different tests. For example, if one school requires a student to pass a basic skills test before graduating, a student who failed this test would be given another chance to pass it. A retake of this test is not the same exam, but it's almost impossible to create two identical but different tests. To be fair, scale scores can help solve the problem. Scores on two tests can be statistically adjusted so that the new scale scores represent a student's performance as if the two tests had been perfectly equal.

scatter When subtest scores vary markedly on any one assessment. Significant scatter within the subtest measurements may indicate a pattern of strengths and weaknesses that should be explored to determine the most effective educational and other treatments. For example, clinicians study profiles of subtest scores from major intelligence tests such as the WISC-III to determine what test score patterns reveal about students' strengths and weaknesses. A pattern in which the student scores lowest on the digit-span and coding subtests, for example, may indicate a significant weakness in short-term memory.

screening Informal assessments and data collection used to identify individuals who may require further assessment to determine if they have LEARNING DISABILITY or developmental delays. Screening is usually done in a group setting with the goal of identifying individuals at risk of having a learning disability. Screening is used also in early education to identify children who may be developmentally delayed in vision, hearing, motor skills, cognitive ability, or social-emotional maturity.

Many school districts use these types of screening for all incoming kindergarten students as a low-cost way of identifying and implementing early intervention strategies. Students with learning problems will typically be screened to determine whether more extensive evaluations to establish learning disabilities are needed.

screen reading program   See KURZWEIL READING MACHINE; SPEECH SYNTHESIZER/SCREEN READERS.

script   See CURSIVE WRITING.

segregated other facility   A SPECIAL EDUCATION placement in which students are removed to a separate school or clinic in which they are no longer exposed to nonhandicapped students. The students go home every day rather than live at the facility. A segregated other facility is considered to be less restrictive than an institutional placement, but more restrictive than a SELF-CONTAINED CLASSROOM.

selective attention   Picking out the most relevant cue among stimuli in the environment, and excluding the rest. It's well established that people don't pay attention to everything; for example, at a party an individual can focus on the voice of one person with whom he is conversing.

Yet while it's clear that people do filter out a great number of stimuli, it's not at all clear how this is done, nor what information is noted unconsciously. In an attempt to find out, psychologists have often used dichotic listening experiments (that is, two different messages are presented separately to each ear), roughly along the lines of the situation at a party.

If a child's "attention" problems are selective—that is, appearing only in certain subjects—it suggests that he is capable of paying attention when the subjects are comprehensible and meaningful.

self-advocacy   An individual's ability to discuss a personal LEARNING DISABILITY and request appropriate accommodations and services. Self-advocacy skills are important to develop in people with learning disabilities so they can take responsibility for their own learning and become empowered in school, work, and life. Individuals with disabilities should be familiar with their learning profile as well as relevant legislation.

Self-advocacy skills should be developed as soon as an individual is old enough to understand the learning process. Parents have a right to include their children who are being considered for special education classification in the multidisciplinary team meeting and in development of the INDIVIDUALIZED EDUCATION PROGRAM. Many high schools encourage students to become self-advocates by discussing their learning style and needs with teachers, and by actively making transition plans from high school to the next environment.

Self-advocacy skills become even more important once an individual leaves school and begins a job or college, where there are no special educators or parents to advocate for them.

self-concept   The way people see themselves, including all the beliefs, feelings, and attitudes about the self. Self-concept can also affect how one feels about others.

Self-concept is a subject that has fascinated philosophers since Socrates. In the field of psychology, self-concept has always been an important and sometimes controversial subject. Both psychologists William James and Mary Calkins used methods of introspection to study the self, while Freud, Jung, and Adler all discussed the development of the self in their writing. The behaviorists who exerted great influence during the first half of the 20th century in the United States questioned the study of self-concept, as the concept was difficult to quantify using the rigorous scientific methods to which they adhered.

During the 1950s and 1960s, the "self-concept" was a central idea in the work of both Abraham Maslow and Carl Rogers. Maslow believed that building self-esteem, an individual's evaluation of self-worth, was a key step in the self-actualization process. Rogers believed that if one had a positive view of the self then one would view the world in a positive way. If the self-view were negative, one would fall short of the goals related to the ideal self. As a part of this perspective, Donald Super developed a related theory of vocational choice. He believed that career satisfaction was related to the degree to which someone could implement his self-concept in the work place.

Social psychologists argue that an individual's self-concept develops through associations with others. Cognitive psychologists study how people think about themselves and how they think about their own thinking. Many criticize the term and its usefulness because it is difficult to quantify or measure consistently. However, it remains an important concept among educators and developmental psychologists. Both groups are concerned with the effects of the educational setting, peers, and family on a child's developing self-concept.

Individuals with LEARNING DISABILITY, not surprisingly, often rate themselves lower than typically achieving students on cognitive ability. Because academic performance is a culturally valued domain, it makes sense that individuals with learning disabilities would also place importance on academic performance.

Some research suggests that for college students with learning disabilities, the availability of a social support network, including clubs, disability services, and interactions with professors,

was a correlate of self-esteem. Other research on successful adults with learning disabilities and the resilience of individuals with learning disabilities, gives insight into how one can nurture emotional health while managing the challenges that having a disability entails. Researchers studied moderately successful and highly successful adults with learning disabilities to identify factors related to success for adults with learning disabilities. Success was defined as high ratings in the following categories: income level, job classification, education level, prominence in one's field, and job satisfaction.

Other research focuses on resilience and its appearance or absence in individuals with learning disabilities. Resilience is a healthy adaptation in the context of severe stress. Despite the challenges and hardships that can accompany having a learning disability, some individuals maintain a positive outlook, achieve success, and avoid emotional problems. Important characteristics of resilient individuals include accuracy of self-appraisal, self-determination, and help from a significant supportive person.

self-contained classroom   A separate classroom within a school designed especially for students with disabilities, to provide a more structured environment and intensive instruction. Most self-contained classes have 12 or fewer students.

Students are placed in a self-contained classroom as the least restrictive environment (LRE), if their needs can't be met in a regular classroom with resource room remedial work and they don't need to be placed in a special school. Students placed in a self-contained classroom spend more than 60 percent of their day in this classroom.

There are two types of self-contained classrooms, sometimes referred to as special classrooms. A classroom designed for only one type of disability is called a categorical classroom; classrooms that contain a variety of children with disabilities (such as emotional, learning, or physical) are called cross-categorical classrooms.

Self-contained classrooms offer some advantages to students with a more severe LEARNING DISABILITY, such as highly specialized learning environments and individual or small-group instruction. This type of classroom allows some students to be mainstreamed with non-special education peers for certain classes, such as art or music.

self-correction Students's ability to detect and correct their own errors. The term is often used while students read aloud and hear themselves make an error but corrects it. Some reading tests consider a self-correction to be an error, which can result in a misleading oral reading score.

self-efficacy The belief that an individual can produce effects through personal effort. Like SELF-ESTEEM, self-efficacy is important in setting and meeting goals for students of all ages.

self-esteem A particularly positive way of experiencing the self that involves emotional, evaluation, and thinking components. Many students with a LEARNING DISABILITY experience poor self-esteem due to years of academic failure. This is why it is especially important to build positive self-esteem by creating opportunities for success, giving sincere praise, and cultivating talents and strengths in individuals with learning disabilities.

Self-esteem is the ability to experience oneself as being competent to cope with the basic challenges of life, and of being worthy of happiness. By extension, it is confidence in our ability to learn, to make appropriate choices and decisions, and respond effectively to change. It also involves the experience that success, achievement, fulfillment, and happiness are right and natural.

While many things can make a person feel good temporarily, if self-esteem is not grounded in reality, it is not self-esteem.

If a teacher treats students with respect, avoids ridicule, deals fairly with students, and projects a benevolent conviction about every student's potential, then that teacher is supporting both self-esteem and the process of learning and mastering challenges. On the other hand, if a teacher tries to nurture self-esteem by empty praise that bears no relationship to the students' actual accomplishments, then self-esteem is undermined and so is academic achievement.

Research indicates that there is a significant relationship between self-esteem and academic achievement, and that if a student's self-esteem can be improved, academic improvement tends to follow. Many factors influence self-esteem, including parents, teachers, and other adults, and biology and life experiences.

See also SELF-CONCEPT.

self-monitoring A strategy in which a student reviews his work to check for errors.

self-regulation The ability to regulate and monitor a person's own actions and behavior. Problems with effective self-regulation are a primary struggle for students with attention and EXECUTIVE FUNCTION problems.

Effective self-regulation depends on a complex interaction of thinking, feeling, and perception. Problems with self-regulation may stem from many different sources. Individuals with ADHD typically have problems with self-regulation due to underlying brain processing difficulties with memory, attention, and executive function, particularly as these affect the ability to control impulses and restrain and monitor internal thoughts. Problems with self-regulation may also be caused by other psychological conditions, such as BIPOLAR DISORDER, conduct disorders, or OBSESSIVE-COMPULSIVE DISORDER.

Development of more effective ways to self-regulate is part of an effective coaching and strategy development program for individuals with ADHD. In general, while self-regulation may be seen as an underlying brain function, it also is learned behavior. Therefore, it's possible to teach individuals how to change patterns of impulsive and reckless behavior.

semantic cueing A strategy used to help an individual retrieve or read a word by giving hints with words of similar meaning. For example, if an individual is trying to remember the word *compliment,* giving the semantic cue *praise* may help make a meaningful connection to the word in question.

Similarly, semantic cueing can be used to help an individual read an unfamiliar word. For example, if a reader stumbles on the word *psychologist,* an instructor may give the semantic cue *a therapist* or *a doctor for your mind* rather than providing a phonetic or decoding cue, such as "*psych* is pronounced 'sike'."

semantic knowledge Information stored in long-term memory regarding information, concepts, and general information.

semantic memory Memory for facts, such as the information that would be contained in a dictionary or encyclopedia with no connection to time or place. People don't remember when or where they learn this type of information.

Semantic memory registers and stores knowledge about the world in the broadest sense; it allows people to represent and mentally operate on situations, objects, and relations in the world that aren't present to the senses. A person with an intact semantic memory system can think about things that are not here now.

Because semantic memory develops first in childhood, before episodic memory, children are able to learn facts before they can remember their own experiences.

The seat of semantic memory is believed to be located in the medial temporal lobe and diencephalic structures of the brain.

See also MEMORY.

semantic network Chunks of information connected into networks by associated meanings. Activation of any one chunk automatically "readies" others that are closely associated with it, with lessening degrees of activation spreading from one network to another. Some scientists believe the semantic network may be the main structural component of long-term memory.

semantics The study of words and sentences and their meanings. An individual with a weak vocabulary may be considered to have a *semantic disorder.* An individual with a semantic disorder may understand concepts, but have difficulty finding the word to express it. Informal activities such as quizzing verbal opposites, word categorization, and classification tasks can be useful ways in which to assess semantic skills.

sensorimotor stage A developmental stage in which a child has little ability with LANGUAGE or the use of symbols, but experiences the world through sensation and movement. It is the first of four stages in the theory of cognitive development as described by child psychiatrist Jean Piaget's, the sensorimotor stage lasts from birth to about age two.

Infants are normally born with a range of reflexes that ensures their survival, such as sucking and grasping. As the infant adapts these reflexes over time, the child can begin to interact with the environment with greater efficiency. By the end of this stage, the child is able to solve simple problems, such as looking for a lost toy or communicating simple needs to a parent or another child. It is also during this stage that the infant develops a sense of object permanence—the awareness that things and people continue to exist even when they cannot be perceived. For example, before the age of two if a parent hides a toy under a pillow in front of the child, the child will not understand that the toy still exists under the pillow. Once a sense of object permanence is developed, the child will understand that the toy hidden under the pillow still exists, and will lift up the pillow to retrieve the toy.

Modern technology was not available in Piaget's time, so he often used motor tasks to test the cognitive understanding of an infant. With the availability of more advanced techniques that can track an infant's eye movements or rate of sucking in response to stimuli, researchers now know that infants reach cognitive milestones such as object permanence at a younger age than Piaget had suspected. However, Piaget's view of the infant as a "little scientist" who comes to understand the world through trial and error experiments remains consistent with recent findings.

sensory diet   A management plan developed by a child and an occupational therapist to help the child learn skills and activities that ease the effects of SENSORY INTEGRATION DYSFUNCTION.

See also SENSORY INTEGRATION.

sensory impairment   Any impairment of the sensory system. The most prominent and predominant forms of sensory impairment are hearing and visual problems. All standard and legal definitions of LEARNING DISABILITY rule out sensory impairment as a contributing cause because those sensory impairments are classified separately in their own handicap categories. However, it's possible for a child with a sensory impairment to also have a learning disability. It's also difficult to tell the difference between the effects of a sensory impairment on learning and those effects that may be associated with a learning disability. It's likely that children with significant sensory problems who also have learning disabilities may generally be underdiagnosed and largely overlooked.

sensory integration   The process of taking in sensory information, organizing this information in the central nervous system, and using the information to function smoothly in daily life.

Sensory integration is a continual process: as children gain competence, their sensory integration improves, so that the more children do, the more they can do.

Sensory experiences include touch, movement, body awareness, sight, sound, and the pull of gravity; as the brain organizes and interprets this information, it provides a crucial foundation for later, more complex learning and behavior. This critical function of the brain is responsible for producing a composite picture of a person's existence, so that the person can understand who he is physically, where he is, and what is going on in the environment around him.

For most people, effective sensory integration occurs automatically and unconsciously, without effort. For others, however, the process is inefficient, demanding effort and attention with no guarantee of accuracy.

For most children, sensory integration develops in the course of ordinary childhood activities. But for some children, sensory integration doesn't develop as efficiently as it should. When the process breaks down, a number of problems in learning, development, or behavior may develop.

The concept of sensory integration comes from a body of work developed by occupational therapist A. Jean Ayres, Ph.D., who was interested in the way in which sensory processing and motor planning disorders interfere with daily life function and learning. This theory has been developed and refined by the research of Dr. Ayres, as well as other occupational and physical therapists. In addition, literature from the fields of neuropsychology, neurology, physiology, child development, and psychology has contributed to theory development and treatment strategies.

Children with sensory integration problems may be bright, but they may have trouble using a pencil, playing with toys, or taking care of personal tasks, such as getting dressed. Some children with this problem are so afraid of movement that ordinary swings, slides, or jungle gyms trigger fear and insecurity. On the other hand, some children whose problems lie at the opposite extreme are uninhibited and overly active, often falling and running headlong into dangerous situations. In each of these cases, a sensory integrative problem may be an underlying factor. Its far-reaching effects can interfere with academic learning, social skills, even self-esteem.

Research clearly identifies sensory integrative problems in children with developmental or learning difficulties, and independent research shows that a sensory integrative problem can be found in some children who are considered learning disabled by schools. However, sensory integrative problems aren't limited to children with learning disabilities; they can affect all ages, intellectual levels, and socioeconomic groups.

A number of situations can trigger sensory integration problems:

Prematurity As more premature infants survive today, they enter the world with easily overstimulated nervous systems and multiple medical problems. Parents need to learn how to give their premature infant the sensory nourishment their child requires for optimal development, and how to avoid harmful over-stimulation.

Developmental disorders Severe problems with sensory processing is a hallmark of AUTISM. Autistic children seek out unusual amounts of certain types of sensations, but are extremely hypersensitive to others. Similar traits are often seen in other children with developmental disorders. Improving sensory processing will help these children develop more productive contacts with people and environments.

Learning disabilities As many as 30 percent of school-age children may have learning disabilities. While most of these children have normal INTELLIGENCE, many are likely to have sensory integrative problems. These children are also more likely than their peers to have been born prematurely, to have had early developmental problems, and to have poor motor coordination. Early intervention can improve sensory integration in these children, minimizing the possibility of school failure before it occurs.

Many studies indicate that children with learning disabilities are at risk for later delinquency, criminal behavior, alcoholism, and drug abuse because of repeated failure in school. By interrupting the vicious cycle of failure, intervention to help children with sensory integration and learning problems may also prevent serious social problems later in life.

Brain injury Trauma to the brain as a result of accidents and strokes can have profound effects on sensory functioning. People who suffer from these effects deserve treatment that will lead to the best possible recovery. In order for this to occur, their sensory deficits must be addressed.

See also SENSORY INTEGRATION DYSFUNCTION.

sensory integration dysfunction (SID) The inefficient brain processing of information received through the senses. A child with SID has trouble detecting, discriminating, or integrating sensations. This complex neurological problem leads to either sensory seeking or sensory avoiding patterns, or a motor planning problem called DYSPRAXIA.

Sensory Seekers

These children have nervous systems that don't always process sensory input that is sent to the brain. As a result, they respond too strongly to sensations. Children who are underresponsive to sensation seek out sensory experiences that are more intense or of longer duration. They may

- be hyperactive as they seek more and more movement input
- be unaware of touch or pain, or touch others too often or too hard (may seem aggressive)
- engage in unsafe behaviors, such as climbing too high

- enjoy sounds that are too loud, such as TV or radio volume

Sensory Avoiders

At the other end of the spectrum of this disorder are those children who have nervous systems that feel sensation too easily or so much so that they are overly responsive to sensation. As a result, they may have "fight or flight" responses to sensation, a condition called "sensory defensiveness." They may

- respond to being touched with aggression or withdrawal
- be afraid of, or become sick with, movement and heights
- be very cautious and unwilling to take risks or try new things
- be uncomfortable in loud or busy environments such as sports events or malls
- be very picky eaters or overly sensitive to food smells

Dyspraxia

These children are clumsy and awkward. They have particular problems with new motor skills and activities. They may have

- very poor fine motor skills, such as handwriting
- very poor gross motor skills, such as kicking, catching, or throwing balls
- trouble imitating movements, such as in the game "Simon Says"
- trouble with balance, sequences of movements, and bilateral coordination

Treatment

Sensory integration dysfunction is a neurological problem that affects behavior and learning. Medicine can't cure the problem, but occupational therapy can address the child's underlying problems in processing sensations. Not stimulant drugs, but a good sensory treatment plan may be a major component in treating the child with SID. Taking a conservative approach often helps the inattentive child whose problem is not ADD, but developmentally delayed sensory processing.

If a child is suspected of having a sensory integrative disorder, a qualified occupational or physical therapist can conduct an evaluation. Evaluation usually consists of both standardized testing and structured observation of responses to sensory stimulation, posture, balance, coordination, and eye movements. After carefully analyzing test results and other assessment data along with information from other professionals and parents, the therapist will recommend appropriate treatment.

If therapy is recommended, the child will be guided through activities that challenge the child's ability to respond appropriately to sensory input by making a successful, organized response. Training of specific skills is not usually the focus of this kind of therapy. Instead, adaptive physical education, movement education, and gymnastics are examples of services that typically focus on specific motor skills training. Such services are important, but they are not the same as therapy using a sensory integrative approach.

The motivation of the child plays a crucial role in the selection of the activities in a sensory integrative approach. Most children tend to seek out activities that provide the best sensory experiences at that particular point in their development. It is this active involvement and exploration that enables the child to become a more mature and efficient organizer of sensory information.

The most important step in promoting sensory integration in children is to recognize that it exists and that it plays an important role in the development of a child. By learning more about sensory integration, parents, educators, and caregivers can provide an enriched environment that will foster healthy growth and maturation.

The goal of occupational therapy is to enable children to take part in the normal "job" of childhood, such as playing, enjoying school, eating, dressing, and sleeping—activities that are often a problem for children with SID. Each child is provided with an individualized treatment plan that directly involves parents.

Occupational therapy usually takes place in a large, sensory-enriched gym with lots of swinging, spinning, tactile, visual, auditory, and taste opportunities.

See also SENSORY DIET.

sequencing skills The ability to order elements correctly. Sequencing skills may be motor (sequencing body movements smoothly) or linguistic (sequencing words appropriately into sentences), as well as keeping track of the correct order of stimuli.

shaken baby syndrome Forceful shaking of an infant or young child by the arms, legs, chest, or shoulders; can cause brain damage leading to MENTAL RETARDATION, speech and LEARNING DISABILITIES, paralysis, seizures, hearing loss and death. It may cause bleeding around the brain and eyes, resulting in blindness.

A baby's head and neck are especially vulnerable to injury because the head is so large and the neck muscles are still weak. In addition, the baby's brain and blood vessels are very fragile and are easily damaged by whiplash motions such as shaking, jerking, and jolting.

About 50,000 cases of shaken baby syndrome occur each year in the United States; one shaken baby in four dies as a result of this abuse. Head trauma is the most frequent cause of permanent damage or death among abused infants and children, and shaking accounts for a significant number of those cases. Some studies estimate that 15 percent of children's deaths are due to battering or shaking and an additional 15 percent are possible cases of shaking. The victims of shaken baby syndrome range in age from a few days to five years, with an average age of six to eight months.

While shaken baby abuse is not limited to any special group of people, 65 percent to 90 percent of shakers are men. In the United States, adult males in their early 20s who are the baby's father or the mother's boyfriend are typically the shaker. Females who injure babies by shaking them are more likely to be baby sitters or child-care providers than mothers.

Severe shaking often begins in response to frustration over a baby's crying or toilet problems. The adult shaker also may be jealous of the attention that the child receives from a partner.

Shaken baby syndrome is also known as abusive head trauma, shaken brain trauma, pediatric traumatic brain injury, whiplash shaken infant syndrome, and shaken impact syndrome.

Diagnosis

Shaken baby syndrome is difficult to diagnose unless someone accurately describes what happens. Physicians often report that a child with possible shaken baby syndrome is brought for medical attention due to falls, difficulty breathing, seizures, vomiting, altered consciousness, or choking. The caregiver may report that the child was shaken to try to resuscitate it. Babies with severe or lethal shaken baby syndrome are typically brought to the hospital unconscious, with a closed head injury.

To diagnose shaken baby syndrome, physicians look for bleeding in the retina of the eyes, blood in the brain, or increased head size indicating buildup of fluid in the tissues of the brain. Damage to the spinal cord and broken ribs from grasping the baby too hard are other signs of shaken baby syndrome. Computed tomography (CT) and magnetic resonance imaging (MRI) scans can reveal injuries in the brain, but are not regularly used because of their expense.

A milder form of this syndrome may be missed or misdiagnosed. Subtle symptoms, which may be the result of shaken baby syndrome, are often attributed to mild viral illnesses, feeding dysfunction, or infant colic. These include a history of poor feeding; vomiting or flu-like symptoms with no accompanying fever or diarrhea; lethargy and irritability over a period of time. Without early medical intervention, the child may be at risk for further damage or even death, depending on the continued occurrences of shaking.

Prognosis

Immediate medical attention can help reduce the impact of shaking, but many children are left with permanent damage. Fewer than 10 to 15 percent of shaken babies recover completely; the rest have a variety of disabilities, including partial or complete loss of vision, hearing problems, seizure disorders, CEREBRAL PALSY, sucking and swallowing disorders, DEVELOPMENTAL DISABILITIES, AUTISM, cognitive or behavior problems, or a permanent vegetative state.

The treatment of survivors falls into three major categories—medical, behavioral, and educational. In addition to medical care, children may need speech and language therapy, vision therapy, physical therapy, occupational therapy, and special education services. Some may need the assistance of feeding experts and behavioral consultants.

sight-word approach A method of teaching reading and spelling in which small numbers of SIGHT WORDS are presented until the child masters them.

While many early readers naturally learn to read words through frequent exposure to them in stories, sight words should often be explicitly taught to individuals with a LEARNING DISABILITY. Sight words can be hard to learn for these children because they frequently have trouble following common spelling and pronunciation patterns, such as *are, were, been,* and *some,* and require a strong visual memory for words.

To avoid such confusions when using the sight-word approach to teach reading and spelling, words should be carefully selected initially to follow consistent spelling patterns.

sight words Words that are recognized instantly, without using word attack skills. The larger the sight-word vocabulary, the more fluent the reading process. Sight words are frequently used words that make up the majority of written text, such as

- the
- just
- had
- from
- about

The Dolch List is a well-known compilation of the 220 most often used words that average learners should know by the end of third grade. When an individual has difficulty recognizing common words by sight, reading is slow and laborious.

See also SIGHT-WORD APPROACH.

simultaneous retrieval memory Recalling multiple items or procedures at the same time. This form of recall is particularly involved in writing tasks. For example, in writing a sentence one must simultaneously recall information about correct spelling, word order and syntactic patterns, and appropriate punctuation. For many individuals with learning disabilities, difficulties in this area may result in performance that does not reflect their actual knowledge of such elements as spelling or punctuation rules. The presence of errors can reflect difficulty in accessing knowledge in long-term memory on demand and simultaneously, rather than in isolation and with time for thought and reflection.

social cognition A term used by social and developmental psychologists to refer to how people come to be concerned about the actions, thoughts, and feelings of others. This area of study examines how social perceptions develop, how individuals make social judgments, and how others affect an individual's self-concept. Many children with learning disabilities have significant deficits in social cognition as well as academic difficulties.

social maladjustment A vague term for a child's chronic misconduct in the absence of emotional disturbance. The INDIVIDUALS WITH DISABILITIES EDUCATION ACT (IDEA) specifically prohibits the classification of children as handicapped because of social maladjustment, although social maladjustment may occur together with legally defined handicaps.

In the past, it was a common practice for schools to place children into special education classes based on their misconduct rather than in the presence of a handicap. Many alleged that public school special education classes became "dumping grounds" for the children whom no one wanted to teach, such as juvenile delinquents and those who defied authority.

social skills problems Children with a LEARNING DISABILITY (especially nonverbal disabilities) may have trouble with social skills as a result of problems with perception. Children in this situation tend to be isolated, with few close friends, and only rarely participate in school activities. They are often rejected by children their own age because of odd behavior or poor school performance.

Teachers tend to rate these children as being easily led and with poor social adjustment. These problems may be caused by poor social comprehension, the inability to understand another's point of view, poor language skills, or misinterpretation of body language.

social skills training A type of behavioral therapy in which a therapist describes and models appropriate behaviors (such as waiting for a turn, sharing toys, asking for help, or responding to teasing). Through role-playing, a child has an opportunity to practice these skills in a therapeutic setting.

social worker A social worker is a mental health professional who provides intervention and treatment to clients who are referred to an agency or through typical school channels. These professionals work as part of a team, pro-

viding consultation regarding further assessment or actions for individuals with medical and/or psychological issues, including parents and children. Social workers must have a degree in social work from a college or university program accredited by the Council on Social Work Education.

The undergraduate degree is the bachelor of social work (B.S.W.); graduate degrees include the master of social work (M.S.W.) and the doctorate in social work (D.S.W.) or Ph.D. An M.S.W. is required to provide therapy. Degree programs involve classroom study as well as practical field experience. The bachelor's degree prepares graduates for generalist entry-level work, whereas the master's degree is for more advanced clinical practice. A D.S.W. or Ph.D. is useful for doing research or teaching at the university level.

Most states require practicing social workers to be licensed, certified, or registered, although standards vary.

sociocultural perspective A psychological approach that explores the social and cultural influences on behavior and learning.

socioeconomic status Class distinctions based on the social and economic status of an individual. Considerations that factor into an individual's socioeconomic status may include level of education, race, social class, or level of income.

Statistics show that families living in poverty have inadequate housing and healthcare, which puts their children at higher risk for disabilities.

sociolinguistics The study of the way people use language in different social situations and the connection between language and society.

Sociolinguistics studies how language influences the social roles in a community. It ranges from the study of the wide variety of dialects across a given region to the analysis of the way men and women speak to one another. Sociolinguistics often shows us the humorous realities of human speech and how a dialect of a given language can often describe the age, sex, and social class of the speaker; it codes the social function of a language.

soft neurological signs Any of a number of minor abnormalities that emerge in childhood and are used as diagnostic indicators of minimal brain damage.

Soft signs are subtle and difficult to detect reliably; they tend to run their developmental course with no clear cause and are not regarded as indicators of any specific neurological disease. The "soft" in the term comes from the difficulties of interpretation and the uncertain association with structural brain damage. Certain soft signs, like those related to fine and gross motor skills, have some predictive value when looking for learning disabilities. Neuropsychological evaluations and psychological evaluations for learning disabilities typically include soft signs assessments such as the ability to walk a straight line, the ability to tell left from right, and the ability to track objects horizontally and vertically.

sound blending The ability to hear sounds in isolation and then blend them into a continuous word. Sound blending requires auditory perception skills to take in information and reproduce the sounds fluently. For example, an instructor may say "put /m/ /a/ /t/ together" to assess if the student can say *mat.* Sound blending is an important skill to develop the awareness of word sounds.

sound/letter/word retrieval The process of reading requires a student to quickly retrieve sounds, letters, and words. Research has shown that a delay in naming pictures, symbols, letters, and words is an accurate predictor of reading problems. Problems in retrieving are probably due to memory retrieval problems that make it difficult to access phonological and verbal information.

Sound, letter, and word retrieval interventions are available, such as computer software programs that slow the pace of language to allow individuals to retrain the pace of language processing.

sound/symbol association The idea that certain sounds are paired with specific symbols.

source memory The memory of where a person obtained information. For example, a child might know that Harrisburg is the capital of Pennsylvania, but not recall where he obtained that information. Many students with learning disabilities have deficient source memory.

space perception The ability to understand on a perceptual level the way in which objects are facing or placed, the direction in which they are moving, and the relation of objects to each other, both in distance and orientation.

spatial ability The ability to imagine objects or symbols in space.

spatial judgment The ability to judge spatial relationships, as between fixed objects or between a moving object and a fixed point. Spatial judgment is involved in activities such as driving a car or playing a sport. Individuals with learning disabilities may have problems with spatial judgment as part of an overall pattern of difficulty with visual-spatial abilities.

spatial-material organizational disorder A problem with organizing materials so that the child constantly struggles for survival within an ordered environment.

A child with this problem has a hard time organizing information on paper. Margins are missing, spacing between words and letters is incorrect, centering is difficult, and the overall appearance of the work is messy. Teachers often have trouble reading the child's work. Often, a child with this problem forgets assignments or books needed to complete assignments. Assignments themselves may be incomplete, or the child can't find completed assignments.

In addition, a child with this problem is often disorganized and has problems following routines or completing tasks. Desk and home environment are usually quite messy and disorganized, although the child may appear to have his own system of organization in his own space.

spatial orientation   The ability to maintain a sense of orientation in a physical space. Difficulties in spatial orientation may be part of a larger pattern of visual-spatial skills deficits that are linked with a LEARNING DISABILITY in some cases. These problems may have a profound effect on an individual's ability to follow physical directions or to locate information or objects within a space.

spatial relationships   The relative positions of objects in a space. Children learn about spatial relationships at an early age as they manipulate toys and other objects. Academically, spatial relationships are involved in the acquisition of reading skills and mathematics: a child must perceive the space between words in a sentence in order to understand the concept of a sentence. In math, understanding spatial relationships is essential for developing many types of math skills such as computation, graphing, and understanding a number line. For example, the child can recognize that the toy is on top of or above the bed; in looking at a picture, a child can recognize that the moon is above the ground. This understanding is often obvious in children's drawings.

spatial sequencing   Refers to the ability to recognize and organize objects in a pattern. For example, spatial sequencing is demanded in the copying of block patterns. Later, spatial sequencing is demanded in reading, in recognizing and interpreting the sequence of letters in words and the spaces between words. At this last level, the skill may be considered cognitive.

special education   Educational services and programs for students with abilities ranging from giftedness to mental retardation, and including various physical, emotional, or learning differences.

The history of special education can be traced at least as far back as Plato's recommendation that children with extraordinary intellectual ability should be provided special leadership training. In more modern times special education was practiced in the 16th century when Pedro Ponce de León taught deaf Spanish children to speak, read, and write. In the 18th century Jean-Marc-Gaspard Itard (1775–1838) developed special education techniques with Victor, the so-called Wild Boy of Avalon. During the late 18th and early 19th centuries, special education procedures for teaching some school skills to pupils with sensory handicaps were supported by Thomas Hopkins Gallaudet. For example, individuals with profound hearing loss were taught meanings for printed words by repeated simultaneous presentations of a printed word and a picture of what the word represented.

About the same time, attempts to educate individuals with mental retardation or with emotional or behavioral disorders increased in number and success, as exemplified in the work of the American educator Samuel Gridley Howe (1801–76). Successful attempts to educate the deaf and blind led to scientific methods to teach the mentally retarded in Europe. For example, Maria Montessori, a pediatrician and innovative educator, used multisensory methods to teach mentally retarded and culturally deprived children in Rome in the late 19th century.

In the 20th century, the enactment and implementation of compulsory education laws led to an increasing need for special education services. In the latter half of the 20th century, great gains have been made in special education. In most developed countries, addressing the educational needs of the disabled has become universal. However, it wasn't until the mid-1970s, with the passage of the EDUCATION FOR ALL HANDICAPPED CHILDREN ACT OF 1975 (PL 94–142), that the education of disabled children carried the force of law in the United States. This revolutionary legislation, guaranteeing a free and appropriate education for all children, paved the way for a rapid expansion of the field of special education that continues to this day.

Public Law 94–142, renamed Individuals with Disabilities Education Act (IDEA) in 1990, requires students with disabilities to be placed in the least restrictive environment (LRE) available in order to avoid segregating students with disabilities.

Schools that comply with the laws receive more money from the federal government to offset part of the costs of providing special education services. The federal government also requires that schools report the number of special education students they serve. During the 1989–90 school year, more than 4.5 million children received such services. About 85 percent of these children were between the ages of six and 17.

Special equipment is used extensively with students who have problems with vision or hearing. Equipment such as computers to convert printed materials into synthetic speech, and special desks, chairs, writing devices, and school buses may help students with physical handicaps. Special ramps and wide doors, swimming pools and schoolrooms specially equipped with hearing aid transmission equipment are all part of special education.

Special services for exceptional individuals include speech training, physical and occupational therapies, counseling, and vocational training for students with mental retardation.

The most common element of special education are the specialized instructional techniques, such as

- sign language
- programmed instruction procedures designed to present information in small steps
- behavior modification techniques such as token economies

While most special education takes place in regular public schools, some classes are provided in special public or private day or residential schools, public or private hospitals, and, in some cases, the homes of individuals whose disabilities prevent them from attending school. Most individuals with disabilities don't require an entire program of services apart from conventional instruction, but rather only a modification of features.

When children are considered able to benefit from participation with other children, they are usually taught in the normal school program. This process, known as mainstreaming, was believed to be consistent with the legal mandate for education in the least restrictive environment. More than two-thirds of students with disabilities receive most of their education in regular education classes.

If a child's handicap is not severe, a special education teacher works with the regular classroom teacher to develop skills. In other cases, an assistant teacher may be able to care for a student's specific needs. For individuals with more serious problems, special education may be provided in a separate classroom for part of the school day; students with severe learning and behavioral problems may remain in a separate special education room all day. The ratio of students to teachers is usually much lower in a special education classroom than in an ordinary classroom.

Special education also includes enhancement for gifted and talented students, and includes special activities beyond the regular curriculum, conventional courses at a faster-than-normal pace, and the opportunity to take college-level courses earlier in the school career.

With the development of assistive technologies, the field of special education continues to evolve, although its goal remains the same as it was from the beginning—to educate and integrate individuals with disabilities into society.

specific language disability (SLD) A severe problem with some aspect of listening, speaking, reading, writing, or spelling, while skills in the other areas are age-appropriate. It is also called specific language learning disability (SLLD).

specific learning disabilities A legal term that plays a central role in legislation governing LEARNING DISABILITIES. As described in PUBLIC LAW 94–142 (amended by PL 101–76), "specific learning disability" means a disorder in one or more of the basic psychological processes involved in understanding or in using spoken or written language. This may manifest itself in an imperfect ability to listen, think, speak, read, write, spell, or to do mathematical calculations.

The term includes such conditions as perceptual handicaps, brain injury, MINIMAL BRAIN DYSFUNCTION, DYSLEXIA, and developmental APHASIA. The term does not include children whose conditions are primarily caused by visual, hearing, or motor problems; MENTAL RETARDATION; emotional disturbance; or due to environmental, cultural, or economic disadvantage.

speech-language pathologist An expert who specializes in the assessment and treatment of speech, language, and voice disorders. Also known as a speech pathologist or speech therapist, the speech-language pathologist evaluates and treats individuals with communication problems resulting from a LEARNING DISABILITY, hearing loss, brain injury, cleft palate, emotional problems, development delays, or stroke. He also provides clinical therapy to help those with speech and language disorders, and helps them and their families understand the disorder and develop better communication skills.

Speech-language pathologists perform screening tests and make recommendations for the type of speech language treatment required. Treatment could include a specific program of exercises to improve language ability or speech, together with support from the client's family and friends.

They conduct research to develop new and better ways to diagnose and treat speech/language problems, work with children who have language delays and speech problems, and provide treatment to people who stutter and to those with voice and articulation problems.

Educational requirements include a master's degree in speech-language pathology, more than 300 hours of supervised clinical experience, and successful completion of a certifying exam. Those who meet the strict requirements of the American Speech-Language and Hearing Association are awarded the certificate of clinical competence.

speech/language specialist An expert who works in the area of speech and LANGUAGE, typically providing individualized work on language areas for children who have been identified as needing services. A speech/language specialist identifies and treats students with speech, language, and related problems, and collaborates with parents, caregivers, teachers, and other professionals in monitoring a student's progress.

speech synthesizer/screen readers Computers designed to convert text into computer-generated speech. Originally designed for individuals with vision problems, as the programs became more sophisticated and affordable, they have been marketed to students with and without a LEARNING DISABILITY.

Many students find screen readers helpful in wading through large reading assignments. For now, getting the reading assignments *into* the computer adds a cumbersome step to the reading process; however, the time saved using the reading software far exceeds the time students take to convert print text into digital text. As college and university publishers move toward web-based textbooks, this accessibility to digital texts may become the standard, making screen readers an essential tool for many students.

Although the quality of computerized voices is continuously improving, at present they can take some adjustment for the user.

Screen readers can be built into a word processing program, or designed as a feature of a voice recognition program. Typically, text can be scanned in, accessed online, or imported from a file. To be used primarily as a reading tool, a scanner is essential in order to enter text that is not already in digital form (such as in a textbook). Many screen readers are used for both reading and writing, though, since they were originally designed to be readers, they tend to be limited as word processors. Screen readers can be invaluable for students with learning disabilities when used in conjunction with other technologies such as word prediction, word processing, and spell checking since they allow students to hear words on the screen.

As reading tools, research has indicated that they enhance both fluency and comprehension. Unlike a print text environment, screen readers empower low decoders by providing flexibility and manipulation of the text. Because users can control how fast the reader reads, and combine both visual and auditory channels for "reading," slow readers can set the speed to much faster than they can read, but not faster than they can comprehend. Since slow readers are exposed to much more text than they would be relying on with traditional reading, studies show that fluency improves.

Not only are screen readers powerful reading tools, they are also useful for students with learning disabilities in the writing process, to hear their papers for proofing and revising.

As with all assistive technology, there are limitations. Although research has shown that college students with learning disabilities were able to find and correct about one-third of their errors with the use of a screen reader, it will not help catch homophone errors such as their/there

that are common for students with learning disabilities.

See also KURZWEIL READING MACHINE.

spell checkers   An electronic computer tool that checks a document for correct spelling. Nearly all word processing programs come with a built-in spell checking tool that can be invaluable for students with a LEARNING DISABILITY, since many written language disabilities include a problem with spelling.

Spell checkers perform two important functions: first, they identify misspelled words and second, they suggest correct spellings.

The process for spell checking is fairly universal. It begins by scanning a document against the program's dictionary and then flagging misspelled words. (Automatic spell checks that identify misspellings as a person types can be visually disruptive for some students. With this system, as it scans the document and flags misspelled words, the spell check will display a list of spelling suggestions. The user then selects the intended word, and it automatically replaces the misspelled word in the document.)

While spell checkers are valuable, they are not without several limitations to students with learning disabilities. First, spell checkers can't identify spelling errors that are real words. Since studies show that up to 40 percent of spelling errors are real words, this can be a problem. For example, in the following sentence the spell checker would miss the underlined words because they are correctly spelled, although incorrect in this context: "After the cloths our finished drying, if you don't fold them they will wriggle." One way to overcome this problem with spell check is to use it together with a synthesized speech program, so the student can hear the words.

Another significant problem with spell checkers for students with learning disabilities is they don't always offer spelling suggestions for badly misspelled words. If the student can't estimate the spelling of the intended word closely enough, then the spell checker is of little use.

Spell checkers may cause problems for students with learning disabilities when a suggested list of words appears in which many words are visually similar. In this case, it is difficult for the user to identify the intended word. In a spell check study done in 1996, students with learning disabilities selected the intended word only 82 percent of the time. A student can avoid selecting the wrong word by cross-checking with a thesaurus or using synthesized speech.

Finally, spell checking tools often flag proper nouns as incorrect, which can be confusing for students with learning disabilities.

Since spelling is often one of the major barriers to writing for students with learning disabilities, most students gladly accept the limitations of spell checking. Spell checkers are most effective with students who have learning disabilities but ample awareness of word sounds, which allows them to approximate the sounds of the intended word. The system is also better suited for those who can distinguish between similar-looking words.

As with all assistive technology, it is extremely important that students with learning disabilities are trained to use the technology in a way that will most empower their writing potential.

spelling   Words in the English language can be difficult to learn to spell because of many irregular spelling patterns. For example "do," "due," and "dew" are all pronounced exactly the same but differ in meaning. While English has 44 sounds, it has only 26 letters.

The letter-sound correspondence is essential for reading, as is the sound-letter correspondence for correct spelling. A difficulty in these relationships results in LANGUAGE DISABILITIES.

Spelling a word is more difficult than reading a word for several reasons. First, passive (receptive) skills such as reading tend to be easier than active, expressive skills such as spelling. In addi-

tion, there are no contextual or structural cues to help with spelling as there are for reading. While spelling can be difficult for average learners, it is particularly difficult for individuals with a weakness in decoding.

SQ3R   An acronym for an active reading method that stands for Survey, Question, Read, Recite, and Review; developed by psychologist Francis Robinson in 1941. To develop this method, Robinson applied the principles of learning theory to the development of reading and study skills. Through extensive research and testing, SQ3R has proven to be an effective reading and study strategy that enhances understanding and recall.

Surveying a passage before reading prepares one mentally to read. Creating questions based on chapter titles, subheading, and vocabulary creates a purpose for reading. Reading, reciting (paraphrasing and margin noting), and reviewing provide repetition of information. Thus, SQ3R combines reading and studying to create an active learning activity.

standard deviation   The measure of how the distribution of test scores varies from the mean. When the scores are tightly bunched together around the mean, the standard deviation is small. When the examples are spread apart, the standard deviation is larger. Computation of the standard deviation is based upon the square of the deviation of each score from the mean.

standardized test   A test that is designed to be administered and scored in a consistent manner in order to provide objective information about performance, ability, or achievement in a specific academic area.

The development process for a standardized test is extensive. Standardized tests typically include comprehensive guidelines for administration and scoring in order to reduce elements that might influence test results. Scores are often norm-referenced. The SAT and ACT are examples of standardized tests.

Unfortunately, as pressure increases on elementary and high schools to provide evidence of success, standardized tests are being used in ways for which they were never designed. A standardized test should never be used as the only criterion in placing a child in a special class, nor as the sole criterion for passing, failing, or graduating.

The two major types of group standardized tests are criterion-referenced tests and norm-referenced tests. Criterion-referenced tests are designed to determine at what level students are performing on various skill areas. These tests assume that development of skills follows a sequence of steps. Criterion-referenced tests try to identify how far along the skills hierarchy the student has progressed. There is no comparison against anyone else's score, only against an expected skill level. The main question that criterion-referenced tests ask is "Where is this child in the development of group skills?"

Norm-referenced tests, in contrast, are typically constructed to compare children in their abilities as to different skill areas. Although the experts who design test items may be aware of skills hierarchies, they are more concerned with how much of some skill the child has mastered, rather than at what level on the skills hierarchy the child is.

Ideally, the questions on these tests range from very simple to extremely difficult. The essential feature of norm-referenced tests is that scores on these measures can be compared to scores of children in similar groups. They answer the question "How does the child compare with other children of the same age or grade placement in the development of this skill?"

Most criterion-referenced tests are created on the state or local level. The major norm-referenced tests include the California Achievement Tests, the Iowa Tests of Basic Skills, the Stanford Achievement Test, the Metropolitan Achievement Tests, and the TerraNova. These generally test several types of reading, language, and mathematics skills along with social studies and science, and together with study and reference skills.

Group standardized tests are designed to assess and compare the achievement of groups—they are NOT designed to provide detailed diagnostic assessments of individual students. This doesn't mean that test information on individual students isn't useful, but it does mean that using these tests to diagnose an individual student is using them for a purpose for which they were not designed. Basically, a group standardized test is simply a way of screening the achievement of many students quickly. Learning problems should not be diagnosed solely on the basis of a group standardized test result, but the results can suggest that a child be referred for more definitive, individual assessments.

A child's group test score should be considered only as a point of information. These scores must be used with other information, such as teacher comments, daily work, homework, class tests, parent observations, medical needs, and social history.

standard scores   The results of most educational tests are reported using standard scores, which are then converted into percentiles. Standard scores are translated from RAW SCORES, generally to allow for greater comparability and ease of interpretation.

Stanford-Binet Intelligence Scale: Fourth Edition (SB:FE or SB-IV)   One type of IQ test that can be used to assess intelligence for individuals between the ages of two and adulthood. First developed in 1910, the test is a standard tool for many school psychologists.

Recently revised, the test now provides multiple IQ scores (called SASs) instead of a single IQ score. In addition to being able to measure the verbal and nonverbal areas of a child's development, the Binet also provides a quantitative score, measuring the child's mathematical reasoning, and a memory score, measuring the child's short-term memory. (While the Wechsler scales also have subtests that measure these areas, they do not provide IQ scores isolating these abilities.)

This test is a good choice for children who are slow at processing information because it contains only one timed subtest. However, this lack of timing can make the testing session extremely long. In addition, this test may score substantially lower than the WAIS-III for very bright individuals over age 16.

One major advantage of the Binet over other IQ tests is that it is useful for assessment of much higher and much lower abilities than most other such tests, extending down to the moderately to the severely deficient and upward to the very superior range. It remains the measure of choice among psychologists assessing possible giftedness.

stanine An approach to grouping standard scores on tests as a means for differentiating between groups of students. "Stanine" is short for *standard nine*—a reference to the fact that stanine scores range from a low of 1 to a high of 9. For instance, a stanine score of 1, 2, or 3 is below average; 4, 5, or 6 is average; and 7, 8, or 9 is above average.

If a child achieves a stanine score that is below average in a particular area, the test reveals an area in which the child needs improvement. If the child achieves an average stanine score, the test indicates that he or she performed at about the same level as the other students who took the test. If the child achieves a stanine score above average, this means that he or she performed better in that area than other students who took the test.

Stanines are similar to percentiles in that they provide a means for assessing an individual's test performance in relation to the various levels of performance. In contrast to stanines, however, percentiles give a more detailed description of how a child compares with others who took the test by showing scores that range from 1 to 99.

For example, if a student scored in the 66th percentile on a test, that student achieved a score that was higher than 66 percent of the other students who took the test. So, if 1,000 students took the test, the student in the 66th percentile scored higher than 660 students who also took the same test.

However, percentiles should not be confused with percentage correct scores. "Percentile" scores allow one student's scores to be compared with a group of students who took the test. "Percentage correct" scores simply reveal the number of items that a student answered correctly out of the total number of items.

While stanines are a fairly popular alternative to percentiles, they are often less precise or informative. Individuals whose percentile rankings are fairly close may be grouped in different stanines, while individuals whose percentiles differ broadly in the middle range may be grouped together.

Stanines and percentiles rely on measuring a student's scores against the scores of a large group of students who also took the same test. This other group of students, or the comparison group, may be composed of other students in a school district who took the test at the same time or of students from a nationally representative sample who took the test earlier.

state education agency The state board of education or other agency primarily responsible for the supervision of public elementary and secondary schools. The state education agencies are responsible for compliance to IDEA within their individual states.

stimulant medications Drugs often used in the treatment of ATTENTION DEFICIT/HYPERACTIVITY DISORDER. RITALIN (methylphenidate) is most commonly prescribed. Other stimulant medications that are frequently prescribed include: Dexedrine (dextroamphetamine), Adderall (amphetamine and dextroamphetamine), and Cylert (pemoline).

For more than 50 years, these drugs have been used to treat the behavior of children with hyperactive symptoms; as many as 80 percent of students with ADHD respond to these drugs. Exactly what makes these medications effective against ADHD is unknown, although experts suspect they affect the rate and balance of specific neurotransmitters in certain areas of the brain. This results in a greater ability to pay attention and stay focused, and a decrease in hyperactivity. Since these children also tend to become less impulsive, aggressive, and destructive, the drugs also help improve social acceptance.

These medications are often used in combination with behavioral and educational interventions.

Individuals who respond positively to stimulant medications generally show improvement in their academic work and in their interactions with others. This change seems to happen right away. (However, there is a lag before Cylert achieves its maximum effect in children.)

Several studies have found that after students with ADHD started taking stimulants, their test scores and accuracy and speed in completing homework improved. The long-term gains are less clear.

Because most stimulant medications are metabolized quickly, often several doses a day are necessary.

Stimulant medications are used by both children and adults, and are taken for as long a period a time as is helpful or necessary. Some children find that as they develop through adolescence the medication is no longer necessary; others find the medication less necessary as their situation changes, for example, in environmental or academic demands. Many find that they face the frustrations of ADHD throughout adolescence and adulthood, and some of these individuals may benefit from using stimulant medication.

Successful treatment with stimulants lies in finding the right drug at the right dosage. It is important to remember that the child with ADHD will remain impulsive and energetic even while taking stimulants, but her ability to pay attention should improve.

Treatment with stimulants for ADHD is a long-term therapy; the government estimates that 80 percent of those who need medication for ADHD in childhood will still need drugs as teenagers, and 50 percent will be helped by stimulants as adults.

Side Effects

The most common side effects include weight loss and appetite loss, together with problems in falling asleep, although these problems may fade away as a student becomes used to the drug. Some studies have found that a child's growth begins to lag, although this growth usually rebounds after the first year in those who are on low or moderate doses. Children taking Dexedrine or high doses of Ritalin may experience prolonged growth lag as long as they remain on the medication, but once the drug is stopped, growth begins again. For this reason, some experts recommend "drug holidays" during vacation to allow a child's growth to catch up.

Less common side effects include stomach problems, headaches, lethargy, irritability, nausea, euphoria, depression, nightmares, dry mouth, constipation, anxiety, hallucinations, nervous tics, and tremors. In children at risk for tic disorders such as Tourette's syndrome, the medication may trigger the condition. Because individual reactions and needs change, it is very important that the use and results of the medication be monitored.

Addiction

While some stimulants can be addictive if abused by teenagers or adults, low doses seem to be safe for children, who don't become addicted nor are likely to be addicts when they are older. On the other hand, some studies suggest that untreated students with ADHD are at higher risk for developing substance abuse in adolescence.

strategy instruction An important educational approach to working with students with a LEARNING DISABILITY. It is based in part on an assumption that individuals with learning disabilities have significant deficits in the area of strategy development. These deficits may be the result of underlying language disabilities and skills deficits, or of problems in acquiring executive procedures and learning strategies.

In any case, a strategy instruction approach assumes that explicit instruction in learning strategies and executive procedures is a fundamental approach to helping students with learning disabilities achieve their potential.

Strategy instruction typically involves teaching procedures for specific academic tasks, such as reading strategies like SQ3R (Survey, Question, Read, Recite, Review). Students learn to perform a sequence of specific activities geared toward a specific task and outcome, practice these procedures in a variety of contexts, and apply them independently.

Strategy instruction has proven effective, particularly in college situations where it allows students to meet course requirements independently.

structural analysis A type of word recognition that identifies structural features such as syllables, prefixes, suffixes, and roots. Other structural elements include compound words (*sunshine*) and contractions (*don't*).

A reader may use a combination of structural analysis and context clues to identify an unfamiliar word. Individuals with learning disabilities benefit from the explicit teaching of structural analysis skills in order to improve spelling and reading comprehension.

See also MORPHOLOGICAL AWARENESS.

study skills Learning strategies that help an individual organize time, materials, and information. Special educators long ago recognized the importance of teaching study skills to students with LEARNING DISABILITIES; such skills have recently become a part of many school curricula starting in the elementary grades.

While some students seem to succeed in school with only basic study skills, many learning disabled students benefit greatly from being taught ideas such as how to maintain a notebook and how to organize materials in each class. Time management is another essential study skill needed to complete long and short assignments on time as well as to schedule time for appointments, friends, and work. Note-taking and active reading strategies are also important study skills for all students, including those with learning disabilities.

stuttering A communication disorder in which the flow of speech is broken by repetitions (li-li-like this), prolongations (lllllike this), or abnormal stoppages (no sound) of sounds and syllables. There may also be unusual facial and body movements associated with the effort to speak. Known medically as dysphemia, stuttering is most obvious in those who don't have control over the timing and rhythm of their speech.

Cause

While experts seem to know all the characteristics of stuttering, they don't agree on the cause. Despite years of research, there are no simple answers to the cause of stuttering, but much has been learned about factors which contribute to its development. Stuttering may occur in the presence of a combination of factors, which may have different causes in different people. It may well be that what causes stuttering differs from what makes it continue or get worse. However, children who stutter are no more likely to have psychological or emotional problems than those who don't, and there is no reason to believe that emotional trauma causes stuttering.

More than 3 million Americans stutter, which affects four times as many boys as girls. About 20 percent of all children go through a stage of development during which they encounter speech fluency problems severe enough to be a concern to their parents.

Treatment

The best prevention is early intervention. Parents should seek help as soon as possible. If the stuttering lasts for more than six months or is particularly severe, a SPEECH-LANGUAGE PATHOLOGIST who specializes in stuttering should be consulted. A speech pathologist can almost always help children make positive changes in their communication skills.

There are a variety of successful approaches for treating children. While therapy won't cure stuttering overnight, a qualified clinician can help children make significant progress toward fluency. Stuttering therapy usually means changing long-standing speech behaviors, emotions, and attitudes about talking and communication in general. As a result, length and type of therapy can vary greatly depending on a person's goals.

substitution   A reading error made when an individual replaces the written word with a different word based on structural or semantic cues.

A structural substitution is when the reader guesses a word based on its visual structure. For example, a reader reads the word "stipulate" as "stimulate" because they look similar.

A semantic substitution occurs when a reader replaces a word with a word that means the same thing. For example, a reader might read "Then they went to her house" as "Then they went to her place," replacing "house" with "place."

Substitution is common in the oral reading of all students and by itself should not be considered as evidence of a reading disability. Tracking reading errors through ERROR ANALYSIS can help to determine reading patterns and problems.

support group   An organization that exists to provide support to individuals struggling with a problem, such as a LEARNING DISABILITY. Some people derive enormous satisfaction by sharing their problems and solutions with others in similar situations.

CHILDREN AND ADULTS WITH ATTENTION DEFICIT/HYPERACTIVITY DISORDER (CHADD) is one of several national organizations with local chapters that offer help to people with learning disabilities.

Belonging to a support group can also help individuals identify which local practitioners are best qualified to diagnose and treat learning disabilities.

survival skills   This term can mean more than one thing depending on the context in which it is used. Survival skills may refer to daily self-help skills necessary to survive in life, such as feeding, dressing, and communicating. In higher education, survival skills often refer to the STUDY SKILLS necessary to be a successful learner.

syllabication   The process of dividing words into syllables. Syllabication is a popular word attack strategy taught to individuals with reading problems. Many PHONICS and structured reading programs teach syllabication.

In English, there are six types of syllables and five principles of syllabication that describe how and where to break a word apart. The six types of syllables include:

1. closed: short vowel followed by a consonant (*con, pan, dis*)
2. open: ends in a single long vowel (*de, o, fi*)
3. silent "e": long vowel/consonant/silent "e" (*hive, ete, ode*)
4. R-controlled: vowel followed by an "r" (*ur, fir, cer*)
5. double vowel: any two vowels that make one sound (*poor, ear, ay*)
6. consonant "le": found at the end of a word with a consonant/le (*kle, dle, ple*).

symbol   Something that represents or stands for an idea, object, or sound. In English, the alphabet is the symbol system for language. Individuals who have difficulty processing or naming symbols will have difficulty reading, since reading is the process of interpreting symbols.

syntax The arrangement of words in sentences, clauses, and phrases. Understanding syntax in the English language is very important because it directly affects comprehension. The following sentences, for example, contain the exact same words, but only the syntax is different—*Liz saw Bob and Bob saw Liz.* The sentences mean very different things.

Students with a LEARNING DISABILITY may have trouble understanding the rules of syntax. When speaking out loud, syntax is more flexible and fluid. Sentences in spoken language tend to be longer, and syntactical errors are often overlooked. In spoken language, difficulties in syntax may lead to the inability to articulate a thought in a complete sentence. Many students with learning disabilities who demonstrate a solid understanding of syntax in spoken language may have considerable difficulties with syntax in written form because of the static nature of text and the rigidity of grammar. In writing, common syntactic errors include run-on sentences, incomplete sentences, subject-verb disagreement, and comma splices.

Syntactic knowledge can have a significant impact on reading and writing. Normal development of syntactic knowledge occurs in the following stages:

- holophrastic stage (10–12 months): children begin uttering one-word sentences to express ideas. For example, "milk" means "I want milk"

- two-word stage (18–24 months): children string two words together to express general ideas. For example, "Mommy sock" could mean "That sock is Mommy's" or "Mommy, the sock is over there"

- expansions (two to nine years): children begin to gradually use more descriptive and grammatically advanced sentences with subjects and verbs. For example a two-year-old may say "Car goes" for "That car goes down the road"

- later stages (nine years through adulthood): after age nine, sentence length continues to increase through early adulthood. In adolescence, average sentence length is about 10 to 12 words. Sentence structure becomes more complex, using complex subjects, interrupters, modals, and so on

Children who don't gain syntactic knowledge in the above stages, may encounter problems with comprehension. Research has discovered that poor readers often have syntactic deficits. Poor readers use fewer complete sentences, they violate subject/verb agreement, use shorter sentences. In writing, they use simple sentences more often than proficient readers.

If an individual is suspected of having problems with syntax, it's important to find out where the breakdown is occurring. There are both formal and informal syntactic assessment procedures that can be carried out by speech pathologists or other such professionals qualified in assessing language skills.

tactile   The sensory system of touch, in which information is transmitted through direct physical contact via the nervous system to the brain.

tactile defensiveness   Being overly sensitive to touch; withdrawing, crying, yelling, or striking out when touched.

tactile perception   Perception through the sensory system of touch, in which direct physical contact is transmitted through the nervous system to the brain.

task analysis   A teaching strategy in which a learning activity is broken down into small sequential tasks. It is an effective strategy used to teach students with a LEARNING DISABILITY because it takes a large learning activity and breaks it into smaller, more easily accomplished tasks. Task analysis is also used as an assessment tool to see precisely at what stage a skill breakdown is occurring. For example, if a student is given an assignment to define 10 vocabulary words, a task analysis might include the following steps:

1. Understand, record, and remember the assignment
2. Read/decode the vocabulary words
3. Use a dictionary/textbook
4. Paraphrase the definition
5. Write the definitions

Breaking an assignment into the five steps can make a difficult and overwhelming project become more manageable.

Similarly, task analysis can be used for instruction where larger skills are broken down into subskills and each subskill taught until mastery.

See also DIRECT INSTRUCTION.

temporal lobe   A part of the brain located above and behind the ears, underneath the frontal and parietal lobes. It is named for the temporal bone at the temple, just above the ear canal. The temporal lobe includes the auditory cortex located near the ear, which is the primary area for processing hearing.

temporal-sequential organization problems   Children with this type of organizational problem have trouble completing long-term assignments, understanding and having a sense of time, and understanding and following directions.

Almost every task a child does involves sequence, whether that involves getting dressed, completing an assignment, or reading a book. Knowing the sequence and being able to follow it are important developmental skills.

School can be overwhelming for students who can't recognize a step-by-step plan needed to master a concept such as memorizing the alphabet, understanding the seasons, or learning the multiplication tables. Spelling can be a particular problem for these children who can't remember the sequence of letters, which is also required for word recognition during reading.

Concepts of time are also very difficult for these children, who have trouble mastering days of the week, months of the year, and how to tell time. The ability to manage time is also compromised, and completing a long-term assignment by the due date is quite a challenge. Because a concept of time is foreign to these children, they easily lose track of time, which can interfere with a child's ability to pace work during a test.

Test of Adolescent and Adult Language–Third Edition (TOAL-3)

This test of language development helps determine areas of relative strength and weakness. The overall score may be accurate, although some of the area scores may not be valid because they are comprised of only two subtest scores. In this test, the individual will

- choose a picture that depicts a dictated word
- choose which sentences with different grammar have the same meaning
- make up and repeat sentences
- write sentences using specific words
- choose words that belong together
- combine sentences

Test of Auditory Comprehension of Language–Revised (TACL-R)

This developmental test assesses auditory comprehension by having children point to the correct picture from among three choices as the examiner dictates single words, words with modifiers, short sentences with different grammatical forms, and complex sentences. A child's score may be lowered if the individual is impulsive or has trouble with perceptual discrimination, even if overall language comprehension is good. This test should be used with tasks that measure the child's expressive language abilities as well.

Test of Language Competence–Expanded Edition (TLC)

A test of language development designed for students aged nine through 18 years, 11 months that measures more sophisti-

cated vocabulary (semantics), sentence structure (syntax), and conversational skills. In this test, the student may be asked to

- identify multiple meanings in a sentence that could mean more than one thing
- choose inferences after related statements
- create a sentence using a picture and three words
- explain metaphors

Test of Language Development–Primary, Third Edition (TOLD-P:3)

A test of language development that measures the younger child's pictorial and oral vocabulary, understanding of sentence structure, repetition of dictated sentences, use of appropriate grammatical forms, and word discrimination and articulation. The test is appropriate for children between ages four years and eight years, 11 months.

Test of Language Development–2 Intermediate (TOLD-2 Intermediate)

A test of language development that measures vocabulary and sentence structure by assessing sentence combinations, oral vocabulary, abstract relationships, the ordering of words within sentences, recognition of grammatically correct sentences, and the correcting of nonsensical sentences.

thalamus   A part of the brain located above the hypothalamus; involved in the relay of information from other regions of the nervous system to the cerebral cortex. It transmits sensory information, including auditory and visual input, in addition to movement information from the cerebellum and basal ganglia to the motor cortex. The thalamus is also involved in the maintenance of consciousness.

thematic maturity   The sophistication of writing. Plot development, sentence structure, and cohesion based on an individual's age and grade are some elements that are considered in evaluating thematic maturity.

thinking skills   The way in which an individual acquires, interprets, organizes, stores, retrieves, and applies information. Known medically as cognitive skills.

tics   Involuntary functions associated with TOURETTE'S SYNDROME that may be either vocal, motor, or mental.

token economy   A behavior therapy procedure in which tokens (such as coins or poker chips) are given for desired behavior. The tokens can then be exchanged for privileges or treats.

Tourette's syndrome   A neurological disorder characterized by tics, or rapid, sudden movements that occur involuntarily and repeatedly in a consistent fashion. To be diagnosed with Tourette's syndrome, an individual must have multiple motor tics as well as one or more vocal tics over a period of more than one year. These need not all occur simultaneously, but in general the tics may occur many times a day, usually in brief, intense groupings, nearly every day or intermittently.

Common simple tics include eye blinking, shoulder jerking, picking movements, grunting, sniffing, and barking. Complex tics include facial grimacing, arm flapping, coprolalia (use of obscene words), palilalia (repeating one's own words), and echolalia (repeating another's words or phrases).

For individuals with Tourette's, tics may vary over time in terms of their frequency and severity, as well as in type and location. In some cases, symptoms may disappear for a period of weeks or even months. Although there is an involuntary quality to the tics experienced by individuals with Tourette's, most persons have some control over their symptoms, at least briefly, and even for hours at a time. However, suppressing

them tends simply to postpone more severe outbursts, since the impulse to express tics is ultimately irresistible. Tics often will increase in response to stress and become less frequent with relaxation or intense focus on a task.

Many patients with Tourette's syndrome have other conditions at the same time, such as ATTENTION DEFICIT/HYPERACTIVITY DISORDER, obsessive-compulsive disorder, or a LEARNING DISABILITY.

Up to 20 percent of children have at least a transient tic disorder at some point. Once believed to be rare, Tourette's syndrome is now known to be a more common disorder that represents the most complex and severe manifestation of the spectrum of tic disorders.

Symptoms

Obsessions, compulsions, impulsive behavior, and mood swings. Tourette's is commonly associated with other syndromes, including attention disorder/hyperactivity disorder, anxiety, mood or panic disorders, obsessive-compulsive disorder, behavior problems, and learning disabilities.

In most children, Tourette's syndrome has a fluctuating course. Anxiety, stress, and fatigue often intensify tics, which are usually significantly reduced during sleep or when the patient is focused on an activity. Psychoactive drugs, particularly cocaine and stimulants, have a tendency to worsen tics.

In most cases, tics peak in severity between ages nine and 11, but between 5 percent and 10 percent of patients continue to have unchanged or worsening symptoms into adolescence and adulthood. In this population, the likelihood of tics continuing for decades is substantial. Patients in their seventh, eighth, and ninth decades of life may have tics that have been present since childhood. In most older patients, the tics tend to become quite stable over time, although occasionally new tics will be acquired. There is no reliable way to predict which children will have a poorer prognosis.

Cause

An abnormal metabolism of the neurotransmitters dopamine and serotonin are linked to the disorder, which is genetically transmitted. Parents have a 50 percent chance of passing the gene on to their children. Girls with the gene have a 70 percent chance of displaying symptoms; boys with the gene have a 99 percent chance of displaying symptoms.

Diagnosis

The single most important component of managing the condition is to get an accurate diagnosis. Tics occur suddenly during normal activity, unlike other movement disorders such as

- chorea: a pattern of nonrepetitive irregular movements
- stereotypy: constant, repetitive behaviors performed for no obvious reason
- dystonias: a slow, constant repetitive behavior

The doctor will want to rule out any secondary causes of tic disorders. A complete general physical examination, with specific attention to the neurologic part of the examination, is important. The thyroid-stimulating hormone (TSH) level should be measured in most patients, since tics often occur together with hyperthyroidism. A throat culture should be checked for group A beta-hemolytic streptococcus, especially if symptoms get worse or better with ear or throat infections. The evidence of strep infection with a single occurrence of worsening tics is not enough to make a diagnosis of streptococcus-induced, autoimmune-caused Tourette's syndrome.

An electroencephalogram is useful only in patients in whom it is difficult to differentiate tics from manifestations of epilepsy. Imaging studies are not likely to be helpful, and the importance of other studies depends on symptoms. For example, a urine drug screen for cocaine and stimulants should be considered in the case of a teenager with sudden onset of tics and inappropriate behavior symptoms. A person with a family history of liver disease associated with a Parkinsonian or hyperkinetic movement disorder should undergo tests of copper levels in the blood to rule out Wilson's disease.

The basic workup is usually appropriate in a patient with a gradual onset of symptoms, a developmental progression of tics, and a family history of tics or obsessive-compulsive disorder.

Treatment

Positive reinforcement programs appear to be most helpful in managing tic disorders. Target behaviors may be categorized into two groups: skill deficiencies, or areas requiring an initial concentration to build social and academic skills, and behavior excesses, in which the goal is to help the patient decrease the frequency of these behaviors. Managing behavior excesses must be handled carefully, however, since some children who undergo behavior modification to directly target the Tourette's symptoms experience a worsening of symptoms.

Drug Treatment

The goal in tic control is to use the lowest dosage of medication that will bring the patient's functioning to an acceptable level. Often this will require only modest levels of tic reduction. The most common drug treatments are haloperidol (Haldol), pimozide (Orap), risperidone (Risperdal), and clonidine (Catapres). Guanfacine (Tenex) is not labeled for use in children under 12 years of age. Less often, clonazepam (Klonopin) may be prescribed. For tics of mild to moderate severity, or in patients who are wary of drug side effects, an initial trial of clonidine or guanfacine may be tried. These medications are modestly effective in tic control and have a range of less specific benefits. Many children taking them may be less irritable or less impulsive, and manifestations of ADHD may improve as well.

Side Effects

These include sedation, weight gain, poor school performance, social anxiety (with school refusal in children), and unusual body movements, including tardive dyskinesias, a potentially irreversible drug-caused movement disorder that may be difficult to distinguish from tics. When pimozide is used, baseline and follow-up electrocardiograms are recommended.

Most patients with Tourette's syndrome require medication for up to one to two years. About 15 percent of patients require long-term medication for tic control. When tics appear to be stable and adequately controlled for a period of four to six months, a slow and gradual reduction in medication should follow. With such a strategy, occasional drug holidays may be possible in some patients as tics lessen. If tics increase, incremental increases in medication may be needed.

Because many patients with Tourette's syndrome have other conditions, treatment for these conditions may be necessary. Treatment of ADHD with Tourette's has been controversial because of reports that stimulants hasten the onset or increase the severity of tics in some patients. This observation alone may not be a contraindication for stimulant treatment in patients with significant symptoms of ADHD. Stimulants alone may not substantially worsen the course or severity of the disorder. In some cases, it may be necessary to treat both the ADHD and the Tourette's syndrome with a stimulant in combination with either clonidine or guanfacine, or with a neuroleptic agent. A trial of clonidine or guanfacine alone may be sufficient to adequately treat both conditions. When possible, multiple drugs should not be used, especially in children.

Treatment of obsessive-compulsive disorder with the antidepressant drug class called selective serotonin reuptake inhibitors (such as Prozac) may be effective. With these medications, there is often a significant delay between start of treatment and response, which may take as long as four to six weeks. Behavior therapy is also effective in the treatment of obsessive-compulsive disorder.

tracking   A process of using a finger or pencil to follow the eyes while reading. Tracking can be a useful strategy for an individual with visual perception difficulties because it incorporates a kinesthetic component to reading. Tracking with a pencil can be beneficial so individuals can physically break long, unfamiliar words into syllables as they read.

See also SYLLABICATION; ABILITY GROUPING.

transition plan   Movement from one place or idea to another. In the context of LEARNING DISABILITIES, a transition plan refers to the change from school to adult life. For disabled students, this may require extra effort and planning for individuals and their support/IEP team. Transition legislation in the INDIVIDUALS WITH DISABILITIES EDUCATION ACT (IDEA) states that transition services and planning be written into the IEP. The contents of a transition plan should include:

- current levels of performance
- interests and aptitudes
- postschool goals
- transition activities—specific steps to be taken (e.g., career/vocational counseling)
- the designation of responsible persons to oversee the transition after high school

transposition   A reading, writing, or numeric error where letters or numbers or words are switched. For example, transposition in mathematics might involve writing or reading the number *258* for *852,* or writing *shinesun* for *sunshine.*

Methods for treating the problem of transposition could include using a multimodal strategy such as asking the student to say the letters as he or she writes the word.

traumatic brain injury   The common general term for brain injuries that impair thinking as a result of physical trauma severe enough to cause loss of consciousness or damage to the brain structure. Of all the problems that can lead to LEARNING DISABILITIES, this is the most preventable. Each year, about 2 million Americans sustain a brain injury—about one every 15 seconds. More than a million of these are sustained by children, 30,000 of whom will have permanent disabilities.

Boys are twice as likely to be injured as girls, especially between the ages of 14 and 24, followed by infants and then the elderly. Children are more likely to incur traumatic brain injury during the spring and summer. Traffic accidents account for almost half of the injuries; about 34 percent occur at home and the rest in recreation areas.

Traumatic brain injury includes both open and closed head injury, both of which can cause severe learning problems. In an open head injury, the force of impact can cause scalp injuries and skull fractures, together with blood clots and bruising. This type of injury usually affects one place in the brain, producing specific problems.

A closed head injury can cause more widespread damage as the force of impact causes the brain to smash against the opposite side of the skull, tearing nerve fibers and blood vessels. This type of "contre-coup" injury may affect the brain stem, causing physical, intellectual, emotional, and social problems. A person's entire personality may be forever changed.

In young children, abuse is the primary cause of this type of injury; 64 percent of babies under age one who are physically abused have brain injuries, usually by shaking. In children under age five, half of brain injuries are related to falls. Cars and biking accidents and suicide attempts are the primary causes of traumatic brain injury in school-age children and adolescents.

Because traumatic brain injury is now included under IDEA, special education services can be provided if the child experiences any problems with thinking or learning skills after the accident. An INDIVIDUALIZED EDUCATION PROGRAM should be prepared to deal with the child's special needs.

Diagnosis

Some patients may experience coma after a brain injury; the degree of the coma severity is measured by the Glasgow Coma Score, or the Rancho Los Amigos Scale, which assigns a number to represent the degree to which patients can open their eyes, move, or speak. X rays and brain scans may help if a skull fracture is suspected.

Symptoms

The signs following a traumatic brain injury may be elusive, but it's important to understand that head injuries tend to get worse over time. Obvious warning signs include

- lethargy
- confusion
- irritability
- severe headaches
- changes in speech, vision, or movement
- bleeding
- vomiting
- seizure
- coma

More subtle signs of head injury may also appear, over time, and may include

- long- and short-term memory problems
- slowed thinking
- distorted perception
- concentration problems
- attention deficits
- communication problems (oral or written)
- poor planning and sequencing
- poor judgment
- changes in mood or personality

Sometimes, certain behavior may appear long after the traumatic brain injury occurs. These behaviors may include overeating or drinking, excessive talking, restlessness, disorientation, or seizure disorders.

Treatment

Rehabilitation should begin as soon as possible after the accident, focusing on the problem areas. They may include physical or occupational therapy, or speech and language therapy.

Prevention

Traumatic brain injury can be prevented by taking appropriate safety precautions, such as insisting that children wear helmets when biking, riding a scooter, or skating, sledding, and skiing. Children should wear seat belts and ride in the back of the car.

See also BRAIN INJURY, TRAUMATIC.

tutoring Instructing a child in a special subject or for a particular purpose. One advantage that small-group or individual tutoring offers to individuals with a LEARNING DISABILITY is that it allows instruction to be individualized to meet the unique needs and learning styles of each learner. Tutors can reinforce subjects that are taught in school as well as teach students how to work independently. Students often become more self-confident after working with a tutor.

Ideally, students with a learning disability should consider scheduling more than one tutoring lesson a week, since these students often need practice and repetition to master skills. Tutoring sessions should include hands-on learning and be very interactive. The tutor should guide the child through direct teaching and practice.

A parent should receive periodic reports from both the tutor and the child's teacher, and show noticeable academic improvement within a few months.

U

United States Code (USC) The code of statutes under which all federal laws are listed.

universal access/design A term originally used in architecture to denote an approach to construction that assures access to all individuals regardless of physical problems such as paralysis, eye problems, or deafness. Such an approach goes beyond assuring that there are ramps for individuals in wheelchairs, or Braille symbols next to elevator buttons. Universal access is an attempt to make every aspect of a building as equally accessible for individuals with disabilities as they may be for those without.

Recently, the concept of universal access or design has been used in educational contexts; the term signifies an approach that provides equal access to appropriate education in a mainstream setting, by assuring that all of the learning needs and styles of individual students are addressed by a variety of teaching techniques.

For example, this would mean students are provided with instructional approaches that use sight, touch, and movements as well as hearing, and that testing as well as instruction allow all students to demonstrate mastery of course material. Highly specific instructional approaches assure that all students in a class are able to use their strengths to respond to course assignments.

Universal design or access represents a new way of thinking about learning disabilities, although there is still a great deal that is undeveloped and unproven regarding the approach.

V

VAKT (Visual–Auditory–Kinesthetic–Tactile)
An acronym for a type of instructional method used primarily for reading that involves sight, hearing, movement, and touch. VAKT is based on the concept that individuals learn better when more than one learning method is stimulated. With this approach to teach reading, students may be asked to *see* the word (visual), *hear* the word (auditory), *write* the word on a surface or in the air using the finger (kinesthetic), and *trace* the word on a textured surface such as sandpaper or a rough board (tactile).

VAKT is not limited to reading instruction, and many special educators use some form of multisensory instruction in every lesson. The Fernald and Orton-Gillingham methods also use the VAKT technique.

See also ORTON-GILLINGHAM APPROACH.

validity An essential way of judging the effectiveness of a test by assessing the extent to which the test accurately measures what it is intended to measure. There are different types of validity according to the nature of the test.

In achievement testing, for example, "content validity" refers to the extent to which the material covered by a test represents a balanced sampling of the information that the test is meant to assess. "Criterion-related" validity refers to the extent to which performance on a specific test accurately predicts future grade performance. Finally, "construct validity" relates to the accuracy with which a test measures some abstract or theoretical idea, such as personality traits or abilities such as critical thinking or interpersonal intelligence.

verbal apraxia Impaired control of proper sequencing of muscles used in speech (tongue, lips, jaw muscles, vocal cords). These muscles are not weak, but their control is defective. With this problem, speech is labored and characterized by sound reversals, additions, and word approximations.

verbal memory Memory for verbal information. Verbal memory is assumed to reflect functioning of the deep structures of the left temporal lobe.

vision training and ADHD Some people believe that visual problems such as faulty eye movements, focus problems, and light oversensitivity of the eyes cause reading disorders. There are few well-designed scientific studies of this approach.

In 1972, a joint statement highly critical of the optometric approach to learning disability treatment was issued by the American Academy of Pediatrics, the American Academy of Ophthalmology and Otolaryngology, and the American Association of Ophthalmology. In the absence of supporting evidence for its effectiveness, most experts warn that this approach should not be used to treat learning disabilities.

visual discrimination The ability to distinguish between visual objects, usually between those with a similar appearance, such as between the letters "p" and "q." Good visual discrimination skills are essential to early reading.

visual memory The ability to take in, store, and retrieve information presented visually. Short-term visual memory is the ability to hold visual information in short-term memory in order to process it, either moving it into long-term memory or shifting focus.

Visual working memory (or nonverbal working memory) involves the ability to hold visual information in mind while considering it, reflecting on it, or in some other fashion processing it.

Long-term memory also involves visual forms, in which images are stored on a long-term basis and available for recall.

visual motor coordination The combination of visual perception with motion; the ability to see something and react with a movement.

visual motor/perceptual test A type of test that measures a child's fine motor skills and perceptual ability in sensory areas. These tests include the

- Beery Developmental Test of Visual Motor Integration
- Bender Visual Motor Gestalt Test
- Detroit Test of Learning Ability–2
- Comprehensive Test of Visual Functioning
- Test of Auditory Perceptual Skills
- Learning Efficiency Test II
- Quick Neurological Screening Test
- Motor-Free Visual Perception Test

visual motor skills A subcategory of perceptual motor skills involving the ability to translate information received by sight into a physical response. In education, visual motor skills are often used when copying information from a blackboard or reproducing letters or numbers. Individuals with problems in this area often have poor handwriting, and may also have more subtle and pervasive difficulties in school performance.

visual perception The ability to recognize and interpret visual information provided to the brain. Difficulties in visual perception are separate from, and unrelated to, impairment in the visual system that may diminish visual acuity or result in visual impairment or blindness. Visual perception involves the determination and discrimination of spatial information, as well as performance on tasks such as the discrimination of letters and words, geometric designs, and pictures.

Visual perception is an essential component of learning, especially in regard to reading development and to acquiring classroom information. Difficulties with visual perception may significantly affect an individual's ability to discriminate letters and words, and to work with mathematical information.

visual perception disabilities Students with visual perception disabilities have trouble making sense out of what they see, not because they have poor eyesight but because their brains process visual information differently.

Children with this problem have trouble organizing, recognizing, interpreting, or remembering visual images. This means that they will have trouble understanding the written and picture symbols they need in school—letters, words, numbers, math symbols, diagrams, maps, charts, and graphs.

Because this type of visual problem is subtle, it is often undiscovered until the child starts having trouble in school. Visual perception problems include the ability to recognize images we've seen before and attach meaning to them; to discriminate among similar images or the words, and to separate significant figures from background details; and to recognize the same symbol in different forms (understanding, for example, that the letter "D" is the letter "D" whether it is uppercase or lowercase, in different colors or fonts). Sequences are another important visual perception skill; a child with a visual sequencing problem may not understand the difference between the words "saw" and "was."

Students with visual perception problems are usually slow to learn letters and numbers, and often make mistakes, omissions, and reversals. They often have trouble with visual memory and visualization and may be extremely slow readers.

voice recognition Computer software that recognizes and creates text and carries out commands as the user speaks. In the past, many students with a LEARNING DISABILITY have depended on parents, teachers, tutors, or friends to transcribe their papers as they dictate. While this has been an effective writing strategy, there are some severe drawbacks to this type of dictation. It makes the student with a learning disability dependent on another person, and it is difficult for the writer to have a sense of the flow of the writing without having the draft to read and reread as each sentence is developed. With new technologies such as voice recognition, students with learning disabilities are now able to become more independent as writers, readers, and learners.

Just a few years ago speech or voice recognition technology was quite expensive and slow. It utilized *discrete speech,* which forced a user to . . . speak . . . like . . . this . . . with . . . long . . . pauses between words. Most voice recognition products now use *continuous speech,* which allows the user to speak at a natural pace.

Voice recognition or speech synthesis software allows students to speak into their computers, which turn their oral language into text. There are various programs available, but all require a significant amount of memory, the software, a microphone, and a headphone.

The obvious advantage of voice recognition for students with learning disabilities who have difficulty expressing themselves in writing is that it sidesteps the transcription process entirely. However, it is by no means a panacea for writing. Voice recognition technology has several distinct limitations. Training the software to recognize a particular voice typically involves reading passages into the computer, which may be difficult for a student who has trouble reading.

Once the initial training is complete (which can be done in less than an hour), the programs are still not accurate. The more the program is used, the better it can recognize a particular voice; however, the user must speak in a consistent voice. For example, a deep sigh into the microphone may be interpreted as a word. Correcting errors such as an unintentional sigh or a misinterpreted phrase is difficult for students with learning disabilities. Some studies have shown that voice recognition software recognized only 75 percent to 80 percent of the words spoken by college students with learning disabilities. While this may be an improvement from having to draft a composition by handwriting or typing, it still means that a student must correct up to a quarter of the document.

As the rapid pace of technology continues to gain momentum, it is likely that voice recognition will replace the use of the keyboard much as the keyboard has replaced the pencil.

Voice recognition technology will most benefit students who can speak their ideas more fluidly than they could write them. By using their more sophisticated vocabulary and syntax, students' written compositions can be a better reflection of their abilities. If a student has severe spelling difficulties, voice recognition allows him to bypass spelling nearly entirely. Students who are fast processors and lose their ideas before they get them out on paper will find voice recognition valuable.

Wechsler Adult Intelligence Scale–Third Edition (WAIS-III)   One of the most widely used IQ tests in the country, designed for older teenagers and adults (from ages 16 through 74 years, 11 months). First introduced in 1939, it was written by David Wechsler and has been updated to reduce bias in testing and scoring. This version is a harder edition of the WECHSLER INTELLIGENCE SCALE FOR CHILDREN–III (WISC-III). Although the WAIS–III will score about four points higher than the WISC-III, the test of choice for 16-year-olds is still the WISC-III because it offers a larger number of valid subtest items to which the teenager can respond.

The WISC-III and the Stanford-Binet Intelligence Test are the two most commonly used IQ tests in U.S. schools. There are many other tests used to assess overall intelligence, academic achievement, and specific LEARNING DISABILITIES.

Wechsler Individual Achievement Test (WIAT)   This achievement test measures achievement in all areas that are specified in the federal law's definition of LEARNING DISABILITIES—oral expression, listening and reading comprehension, basic reading skills, written expression, mathematics calculation, and mathematical reasoning. The test is designed for students between ages five years and 19 years, 11 months.

Oral expression: children describe scenes, give directions, and explain steps in a process while looking at pictures.

Listening comprehension: examiner presents word and children identify the picture; examiners present passages and children respond orally to questions.
Reading comprehension: children read passages and respond to oral questions.
Basic reading skills: children read words on a list in 10 seconds.
Written expression: children write spelling words and a short passage.
Mathematics calculation: children complete math problems.
Mathematics reasoning: children use math reasoning in response to practical questions.

Wechsler Intelligence Scale for Children–III (WISC-III)   The IQ test of choice for most situations, appropriate for children between the ages of six years and 16 years, 11 months. This test does a good job of measuring the ability to process visual and verbal information, allowing the child to demonstrate strengths and weaknesses in several areas. These include

- interpretation and problem solving with words or visual images
- speed of information processing
- planning and organization
- attention
- short-term and long-term memory

See also WECHSLER PRESCHOOL AND PRIMARY SCALE OF INTELLIGENCE–REVISED; WECHSLER ADULT INTELLIGENCE SCALE–REVISED.

Wechsler Preschool and Primary Scale of Intelligence–Revised (WPPSI-R) A simpler version of the WECHSLER INTELLIGENCE SCALE FOR CHILDREN–III (WISC-III) that is designed for young children from ages three years through seven years, three months. While six- and seven-year-olds usually score higher on the WISC-III, those who are below average intellectually have more of an opportunity to demonstrate their range of problem-solving skills on this test than on the WISC-III. The latest revision of this test (the WPPSI-III) will be published soon.

See also WECHSLER ADULT INTELLIGENCE SCALE–REVISED.

Wernicke's area A part of the brain located in the temporal lobe near the primary auditory cortex that is critical to language comprehension, especially at the level of the meaning of individual words (rather than syntax, which is regulated by BROCA'S AREA).

Damage to this part of the brain results in Wernicke's aphasia, which makes individuals unable to understand words while listening, and unable to produce meaningful sentences.

whole language approach An educational philosophy that believes language learning is a natural outgrowth of a child-centered process that integrates speaking, listening, reading, and writing. The whole language approach emphasizes that reading is closely linked to spoken language, so students are exposed to language-rich classrooms to help make better readers and writers.

The way American schools teach children to read and write has for many years been affected by the influence of two powerful schools of thought. A conventional curriculum tends to rely on phonics and basic readers. This traditional theory of learning, which became widespread in the 19th century, is based on the idea that children learn a complex skill like reading by first making sense of letters and then pro-

gressing to sounds, words, and sentences. Proponents of this theory believe that children learn to read by learning to decode the language; understanding follows after they break the code and master the parts. Traditional American education begins with reading lessons that focus on phonics (sounding out first letters, then combinations of letters), tightly controlled vocabulary, and short basic reading passages, followed by exercises, each with only one correct answer.

Whole language represents a different philosophy about teaching, learning, and the role of language in the classroom, emphasizing the idea that children should use language in ways that relate to their own lives and cultures. In the whole language classroom, the final answer isn't as important as the process. Children are encouraged to decode words by their context.

Whole language advocates point out that the average first grader has already acquired a vocabulary of 10,000 words and inherently understands many of the rules of grammar without being formally taught. The common techniques of whole language teaching, which include daily journal and letter writing plus lots of reading of real literature, represent that philosophy in action.

The rise of the whole language approach has been so dramatic that some teachers complain they can't find basic readers anymore. In addition, many new teachers say their instructors at colleges of education no longer discuss how to teach phonics.

Critics feel that whole language overemphasizes understanding at the expense of accuracy. The whole language movement had a significant impact on reading and writing instruction in the 1980s and 1990s, when the appeal of whole language instruction influenced many schools to revise their curriculums. As a result of this movement, a vigorous debate emerged amongst educators over how children learn language. Many special educators felt that whole language was flawed by its neglect of explicit language skills such as phonics, spelling, and grammar. Since a language-rich classroom does not help many students, especially those with learning disabilities, learn to read and spell, a "back to basics" movement in education began to turn trends back to explicit skill instruction.

Advocates of the whole language approach say that an overemphasis on rules and rote learning is stifling and leads children to see reading and writing as boring and difficult chores, rather than as an interesting way of gathering information.

Research strongly indicates that students will be the most successful if a balanced approach is used, teaching phonics in a systematic fashion within the context of real stories. Today, many classrooms use this combination approach of elements of both whole language and phonics, spelling and grammar.

Woodcock-Johnson, Third Edition (WJ-III)

The recent version of an individually administered assessment system that educators and psychologists have found useful in assessing intelligence and achievement. The WJ-III, which is designed for people from two years through 90+ years, includes two forms:

- WJ-III Tests of Achievement (WJ-III ACH)
- WJ-III Tests of Cognitive Abilities (WJ-III COG)

The highly flexible system assesses the widest array of cognitive and achievement abilities among major available test systems and allows for administration of the entire battery or selected subtests. The WJ-III is the first major cognitive or achievement battery to assume that the person giving it has access to a computer: those administering the tests can only score the WJ-III with specialized software included in each test kit.

If the complete battery is administered, the WJ-III provides assessments in the following individual subtests:

- Verbal Comprehension
- Visual-Auditory Learning
- Spatial Relations
- Sound Blending
- Concept Formation
- Visual Matching
- Numbers Reversed
- Incomplete Words
- Auditory Work Memory
- General Information
- Retrieval Fluency
- Picture Recognition
- Auditory Attention
- Analysis-Synthesis
- Decision Speed
- Memory for Words
- Rapid Picture Naming
- Planning
- Pair Cancellation
- Letter-Word Identification
- Reading Fluency
- Story Recall
- Understanding Directions
- Calculation
- Math Fluency
- Spelling
- Writing Fluency
- Passage Comprehension
- Applied Problems
- Writing Samples
- Story Recall—Delayed
- Word Attack
- Picture Vocabulary
- Oral Comprehension
- Editing
- Reading Vocabulary
- Quantitative Concepts
- Academic Knowledge
- Spelling of Sounds

- Sound Awareness
- Punctuation & Capitals

Depending on which individual subtests are administered, the WJ-III groups results into the following cognitive clusters:

- Verbal Ability
- Thinking Ability
- Cognitive Efficiency
- Comprehensive Knowledge
- Long-Term Retrieval
- Visual-Spatial Thinking
- Auditory Processing
- Fluid Reasoning
- Processing Speed
- Short-Term Memory
- Phonemic Awareness
- Phonemic Awareness III
- Working Memory
- Broad Attention
- Cognitive Fluency
- Executive Processes
- Knowledge

The WJ-III also groups individual tests into the following achievement clusters:

- Oral Language
- Oral Expression
- Listening Comprehension
- Total Achievement
- Broad Reading
- Broad Math
- Broad Written Language
- Basic Reading Skills
- Reading Comprehension
- Mathematics Calculation Skills
- Mathematics Reasoning

- Basic Writing Skills
- Written Expression
- Academic Skills
- Academic Fluency
- Academic Applications
- Academic Knowledge
- Phoneme/Grapheme Knowledge

Given the large number of areas tested, the WJ-III can provide extensive information on a wide range of cognitive and academic strengths and weaknesses. The WJ-III provides a very reliable and valid means of determining "discrepancies between potential and achievement" required by federal law for determination of learning disabilities.

word attack skills   The ability to read a word using phonetic, structural, or context cues. Word attack skills using phonetic cues require a child to understand the sound-symbol relationship. Phonetic word attack skills can be assessed by asking a child to read nonsense words (such as "thrump").

Word attack skills using structural cues require individuals to identify prefixes, suffixes, and roots, or to break up a word by syllables. These skills are assessed by asking a child to divide a word into syllables (such as *com/pre/hend*) or break a word into meaningful word parts (such as *un/happy*).

Good readers use contextual cues when they rely on the context of a sentence to decode a word. Poor word attack skills are one of the most common reading problems among children with a LEARNING DISABILITY; therefore, poor word attack skills are often improved by using phonics-based word attack instruction.

word-finding deficits   See SOUND/LETTER/WORD RETRIEVAL.

word prediction   A type of software that supports word processing by predicting what word the user will write next—based on syntax, the first letters typed, and frequency of use. A list of words appears in a window on the computer screen. If the list contains the intended word, the user can select the word by entering the number next to the word, point and click, or scroll down the list until the correct word is selected. The word is then automatically inserted into the text and the next word will be predicted even before a letter has been typed. If the intended word is not shown in the prediction list after the first letter is typed, the program continually revises the list after each letter is typed. If the intended word is not in the prediction program, the user can add words to the dictionary.

Different word prediction programs vary slightly. Many are now available with synthesized speech to read the word list aloud, which is useful for students with difficulty distinguishing between words that look similar. Some word prediction programs are more sophisticated and offer a more extensive dictionary.

However, while this program can be useful for creating sophisticated writing, it can also be more confusing to the user by offering too many word choices.

With regard to spelling, word prediction programs can be either liberating or limiting. For students who can write the first several letters of a word with relative accuracy, it can be very helpful in predicting longer, more difficult words. On the other hand, word prediction does not recognize phonetic similarities; therefore, it can be quite limiting for students who do not have strong sound-symbol skills. For example, if a student using word prediction is attempting to write *philosophically* and first types in *fil . . .* , the program will not include words that started with *phil-*. Word prediction assumes that students have the ability to interrupt the flow of writing to sound out the beginning of a word. This can cause problems for students who find sounding out words laborious and disruptive to the writing process.

Word prediction programs offer several advantages. For some students with poor typing skills, the program can minimize the number of keystrokes and help students who have problems choosing the right words. Since the programs use syntax to predict words, the predicted list may act as a necessary prompt to locate the suitable word. Not only is this useful for word retrieval, it also can help students who misuse words due to syntactical errors.

On the other hand, some students with learning disabilities may find word prediction programs frustrating. For students who don't want to interrupt the logical flow of their writing, word prediction may be distracting by requiring the student to stop and choose words, especially if the individual has good typing skills. If a student has trouble recognizing words, word prediction won't be very useful unless it's used in conjunction with synthesized speech.

word processing   Using a computer program as a writing tool. Word processing offers many advantages for children with a LEARNING DISABILITY. First, editing is considerably easier on a word processor, making it possible for individuals to focus on creating meaning rather than the mechanics of writing. Also, the use of a word processor allows individuals to create neat and legible documents rather than messier versions written out conventionally on paper.

The significance of creating more professional-looking compositions has proven to motivate individuals to create longer written pieces.

In addition, word processors make writing more visible. For many students with learning disabilities, reading their own handwriting is difficult and frustrating. In addition, instructors can better read student writing in class when it is projected on a screen. Because word processors make editing and spelling considerably easy to repair, it allows individuals to concentrate on generating meaning rather than mechanics. This liberation from the "nuts and bolts" aspect of writing can lead to better compositions.

In addition to physical writing problems, students with visual problems often find word processors make writing easier. Digital text can be made large and colored for easier understanding. Individuals with short-term memory weaknesses can also be empowered by a word processor because the time lapse between having an idea and getting it on paper or on screen is dramatically diminished. The burden of arranging a sentence and spelling words in a fixed way on paper is eliminated when one can write with a word processor and easily revise the idea once it is expressed.

word recognition An ability to apply any number of strategies to recognize and understand a word. Word recognition strategies include:

configuration – using visual cues such as the shape and size of the word

context analysis – using surrounding information (including pictures) to predict a word

sight words – instant recognition of a word without further analysis

phonemic analysis – "sounding out" a word

syllabication – dividing a word into syllables

structural analysis – using morphological information such as prefixes, suffixes, and roots

See also SIGHT WORDS; SYLLABICATION; WORD ATTACK SKILLS.

word retrieval See SOUND/LETTER/WORD RETRIEVAL.

writing process A writing process approach to writing instruction has become common in school systems and colleges in the past 20 years. There are many different meanings of the phrase "writing process," but most refer to the concept that writing is part of a thinking process involving many different mental activities over a period of time. Effective instruction in writing teaches students how to generate, organize, and revise their writing, rather than focusing solely on written language structures.

In its early years of development, the process theory of writing instruction focused largely on individual expression and the facilitation of the development of a student's "voice." This approach to the writing process was in many ways a reaction to traditional methods of writing instruction, which focused mainly on structural and mechanical elements such as grammar, punctuation, and following paragraph and essay models.

In the early 1980s, Linda Flower and John Hayes developed a theoretical model of writing as a thought process involving a number of different mental activities, including planning, generating, organizing, translating, reviewing, and editing. In their model, any given activity might interrupt any other one at any stage. The Flower/Hayes model continues to be useful, especially for understanding the writing problems of students with learning disabilities and attention disorder. However, the primary contemporary model of writing as a process is social, emphasizing the ways in which writing is a social practice, and focusing on collaborative approaches to developing writing skills and producing written work.

In practical terms, effective writing instruction involves an understanding that writing involves different activities of generating, organizing, drafting, and revising and that incorporates collaborative activities in helping students develop a sense of voice, audience, and using writing as a communication tool.

A process approach to writing is particularly vital for students with learning disabilities, in that it enables them to take the different cognitive tasks involved in writing and spread them over a series of steps and periods of time. For example, a student with DYSLEXIA may benefit from putting off any attention to editing and spelling until late in the process, instead focusing mainly on generating ideas and language first.

Likewise, a student with attention deficit disorder may benefit from taking a highly specific approach to planning a paper and mapping out the steps that will be involved, using a checklist to monitor completion of each step.

written expression, disorders of   Problems in producing writing that don't seem to be linked to a child's overall intelligence. Individuals with writing disorders typically have problems in several areas of the writing, such as sentence structure, punctuation, spelling, or generating ideas and language in written form. Their ability to express concepts in writing may generally be far more limited than their ability to do so in spoken language, or it may be consistent with their oral-language functioning. In some cases the quality of the writing produced may be the primary difficulty; this might include problems with syntax, word meanings, spelling, grammar, or structure and organization.

In other cases, some children have problems with the ability to produce written text fluently and continuously in response to prompts; in this case, the child may be able to produce good writing sometimes, while at other times be unable to respond effectively at all.

Sometimes both the quality and production of writing may be impaired. Handwriting may also be a problem area. However, problems in only one area, such as spelling or handwriting, exclude this diagnosis.

Disorders of written expression may have a significant impact on an individual's school or job functioning, and may have a particularly severe impact on success in high school and college.

Diagnosis

As with other learning disorders, the assessment of a writing disorder is based on problems that aren't related to intelligence, age, education, or other disorders. Disorders of written expression are generally diagnosed together with reading and mathematics disabilities, and they are more often discussed and studied under the general category of LEARNING DISABILITIES than in isolation.

Significant problems with written fluency and production may also be linked to a more general learning disability, but are often associated with a diagnosis of ATTENTION DEFICIT/HYPERACTIVITY DISORDER. Written-output difficulties linked to deficits in attention and executive function are often diagnosed as DYSGRAPHIA.

Because "disorders of written expression" is a general diagnostic term, determining effective educational practices depends on a closer analysis of the individual's pattern of deficits and strengths.

For those whose disorder of written expression appears along with a general expressive-language disorder or a reading disability, the development of effective writing skills begins with developing more basic language abilities. These may include intensive study and practice of oral language syntax and vocabulary in order to provide a foundation for the development of written-language skills.

In those individuals who also have a reading disorder, the development of decoding skills through practice in awareness of word sounds, discrimination, and phonics, may be an essential starting point. Reading and language enrichment activities on a whole language model may boost comprehension and critical reasoning skills.

Until these skills are developed, direct remediation of written-language deficits won't be effective and may in fact lead to frustration and resistance. At the same time, it is important that some work in the area of writing development begin simultaneously with instruction in oral communication and reading development, in order to reinforce and extend the skills acquired in those areas. Such work should focus primarily on the generation of expressive writing, drawing linkages between oral language abilities and their manifestation in writing.

The concept of writing as a process, and the gradual introduction of various strategies for generating, planning, and organizing text, should all play a central role in instruction. In addition, simple elements such as sentence and paragraph concepts should be introduced. Examples of the mechanics of language, such as punctuation or sentence structure, also may be introduced.

As much as possible, work in spelling should be linked to work in the area of reading development, and spelling should generally be deemphasized within the context of writing instruction, except as reinforcement and a reminder to apply newly learned skills.

For individuals whose written expression disorder may be associated with a reading and/or spelling disability, but not with an expressive language disorder, instruction should focus first on the introduction of the concept of writing as a recursive process, and on continuing practice with various strategies for planning, generating, and organizing writing. In most cases, engaging generating strategies that draw on oral-communication strengths, such as talking out ideas before writing, will play an effective part in writing development. Students with this pattern of abilities will also benefit from direct instruction in written language structures, rules, and conventions, and from continual reinforcement and practice of this knowledge in writing assignments. Instruction in written language structures and rules, if embedded appropriately into a process-based classroom, may actually have a facilitative and generating power, rather than serve as a constraint on imagination and the free flow of ideas.

Individuals whose disorder of written expression is linked primarily to problems with written output are often also diagnosed with ADHD, and may often possess very strong oral communication and reading skills, as well as the ability to demonstrate excellent basic writing abilities in some contexts. The difficulties such individuals experience with writing may primarily stem from deficits in attention, executive function, and active-working memory that severely constrain the process of writing and result in impaired writing production, particularly on complex and unfamiliar tasks. While some direct instruction in written language structures may be appropriate for such individuals, in general, writing instruction should use a coaching model.

written language   Printed text. Production of written language requires many subskills such as handwriting or typing, spelling, grammar, organizing, planning, and revising. Related skills such as fluent spoken language, reading, and vocabulary are also important in competent writers. Individuals with a LEARNING DISABILITY often have trouble with one or more of the skills necessary to communicate effectively using written language.

Y

yeast A controversial theory of ATTENTION DEFICIT/HYPERACTIVITY DISORDER links the condition with toxins produced by yeast overgrowth that weaken the immune system, making the body susceptible to ADHD and other disorders. There is no evidence from controlled studies to support this theory, and it is not consistent with what is currently known about the causes of ADHD.

zone of proximal development (ZPD) The gap between the level of a student's independent function and how he may perform learning tasks with help. This term was coined by Russian psychologist Lev Vygotsky (1896–1934) and refers to the fact that it is crucial to provide help before a child gets frustrated. Failure can be avoided when teachers are aware of a student's zone of proximal development and provide just enough support to enable students to achieve a goal that would not have been possible independently.

This concept may play a key role in educational approaches, in that it represents a way of thinking about what is involved in meeting students' needs, and of understanding teaching and learning as a dynamic and developmental process, rather than as a static juxtaposition of instruction and learning readiness.

This theory allows a teacher to see a student's learning problems not as impediments but rather as a starting point for a process of development that challenges students within the scope of what they are able to master successfully with appropriate instruction. An approach to teaching that incorporates this concept must also mean that a teacher begins to teach a child at his current level, rather than at arbitrary curricular standards.

APPENDIXES

APPENDIX I
NATIONAL ORGANIZATIONS

ADD/ADHD

Attention Deficit Disorder
Website only
http://www.ADD.ldsite.com

Website offering information on ADD, ADHD, ODD, and OCD for parents, teachers of affected children.

Attention Deficit Information
Network, Inc.
475 Hillside Avenue
Needham, MA 02194
(781) 455–9895
http://www.addinfonetwork.com

Nonprofit organization that offers support and information to families of children with ADD, adults with ADD, and professionals.

Children and Adults with Attention Deficit Disorder
(CHADD)
8181 Professional Place
Suite 201
Landover, MD 20785
(301) 306–7070
http://www.chadd.org

Through family support and advocacy, public and professional education and encouragement of scientific research, CHADD works to ensure that those with ADD reach their inherent potential. Local chapters hold regular meetings providing support and information.

National ADD Association (NADDA)
9930 Johnnycake Ridge Road, Suite 3E
Mentor, OH 44060
(800) 487–2282 for information packet; (440) 350–9595
http://www.add.org

National nonprofit organization focusing on needs of adults, young adults, and families with ADD, offering information, resources on treatment and research, as well as workplace, relationship, parenting, and educational information.

One ADD Place
Website only
http://www.greatconnect.com/oneaddplace

Website virtual neighborhood offering information on ADD/ADHD, including articles, products and services, and information on seminars, workshops, and links to other ADD-related websites.

AMERICANS WITH DISABILITIES ACT (ADA) RESOURCES

ADA Homepage
U.S. Department of Justice
http://www.usdoj.gov/crt/ada/adahoml.htm

Online page that offers information on the Americans with Disabilities Act.

ADA Information Center Online
http://www.public.iastate.edu/%7Esbilling/ada.html

On-line source offering information on ADA resources and general disability information.

ANGELMAN SYNDROME

Angelman Syndrome Foundation
414 Plaza Drive
Suite 209
Westmont, IL 60559
(800) IF.ANGEL or (630) 734–9267
http://www.angelman.org

Foundation provides information on diagnosis, treatment, management, and offers support and advocacy.

APHASIA

National Aphasia Association
PO Box 1887
Murray Hill Station
New York, NY 10156
(800) 922–4622
http://www.aphasia.org

A nonprofit organization that promotes research and offers rehabilitation, education, and support services.

APRAXIA

Apraxia-Kids website
http://www.avenza.com/~apraxia/index.html

Beginning as a listserv for parents of children with apraxia of speech, it grew to become a forum for parents, therapists, and professionals all over the world.

ASPERGER DISORDER/SYNDROME

Asperger Syndrome Coalition of the United States
PO Box 49267
Jacksonville Beach, FL 32240–9267

A national nonprofit support and advocacy organization for Asperger Syndrome and related disorders committed to providing the most up-to-date and comprehensive information on Asperger Syndrome and related conditions.

Asperger's Disorder Home Page
Website only
http://www.aspergers.com

Website offering list of U.S. specialists, bibliography, and links.

ASSESSMENT

ERIC Clearinghouse on Assessment and Evaluation
1131 Shriver Lab, Building 075
University of Maryland
College Park, MD 20742
(800) 464-3742; (301) 405-7449
http://www.ericae. net

Balanced information on educational assessment, evaluation, and research methodology. Provides resources to encourage the responsible use of educational data.

ASSISTIVE TECHNOLOGY

See Appendix III.

ATAXIA

The National Ataxia Foundation
2600 Fernbrook Lane
Suite 119
Minneapolis, MN 55477
(612) 553–0020
http://www.ataxia.org

Nonprofit organization with 45 chapters that supports research and offers information and educational programs.

ATTENTION DEFICIT DISORDER

See ADD/ADHD, above.

AUTISM

Autism Network International
PO Box 448
Syracuse, NY 13210
(315) 476–2462

Self-help group dedicated to supporting people with autism, offering peer support, tips, problem solving, and information and referrals.

Autism Research Institute
4182 Adams Avenue
San Diego, CA 92116
(619) 281–7165
http://www.autism.com/ari/contents.html

Research organization investigating autism, offering information to families by mail or phone.

Autism Resources on the Internet
Website only
http://web.syr.edu/~jmwobus/autism/#general

Website offering resources about autism and an index of resources for autism and Asperger's disorder.

Autism Society of America
7910 Woodmont Avenue
Suite 650
Bethesda, MD 20814–3015

(800) 3AUTISM, x150; (301) 657–0881
http://www.autism-society.org

A nonprofit organization that seeks to promote life-long access and opportunities for persons within the autism spectrum and their families, to be fully included, participating members of their communities through advocacy, public awareness, education, and research related to autism.

Families for Early Autism Treatment
PO Box 255722
Sacramento, CA 95865
http://www.feat.org

Nonprofit organization of parents and professionals offering support and information.

National Alliance for Autism Research
414 Wall Street, Research Park
Princeton, NJ 08540
(888) 777–NAAR; (609) 430–9160
http://babydoc.home.pipeline.com/naar/naar.htm

Nonprofit organization dedicated to research and treatment.

BRAIN INJURY/RESEARCH

Brain Injury Association
105 North Alfred Street
Alexandria, VA 22314
(703) 236–6000
http://www.biausa.org

Organization offering advocacy, support services, and research.

Children's Brain Tumor Foundation
274 Madison Avenue
Suite 1301
New York, NY 10016
(212) 448–9494
http://www.childrensneuronet.org

Group that seeks to improve treatment and outlook for children with brain and spinal cord tumors through research and treatment, education and support.

Dana Alliance for Brain Initiatives, The
745 Fifth Avenue, Suite 700
New York, NY 10151

The Dana Alliance, a nonprofit organization of 150 neuroscientists, was formed to help provide informa-tion about the personal and public benefits of brain research.

National Brain Tumor Foundation
785 Market Street
Suite 1600
San Francisco, CA 94103
(415) 284–0208; (800) 934–2873
http://www.braintumor.org

Foundation that offers resources and support, plus research. Affected patients can receive referrals to a network of support groups.

CAMPS

Camps for Children and Adults with Attention Deficit Disorder
499 NW 70th Avenue
Suite 101
Plantation, FL 33317
(954) 587–3700

Call for state-by-state listing of special camps.

Courage Camps
Website only
http://www.couragecamps.org

Website offering information on safe camps for chil-dren and adults with a range of disabilities.

Directory of Summer Camps for Children with Learning Disabilities
Learning Disabilities Association
4156 Library Road
Pittsburgh, PA 15234
(412) 341–1515
http://www.ldanatl.org/store/LD_Directories.html

Kids Camps
Website only
http://www.kidscamps.com

Website offering all types of special needs camps around the country.

CEREBRAL PALSY

United Cerebral Palsy Association
1522 K Street, NW
Suite 1112
Washington, DC 20005

(800) 872–5827; (202) 776–0406
http://www.ucpa.org

Nonprofit group providing referral services, advocacy, research, and information.

COMMUNICATION

(See also Stuttering, below.)

American Speech–Language–Hearing
Association (ASHA)
10801 Rockville Pike
Rockville, Maryland 20852
(800) 498–2071 (voice) or 301–897–5700 (TTY)
http://www.asha.org

Membership organization comprised of speech/language pathologists and audiologists that provide information and referrals to the public on speech, language, communication, and hearing disorders.

DEAFNESS/HARD OF HEARING

Alexander Graham Bell Association for the Deaf, Inc.
3417 Volta Place, NW
Washington, DC 20007
(202) 337–5220 (Voice/TT)
http://www.agbell.org

American Society for Deaf Children
PO Box 3355
Gettysburg, PA 17325
(800) 942–2732 (Voice/TTY); (717) 334–7922 (TTY)
Web: www.deafchildren.org

Laurent Clerc National Deaf Education Center
and Clearinghouse
KDES PAS-6, Gallaudet University
800 Florida Avenue, NE
Washington, DC 20002–3695
(202) 651–5051 (Voice); (202) 651–5052 (TT)
http://clerccenter.gallaudet.edu/infotogo/index.
html

National Institute on Deafness and Other
Communication Disorders
Clearinghouse
One Communication Avenue
Bethesda, MD 20892–3456
(800) 241–1044 (Voice); (800) 241–1055 (TT)
http://www.nih.gov/nidcd

Self Help for Hard of Hearing People (SHHH)
7910 Woodmont Avenue
Suite 1200
Bethesda, MD 20814
(301) 657–2248 (Voice); (301) 657–2249 (TT)
http://www.shhh.org

DEVELOPMENTAL DISABILITIES

(See also Down Syndrome, below.)

American Association on Mental Retardation
444 North Capitol Street, NW
Suite 846
Washington, DC 20001
(800) 424–3688; (202) 387–1968
http://www.aamr.org

National organization providing information, services, and support, plus advocacy.

American Association of University
Affiliated Programs for Persons with
Developmental Disabilities
8630 Fenton Street
Suite 410
Silver Spring, MD 20910
(301) 588–8252
http://www.aauap.org

National association with sites at major universities and teaching hospitals that support the independence, integration, and inclusion of people with developmental disabilities and their families.

Arc (formerly Association for Retarded Citizens)
500 East Border Street
Suite 300
Arlington, TX 76010
(800) 433–5255; (817) 261–6003
http://thearc.org

Volunteer organization committed to the welfare of all children and adults with mental retardation, offering information, books, and an annual conference.

Developmental Delay Resources
7801 Norfolk Avenue
Suite 102
Bethesda, MD 20814
(301) 652-2263
http://www.parenting-qa.com/cgi-bin/detail/
specialneedsdisabilities/developmentallydelayed/
4535.core.organization

National nonprofit membership organization providing information and networking opportunities to parents and professionals working with children who have developmental delays.

National Institute for People with Disabilities
460 West 34th Street
New York, NY 10001
(212) 563–7474
http://www.yai.org

Nonprofit agency serving children and adults with developmental disabilities in New York, including information and referrals.

Voice of the Retarded
5005 Newport Drive
Suite 108
Rolling Meadows, IL 60008
(847) 253–6020

Organization that provides support, information, and advocacy, with a large collection of research files.

DISABILITIES

Association on Higher Education and
Disability (AHEAD)
University of Massachusetts/Boston
100 Morrissey Boulevard
Boston, MA 02125–3393
(617) 287–3880
Website http://www.ahead.org

International, multicultural organization of professionals committed to full participation in higher education for persons with disabilities.

American Association of People with Disabilities
1819 H Street, NW
Suite 330
Washington, DC 20006
(800) 840–8844; (800) 235–7125
http://.aapd-dc.org

Organization offering support and information, and supporting full implementation and enforcement of disability nondiscrimination laws.

Association for the Severely Handicapped
29 West Susquehanna Avenue
Suite 210
Baltimore, MD 21204

(410) 828–8274
http://www.tash.org

An international advocacy association of people with disabilities, their families and others; with 38 chapters throughout the world. It actively promotes the full inclusion and participation of those with disabilities and seeks to eliminate physical and social obstacles that interfere with quality of life.

Children's Defense Fund
25 East Street, NW
Washington, DC 20001
(202) 628–8787
http://www.childrensdefense.org

A nonprofit research and advocacy organization that provides a strong voice for children who can't speak for themselves, including children with disabilities. The organization has regional offices throughout the country.

Commission on Mental and Physical Disability
Law–American Bar Association
740 15th Street, NW
Washington, DC 20005
(202) 662–1570
http://www.abanet.org/disability/home.html

This ABA affiliated group is committed to justice for those with physical disabilities, and maintains resources and references for helping the disabled community.

Disability Rights Advocates
449 15th Street
Suite 303
Oakland, CA 94612
(510) 451–8644
http://members.aol.com/dralegal

Nonprofit civil rights organization for people with disabilities.

Disability Rights Education and Defense Fund, Inc.
2212 Sixth Street
Berkeley, CA 94710
(510) 644–2555
http://www.dredf.org

A national law and policy center dedicated to protecting and helping people with disabilities through legislation, litigation, advocacy, technical help, and education.

Family Resource Center on Disabilities
20 East Jackson Boulevard
Room 300
Chicago, IL 60604
(800) 952–4199; (312) 939–3513

Coalition of parents, professionals, and volunteers dedicated to improving services for all children with disabilities.

National Association of Protection and
Advocacy Systems
900 Second Street, NE
Suite 211
Washington, DC 20002
(202) 408–9514
http://www.protectionandadvocacy.com/napas.htm

A national membership organization for the federally mandated nationwide network of disability rights agencies, protection and advocacy systems, and client assistance programs.

National Clearinghouse on Women and Girls
with Disabilities
114 E. 32nd Street
Suite 701
New York, NY 10016
(212) 725–1803
http://www.onisland.com/eec

Clearinghouse that provides catalog of manuals, supplements, videos, and directories, many of which deal with sexual issues faced by women and girls with disabilities.

National Information Center for Children and Youth
with Disabilities
1875 Connecticut Avenue
8th floor
Washington, DC 20009
(800) 695–0285
http://www.aed.org/nichcy

An information clearinghouse that provides free information on disabilities and disability-related issues.

National Information Center for Children and Youth
with Disabilities
PO Box 1492
Washington, DC 20013
(800) 695–0285
http://www.nichcy.org

Information clearinghouse that provides free information on disabilities and related issues, focusing on children and youth (birth to age 25). Free services include: personal responses, referrals, technical assistance, and information searches.

National Library Service for the Blind and
Physically Handicapped
Library of Congress
Washington, DC 20542
(202) 707-5100
http://www.leweb.loc.gov/nls/index.html

Voice mail system. Operators provide information on audiocassette, large print, and Braille books and magazines. Callers with learning disabilities must meet certain guidelines to use these services.

National Organization on Disability
910 16th Street, NW
Suite 600
Washington, DC 20006
(202) 293–5960
http://www.nod.org

National disability network group concerned with all disabilities of all ages.

National Parent Network on Disabilities
1130 17th Street, NW
Suite 400
Washington, DC 20036
(202) 434–8686
http://www.npnd.org

Membership advocacy organization open to all agencies, organizations, parent centers, parent groups, professionals, and individuals concerned with the quality of life for people with disabilities. Provides weekly email newsletter with legislative news and more.

National Center on Secondary Education and
Transition (NCSET)
University of Minnesota
Pattee Hall, 150 Pillsbury Drive SE
Minneapolis, MN 55455
(612) 624-2097
http://ici.umn.edu/ncset

NCSET is comprised of six organizations that work with national, state, and local agencies and organizations to improve secondary education and transition for youth with disabilities and their families.

Protection and Advocacy
100 Howe Avenue
Suite 185-N
Sacramento, CA 95825
(800) 776–5746
http://www.pai-ca.org

Nonprofit agency that provides legal assistance to those with physical, developmental, and psychiatric disabilities. Services include information and referral to other help, peer and self-advocacy training, representation in administrative and judicial proceedings, investigation of abuse and neglect, and legislative advocacy.

Sibling Support Project
Children's Hospital and Medical Center
PO Box 5371 CL-09
Seattle, WA 98105
(206) 368–0371
http://www.chmc.org/department/sibsupp/default.htm

National program dedicated to interests of brothers and sisters of those with special health and developmental needs.

World Institute on Disability
510 16th Street
Suite 100
Oakland, CA 94612
(510) 763–4100
http://www.wid.org

Nonprofit public policy center dedicated to independence and inclusion of people with disabilities.

DOWN SYNDROME

(See also Developmental Disabilities, above.)

International Resource Center for Down Syndrome
1621 Euclid Avenue
Suite 514
Cleveland, OH 44115
(216) 621–5858; (800) 899–3039

Center provides research, information, education, and parental support.

National Down Syndrome Congress
1605 Chantilly Drive, NE
Suite 250
Atlanta, GA 30324

(800) 232–NDSC; (404) 633–1555
http://members.carol.net/ndsc

National advocacy organization for Down syndrome, offering research, education, and resources.

National Down Syndrome Society
666 Broadway
Suite 810
New York, NY 10012
(800) 221–4602; (212) 460–9330
http://www.ndss.org

National organization that sponsors research and offers support, resources, information, and advocacy.

DYSLEXIA

Davis Dyslexia Association
International
1601 Bayshore Highway
Suite 260
Burlingame, CA 94010
(800) 729-8990; (650) 692-8990
http://www.davisdyslexia.com/

DDAI is based in the United States. Affiliated organizations have been established in France, Germany, Holland, Switzerland, Mexico, and the United Kingdom.

Hello Friend/Ennis William Cosby Foundation
P.O. Box 4061
Santa Monica, CA 90411
http://www.hellofriend.org

Foundation dedicated to dyslexia resources and information for parents, students, and educators.

The International Dyslexia Association (IDA)
(formerly The Orton Dyslexia Society)
8600 LaSalle Road
Chester Building
Suite 382
Baltimore, MD 21286–2044
(800) ABC–D123 (for general information);
(410) 296–0232 (for detailed information)
http://interdys.org

With 11,000 members in 45 branches around the world, IDA offers an international network that brings professionals in the field of dyslexia and parents together for a common purpose. The group offers informational meetings and support groups, referrals, journals, and publications regarding dyslexia.

Recording for the Blind and Dyslexic, Inc.
20 Roszei Road
Princeton, NJ 08540
(609) 452-0606
http://www.rfbd.org/

Operators provide information on over 80,000 recorded textbooks and other classroom materials, from fourth grade through postgraduate levels, available for loan. Callers with learning disabilities are eligible to participate but must complete the certification requirements.

World Dyslexia Network Foundation
http://webukonline.co.uk/wdnf/index.html

Information and links for learning disabilities, multilingual and multicultural learning issues.

EDUCATION

Association of Educational Therapists
1804 West Burbank Boulevard
Burbank, CA 91506
(818) 843-1183

National membership organization that provides referrals to local educational therapists.

Association on Higher Education and Disability
PO Box 21192
Columbus, OH 43221
(614) 488-4972
http://www.ahead.org

Organization of professionals committed to full participation in higher education for those with disabilities, offering education and training.

Center on Accelerating Student Learning
http://www.vanderbilt.edu/CASL

Designed to accelerate learning for students with disabilities in the early grades and thereby to provide a solid foundation for strong achievement in the intermediate grades and beyond. CASL is a five-year collaborative research effort supported by the U.S. Department of Education's Office of Special Education

Programs (OSEP). Participating institutions are the University of Maryland, Teachers College of Columbia University, and Vanderbilt University.

HEATH Resource Center
One Dupont Circle
Suite 800
Washington, DC 20036
(800) 544–3284

HEATH (Higher Education and Adult Training for People with Handicaps) is a national clearinghouse that provides free information on postsecondary education and related issues for individuals with learning disabilities.

National Association for the Education of Young Children (NAEYC)
1509 16th Street, NW
Washington, DC 20036-1426
http://www.naeyc.org/default.htm

National membership organization that focuses on children from birth to age eight. Sponsors an annual conference, publishes a bimonthly journal, and has a catalog of books, brochures, videos, and posters.

National Association for Private Schools for Exceptional Children
1522 K Street, NW
Suite 1032
Washington, DC 20005
(202) 408–3338
http://www.spedschools.com/napsec.html

Referral services for those interested in private special education in the United States, including publications and conferences.

National Center on Educational Outcomes
University of Minnesota
350 Elliott Hall
75 East River Road
Minneapolis, MN 55455
(612) 626-1530
http://www.coled.umn.edu/NCEO

Provides national leadership in the participation of students with disabilities and limited English proficient (LEP) students in national and state assessments, standards-setting efforts, and graduation requirements.

National Head Start Association
1651 Prince Street
Alexandria, VA 22314
(703) 739–0875
http://www.nhsa.org

A not-for-profit membership organization representing the 835,000 children and the more than 170,000 staff and 2,051 Head Start programs in America. NHSA provides a national forum for the continued enhancement of Head Start services for poor children from birth to age five years, and their families. It is the only national organization dedicated exclusively to the concerns of the Head Start community.

Parent Advocacy Coalition for Educational Rights
8161 Normandale Boulevard
Minneapolis, MN 55437
(952) 838-9000
http://www.pacer.org

Parent-to-parent organization with lots of resources for parents of children with disabilities, including training programs for parents and youth, technical assistance, and advocacy.

EMPLOYMENT

Foundation on Employment and Disability
3820 Del Amo Boulevard
Suite 201
Torrance, CA 90503
(213) 214–3430

Offers information on transition services from school and vocational training to job.

FETAL ALCOHOL SYNDROME

National Organization on Fetal Alcohol Syndrome
216 G Street, NE
Washington, DC 20002
(202) 785-4585
http://www.nofas.org

FRAGILE X SYNDROME

National Fragile X Foundation
1441 York Street
Suite 303
Denver, CO 80206

(303) 333–4369
http://www.nfxf.org

Nonprofit organization that provides advocacy, consultation, information, research, newsletters, referrals, and education.

HYPERLEXIA

American Hyperlexia Association
479 Spring Road
Elmhurst, IL 60126
(708) 530–8551
http://www.hyperlexia.org

Nonprofit organization dedicated to offering information and education to parents and professionals.

LEAD POISONING

The Environmental Protection Agency Safe Drinking Water Hotline
(800) 426–4791

For information on laboratories certified to test for lead in water.

The National Center for Lead-Safe Housing
205 American City Building
Columbia, MD 21044
(410) 964–1230

For information about lead in housing.

The National Lead Information Center
(800) LEAD-FYI (800–532–3394)

Materials about lead poisoning are available in Spanish and English.

LEARNING DISABILITIES

Association for Children and Adults with
Learning Disabilities
4156 Library Road
Pittsburgh, PA 15234
(412) 341–8077

Council for Exceptional Children and the Division
for Learning Disabilities
1920 Association Drive
Reston, VA 22091–1589
(800) 328–0272; (703) 620–3660

Council for Exceptional Children: www.cec.
sped.org
Division for Learning Disabilities: www.dldcec.org

An international, professional association with over
52,000 educator members. Their principal purpose is
to advance the education of all exceptional children
and youth—those with disabilities and those who are
gifted. DLD is the division of the CEC that focuses on
the special needs of individuals with learning disabilities. This membership organization has 17 specialized
divisions including the Division of Learning Disabilities, which is dedicated to the field of learning disabilities. CEC conducts an annual conference, publishes a
newsletter and magazines.

Council for Learning Disabilities
PO Box 40303
Overland Park, KS 66204
(913) 492–2546
www.cldinternational.org

The CLD is an international organization of and for
professionals who establish standards of excellence
and promote innovative strategies for research and
practice through collaboration and advocacy.

Learning Disabilities Association of America
4156 Library Road
Pittsburgh, PA 15234
(888) 300–6710
http://www.ldanatl.org

National nonprofit membership organization with
more than 60,000 members and 600 state and local
affiliates in 50 states, Washington, D.C., and Puerto
Rico. Members gather for education, networking, and
advocacy; conducts an annual conference and offers
information and various publications.

Learning Resources Network
1550 Hayes Drive
Manhattan, KS 66502
(800) 678–5376
http://www.lern.org

Organization providing information and support
about learning disabilities and those who teach adult
education.

LD On-Line
Website only
http://ldonline.org

A to Z database on all aspects of learning disabilities
and children.

National Center for Learning Disabilities
381 Park Avenue South
Suite 1401
New York, NY 10016
(888) 575–7373 (for general information);
(212) 545–7510 (for detailed information)
http://www.ncld.org

Develops training and educational materials for parents and practitioners including Every Child Is Learning, a training program to help preschool teachers and
parents recognize the early warning signs of learning
disabilities. NCLD seeks to raise public awareness and
understanding, furnish national information and
referrals, and arrange educational programs and legislative advocacy. NCLD provides educational tools to
heighten understanding of learning disabilities,
including the annual publication called *Their World,*
quarterly newsletters, informative articles, specific
state-by-state resource listings, and informative videos
regarding learning disabilities.

Nonverbal Learning Disorders Association
2446 Albany Avenue
West Hartfor, CT 06117
(860) 570-0217
http://www.nlda.org/

A nonprofit corporation dedicated to research, education, and advocacy for nonverbal learning disorders.

Schwab Foundation for Learning
1650 South Amphlett Boulevard
Suite 300
San Mateo, CA 94402
(800) 230–0988
www.schwablearning.org

Group that provides services to parents and educators
to help students with learning differences succeed.
Services include a lending library and *Bridges to Reading,* a step-by-step guide to understanding, identifying, and addressing reading problems.

LOWE SYNDROME

Lowe Syndrome Association
222 Lincoln Street
West Lafayette, IN 47906

(765) 743–3634
http://www.lowesyndrome.org

Voluntary health organization of parents, professionals, and others to provide information and support, and to support research and treatments.

MENTAL RETARDATION

(See also Developmental Disabilities and Down Syndrome, above.)

PRADER-WILLI SYNDROME ORGANIZATIONS

Prader-Willi Syndrome Association
5700 Midnight Pass Road
Suite 6
Sarasota, FL 34242
(800) 926–4797; (941) 312–0400
http://www.pwsausa.org

Organization providing information, education, and support services to members.

RETT SYNDROME

International Rett Syndrome Association
9121 Piscataway Road
Suite 2B
Clinton, MD 20735
(800) 818–7388; (301) 856–3334
http://www2.paltech.com/irsa/irsa.htm

Promoting research and offering information, advocacy, referrals to support groups, genetic counseling, and other services.

Rett Syndrome Research Foundation (RSRF)
4600 Devitt Drive
Cincinnati OH 45246
(513) 874–3020
http://www.rsrf.org

Promoting research and offering information, advocacy, referrals to support groups, genetic counseling, and other services.

SPECIAL EDUCATION

Center for Special Education Finance
American Institutes for Research
1791 Arastradero Road
Palo Alto, CA 94304-1337

(650) 843-8136
http://csef.air.org

Provides information and research on issues regarding special education spending. Publishes newsletter, policy papers, state analysis series, briefs, and reference documents.

Council of Educators for Students with
Disabilities (CESD)
9801 Anderson Mill Road
Suite 230
Austin, TX 78750
(512) 219-5043
http://www.504idea.org/

Provides information and training to assist educators in complying with federal laws protecting students with disabilities, including IDEA '97 and Section 504 of the Rehabilitation Act of 1973.

Disability Resources, Inc.
http://www.disabilityresources.org

A nonprofit organization that offers alphabetical listings by disability and/or state of local and national resources.

Edlaw, Inc.
1426 Harvard Street
#466
Seattle, WA 98122-3813
http://www.edlaw.net

Source for information on special education law; download laws, regulations, and more.

ERIC Clearinghouse on Disabilities and
Gifted Education
110 North Glebe Road
Arlington, VA 22201-5705
(800) 328-0272
http://www.ericec.org

Information on learning disabilities, parenting, and teaching.

STUTTERING

(See also Communication, above.)

National Center for Stuttering
200 E. 33rd Street
Suite 17C
New York, NY 10016

(800) 221–2483
http://www.stuttering.com

Center that offers information, a hotline, treatment, continuing education, and research.

TOURETTE'S SYNDROME

Tourette's Syndrome Association
4240 Bell Boulevard
Suite 205
Bayside, NY 11361
(718) 224–2999; (800) 237–0717
http://tsa.mgh.harvard.edu

Organization offers information, resources on Tourette's syndrome.

VOCATIONAL EDUCATION

ERIC Clearinghouse on Adult, Career & Vocational Education at the Center for Employment, Education & Training at Ohio State University
Ohio State University College of Education
1900 Kenny Road
Columbus, OH 43210-1090
(614) 292-7069; (800) 848-4815, ext. 2-7609
http://www.ericacue.org

ERIC Clearinghouse representatives are available to provide information, ERIC Digests, annotated bibliographies, and assorted publications, some with information on LD. ERIC does not answer specific questions on disabilities, local programs, or jobs.

APPENDIX II
GOVERNMENT SOURCES OF INFORMATION, HELP

Americans with Disabilities Act (ADA) Hotline
(800) 949-4232

The ADA Hotline provides technical assistance, information on services, and outreach regarding the Americans with Disabilities Act (ADA). Operators are equipped with a listing of LD associations and can answer questions about how ADA protects individuals with LD. An answering machine is available during non-business hours, and follow-up calls are placed the next working day.

Comprehensive Regional Assistance Centers
(800) USA-LEARN; (800) 437-0833 (tty)

Sponsored by the U.S. Department of Education, the 15 Comprehensive Centers are part of an emerging network of organizations that support and assist states, districts, and schools in meeting the needs of children served under the Improving America's Schools Act (1994).

Department of Education
400 Maryland Avenue, SW
Washington, DC 20202
(800) USA–LEARN
http://www.ed.gov

Department administers more than 200 programs involving education.

IDEA 97
http://www.ed.gov/offices/OSERS/IDEA/

(U.S. Department of Education)

Complete information on the Individuals with Disabilities Education Act amendments of 1997.

Knowledge Exchange Network
P.O. Box 42490
Washington, DC 20015
(800) 789-2647
http://www.mentalhealth.org

Center for Mental Health Services, Substance Abuse, and Mental Health Services Administration
Information and resources on mental health including database of community resources, extensive catalog, events, and more.

National Institute of Child Health and Human Development (NICHD)
6100 Building
9000 Rockville Pike
Bethesda, MD 20892
(301) 496–5133
http://www.nih.gov/nichd

Institute that supports research into the health of children and offers information on a wide variety of topics relevant to children and maternal health.

National Institute of Mental Health (NIMH)
5600 Fisher Lane
Rockville, MD 20857
(301) 443–4513
http://www.nimh.nih.gov

Foremost mental health research organization in the world.

National State Policy Database
http://www.nasdse.org/national_state_policy_database.htm

Contains special education regulations for 30 states. To access information on the site enter search terms on the main page. This site is under development.

Office of Civil Rights
U.S. Department of Education, OCR
330 C Street, SW
Suite 5000
Washington, DC 20202–1100
(202) 205–5413
http://www.ed.gov/offices/OCR

Agency ensures equal access to education, and enforces civil rights. To file a formal civil rights complaint (a Section 504 complaint), contact this office or the regional office servicing your area.

Office of Special Education and Rehabilitation Services
Switzer Building
330 C Street, SW
Suite 3006
Washington, DC 20202
(202) 205–5465
http://www.ed.gov/offices/OSERS

Office supports programs that help in educating children with special needs and also supports research. OSERS includes the Office of Special Education Programs, Rehabilitation Services Administration, and the National Institute on Disability and Rehabilitation Research.

Office of Special Education Programs
Switzer Building
330 C Street, SW
Suite 3086
Washington, DC 20202
(202) 205–5507

The OESP administers programs relating to education of all children, youth, and adults with disabilities, through age 22.

Rehabilitation Services Administration
Switzer Building
330 C Street, SW
Suite 3026
Washington, DC 20202
(202) 205–5482
http://www.ed.gov/offices/OSERS/RSA/rsa.html

RSA guides programs that help those with physical or mental disabilities get hired by providing counseling, health services, job training, and other support.

National Institute on Disability and Rehabilitative Research
Switzer Building
330 C Street, SW
Suite 3060 MES
Washington, DC 20202
(202) 205–8134
http://www.ed.gov/offices/OSERS/NIDRR/nidrr.html

NIDRR conducts research and administers ADA technical assistance centers.

Office of Educational Research and Improvement
555 New Jersey Avenue, NW
Washington, DC 20208
(202) 219–1385
http://www.ed.gov/offices/OERI

Provides support for educational research and statistics and offers a variety of services. Its agencies include the National Center for Educational Statistics; the National Institute on Early Childhood Development and Education; National Institute on the Education of AT Risk Students; National Institute on Student Achievement, Curriculum, and Assessment.

APPENDIX III
ASSISTIVE TECHNOLOGY RESOURCES

ABLEDATA website
National Institute on Disability and Rehabilitative Research
8455 Colesville Road
Suite 935
Silver Spring, MD 20918
(800) 277–0216; (301) 608–8998
http://www.abledata.com

Electronic database of information on assistive technology and rehabilitation equipment in the United States, including more than 23,000 products.

Adaptive Computing Technology Center
Website only
http://www.missouri.edu/~ccact

Website that provides information on technology that combines adaptive devices with standard computer equipment.

Alliance for Technology Access
2175 East Francisco Boulevard
Suite L
San Rafael, CA 94901
(800) 455–7970; (415) 455–4575
http://www.ataccess.org

Network of community-based resource centers around the country offering information and support to children and adults with disabilities on standard assistive and information technology.

Apple Computer's Worldwide Disability Solutions Group
Website only
http://www.apple.com/disability/welcme.html

Website that offers help for people with disabilities who want to use a Macintosh computer, including links to organizations and manufacturers and software programs.

Assistive Technology Devices on the Internet
Website only
http://www.asel.udel.edu/at-online/devices

Website providing an A to Z list of manufacturers and devices.

Assistive Technology Industry Association
526 Davis Street
Suite 217
Evanston, IL 60201-4686
(877) 687-2842; (847) 869-1282
http://www.atia.org

A not-for-profit membership of organizations manufacturing or selling technology-based assistive devices for people with disabilities, or providing services associated with or required by people with disabilities. Among its primary goals is the establishment and continuation of an assistive device technology conference on an annual basis.

Association for the Advancement of Rehabilitation Technology
1700 North Moore Street
Suite 1540
Arlington, VA 22209
(703) 524–6686
http://www.resna.org

Resource for those interested in assistive technology.

Center for Applied Special Technology
39 Cross Street
Peabody, MA 01960
(978) 531-8555
http://www.cast.org/

Nonprofit organization whose mission is to expand opportunities for people with disabilities through innovative multimedia computer technology.

Center for Electronic Studying

5265 University of Oregon
Eugene, OR 97403-5265
(541) 346-2544
http://www.ces.uoregon.edu/

Center investigating ways in which computer technology can be used to enhance students' efforts to study and learn content-area material. Funded by the U.S. Department of Education, the Center has launched three projects blending portable computer technology with instruction on computer-based study strategies.

Center for Information Technology Accommodations

Website only
http://www.gsa.gov:80/coca

Government clearinghouse for information systems.

Closing the Gap

P.O. Box 68
526 Main Street
Henderson, MN 56044
(507) 248-3294
http://www.closingthegap.com

Internationally recognized source for information on the use of microcomputer-related technology by and for exceptional individuals. Publishes newsletter, resource directory and holds annual international conference each fall in Minneapolis, Minnesota.

Disability Resources on the Web

Website only
http://www.geocities.com/~drm/AT.html

Website provides on-line information about assistive technology products and services.

DREAMMS for Kids

Website only
http://users.aol.com/dreamms/main.html

Nonprofit parent-professional agency that offers information and research in assistive technology. Services include newsletters, Tech Paks, and special programs aimed at kids and computers.

LD OnLine's Assistive Technology Resources Guide

http://www.ldonlin.org/ld_indepth/technology/techguide.html

A comprehensive listing of assistive technology devices by type, and links to sources and information about the devices.

Equal Access to Software and Information

Website only
http://www.isc.rit.edu/~easi

EASI offers information and guidance in access-to-information technologies by individuals with disabilities.

National Center to Improve Practice

http://www2.edc.org/NCIP/

Promotes the effective use of technology to enhance educational outcomes for students with sensory, cognitive, physical, and social/emotional disabilities. Funded by the U.S. Department of Education.

RESNA Technical Assistance Project

1700 North Moore Street
Suite 1540
Arlington, VA 22209-1903
(703) 524-6686
http://www.resna.org/tapproject/

Information and consultation to assistive technology programs in states and territories funded under the Technology-Related Assistance for Individuals with Disabilities Act Amendments of 1994 (PL 103–218).

Speak to Write

http://www.edc.org/spk2wrt/

Federally funded project studying the use of speech recognition technology by secondary students with disabilities. Includes email discussion forum (listserv) of the educational issues associated with using speech recognition technology to support students with disabilities in home and school settings.

Tech IDEAs

http://www.air-de.org/techideas/default.htm

Developed by the U.S. Department of Education, Office of Special Education Programs (OSEP), this website is designed to provide information on the use of technology to support the education of students with disabilities.

UNLV Assistive Technology Curriculum Project

Department of Special Education
University of Nevada, Las Vegas
4505 Maryland Parkway
Box 3014
Las Vegas, NV 89154-3014
(702) 895-1106
http://www.jsrd.or.jp/dinf_us/csun_98/csun98_114.htm

This project has integrated knowledge of the ADA, assistive technology, and disability issues into a university curriculum.

APPENDIX IV
HOTLINES

American Association for Vocational and Instructional Materials
(800) 228–4689

An operator is available from 8 A.M. to 5 P.M. EST, Monday through Friday, to provide information on educational materials (software, videos, manuals), including a listing of Category L modules that deal with teaching students with special needs. Products are available for purchase.

Equal Employment Opportunity Commission
(800) 669–3362

Voice mail directs calls from 7 A.M. to 5:30 P.M. EST, Monday through Friday. Operators accept orders for publications, fact sheets, posters, and a resource directory for people with disabilities, including learning disabilities. They do not answer questions relating to employment but can give referrals to local EEOC offices.

ERIC Clearinghouse on Adult, Career, and Vocational Education Center for Employment, Education & Training
(800) 848–4815

A 24-hour voice mail service that provides information on ERIC digests, annotated bibliographies, and assorted publications, some with information on learning disabilities. ERIC does not answer specific questions on disabilities, local programs, or jobs.

Federal Student Aid Information Center Hotline
(800) 433–3243

Provides information from 9 A.M. to 8 P.M. EST, Monday through Friday, on eligibility, benefits, applications, and other questions about student aid. Voice mail directs calls during business hours.

GED Hotline
(800) 629–9433

A 24-hour operator service provides information on local GED classes and testing services; offers an accommodations guide for people taking the GED who have a learning disability.

International Dyslexia Association
(800) 222–3123

A 24-hour voice mail service to receive information requests.

and
(410) 296–0232

From 8:30 A.M. to 4:30 P.M. EST, Monday through Friday, staff provide information on appropriate materials on dyslexia, referrals for testing and tutors, branches of IDA, and workshops and conferences.

Job Accommodation Network
(800) 526–7324

A free consulting service from 8 A.M. to 8 P.M. EST, Monday through Thursday, and 8 A.M. to 5 P.M. EST on Friday to provide information on: equipment, methods, and modifications with which persons with disabilities can improve their work environment. All information is specific to the disability, including learning disabilities.

Learning Resources Network
(800) 678–5376

An operator service from 8 A.M. to 5 P.M. EST, Monday through Friday, to provide information to practitioners of adult continuing education, give consulting information, take orders for publications, and provide phone numbers of associations and organizations that deal with learning disabilities.

National Center for Research in Vocational Education
(800) 762–4093

An operator is available from 8 A.M. to 5 P.M. Pacific Time, Monday through Friday, to provide information on products, electronic services, and vocational education. A catalog and newsletter are also available. The Office of Student Services produces materials on learning disabilities and a subcatalog for special populations.

National Clearinghouse on Postsecondary Education for Individuals with Disabilities
HEATH Resource Center
(800) 544–3284

Information specialists available from 9 A.M. to 5 P.M. EST, Monday through Friday, to provide resource papers, directories, information on national organizations, and a resource directory for people with learning disabilities.

National Library of Education at the U.S. Office of Educational Research and Improvement
(800) 424–1616

An operator is available from 9 A.M. to 4 P.M. EST, Monday through Friday, to provide statistical information on education and schools, publications, references to other agencies, and references to a specialist on learning disabilities.

National Library Services for the Blind and Physically Handicapped
(800) 424–8567

A voice mail system directs calls from 8 A.M. to 4:30 P.M. EST, Monday through Friday; operators provide information on audiocassette, large print, and Braille books and magazines for recreational reading. Callers with learning disabilities must meet certain guidelines to use these services.

National Literacy Hotline
(800) 228–8813

A 24-hour bilingual (Spanish/English) operator service to provide information on literacy/education classes, GED testing services, volunteer organizations, and learning disabilities.

Recording for the Blind and Dyslexic, Inc.
(800) 221–4792

Operators are available from 8:30 A.M. to 7 P.M., Monday through Friday, to provide information on more than 80,000 recorded textbooks (in four-track cassette or computer disk) and other classroom materials, from fourth grade through postgraduate levels, available on loan. There is an application and certification process and one-time fee ($37.50). Callers with learning disabilities are eligible to participate but must complete the certification requirements.

Social Security Administration
(800) 772–1313; (800) 325–0778 (TT)

Representatives answer calls from 7 A.M. to 7 P.M. EST, Monday through Friday, to provide information on Social Security and Supplemental Security Income matters. A limited number of automated services are available 24 hours a day. Bilingual (Spanish/English) services are also available.

APPENDIX V
COMMERCIAL TECHNOLOGY RESOURCES

Each of these websites has a variety of products and information about assistive technology:

Adaptive Technology Consulting, Inc.
http://www.adaptivetech.net/

Provides, installs, and trains in the use of equipment for the blind, visually impaired, and individuals with reading difficulties.

Adaptive and Assistive Technology@Rehab Tool.com
http://www.rehabtool.com/

Offers a variety of high-tech assistive and adaptive technology products, augmentative and alternative communication devices, computer access equipment, multilingual speech synthesis and voice recognition software.

Apple Computer Disability Resources
http://www.apple.com/disability/

Innovative products and programs designed to help individuals with disabilities lead independent lives.

Assistive Technology, Inc.
http://www.assistivetech.com

Provides innovative solutions to help people with learning, communication, and access difficulties lead more independent and productive lives.

Don Johnston
http://www.donjohnstone.com

Computer products designed to provide a means for people with special needs to discover their potential and experience success.

Evan Kemp Associates Disability Resources, Products, Service
Solutions@disability.com, linking people with disabilities and chronic health conditions to resources, products, and services that promote active, healthy, independent living.

Freedom Scientific
11800 31st Court North
St. Petersburg, FL 33716-1805
(800) 444-4443
http://www.freedomscientific.com

A nonprofit organization whose goal is to deliver information access through technology. From reading machines to talking GPS-based personal locators, Freedom Scientific has solutions to make its users successful in the real world.

IntelliTools
http://www.freedomscientific.com

Quality computer products for people with disabilities.

Super School Software
1857 Josie Avenue
Long Beach, CA 90815-3432
(562) 594-8580
http://www.superschoolsoftware.com

Software and IEP Writer.

Able Generation
http://www.ablegeneration.com

Pediatric therapeutic furniture for children with special needs.

APPENDIX VI
BULLETIN BOARD LISTSERVS ABOUT LD AND ADHD

LD-List

A general discussion of LD issues by parents, educators, and LD individuals
Send message to majordomo@curry.edu
Message: "subscribe ld-list"

National Institute for Literacy's LD Adults List

For adults with learning disabilities
Send message to: listproc@literacy.nifl.gov
Message: "subscribe nifl-ld firstname lastname"

Childhood ADD List

For parents of children with ADD
Send message to listserv@n7kbt.rain.com
"subscribe ADD-PARENTS (your name)"

Postsecondary LD-List

For postsecondary students with LD
Send message to listserv@listserv.acsu.buffalo.edu
with "subscribe swdhe-1" in the message body

DADVOCAT List

For dads of children with disabilities or special health needs

Subscription address: listserv@lsv.uky.edu
Send message to: dadvocat@lsv.uky.edu

Women and Learning Disabilities/ADHD List

A listserv for professionals in the fields of education, student services, psychology, and health services, with an emphasis on postsecondary education. Women with learning differences are especially welcome.

Send message to: listserv@home.ease.lsoft.com subscribe WLDADD (your name)

Teaching Writing and LD/ADHD List

For professionals engaged in the challenges and rewards of teaching writing skills to individuals with learning disabilities and/or ADHD. The emphasis is on postsecondary education but teachers of younger students are also welcome. Send message to: listserv@home.ease.lsoft.comsubscribe LDCOMP (your name)

APPENDIX VII
BOOKS OF INTEREST TO PEOPLE WITH LEARNING DISABILITIES

BOOKS FOR CHILDREN AND TEENS WITH LEARNING DISABILITIES

Fisher, G., and Cummings, R. *The Survival Guide for Kids with LD.* Minneapolis: Free Spirit Publishing, 1990.

Gehret, J. *Learning Disabilities and the Don't-Give-Up-Kid.* Fairport, N.Y.: Verbal Images Press, 1990.

Landau, E. *Dyslexia.* New York: Franklin Watts, 1991.

Levine, M. *Keeping a Head in School: A Student's Book about Learning Abilities and Learning Disorders.* Cambridge, Mass.: Educators Publishing Services, 1990.

BOOKS FOR COLLEGE-BOUND STUDENTS WITH LEARNING DISABILITIES

Mangrum, Charles T., II, and Strichart, Stephen S., eds. *Peterson's Colleges with Programs for Students with Learning Disabilities.* 4th ed., 1994.

A comprehensive guide to more than 800 colleges and universities in the United States and Canada, including two-year, four-year, and graduate programs. Available for $31.95, plus $6.75 shipping and handling, from Peterson's Guides, PO Box 2123, Princeton, NJ 08543; (800) 338–3282.

Kravets, Marybeth, and Wax, Imy F. *The K&W Guide to Colleges for the Learning Disabled.* 3rd ed., 1995.

An analysis of more than 200 U.S. colleges offering programs and services specifically geared to students with learning disabilities. Available for $28 plus $3.00 shipping and handling, from Educators Publishing Service, Inc., 31 Smith Place, Cambridge, MA 02130; (800) 225–5750.

BOOKS FOR ADULTS WITH LEARNING DISABILITIES

Adelman, P., and Wren, C. *Learning Disabilities, Graduate School, and Careers: The Student's Perspective.* Lake Forest, Ill.: Learning Opportunities Program, Barat College, 1990.

Cordoni, B. *Living with a Learning Disability.* Carbondale: Southern Illinois University Press, 1987.

Kravets, M., and Wax, I. *The K&W Guide: Colleges and the Learning Disabled Student.* New York: HarperCollins, 1992.

Mangrum, C., and Strichart, S., eds. *Colleges with Programs for Students with Learning Disabilities.* Princeton, N.J.: Peterson's Guides, 1992.

BOOKS FOR PARENTS

Directory of Facilities and Services for the Learning Disabled, 17th ed. Novato, Calif.: Academic Therapy, 1998.

Greene, L. *Learning Disabilities and Your Child: A Survival Handbook.* New York: Fawcett Columbine, 1987.

Mackenzie, L. *The Complete Learning Disabilities Directory.* Lakeville, Conn.: GreyHouse, 1997.

Novick, B., and Arnold, M. *Why Is My Child Having Trouble in School?* New York: Villard Books, 1991.

Pierangelo, Roger, and Crane, Rochelle. *The Special Education Yellow Pages.* Upper Saddle River, N.J.: Prentice Hall, 2000.

Silver, L. *The Misunderstood Child: A Guide for Parents of Children with Learning Disabilities,* 3rd ed. New York: Time Books, 1998.

Silver, L. *Dr. Silver's Advice to Parents on Attention-Deficit Hyperactivity Disorder.* Washington, D.C.: American Psychiatric Press, 1993.

Smith, S. *No Easy Answers,* rev. ed. New York: Bantam Books, 1995.

Vail, P. *Smart Kids with School Problems.* New York: E. P. Dutton, 1987.

Weiss, E. *Mothers Talk About Learning Disabilities.* New York: Prentice Hall, 1989.

BOOKS AND PAMPHLETS FOR TEACHERS AND SPECIALISTS

Adelman, P., and Wren, C. *Learning Disabilities, Graduate School, and Careers.* Lake Forest, Ill.: Learning Opportunities Program, Barat College, 1990.

Silver, L. *ADHD: Attention Deficit-Hyperactivity Disorder, Booklet for Teachers.* Summit, N.J.: CIBA-GEIGY, 1989.

Smith, S. *Success Against the Odds: Strategies and Insights from the Learning Disabled.* Los Angeles: Jeremy Tarcher, 1991.

RELATED PAMPHLETS AVAILABLE FROM THE NATIONAL INSTITUTES OF HEALTH

Facts About Dyslexia
National Institute of Child Health and Human Development
Building 31, Room 2A32
9000 Rockville Pike
Bethesda, MD 20892
(301) 496–5133

Developmental Speech and Language Disorders—Hope through Research
National Institute on Deafness and Other Communicative Disorders
PO Box 37777
Washington, DC 20013; (800) 241–1044

GLOSSARY

abstraction The ability to relate ideas or understand concepts at a higher level than the literal or concrete meaning.

adaptive physical education A special physical education program developed to fit the limits and disabilities of persons with handicaps.

afferent Movement of impulses toward the brain.

amphetamines A group of drugs used to stimulate the cerebral cortex of the brain that are sometimes used to treat hyperactivity.

anosmia Absense of sense of smell.

articulation The production of speech sounds resulting from the movements of the lips, jaw, and tongue as they modify air flow.

association Ability to relate concepts presented through the senses (visual, auditory, tactile, or kinesthetic).

basal ganglia Size of brain where extrapyramidal system originates; includes caudate nucleus, globus pallidus, and putamen; thalamus, subthalamus, substantia nigra, and red nucleus sometimes included.

basic skill area Subjects such as reading, writing, spelling, mathematics.

bilateral Refers to using both sides of the body or the arms or leg (extremities) on both sides of the body.

body image The concept and awareness of a person's own body as it relates to space, movement, and other objects.

brain stem Composed of midbrain, pons, and medulla; contains reticular activating system and other key centers.

cognition The process of recognizing, interpreting, judging, reasoning, and knowing. Perception is considered a part of cognition by some psychologists, but not by others.

cognitive The process of knowing in the broadest sense, including perception, memory, and judgment.

cognitive ability Intellectual ability; thinking and reasoning skills.

cognitive deficit A perceptual, memory, or conceptual problem that interferes with learning

cognitive retraining Developing or relearning the processes involved in thinking.

cognitive style A person's typical approach to learning activities and problem solving.

compensation The process by which a person is taught how to cope with learning problems by focusing on personal strengths, and how to work around abilities that may be weak.

conceptualization The process of forming a general idea from what is observed, such as seeing peas, beans and tomatoes and recognizing that they are all vegetables.

conceptual disorder Disturbances in thinking, reasoning, generalizing, or memorizing.

confidential file A file maintained by the school that contains evaluations of whether a child is handicapped, as well as any other information related to special education placement. Parents

277

have the right to inspect the file and have copies of any information contained in it.

configuration The visual shape or form of words; may be used as a cue in word-attack skills.

congenital A condition existing at birth or before birth but that does not imply an inherited problem.

coordination The harmonious functioning of muscles in the body to perform complex movements.

coping skills The ability to deal with problems and difficulties by attempting to overcome them or accept them.

cross-categorical A system in which a teacher addresses more than one handicapping condition within one instructional period.

cross dominance A condition also known as mixed dominance in which the preferred eye, hand, or foot are not on the same side of the body. For example, a child may be right-footed but left-handed.

cumulative file A general file maintained by a school for every student. Parents have a right to inspect the file and have copies of any information contained in it.

decoding The process of getting meaning from written or spoken symbols.

developmental lag A delay in some aspect of physical or mental development.

directionality The ability to know right from left, up from down, forward from backward, and direction and orientation.

discrimination The ability to discern fine differences among stimuli, whether visual, auditory, tactile, and so on.

disinhibition A lack of restraint in responding to a situation. A child who is disinhibited reacts impulsively and often inappropriately.

distractibility Shifting of attention from a task to other stimuli.

echolalia Repetition of words or phrases.

emotional lability Exhibiting rapid and drastic changes in emotions (such as laughing, crying, anger) without apparent reason.

frustration tolerance The ability to deal with frustrating events in daily life without becoming angry or aggressive.

insertions The addition of letters or numbers that don't belong in a word or numeral, such as "wheare" for "where."

inversions Mistakes in reading, spelling, or math that involve confusion of up-down directionality of letters or numbers, such as *m* for *w* or *6* for *9*.

itinerant teacher A special education teacher who is shared by more than one school.

kinesthetic Pertaining to the muscles.

kinesthetic method A way of teaching words by using the muscles. For example, a student might trace a word with a finger in sand while saying aloud the word or its letters.

laterality The tendency to use the hand, foot, eye, and ear on the left or right side of the body.

motor Term that refers to the origin or execution of muscular activity.

perseveration Repeating words, motions, or tasks. A child who perseverates often has trouble shifting from one task to another, and continues working on an old task long after classmates have moved on.

prefrontal area Brain location of processes of foresight, abstract thinking, and judgment.

premorbid A term to describe the patient's condition before an injury.

psychomotor A term that relates to the motor effects of psychological processes. Psychomotor tests are tests of motor skill which depend upon sensory or perceptual motor coordination.

readiness The acquisition of skills considered prerequisite for academic learning.

registration A very brief sensory/memory function by which information enters the memory system. It is then entered into short-term memory or decays and is lost. Registration is very resistant to impairments.

reversals Trouble in reading or reproducing letters by themselves, letters as contained in words, or words in sentences in their proper order. The term also may refer to a reversal of mathematical concepts (adding for subtracting, or multiplying for dividing).

sensorimotor   The relationship between sensation and movement.

strabismus   Weakness of eye muscles allowing eyes to cross.

subdural   Beneath the tough membrane (dura) covering the brain and spinal cord.

syntax   Grammar, sentence structure, and word order in oral or written language.

syndrome   A set of symptoms that indicates a specific disorder.

tactile   The ability to receive and interpret stimuli through contact with the skin.

unilateral   Pertaining to only one side.

ventricles   Four natural cavities in the brain that are filled with cerebrospinal fluid.

BIBLIOGRAPHY

Anderson, Elizabeth, and Emmons, Pauline. *Unlocking the Mysteries of Sensory Dysfunction.* Arlington, Tex.: Future Horizons, 1996.

Anderson, M. "Annotation: Conceptions of Intelligence," *Journal of Child Psychology and Psychiatry* 42, no. 3 (March 2001): 287–98.

Armstrong, Thomas. *The Myth of the A.D.D. Child: 50 Ways to Improve Your Child's Behavior and Attention Span without Drugs, Labels, or Coercion.* New York: Plume 1997.

Ball, S., et al. "Early Screening for Dyslexia—A Collaborative Pilot Project," *International Journal of Language and Communication* Disorders 36 (2001): 75–76.

Barkley, Russel A. *Attention Deficit Hyperactivity Disorder: A Handbook for Diagnosis and Treatment.* New York: Guilford Press, 1990.

Batshaw, Mark L., and Perret, Yvonne. *Children with Disabilities: A Medical Primer.* Atlanta: Paul L. Brookes, 1992.

Behrmann, M., et al. "The Eye Movements of Pure Alexic Patients during Reading and Nonreading Tasks," *Neuropsychologia* 39, no. 9 (2001): 983–1002.

Berenbaum, S. A. "Cognitive Function in Congenital Adrenal Hyperplasia," *Endocrinology and Metabolism Clinics of North America* 30, no. 1 (March 2001): 173–92.

Bishop, D. V. "Genetic Influences on Language Impairment and Literacy Problems in Children: Same or Different?" *Journal of Child Psychology and Psychiatry.* 42, no. 2 (February 2001): 189–98.

Block, Mary Ann. *No More Ritalin: Treating ADHD without Drugs.* New York: Kensington Publishing Co., 1997.

Boone, K. B. et al. "Neuropsychological Profiles of Adults with Klinefelter Syndrome," *Journal of the International Neuropsychological Society* 7, no. 4 (May 2001): 446–56.

Bos, Candace S., and Vaughn, Sharon. *Strategies for Teaching Students with Learning and Behavior Problems.* Needham Heights, Mass.: Allyn & Bacon, 1997.

Boyles, Nancy S., and Contadino, Darlene. *Parenting a Child with Attention Deficit Hyperactivity Disorder.* Los Angeles: Lowell House, 1996.

———. *The Learning Differences Sourcebook.* New York: NTC Contemporary, 1998.

Bradley, W. et al., eds. *Neurology in Clinical Practice: Principles of Diagnosis and Management.* Vol. 1. 2nd ed. Boston: Butterworth-Heinemann, 1996.

Briskman, J.; Happe, F.; Frith, U. "Exploring the Cognitive Phenotype of Autism: Weak "Central Coherence" in Parents and Siblings of Children with Autism: II. Real-Life Skills and Preferences," *Journal of Child Psychology and Psychiatry* 42, no. 3 (March 2001): 309–16.

Brook, U., and Geva, D. "Knowledge and Attitudes of High School Pupils Towards Peers' Attention Deficit and Learning Disabilities," *Patient Education and Counseling* 43, no. 1 (April 2001): 31–36.

Brown, W. E., et al. "Preliminary Evidence of Widespread Morphological Variations of the Brain in Dyslexia," *Neurology* 56, no. 6 (March 27, 2001): 781–83.

Butler, F. M., et al. "Teaching Mathematics to Students with Mild-to-Moderate Mental Retardation: A Review of the Literature," *Mental Retardation* 39, no. 1 (February 2001): 20–31.

Butterworth, B.; Cappelletti, M.; Kopelman, M. "Category Specificity in Reading and Writing: The Case of Number Words," *Nature Neuroscience* 4, no. 8 (August 2001): 784–86.

Cahall, Jeanne S. *Stages of Reading Development.* 2nd ed. New York: Harcourt Brace, 1996.

Campbell, Linda. *Teaching and Learning Through Multiple Intelligences.* Needham Heights, Mass: Allyn & Bacon, 1996.

Chabot, R. J.; di Michele, F.; Prichep, L.; John, E. R. "The Clinical Role of Computerized EEG in the Evaluation and Treatment of Learning and Attention Disorders in Children and Adolescents," *Journal of Neuropsychiatry and Clinical Neuroscience* 13, no. 2 (Spring 2001): 171–86. Review.

Comings, David E. *Tourette Syndrome and Human Behavior,* Duarte, Calif.: Hope Press, 1990.

Como, P. G. "Neuropsychological Function in Tourette Syndrome," *Advances in Neurology.* 85 (2001): 103–11.

Daly, E.; MacDermott, E.J.; Green, A. "Diagnostic Review of 66 Children with Learning Disability Attending a Single Center," *Irish Medical Journal*. 94, no. 6 (June 2001): 184–85.

Davis, B.; Krug, D.; Dean, R. S. "Neuropsychological Clusters within Intelligence Levels for Learning Disabled Children," *International Journal of Neuroscience* 106, nos. 3–4 (2001): 239–51.

Davis, Ronald D., and Braun, Eldon M. *The Gift of Dyslexia: Why Some of the Smartest People Can't Read and How They Can Learn*. New York: Perigee, 1997.

Doyle, A. E., et al. "Separating Attention Deficit Hyperactivity Disorder and Learning Disabilities in Girls: A Familial Risk Analysis," *American Journal of Psychiatry* 158, no. 10 (October 2001): 1666–672.

Ewing-Cobbs, L.; Fletcher, J. M.; and Levin, H. S. "Traumatic Brain Injury." In B. P. Rourke, ed. *Syndrome of Nonverbal Learning Disabilities: Neurodevelopmental Manifestations*. New York: Guilford Press, 1995, pp. 433–59.

Fischman, J. "New Reading Programs Spell Help for Frustrated Kids," *U.S. News & World Reports*. 16, no. 130 (April 16, 2001): 48–50.

Flanagan, O., and Nuallain, S. O. "A Study Looking at the Effectiveness of Developmental Screening in Identifying Learning Disabilities in Early Childhood," *Irish Medical Journal* 95, no. 5 (May 2001): 148–50.

Gaddes, William H., and Edgell, Dorothy. *Learning Disabilities and Brain Function: A Neuropsychological Approach*. New York: Springer-Verlag, 1994.

Gardener, Howard. *Multiple Intelligences*. New York: Basic Books, 1993.

———. *Leading Minds: Anatomy of Success*. New York: Basic Books, 1995.

Gates, B.; Newell, R.; Wray, J. "Behavior Modification and Gentle Teaching Workshops: Management of Children with Learning Disabilities Exhibiting Challenging Behaviour and Implications for Learning Disability Nursing," *Journal of Advanced Nursing* 34, no. 1 (April 2001): 86–95.

Goodley, D., and Rapley, M. "How Do You Understand "Learning Difficulties"? Towards a Social Theory of Impairment," *Mental Retardation* 39, no. 3 (June 2001) 229–32.

Gross-Tsur, V., et al. "Cognition, Attention, and Behavior in Prader-Willi Syndrome," *Journal of Child Neurology* 16, no. 4 (April 2001): 288–90.

Hagberg, B. A. "Rett Syndrome: Clinical Peculiarities, Diagnostic Approach, and Possible Cause," *Pediatric Neurology* 5, no. 2 (1989): 75–83.

Hall, D. A.; Humphreys, G. W.; Cooper, A. C. "Neuropsychological Evidence for Case-Specific Reading: Multi-Letter Units in Visual Word Recognition," *The Quarterly Journal of Experimental Psychology* 54, no. 2 (May 2001): 439–67.

Hallowell, Edward M., and Ratey, John J. *Driven to Distraction: Recognizing and Coping with Attention Deficit Disorder from Childhood through Adulthood* New York: Simon & Schuster, 1995.

Harnadek, M. C. S., and Rourke, B. P. "Principal Identifying Features of the Syndrome of Nonverbal Learning Disabilities in Children," *Journal of Learning Disabilities*. 27 (1994): 54.

Hasselbring, T. S., and Glaser, C. H. "Use of Computer Technology to Help Students with Special Needs," *Future Child* 10, no. 2 (Winter 2000): 102–22.

Izard, C., et al. "Emotion Knowledge as a Predictor of Social Behavior and Academic Competence in Children at Risk," *Psychological Science* 12, no. 1 (January 2001): 18–23.

Jenkins, R. "Use of Psychotropic Medication in People with a Learning Disability," *British Journal of Nursing* 9, no. 13 (July 13–26, 2001): 844–50.

Kamhi, A. G.; Allen, M. M.; Catts, H. W. "The Role of the Speech-Language Pathologist in Improving Decoding Skills," *Seminars in Speech and Language* 22, no. 3 (2001): 175–84.

Kelly, Kate, and Ramundo, Peggy. *You Mean I'm Not Lazy, Stupid or Crazy?! A Self-Help Book for Adults with Attention Deficit Disorder*. New York: Fireside, 1996.

Kher, U. "Deconstructing Dyslexia. Blame It on the Written Word," *Time* (March 26, 2001), p. 56.

Kirkendall, D. T.; Jordan, S. E.; Garrett, W. E. "Heading and Head Injuries in Soccer," *Sports Medicine* 31, no. 5 (2001): 369–86.

Klin, A.; Sparrow, et al. "Asperger Syndrome." In B. P. Rourke, ed. *Syndrome of Nonverbal Learning Disabilities: Neurodevelopmental Manifestations*. New York: Guilford Press, 1995.

Kranowitz, Carol Stock. *The Out-of-Sync Child: Recognizing and Coping With Sensory Integration Dysfunction*. New York: Perigee, 1998.

Laforce, R. Jr.; Hayward, S.; Cox, L. V. "Impaired Skill Learning in Children with Heavy Prenatal Alcohol Exposure," *Journal of the International Neuropsychology Society* 7, no. 1 (2001): 112–14.

Lannetti, D. W. "Extending Coverage of the Americans with Disabilities Act to Individuals with Attention Deficit Hyperactivity Disorder: A Demonstration of Inadequate Legislative Guidance," *Tort & Insurance Law Journal* 35, no. 1 (Fall 1999): 155–73.

Lerner, Janet W. *Learning Disabilities: Theories, Diagnosis, and Teaching Strategies*. Boston: Houghton-Mifflin, 2000.

Levelt, W. J. "Defining Dyslexia," *Science* 292, no. 5520 (May 2001): 1300–1.

Little, L. "Peer Victimization of Children with Asperger Spectrum Disorders," *Journal of the American Academy of Child and Adolescent Psychiatry* 40, no. 9 (September 2001): 995–96.

Martin, C. S., Romig, C. J., Kirisci, L. "DSM-IV Learning Disorders in 10- to 12-Year-Old Boys with and without a Parental History of Substance Use Disorders," *Prevention Science* 1, no. 2 (June 2000): 107–13.

Mather, D. S. "Does Dyslexia Develop from Learning the Alphabet in the Wrong Hemisphere? A Cognitive Neuroscience Analysis," *Brain Language* 76, no. 3 (March 2001): 282–316.

McArthur, G. M., and Hogben, J. H. "Auditory Backward Recognition Masking in Children with a Specific Language Impairment and Children with a Specific Reading Disability," *Journal of the Acoustical Society of America* 109, no. 3 (March 2001): 1092–100.

McCann, B. S., Roy-Byrne, P. "Attention-Deficit/ Hyperactivity Disorder and Learning Disabilities in Adults." *Seminars in Clinical Neuropsychiatry* 5, no. 3 (July 2000): 191–97.

Mercer, Cecil D., and Mercer, Ann R. *Teaching Students with Learning Problems.* Upper Saddle River, N.J.: Prentice Hall, 1997.

Mooney, Jonathan, and Cole, David. *Learning Outside the Lines: Two Ivy League Students with Learning Disabilities and ADHD Give You the Tools for Academic Success and Educational Revolution.* New York: Simon & Schuster, 2000.

Motsch, S., and Muhlendyck, H. "Frequency of Reading Disability Caused by Ocular Problems in 9- and 10-Year-Old Children in a Small Town," *Strabismus* 8, no. 4 (December 2000): 283–85.

Mulrine, A. "Are Boys the Weaker Sex?" *U.S. News & World Reports.* 131, no. 4 (July 30, 2001): 40–47.

Murphy, Kevin R., and Levert, Suzanne. *Out of the Fog: Treatment Options and Coping Strategies for Adult Attention Deficit Disorder.* New York: Hyperion, 1995.

Neville, B. G., "Mental Health Services for People with Learning Disabilities. Medical Needs Are Important Too," *British Medical Journal* 322, no. 7281 (February 3, 2001): 302.

Nyden, A., et al. "Neurocognitive Stability in Asperger Syndrome, ADHD, and Reading and Writing Disorder: A Pilot Study," *Developmental Medical Child Neurology* 43, no. 3 (March 2001): 165–71.

Paulesu, E., et al. "Dyslexia: Cultural Diversity and Biological Unity," *Science* 291, no. 5511 (March 16, 2000): 2165–167.

Percy, A. K., "Research in Rett Syndrome: Past, Present, and Future," *Journal of Child Neurology* 3 (1988): 572–75.

Ramus, F. "Dyslexia. Talk of Two Theories," *Nature* 412, no. 6845 (July 26, 2001): 393–95.

Rashid, F. L.; Morris, M. K.; Morris, R. "Naming and verbal memory skills in adults with Attention Deficit Hyperactivity Disorder and Reading Disability," *Journal of Clinical Psychology* 57, no. 6 (June 2001): 829–38.

Richek, M. A., et al. *Reading Problems: Assessment and Teaching Strategies.* Boston: Allyn & Bacon, 2001.

Rickards, H. "An International Perspective on Tourette syndrome," *Developmental Medical Child Neurology* 43, no. 6 (June 2001): 428–29.

Ricker, J. H.; Hillary, F. G.; DeLuca, J. "Functionally Activated Brain Imaging (O-15 PET and fMRI) in the Study of Learning and Memory after Traumatic Brain Injury," *Journal of Head Trauma Rehabilitation* 16, no. 2 (April 2001): 191–205. Review.

Russell, J., Hill, E. L. "Action-Monitoring and Intention Reporting in Children with Autism," *Journal of Child Psychology and Psychiatry* 43, no. 3 (March 2000): 317–28.

Sakurai, Y.; Ichikawa, Y.; Mannen, T. "Pure Alexia from a Posterior Occipital Lesion," *Neurology* 58, no. 6 (March 27, 2001): 778–81.

Smith, Corrine, and Strick, Lisa. *Learning Disabilities: A to Z.* New York: Simon & Schuster, 1997.

Snowling, M. J. "From Language to Reading and Dyslexia," *Dyslexia* 7, no. 1 (January–March 2001): 37–46.

Stein, David B. *Ritalin Is Not the Answer: A Drug-Free, Practical Program for Children Diagnosed With ADD or ADHD.* San Francisco: Jossey-Bass, 1999.

Stein, M. T.; Levine, M. D.; Reiff, M. I. "School Underachievement in the Fifth Grade," *Journal of Developmental and Behavioral Pediatrics.* 22, no. 2 (April 2001): S117–21.

Stein, M. T., et al. "A School-Aged Child with Delayed Reading Skills," *Journal of Developmental and Behavioral Pediatrics.* 22, no. 2 (April 2001): S111–15.

Stevens, Laura J., and Crook, William G. *12 Effective Ways to Help Your ADD/ADHD Child: Drug-Free Alternatives for Attention-Deficit Disorders* New York: Penguin Putnam, 2000.

Strichart, Stephen S., and Mangrum II, Charles T., eds. *Peterson's Colleges With Programs for Students with Learning Disabilities or Attention Deficit Disorders (Peterson's Colleges with Programs for Students).* Boston: Peterson's Guides, 2000.

Sudderth, David, and Kandel, Joseph. *Adult ADD: The Complete Handbook: Everything You Need to Know About How to Cope and Live Well with ADD/ADHD.* Roseville, Calif.: Prima, 1997.

Swanson, H. L., and Sachse-Lee, C. "Mathematical Problem Solving and Working Memory in Children with

Learning Disabilities: Both Executive and Phonological Processes are Important," *Journal of Experimental Child Psychology* 79, no. 3 (July 2001): 294–321.

Taylor, K. E.; Richardson, A. J.; Stein, J. F. "Could Platelet Activating Factor Play a Role in Developmental Dyslexia?" *Prostaglandins, Leukotrienes, and Essential Fatty Acids.* 64, no. 3 (March 2001): 173–80.

Townes, B. D. "Adult Outcome of Verbal Learning Disability: An Optimistic Note," *Seminars in Clinical Neuropsychiatry* 5, no. 3 (July 2000): 210–11.

Vicari, S.; Bellucci, S.; Carlesimo, G. A. "Procedural Learning Deficit in Children with Williams Syndrome," *Neuropsychologia* 39, no. 7 (2000): 665–77.

Willcutt, E. G., et al. "A Comparison of the Cognitive Deficits in Reading Disability and Attention-Deficit/Hyperactivity Disorder," *Journal of Abnormal Psychology* 110, no. 1 (February 2001): 157–72.

Winner, B. J. "Disability and the ADA: Learning Impairment as a Disability," *Journal of Law and Medical Ethics* 28, no. 4 (Winter 2000): 410–11.

Wolf, L. E. "College Students with ADHD and Other Hidden Disabilities. Outcomes and Interventions," *Annals of the New York Academy of Science* 931 (June 2001): 385–95.

INDEX